WITHDRAWN

OLD HISTORIC CHURCHES

OF AMERICA

THE MACMILLAN COMPANY
NEW YORK · BOSTON · CHICAGO · DALLAS
ATLANTA · SAN FRANCISCO

MACMILLAN & CO., Limited
LONDON · BOMBAY · CALCUTTA
MELBOURNE

**THE MACMILLAN COMPANY
OF CANADA, Limited**
TORONTO

Christ Church, Alexandria, Va. The church of Washington and Lee.
Photo by Homeier-Clark Studio.

Old Historic Churches of America

Their Romantic History and Their Traditions

By

EDWARD F. RINES

PUBLISHED UNDER THE AUSPICES
OF THE NATIONAL SOCIETY OF
COLONIAL DAMES OF AMERICA

NEW YORK
THE MACMILLAN COMPANY
1936

PRINTED IN THE UNITED STATES OF AMERICA
BY THE STRATFORD PRESS, INC., NEW YORK

9450

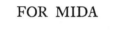

FOR MIDA

INTRODUCTION

ALTHOUGH always an admirer of old churches, the idea of writing a book about them came rather suddenly and was the direct result of visits paid to St. Paul's Chapel, New York City, and Old Christ Church, Alexandria, Virginia, in the spring of 1931, and the wish to share my enthusiasm with others.

Presently began the excursion which has ended in this book. One church led to another; one state to another; one whole section of the country to another. It was not difficult to unearth material on St. Paul's Chapel and Old Christ Church, but there were many, many other historic old structures whose stories had never been told and much of whose history was in danger of being lost. In numerous cases only ancient neighborhood traditions were extant; oftentimes these were not even written down but simply preserved in the mind of an old member. In certain cases, however, these traditions could be partially verified when the earlier parish registers were dug out and examined or old newspapers consulted. It was with a desire to record in permanent form such of this history and these traditions as seemed worthy of preservation that this book was first undertaken.

Only recently, several months after the completion of this work, the historic importance of old churches has received the attention of the Federal Government and there is under way at the present time a government survey of historical churches. President Roosevelt is taking a great personal interest in this survey and has suggested several structures to be included.

These old historic churches of ours are more than mere ancient buildings, preserved through the years; they are a vital, important part of our very history of existence. Many times the church was the main force back of colonization effort. If this was especially true in New England, Maryland, and Pennsylvania, it was equally true of the Missions of California.

Introduction

Generally speaking, it can be safely said that the history of any part of the country becomes at some time or another the religious history of that part of the country.

"One of the first acts of the early settlers was to erect a meeting house or church. . . ."

How many times we come across those words: at Jamestown, where the colonists stretched canvas across the branches of a tree and under this rude shelter held services; at St. Mary's, where the Maryland Pilgrims had a place of worship before they had a place of abode; at San Fernando, where a military barrack was hastily turned into a chapel. It was equally true in the cane-brake section of Kentucky; by the shores of the Great Salt Lake; in isolated sections of New Mexico and Arizona; in French St. Louis and Spanish St. Augustine.

Old meeting houses and old shrines of worship played an important part in the shaping of America's destiny. Thus, for instance, a church played its part in Paul Revere's ride and it was in a church that Patrick Henry exclaimed, "Give me liberty or give me death." Almost every battle of the Revolution was followed by a church receiving its baptism of history by being turned into a temporary hospital for the care of the sick and the wounded; this was also true of the War Between the States.

But in addition to playing their part in historic happenings, many of these old religious organizations were pioneers in the matter of education and numerous indeed are the flourishing schools and colleges of today which had their inception in a humble little class taught by a missionary clergyman.

A word about this book. It is concerned primarily with old church buildings; the actual structures in which the historic happenings took place. There are only a few deviations from this and even in most of these there is at least some portion of the original church preserved in the structure as it exists today.

EDWARD F. RINES

CONTENTS

ILLUSTRATIONS

Illustrations

OLD HISTORIC CHURCHES

OF AMERICA

CHAPTER I

CHURCHES OF THE CAVALIERS

By faith Moses refused to be called the son of Pharaoh's daughter, choosing rather to suffer the affliction with the children of God for he endured as seeing Him who is invisible.

ENGLISH America, which was the America of the Revolution, actually began with the landing of the first colonists at Jamestown, Virginia, on May 13, 1607. This was the real start of the first permanent settlement by the English and as it took place some thirteen years before the landing of the Pilgrims at Plymouth, a fact that is sometimes forgotten by readers and not infrequently by historians as well, it would seem but fair that any discussion of historic churches should begin in Virginia. As a matter of fact we shall begin at Jamestown although there is not so much there as one might perhaps wish.

When the first colonists disembarked, on that May day three hundred and twenty-nine years ago, a board was carried ashore and nailed between two trees for a reading desk, canvas spread across the branches overhead and under this rude shelter, religious services were held, except in "foule" weather when the congregation shifted into an old tent.

"This was our church," wrote Captain John Smith, a gentleman well known in history, "till we built a homely thing like a barne, set upon cratchets, covered with rafts, sedge and earth; so was the walls. The best of our houses (were) of like curiosity; but the most part far much worse workmanship, that neither could well defend (from) wind nor raine. Yet we had daily Common Prayer, morning and evening; every Sunday two sermons; and every three months the Holy Communion, till our minister died; but our prayers daily with an Homily on Sundaies we continued two or three years after till our preachers came." This humble little house of worship described by Captain John Smith was, of course, the first church building of the Church of England in America.

For many years the ruins of its tower were the only remnants left at Jamestown of the historic church which once flourished there and even this was in danger of perishing with the passing of time. But when the Jamestown site came under the control of the Society for the Preservation of Virginia Antiquities, a memorial chapel was erected, utilizing the old tower and following the outline of the foundations uncovered; in this manner preserving both.

In all there were five churches erected at Jamestown. The first three were frame buildings and each was burned in turn. The foundations of the third church, erected some time between 1617 and 1619, were discovered by the careful explorations of the Society and lie within the foundations of the present memorial chapel. This is mentioned because it was in this third little frame church that the first House of Burgesses met in July 1619—the first representative body of English lawmakers to assemble in America.

The first brick church was built about 1639 and was used until September 1676 when it was burned along with the rest of Jamestown by Nathaniel Bacon and his men during "Bacon's Rebellion." It has been suggested, however, that enough of the tower and the walls remained standing to be utilized in the building of a new church upon the same spot some time between 1676 and 1686.

This is, of course, merely an assumption, although not an unfair one; the existing old tower may have been built in 1639 or it may date from as late as 1686. The church of which it was a part continued to be used for many years. After 1699 the meetings of the House of Burgesses were no longer held in Jamestown, but removed to the new capital of Williamsburg and the residents of Jamestown became very few and the congregation of the Jamestown Church was likewise greatly reduced. The structure was in ruins before 1812 and presently the old tower alone was left. This has now been saved from a similar fate and, as a part of the Jamestown Memorial Chapel, is in the nature of an appropriate marker for one of the most historic spots of all—the site of the first permanent English settlement in America.

Churches of the Cavaliers

After the destruction of the State House in 1698 it was decided to remove the seat of government to a more healthful spot, less afflicted with malaria and mosquitoes. The site chosen was the little village of Middle Plantation, situated upon high ground about seven miles back from Jamestown and the river. The name was promptly changed to Williamsburg after the reigning King of England and the continuity of the first permanent English settlement was unbroken, Williamsburg merely becoming an extension of the earlier site and continuing on down to this day. In like manner old Bruton Parish Church, at Williamsburg, became but an extension of the religious organization at Jamestown and today bears witness to the continuity of the life of the church established there.

Bruton Parish Church is the oldest Episcopal Church in continuous use in the United States. The present building, begun in 1710, is the third of a series of churches located on the same spot but nothing definite is known concerning its designer. It is said that Alexander Spotswood, then governor of the colony, made the drawings and it seems quite likely that this is true.

The exterior is of the typical Virginia type, built in the form of a Roman Cross with a square entrance of red glazed brick and a somewhat heavy tower. The interior, although very simple, is one of the most artistic of its kind in the world. The parish was not called Bruton until some years after it was founded and is thought to have been so named as a mark of respect to an early parishioner, Sir Thomas Ludwell, who was born in Bruton, England.

The first known rector of Bruton Church was the Reverend Rowland Jones, an ancestor of Martha Washington, who is listed as minister in the vestry book of 1674, the oldest record book that has been preserved, and prominent among the early vestrymen may be found George Wythe, the first professor of a law course given in a college in America, and Henry Tyler, great-great-grandfather of President Tyler. Washington was in George Wythe's home many times and during the period that he was in Williamsburg, he always worshiped at Bruton Parish Church, as did also Patrick Henry and George Mason. Washington's name appears fourteen times on the record books.

The west and part of the south galleries were reserved for students of William and Mary College. In these galleries, while students, sat Presidents Jefferson, Monroe, and Tyler, Chief Justice John Marshall, Governor Edmund Randolph, General Winfield Scott and Peyton Randolph, President of the Continental Congress.

In 1715 Bruton Church became the Court Church of Colonial Virginia and when Virginia was about to go to war with Great Britain the House of Burgesses on June 1, 1774 proceeded to the church for fasting, humiliation and prayer.

In 1839 the interior of the church was entirely altered and divided up by partitions regardless of artistic effect. Pews were rearranged and even the graves of many eminent persons who rested within the sanctuary were transferred elsewhere!

Happily, in 1905–1907, the structure was at least partially restored. The foundations and roof timbers were renewed and the bell presented to the parish in 1761 was rehung in the tower. A rich velvet curtain, embroidered with the name of Alexander Spotswood, was placed in proper position over the Governor's seat, the high pulpit relocated in its original position and the aisles of the church paved with white marble in which stones were properly marked to designate the graves which had been so rudely removed back in 1839. King Edward VII gave the new pulpit Bible and President Theodore Roosevelt the lectern upon which it rests. The present Prayer Desk Bible was presented by President Woodrow Wilson.

This restoration was incomplete and, in the light of further research, is now known to have been in some respects inaccurate. By reason of the perfection of the restoration work since done in Williamsburg, and also because of other reasons, practical and compelling, it is now planned to complete and perfect the restoration of Old Bruton, its ancient churchyard, and its churchyard wall.

In the old, moss-covered churchyard are buried three Colonial governors, the great-grandfather, the grandfather, and the grandmother of Martha Washington; also two of her children.

The bell in the tower is one of the most historic in the entire country. It rang with the repeal of the Stamp Act in 1766, with the first act of sovereignty by any of the colonies, on May 15, 1776, being thus six weeks ahead of the Philadelphia bell in proclaim-

Interior Bruton Parish Church, Williamsburg, Va. The court church of Colonial Virginia.
Photo by Homeier-Clark Studio.

St. Luke's, near Smithfield, Va. The oldest church of English construction in the United States.

Photo by Homeier-Clark Studio.

ing American Independence; it rang with the hauling down of the Union Jack from the old Williamsburg Capitol; it rang at the surrender of Cornwallis at Yorktown, and it celebrated the peace with Great Britain proclaimed at Williamsburg May 1, 1783!

The baptismal font in the church is said to have been the one used in the Jamestown Church where Pocahontas was baptized and a great deal of its communion service came as gifts from British sovereigns.

There are in fact three notable communion services, the most interesting being the one brought from the church at Jamestown. It consists of chalice, paten and alms basin presented to Jamestown Church by Francis Maryson, Acting Governor of Virginia. The paten and chalice are marked "Mixe not holy thinges with profane. Ex dono Francisci Morrison Armigeri Anno Domi 1661" and the basin is marked with arms and "For the use of James City Parish Church."

It is largely due to the efforts of the Reverend W. A. R. Godwin, D.D., the present rector of Old Bruton, that the city of Williamsburg is now being restored to its original Colonial charm for it was Dr. Godwin, who, fired by the vision of Williamsburg as it had existed in the days of the colonies, carried his dream to John D. Rockefeller, Jr., and interested him in the project.

Many Presidents of the United States have worshiped at Old Bruton, the last being Woodrow Wilson, while Presidents Harding, Coolidge, and Franklin D. Roosevelt have visited the church during their terms of office.

The ancient brick church of St. Luke's, near Smithfield, was erected in 1632. This date, long insisted upon by tradition, was apparently verified in 1887 when read in some bricks that fell from the walls. From this it appears likely then that St. Luke's is the oldest building of English construction in the United States.

The builder was one Joseph Bridger, about whom very little is known, although his son was a councillor of State to Charles II and prominent in the early life of the colony.

From existing records, St. Luke's appears first to have been known as "The Old Brick Church" and its present designation not to have come until later. The oldest vestry book is dated 1727, an earlier book having been destroyed. It is said this earlier book contained the statement that the church was built in 1632 and several persons who had the privilege of reading the book before it crumbled to dust confirmed this fact in writing.

St. Luke's is a small but solid and substantial-looking structure. It is a pronounced Gothic building and exceedingly well proportioned, although as is the case in a great many early Colonial churches, the entrance tower seems a little too rugged for the remainder of the structure.

One of the most interesting features of the church is the famous chancel window which is in reality seventeen distinct windows, separated by brick mullions. It contains both circular and pointed panes, the whole forming a large rounded window that is at once very graceful and very beautiful. The stained glass for this window was made in England and given, duty free, by Queen Victoria. In the woodwork of the chancel is now firmly embedded the brick containing the figures 1632, verifying this date as the year in which the church was erected.

Beneath the shade of giant oaks which surround the ancient building Tarleton's British troopers are said to have rested during the Revolutionary War, the Virginia militia, in the War of 1812, bivouacked around it, as did also Confederate troops in 1861. According to one tradition, somewhat vague I am afraid, Washington is said to have visited the church and Cornwallis, with his troops, rested for an afternoon under the branches of the trees within its yards.

In the early days of its existence, St. Luke's was a thriving and active parish attended by families for miles around but as the years went by many of these families moved away, others preferred to attend church in Smithfield and through lack of finances the old building began to fall into a neglected state.

Finally in 1836 after two hundred years of service, St. Luke's was abandoned as a place of worship and for nearly half a century remained closed. During this time the building was preyed upon by relic hunters and the doors, windows and all removable portions of the interior carried away.

In 1884 the roof caved in bringing down with it a portion of the east wall. It was at this time that the Reverend David Burr, the rector of a neighboring church, visited the parish and, realizing the importance of the old building to American history, determined upon a restoration. It was due to his untiring efforts in the face of many difficulties and to the efforts of the architect, Dr. E. J. N. Stent, that this restoration was successfully carried to completion. Mr. Stent contributed his services and even helped collect money to aid in the work.

Happily the walls were still intact with the exception of a portion of the east wall which had fallen with the roof so that the design of the church as it exists today is undoubtedly very much as it was at the beginning.

The families of early communicants who had moved away to other states aided generously in the restoration and in order to retain in the structure as much as possible of the original building, the chancel railing was constructed from the wood of the roof which had caved in.

While keeping as true to the traditions and style of the original structure as possible, twelve new memorial windows were added. Among those so honored are George Washington, General Robert E. Lee, Captain John Smith and the already mentioned Joseph Bridger who himself lies buried not far from this ancient church that he designed.

In addition to the Old Brick Church of Isle of Wight County, there remain at least six Virginia structures, and there may be more, which claim a seventeenth-century date for their existing church buildings. Some of these depend upon tradition alone in support of this claim; others have various bits of evidence to offer in addition.

The tradition in regard to St. Mary's White Chapel, Lancaster County, named for St. Mary's Church in Whitechapel District in London, is rather vague but it is thought to have been built about 1669. This is the ancient church of the Ball family, the ancestors of George Washington's mother, and in the churchyard are a number of old tombs of massive marble, bearing dates in the seventeenth and eighteenth centuries and nearly all of the oldest inscribed with the name of Ball.

St. Mary's was first built in the form of a cross, with three galleries, one of which was for the use of the slaves, but in 1740 the structure was almost entirely rebuilt; a new roof was put on, the two arms of the church taken down and the remaining parts made into an oblong structure, sixty feet long, thirty feet broad, twenty-four feet high, with an oval ceiling. One gallery alone remains, over the south door.

This little church underwent no depredations during the War Between the States although its vestry book was destroyed at this time. Also bomb shells thrown from the Federal gunboats coming up the Rappahannock River fell close by, cutting off the tree tops but not hitting the church itself. The interior underwent various changes during the nineteenth century, the old pews were cut down and the high pulpit removed; however, the tablets placed above the Communion Table in 1669 are still in use.

Like St. Mary's, St. George's Church, Accomac County, is but a shadow of its former self. It was also at first cruciform but after being used as a stable by the Federal troops during the War Between the States was left almost a complete wreck. After being abandoned for twenty-five years, during which time cows grazed on the grass growing in its brick paved aisles, the structure was repaired by taking down the arms of the cross and using the bricks to rebuild the main portion. With its classic pediment and square belfry, St. George's resembles more a New England house of worship rather than a Virginia church of 1652, the date usually assigned for its erection. The explanation is, of course, that these features were not a part of the church originally but nineteenth century additions.

The little church of Merchant's Hope, Prince George County, takes its quaint and suggestive name from the old plantation on which it stood, this plantation in turn having received its title from a bark called *Ye Merchant's Hope* which was plying between England and Virginia in 1634. The church is sixty feet long and thirty feet wide with walls twenty-two inches thick and rafters of such huge size that about the middle of the last century the walls were braced by iron rods to prevent threatened damage. On one of these rafters the date 1657 was found and this was taken to be the year of the church's erection. Some changes have been made in the interior. The chancel furniture and pulpit were destroyed during the war of the sixties and have been replaced. The original flagstone aisles are still in use. On replacing one of these tiles it was found to bear on its under surface a crown in the stone as a sort of stamp or trademark, leading some to infer that they were imported from England. The great age of this little building is apparent. Many believe it to be the oldest church standing in Virginia. The Merchant's Hope tract was at one time owned by Richard Quiney, the brother of Thomas Quiney who married Shakespeare's daughter Judith.

Ware Church, Gloucester County, is thought to have been built some time not later than 1690 and the parish goes back to the middle of the seventeenth century. Like most Virginia churches no provisions seem to have been made for heating the building, it being left to each family or person to come prepared to face the cold, or else worship regardless of whatever discomfort was experienced. Or perhaps the spiritual warmth furnished by the sermons of the early parsons was deemed sufficient to provide comfort. The interior of Ware has been "modernized." This consisted in removing the tall pulpit from the side wall, the square pews, and the flagstones from the aisles. The chancel floor was built over to cover the tombstones placed in the pavement in front of the altar, while a vestibule was built under what had originally been the servants' gallery. The church suffered somewhat during the War Between the States, the communion table being stolen during this period.

About 1691 was built Hungar's Church in Northampton County. Prior to the Revolution its interior furnishings were among the finest in the colony, all coming from England and most of them being gifts from Queen Anne. Following the war, in the general antagonism to everything English, the building was pillaged and desecrated. The large pipe organ was carried from the church and destroyed. According to tradition the metal was used by the fishermen in the neighborhood as sinkers for their nets. The beautiful chancel draperies of dark crimson velvet, with gold embroidery and bullion fringe, were cut to pieces, while doors and windows were allowed to fall from their hinges. The exterior of the church remained unchanged but the interior never regained its Colonial splendor and the furnishings and drapes afterwards installed were simple and inexpensive.

About 1850 the building was pronounced unsafe. Cracks had appeared in one of the gables and the walls were slightly out of plumb. Attempts to draw the walls back into place having proved unsuccessful, the cracked gable was pulled down together with a portion of each side wall, reducing the size of the structure about one-third. At the same time the interior was somewhat altered. The congregation still has in its possession silver and an altar cloth given by Queen Anne, which in some manner escaped the destroying hands of the post-Revolutionary period.

Grace Church, Yorktown, was probably built in 1696 and the structure is undoubtedly the same one to whose building fund Governor Nicholson subscribed at that time, however only the walls of the main portion of the original church stand. These are constructed of a kind of marl stone and when the building was burned in 1815, the action of the fire made the stone firmer than ever, rendering the task of rebuilding fairly easy. The old structure, we are told, was in the "shape of a T situated east and west." When the church was rebuilt the wings of the T were left off, making only a nave sixty by thirty feet.

During the siege of Yorktown Cornwallis used the structure as a magazine, damaging it to the extent of one hundred and fifty pounds. During the Civil War the church suffered again. Standing as it did on a favorably-high position, a signal tower was erected on top of the roof and the interior dismantled. When the building burned, the bell in this church was broken and the pieces laid aside in the vestry room. These fragments disappeared during the Civil War but were afterwards found in Philadelphia, returned to the church and recast in a new bell which is still in use.

The Reverend David Mossom, who was rector of St. Peter's Church, in New Kent County, from 1727 to 1767, was the first American admitted to the office of presbyter in the Church of England. He was also the minister who married General Washington and Mrs. Martha Custis on January 6, 1759, tradition making the scene of the marriage in the church itself and historians pretty generally placing it at the Custis homestead, known as the White House, not far away, until it has even been written that St. Peter's is famous as "the church in which Washington was not married."

But aside from this disputed point St. Peter's has other claims for remembrance and honor at this late date. It is one of the oldest church buildings in Virginia and as such is intimately connected with early life in the colony.

In those days there was no great distinction between civil and moral law and an examination of the parish records shows that the vestry exercised what would now be termed police power over the members. Perhaps drastic action was necessary for an early minister, the Reverend Nicholas Moreau, in writing to the Bishop of London, said, "I have got into the very worst parish of Virginia and most troublesome." Mr. Moreau was also strongly in favor of a Bishop in Virginia—something to which the vestries and the council stood firmly opposed—and in the same letter to his Bishop he pleads, "an eminent Bishop being sent over here will make hell tremble, and settle the Church of England here forever."

Work on the present structure started in 1701 and two years later services were commenced. The architect was one Will Hughes but his name is the only fact we have concerning him. The outside of the building is not greatly unlike St. Luke's at Smithfield, commenced some sixty-eight years earlier. The lower part of the tower entrance is broken up by three arched openings and the upper portion of this tower is treated somewhat differently from that of the earlier church. The windows also are rectangular and plainer.

Inside, the church is almost austere in its simplicity but as has been pointed out, it at least offers no distraction to the worshiper!

During the Civil War St. Peter's like so many churches in Virginia, suffered defacement by soldiers and was turned into a stable. A relic of these stormy days is found in the names of soldiers from Connecticut carved upon the walls of the porch. After the war the few parishioners left set to work to repair the building and save it from falling into further decline so that today it looks very much as it must have looked in the early part of the eighteenth century. Services are still held there one Sunday in each month.

Of all the ministers who have officiated at St. Peter's, the Reverend David Mossom, already referred to, is perhaps best remembered. He was hardly an ideal rector but his frequent outbursts of temper lent color to his forty years of service and help to keep his memory green. Bishop Meade in his book on Virginia families and churches "gently apologizes" for Parson Mossom by informing us, "He was married four times, and much harassed by his last wife, as Colonel Bassett has often told me, which may account for and somewhat excuse a little peevishness."

At one time he had a quarrel with the clerk of the parish and this quarrel reached such an intensity that the offender was assailed in a sermon from the pulpit and threatened with a beating, no doubt a very exciting Sunday morning for the members of the congregation present on that occasion. Undaunted, the clerk struck back by giving out the Second Psalm containing the lines:

> *With restless and ungovern'd rage,*
> *Why do the heathen storm?*
> *Why in such rash attempts engage,*
> *As they can ne'er perform?*

Westmoreland County is identified with the very early history of Virginia and one of its churches, Yeocomico, bearing the Indian name of a close-by river, is one of the oldest church structures in the state. It was built in the year 1706 and is a cruciform structure, simply but very strongly built of colonial brick, with a steep shingled roof and large square windows, protected by heavy old-fashioned shutters.

The old church has suffered greatly from the scars of war. During the War of 1812 it was used as a barracks and later a company of the home militia camped there. The communion table was removed to the yard, where it served as a butcher's block and was almost entirely defaced. The baptismal font was taken some miles from home and used as a punch bowl. This was afterwards returned to the church and is in use even today. The canvas on which the Ten Commandments, the Lord's Prayer, and the Credo were impressed was so torn by the soldiers that it was necessary to remove it.

The old building remained in ruins until 1820 when it was restored through the generosity of a worthy gentleman of New York. During the Civil War it afforded shelter for the home guard and since then repairs have been carefully made from time to time. The original pews have been replaced by more modern ones and the old pulpit with its sounding board is gone. The baptismal font and communion table alone remain of the original furnishings.

Christ Church, Middlesex County, was erected about 1712, but although the community was a very prosperous one prior to the outbreak of the Revolution, the parish afterwards declined to such an extent that the church was abandoned as a place of worship. The Revolutionary pastor was a man of deep piety but his successor was not and his ministry helped to complete the wreck already well started by the war.

However, in spite of this and similar instances that not infrequently come to light in the study of the Colonial church, it can be said that such cases were the exception rather than the general rule. Notwithstanding all the best efforts exercised by the vestries of the various churches, many unworthy men and some impostors did creep in but these instances were much less frequent than has sometimes been represented.

Christ Church was first restored in 1840, at which time Bishop Meade wrote the following description of the building's appearance:

More, perhaps, than fifty years ago it was deserted. Its roof decayed and fell in. Everything within it returned to its native dust. But nature abhors a vacuum. A sycamore tree sprung up within its walls. All know the rapidity of that tree's growth. It filled the void. Its boughs soon rose over and overspread the walls.

Bishop Meade also recorded how this tree was removed piecemeal and the "rich mould of fifty years' accumulation, to the depth of two feet," dug up before the chancel floor and the stone aisles could be reached.

The present St. John's Church, Hampton, was erected in the year 1727 but the parish in which it is situated had a long and interesting history prior to this time, going back to the settlement founded by the early colonists on the site of the ancient Indian village of Kecoughtan.

The first church was erected about 1610 but aside from the supposition that it was very likely a wooden structure, as were most of the early colonial buildings, little else is known of this early house of worship, however, it is considered probable that Pocahontas worshiped within its walls.

In 1619 the name of the town was changed to Elizabeth City and in 1623 it is recorded that the first English couple married in Virginia, John and Anna Layden, lived within the bounds of the parish. Their first child, Virginia Layden, was the first English child born in America after Virginia Dare of Roanoke Island, whose history, as we know, ends with her birth.

In 1727 the parish was without a church and the matter being referred to the Governor, it was decided that the new church should be built within the "precincts of the town of Hampton." The new church prospered until the Revolutionary War when it suffered the usual irreverent treatment; also during that time the belfry was struck by lightning and the royal coat of arms hurled to the ground. This was very pleasing to the patriots who seemed to see in it a sign very favorable.

Hardly had repairs been made and services resumed than the town of Hampton was plundered by the British in 1812 and St. John's Church desecrated and turned into barracks. Following the war the structure became a refuge for owls and bats "while cattle roamed in the yard which was used as a slaughter ground for the butcher and an arena for pugilistic contests." The building fell more and more into decay until nothing was left but the bare walls and a roof that was about ready to cave in.

In 1824 Bishop Moore held a service in the ruins and plans were laid to repair the historic old building. Six years later Bishop Moore consecrated the restored structure and the church once more prospered until 1861 when it again fell upon evil days.

On the nights of August 7th and 8th, upon the approach of the Federal troops, the inhabitants of Hampton set fire to their own homes as proof of their confidence in the Southern cause and to prevent the buildings from falling into the hands of the opposing forces. In this fire St. John's also was burned. Only the walls were left standing and once more they became a refuge for owls and bats and a shelter for cattle. Later a group of squatters moved in and built their shacks against the walls.

As soon as possible after peace was declared the members of Elizabeth City Parish set about to rebuild their church. The walls were intact but the roof and tower were gone. The work was finally completed in 1869 under the ministration of the Reverend Mr. McCarthy, a retired chaplain of the United States Army, who freely gave his services for a period of two years. A tower was added some time later and a new organ installed.

The communion service in the keeping of the parish was made in London in 1618 and the chalice and paten have been in longer use than any other English church vessels in America. They are relics of a church established for the Indians, which was destroyed in the great massacre of 1622. The vessels were taken to Jamestown by Governor Yeardley and afterwards given to the parish of Elizabeth City.

Probably no one book has caused more consternation than Bishop Meade's "Old Churches and Families of Virginia." It is an encyclopedia on what does and what does not comprise a "First" Family of Virginia, and the failure of a Virginian to find one or more of his forbears listed therein has been the cause of much distressed feeling. One can only say that Bishop Meade's book is an amazing one for the matter of F. F. V's is an intricate study at best and to tackle it meant to brave the wrath to come! However, so well did he do the job that his book yet remains the final authority on the subject.

"Old Churches and Families of Virginia" contains a great wealth of church history and much delightful detail, including some of the good Bishop's experiences with the old high pews and tall pulpits of the Colonial churches, which allowed both minister and congregation to enjoy deep seclusion, and how he frequently had to erect temporary platforms of brick or stone, in the pulpits, to enable him to see those who had come to worship.

Such a condition always awaited him at Vauter's Church in Essex County, a cruciform brick structure erected in 1731, or earlier. The old box stall pews were long ago cut down to nearly half of their former height but, although the chancel is now equipped with two modern stands or lecterns, the tall crimson-draped pulpit with its winding stairway and reading desk on the first landing was left standing against the wall.

Following the Revolutionary War Vauter's seemed likely to suffer the fate of other houses of worship and it was only due to the friendship of Mrs. Muscoe Garnett that it was spared. Hearing that persons had commenced carrying away the paving stones of the aisles, she claimed the building as her own, insisting that it stood upon her ground, and threatening prosecution to the next offender. Mrs. Garnett did in fact own land adjacent to the church but apparently no one challenged her claim and the little building was saved from despoiling hands.

Christ Church, Lancaster County, has been called "The most perfect example of Colonial church architecture now remaining in Virginia" and aside from a few minor alterations and repairs, the building remains today almost exactly as it was when first erected in 1732. The first church on this site was built in 1670. This place of worship becoming too small for the congregation, a larger one, together with a new location, was considered.

Robert Carter, of Corotoman, generally known, on account of his estate and wealth, as "King Carter," offered to build a new church at his own expense, provided the old site was retained and, to quote from his will, "Provided always the chancel be preserved as a burial place for my family, as the present chancel is, and that there be preserved for my family a commodious pew in the chancel."

The ancient records show that he bore the entire cost of construction, reserving one-fourth of the church for his servants and tenants and a large pew near the chancel for his family. According to tradition the congregation did not enter on Sunday until the arrival of his coach, at which time they followed the "King" into church. Even before the present church was built the Carters were accustomed to write their names in the vestry book ahead of the minister's name!

Colonel Carter was married five times, one of his wives surviving him, and because of the confused manner in which his wives and children are mentioned, the epitaph on his tomb, to be found in the church at the side of the chancel, always creates comment.

Christ Church is in the form of a cross with brick walls three feet thick. The interior walls are panelled with black walnut as high as the tops of the pew backs, above which they are plastered. The pews are the old square variety and some of these seat twenty persons with ease. Not many years ago the structure was re-shingled, broken panes of glass replaced and other necessary repairs made. Occasional services are still held in the old building.

St. John's, King William County, was built in 1734. It is a rather typical example of the colonial cruciform church and has but recently been rescued from a desolate state and at least partially repaired. The original furnishings are all gone, the high-backed pews having given way to benches, and other changes made. Carter Braxton, signer of the Declaration of Independence, was a member of St. John's, the "Mother Church of St. John's Parish."

The old town of Petersburg has many historic associations but probably its most famous treasure is Old Blandford Church, for many years a picturesque ivy-draped ruin in the midst of a beautiful moss-covered cemetery, but now restored into a Confederate Museum.

Before the Revolution the town of Blandford, now a part of Petersburg, was a very busy port and one of the leading tobacco shipping points in Virginia. The old vestry book indicates that in 1735 it was "order'd that a Church be built of Brick on Wellses Hill to be 60 foot by 25 foot in the Clear and 15 foot to the spring of the Arch from the floor." This is the church now known as Old Blandford; in the early days it was always known as "The Brick Church on Wells' Hill," and for a long period is so referred to in the church records. In the years 1752–64 radical changes were made, additions on the south and north sides making the structure cruciform, but from the time these changes were completed until the building was finally abandoned as a place of worship, "The Brick Church on Wells' Hill" remained practically unaltered. In this old church George Whitefield, the great English evangelist, once preached and here also was heard William Stith, the Virginia historian.

After the Revolution the old town of Blandford declined in importance while the newer town of Petersburg grew steadily; finally, with the building of a new church in Petersburg in 1808 the fate of the old brick church was sealed. Services were held there intermittently but at last even infrequent services were discontinued and the ancient building allowed to fall into ruins. The churchyard continued to be, and still is, the town cemetery of Petersburg. It was as a melancholy, moss-grown ruin that Old Blandford became famous and the subject of some half dozen or more printed poems. Probably none of these more feelingly tells the story than the beautiful lines found inscribed upon the walls of the church about 1841, which start out:

> *Thy art crumbling to the dust, old pile,*
> *Thy art hastening to thy fall,*
> *And 'round thee in thy loneliness*
> *Clings the ivy to thy wall.*
> *The worshipers are scattered now,*
> *Who knelt before thy shrine;*
> *And silence reigns where anthems rose,*
> *In days of "Auld Lang Syne."*

According to tradition the English General Phillips was laid to rest in the southeast corner of Blandford Cemetery. As he lay dying the town was being bombarded by the Americans under Lafayette and the noise of battle is said to have disturbed his last hours.

Not far away from the ancient edifice are the remnants of the earthworks held by the Confederate forces during the famous siege of Petersburg which lasted from the 9th of June, 1864, to the 2nd of April, 1865, and for many years bullets were to be found in the cemetery and close up to the old churchyard wall.

Some time during the eighties the walls of Old Blandford were reroofed to preserve the ruins from utter destruction and the restored church has since been converted into a Confederate Memorial Chapel to which each of the states of the Southern Confederacy has contributed a memorial window.

Old Fork Church, Hanover County, was built in 1735 and the popular name by which it is now known came about from its location at the forks of the Pamunkey River, as the two little streams, the North Anna and South Anna, were called in many legal documents of early times.

The church is built of the old familiar glazed-end brick and the building is about seventy-five by twenty-five feet. The rather severe style of architecture is relieved somewhat by the colonial porticos of harmonious proportions found over both the front and the side, or minister's door.

Old Fork has had many notable members, among these being Patrick Henry who attended there in his youth and in later life while living at "Scotch Town" an old structure some five miles distant. From "Scotch Town" also came Henry's cousin Dorothea, better known as Dolly, to attend services but it is quite certain that the little girl who then sat in one of the old high-backed pews little dreamed that she would one day be the wife of James Madison, President of the United States, and become known as one of the most gracious of our First Ladies. Another distinguished member who attended this church in his youth and early manhood was Thomas Nelson Page, the well-known writer. Both the Page and Nelson families have been among the church's most staunch supporters for generations.

Old Fork has in its possession a very beautiful communion service bearing the following inscription: "For the use of the churches in St. Martin's Parish, in Hanover and Louisa counties, Virginia, 1759." Unfortunately the history of this service is lost but according to one story it was presented by the church of St. Martin-in-the Fields, London, and by another that it was presented by William Nelson, President of the Council, and brought over by his son, Thomas, afterwards Governor Nelson, upon his return from England that year.

We are accustomed to associate the witchcraft delusion almost wholly with New England but this belief existed elsewhere as well. Lynnhaven Parish, Princess Anne County, had several witchcraft trials, perhaps the most notable being the case of Grace Sherwood who as early as 1698 was suspected of practicing black magic. One neighbor declared that Grace had in fact bewitched his cotton; another that she was capable of going out of a keyhole and through the crack of a door like a black cat. Mrs. Sherwood seems to have emerged safely from these difficulties only to suffer the same accusation some seven years later.

This time she was judged by "a jury of Anciente and knowing women" but the matter was not settled and Grace was at last ordered to be tried in the water. The spot on the Lynnhaven River where she was bound and put in, that her judges might "try her how she swims," is still called Witch Duck. Even this trial was not deemed conclusive and so poor Grace was again placed before more "Anciente and knowing women" who declared that "she was not like them, nor like any other woman that they knew." And here I think we may leave Grace Sherwood although her troubles were not completely over. There remained the threat of a further trial but as to whether or not this ever took place, the records remain silent. Probably not and perhaps Grace was allowed to go about unmolested from then on. Her will was not recorded until 1740 so she undoubtedly outlived many of the "Anciente" women who made up her trial jury. It would certainly seem that she earned whatever rest then came her way.

In addition to her apparent proclivity to witchcraft accusations, Grace Sherwood is remembered for another reason; it being the common tradition that she brought rosemary across the sea in an egg-shell. The fragrant shrub still flourishes in Princess Anne County.

The old Donation Church in Princess Anne County, Lynnhaven Parish, was built in 1736 when an older church was destroyed in a curious way. Some of the parishioners were fishermen and in order to save themselves a long roundabout journey, cut a short and narrow waterway from the Lynnhaven River to the bay; the winter storms caused a swift deep current which cut its way into the churchyard. Before very long the entire churchyard was submerged and found a tragic resting place at the bottom of the Lynnhaven River.

The name of the new church came from its being near a donation of land given by a subsequent rector. There was some rather violent dissatisfaction with the manner in which the vestry assigned the pews, leading that august body to declare "that who or whatsoever person or persons shall assume to themselves a power or take the liberty to place themselves or others in any other seats or pews in ye said church, shall be esteemed a disorderly person, and may expect to be dealt with according to law."

For many years Donation Church stood in a state of picturesque ruin, with big trees growing up within its walls in the lonely woods, but the structure has now been thoroughly restored. The Eastern Shore Chapel in the same county and parish was built in 1754. The church still has in its possession the original communion vessels, consisting of a handsome cup, paten and flagon, all bearing the date 1759.

Farnham Church, Richmond County, has had a very unique history, being, so far as I know, the only Virginia church which has ever seen service as a distillery in its long period of existence. It was probably built about 1737 and during the Revolutionary War was used as a stable by the British troops. Gapping openings were left in the walls so that the domestic beasts of the field, such as cattle and hogs, could wander through at will. The bricks of the wall which originally surrounded the churchyard were taken away piecemeal by anybody in the neighborhood who wanted to build a chimney or repair a hearth or foundation and the building was turned into a distillery of what Bishop Meade calls "poisonous liquors," but which, it has been pointed out, evidently refers to the usual kind, the term "poisonous" quite obviously merely expressing ecclesiastical disapproval of all liquor in general.

It was during this period that the doors were broken down to make way for bringing a wagon into the building and the baptismal font "was used to prepare materials for feasting and drunkenness," probably for making mash or to harbor punch. Happily though this bowl was afterwards rescued from its sacrilegious uses and returned to its rightful place as a baptismal font. The last time the building was restored only the bare walls remained of what had once been a very handsome church on the cruciform order. During the War of 1812 a skirmish occurred around the church between the Richmond County Militia and raiders from Admiral Cockburn's fleet sailing up the Potomac to attack the city of Washington. The walls of the church still show the marks of bullets fired in this skirmish.

Probably the most interesting feature connected with the Glebe Church, Nansemond County, is the bit of Revolutionary War history that has come down to us. The minister at that time, the Reverend Mr. Agnew, was a pronounced loyalist and made no effort to keep his views in the background. In the spring of 1775 he visited among his congregation urging their presence upon a particular Sunday. A large crowd assembled but in spite of the known feelings of this congregation, no word of disapproval was heard when Parson Agnew recited the prayer for the King. But when he announced the text of his sermon, "Render unto Caesar the things that are Caesar's," his listeners undoubtedly pricked up their ears and waited apprehensively for what was coming. In the midst of the sermon in which was decried the sins of disloyalty, Mr. William Cowper, a vestryman and magistrate, left his seat and mounting the pulpit stairs, ordered the minister to come down.

Replied Mr. Agnew, "I am doing my Master's business."

"Which master?" shouted back the angry Mr. Cowper, "your Master in heaven or your master over the seas? You must leave this house, or I will use force."

Under this threat Parson Agnew capitulated. "I will never be the cause of breeding riot in my Master's house," he answered and with this he stepped down from the pulpit, walked down the aisle and through the crowd at the church door. Here he entered a carriage and drove away. This was the last of Parson Agnew in so far as the Glebe Church was concerned but it was by no means the last of Parson Agnew. He continued his activities against the impending revolution and was finally imprisoned by the county committee. Some time during 1776 he left Nansemond County and entered the British service, becoming Chaplain of the Queen's

Rangers. Later he was taken prisoner and carried to France. William Cowper became very popular because of his defiance of Parson Agnew and was chosen to represent the county in the Virginia Convention of May, 1776, which gave to the state its first constitution.

The present Glebe Church—the same building in which the Reverend Mr. Agnew officiated that stirring Sunday morning in 1775—was built in 1738 and stands in a good state of preservation. Another church of this parish, that of Suffolk, is St. John's, built in 1755 near the site of its predecessor of far more ancient birth. The church was not called St. John's until 1845, before this being known as Chuckatuck Church. In this church the law was strictly observed requiring the name of the parish to be sewn on the sleeves of those receiving aid from the church.

The present church of St. Paul's, Norfolk, was erected in 1739 and in general outline follows the simple lines of village churches of the period in England. This connection of the old world with the new is one of the many things that makes the early Colonial churches of Virginia so very interesting.

The land for the church was given by one Samuel Boush and it is thought that the letters S. B. appearing in raised brick on the south wall signify his initials. Above these initials is inscribed the date of the church's erection.

The rector of St. Paul's during the Revolution was the Reverend Thomas Davis, an ardent patriot, President of the Sons of Liberty and Chairman of the town meeting held to protest against the notorious Stamp Act.

When the British under Lord Dunmore bombarded the city some ten years after this meeting the town was almost completely destroyed, the walls of St. Paul's alone resisting the attack. A cannon ball, fired from the frigate *Liverpool*, is today cemented in the south wall of the church in the indenture it made when it struck the building, and serves as a relic of the British onslaught. This ball after striking the church fell to the ground beneath and was covered up for many years—was not discovered in fact until as late as 1848.

After the close of the Revolution the building was only partially restored and some time shortly after 1800 was used for a while by the Baptists and then by the colored people of that church but in 1832 was again taken over by the Episcopalians and a more thorough restoration made.

The church had no more than recovered from the ill effects of the War of the Revolution than the congregation was swept into the War Between the States and dark days set in once more. After the capture of Norfolk by the Federal troops, St. Paul's was taken possession of by the military forces and when restored to the congregation in 1865 was in a terrible state of disrepair. Years later the United States Government reimbursed the church for damage done during that period.

The churchyard is one of the prettiest to be found anywhere. A wealth of rich ivy covers the war-scarred monuments which are guarded and watched over by the giant elms and willows. There are flowers in abundance and much shrubbery and the whole effect is one of quiet and complete rest. In this churchyard are buried many pioneers of Virginia as well as many who fought in the War of the Revolution and in the War Between the States.

Various changes were made in the interior of the church from time to time but in 1892 a complete restoration to its earlier appearance was effected.

One of the most interesting relics to be found here is the chair in which John Hancock sat when he signed the Declaration of Independence, a mahogany arm-chair, upholstered in leather and appropriately marked with a silver plate reading as follows:

This chair was occupied by John Hancock when he signed the Declaration of Independence. It was bought by Colonel Thomas M. Bayly, of Accomac County, Va. At his death it became the property of his daughter Ann, who subsequently intermarried with the Rev. Benjamin M. Miller, once rector of St. Paul's church, Norfolk, Va., who presented it to the parish.

The marble font of the church is also quite interesting, as is the communion table. This table, of English oak, is a copy of one in Yorkshire, England, of the date of 1680.

Westover, Charles City County, the little church of the Byrd

family, was built in its present form about 1740, having been removed brick by brick by "Mrs. Byrd to her land Evelyngton"
about this date. The original church stood near the great Westover
House, about a quarter of a mile up the river bank, but owing to
the unfortunate loss of the early parish records some confusion
exists as to when a church was first built there. The earliest tomb
in what was once the churchyard is dated 1671. Bishop Meade
recorded some of the church's history as it existed in his time:

> The old Westover church still stands, a relic and monument of ancient
> times. It is built of the glazed-end bricks, generally used in Colonial
> structures. It has been subject to terrible mutilation, having been used
> in the days of general depression in the Episcopal Church in the begin-
> ning of the 19th century as a barn. Repaired then by the families of
> Berkeley and Shirley, and again repaired just prior to the war, it was
> used by the Federal troops as a stable.
>
> In 1867 the Westover church was opened and used again for the
> first time since the close of the war. Not a door, window, or floor was
> left, but by the blessing of good God and kind friends, we have repaired
> it.

The oldest portion of Old Hebron Lutheran Church, Madison
County, was built in 1740, and the building is now the oldest
Lutheran Church in the country still *owned and used* by that
denomination.

The first German settlers came to Virginia in 1714 under the
sponsorship of Governor Alexander Spotswood and settled at
Germania on the Rapidan River. In 1717 a shipload of Germans
bound for Pennsylvania was driven into the Chesapeake and sold
by the captain to cover the cost of their passage, not an unusual
procedure and one of the means adopted of supplying indentured
servants to the plantations. It had been a troublous journey from
the start. When the ship stopped at London the captain had been
imprisoned for debt for several weeks. By this delay part of the
ship's provisions were consumed. What remained was not sufficient to meet the demands of the passengers and many died of
hunger while the rest never reached their intended destination.

Governor Spotswood purchased the whole unfortunate shipload and settled them near the first group. When their term of

service was over they and others who had come from the Father-
land in the meantime, moved west, settling in the Valley of
Robinson River and White Oak Run in what is now Madison
County. There they built a log church in about 1726 to be followed
in 1740 by the main portion of the church which still stands and
which later came to be known as Hebron Church.

When the time came to build this church the pastor and two
members of the congregation went all the way across the ocean
to Germany to collect the money necessary. About three thousand
pounds were donated by friends in the old country, one-third of
which was used for traveling expenses, the remainder building
the church and buying the glebe lands. Negro slaves were purchased by the congregation, between 1739 and 1743, to work the
church lands, this being "one of the rare cases wherein Germans
departed from their dislike of the institution of slavery."

Originally the building was in the form of a rectangle fifty feet
long by twenty-six feet wide. There was a door at both ends and
in the south wall, a large vase-like pulpit and the customary high
pews. Near the end of the century of its birth the church was
altered by two additions built at right angles to the old part,
making the structure cruciform. Later improvements changed the
original curved ceiling to the present flat one and substituted the
modern pulpit and pews in place of the old. German names continue to predominate in the neighborhood and Old Hebron, after
nearly two hundred years of active service, continues to flourish
and to prosper.

In the early days when it was the largest public building in
Richmond, St. John's Church, Henrico Parish, was occasionally
used for political and patriotic meetings. On March 20, 1775, the
Virginia convention met in the church and through the entrance
door that day passed such men as George Washington, George
Mason, Thomas Jefferson, Richard Henry Lee, Peyton Randolph,
George Wythe. . . .

In the third pew on the north side sat Patrick Henry. His eyes
revealed a hidden fire burning within him but when his time
arrived and he arose to speak, his opening words were almost calm;
then as he continued, his suppressed excitement sought an out-

let and the muscles in his face and neck contracted and were drained of all color while his voice boomed out louder and louder.

An electric tension swept over the audience . . . the faces of his listeners became as pale as his own . . . finally he finished:

Gentlemen may cry peace, peace—but there is no peace. The war is actually begun! The next gale that sweeps from the north will bring to our ears the clash of resounding arms! Our brethren are already in the field! Why stand idle here? What is it that gentlemen wish? What would they have? Is life so dear, or peace so sweet, as to be purchased at the price of chains and slavery? Forbid it, Almighty God! I know not what course others may take, but as for me, give me liberty, or give me death!

No applause followed and for some seconds there was complete silence. The former opponents of the man were struck dumb, and willingly. Everyone in the group assembled there believed for the moment and felt just as this man who had addressed them believed and felt.

Then the silence grew protracted and the tension in the room mounted. Suddenly a man, seated in one of the east windows, sprang down to the floor and cried out with emotion, "Let me be buried at this spot!"

This man was Colonel Edward Carrington and his grave may now be found beneath the very east window in which he sat that memorable afternoon while a bronze tablet marks the pew in which Patrick Henry stood to deliver his immortal address.

St. John's Church was first opened in 1741, probably in June, although the exact month is unknown. It was a wooden structure painted white, plain and less beautiful than other colonial churches of the period. It stood on the top of Richmond Hill with the city to the west and the James River to the south.

Some time after the Revolutionary War it was enlarged and made into the shape of a cross and although various changes have been made from time to time, a great deal remains unchanged. The original pews are still in use although their high backs have been cut down. The hinges on the pew doors are the handwrought ones first placed there while the original weather-boarding still adorns that part of the outside which is the oldest and the window sashes are those first put in. Anyone examining the exterior will easily recognize the original weather-boarding. It is thicker and wider than that found on the newer part of the church and fastened with nails wrought on the anvil with heads half an inch thick.

The bowl of the baptismal font is a relic of Curle's Chapel, the principal church in the parish at the time St. John's was erected. Curle's Church was located some miles below Richmond on the north side of the James River and the structure disappeared during the Civil War. The bowl of the baptismal font was located in the cellar of a near-by house where it was being used as a mortar for beating hominy!

During the Revolutionary War when the British took possession of Richmond, St. John's became a barracks for Arnold's men but the church did not suffer defacement as did so many during this period.

In the old burying ground will be found many ancient tombstones, the oldest dating from 1751. George Wythe who in addition to being the first professor of a law course given in a college in America is also famous as one of the Signers of the Declaration of Independence, and Elizabeth Arnold Poe, mother of Edgar Allan Poe, are buried here. Many of the moss-covered tombstones contain quaint, prim epitaphs, of which the following is characteristic:

> *Return my friends and cease to weep,*
> *While in Christ Jesus here I sleep.*
> *Prepare yourselves, your souls to save,*
> *There's no repentance in the grave.*
> *Stop my friends as you pass by,*
> *As you are now so once was I,*
> *As I am now you soon must be;*
> *Prepare yourselves to follow me.*

Abingdon Church, Gloucester County, was probably built about 1755; at least this is the date usually assigned for its completion. Just when the work was started is not definitely known. The church

St. John's Church, Richmond, Va., where Patrick Henry said, "Give me liberty or give me death." *Photo by Homeier-Clark Studio.*

Interior Pohick Church, near Alexandria, Va. The parish church of Mount Vernon and designed by George Washington. *Photo by Alexandria Studio.*

is in the form of a square or Greek cross, with walls two feet thick. The parish is, of course, much older than the present church structure and the handsome communion set still in use was presented by Major Lewis Burwell, of Carter's Grove, in 1703. This consists of a flagon, cup and two patens, engraved "The gift of L. B. to Abingdon Parish" and stamped as being made in London in 1702. Some years later Miss Rebecca Burwell of Carter's Grove was to dance with Thomas Jefferson at the Raleigh Tavern in Williamsburg and very nearly break that young man's heart.

Abingdon was first repaired in 1841 at which time very probably the present beautiful reredos, representing in bas-relief the façade of a Greek temple, was placed in the chancel. During the Civil War the building was used as a stable by the Federal troops. Some of the Colonial pews served as stalls for horses; others were destroyed. One of the donors of the land upon which the present church stands was Colonel Augustine Warner, great-grandfather of General Washington.

Timber Ridge Presbyterian Church is located on the side of a hill that is covered with a heavy growth of fine timber—from these surroundings comes its name.

It is a fine old stone church, built of native limestone quarried from the hill a few hundred feet away. The style of architecture is massive Roman. The pulpit was built across the north wall and there were two galleries, the one at the east end for the white members and the other, along the south wall, for the slaves. Entrance to these galleries was by a stone stairway outside and over the south door.

The church was erected in 1756 and tradition tells us that the women helped in the work of construction, going with the men, holding bags and scooping in the sand. Then they rode, each with a bag of sand across her horse. Pack horses laden with sand followed. Men on foot and carrying rifles accompanied them through the Indian-infested forest as a protection against sudden attacks. Today these women who with their own hands helped to build this historic old church are commemorated by a tablet in the north end of the building, placed there by their descendants.

When first erected, the bare earth served as a floor. Later a "puncheon floor," split logs, hewn smooth and placed face up-wards, was installed; still later sawed boards, hand planed, tongued and grooved were put in. Until the Revolutionary War period logs with the top side flattened were used for seats, at which time these crude benches were replaced by high-backed pews. When trouble afterwards arose as to the assignment of pews, this was settled by assigning to each family the pew standing where its family log had been located.

Because of its massive stone walls Timber Ridge Church was used, in Indian times, as a fort. On July 17, 1763, Cornstalk and his band of Shawnee Indians invaded the little settlement of Kerr's Creek and massacred a number of men, women and children. A number escaped because they were in attendance at a religious meeting at Timber Ridge Church.

Timber Ridge is the cradle of Washington and Lee University. In October, 1774, the Presbytery agreed to adopt the grammar school taught by the Reverend John Brown. This was the school which had been started by Robert Alexander twenty-five years before.

In 1776 the school was moved to Mount Pleasant, near Fair-field, but the following year, a new building known as Liberty Hall having been completed, the school came back to Timber Ridge. Three years later Liberty Hall Academy, as the institution was now called, was again moved, this time to Lexington, Virginia. Later this school grew into the present Washington and Lee University.

Between the years 1800 and 1814 a great revival of religious fervor swept over the country. It was accompanied by violent con-tortions of the body, known as "jerks" and was looked upon with disfavor by the more staid and sturdy church fathers who thought it the work of the devil; the more progressive members looking upon this new phenomenon as the work of the Holy Spirit.

It is said that only a few such cases occurred in Timber Ridge Church. On August 4, 1805, one Ann Henderson was taken with the "jerks." Old Major Houston, the father of General Sam Hous-ton of Texas fame, and a leading member of the church, gave notice that the next case would be picked up bodily and carried out. This threat, incidentally, never had to be put into effect and there is no further mention of any case of the "jerks" in the records of Old Timber Ridge Church.

Some changes have been made in the building. In 1871 the door on the cemetery side was closed and a front entrance, called a vestibule, was built to the north end. In 1900 the church was extended and two wings added, this being done in such a manner as to harmonize perfectly with the architecture of the old building. New and more comfortable pews were also installed at this time, and the historic edifice rededicated on Sunday, December 2, 1900.

A number of old tombs are to be found near the church. On one of them may be found an epitaph which quaintly warns the passer-by:

Remember man, As you pass by,
As you Are Now so once was I
As I Am Now you soon will be,
Therefore think on Eternity&c

Augusta Church, located about eight miles from Staunton, was completed in 1749. It is also an old stone Presbyterian church and like the Timber Ridge structure, the women members are said to have aided the men in its construction, bringing the sand for the mortar on "pack horses."

In the early days of its existence a fort was erected around the church to protect it from attacks by the Indians and in the rear of the building a ridge may still be seen which marks the foundation and shows the size of the old fort. While so used, the Virginia authorities called the spot Fort Defiance. Today the church is sometimes called Fort Defiance Old Stone Church.

The building has been remodeled from time to time and in 1922 was considerably enlarged so as to seat comfortably the students attending Augusta Military Academy and a portico entrance added at the front. The result is a very pleasing structure, the new additions blending nicely with the old.

One of the most interesting features of Aquia Church, Stafford

County, is the old "three decker" pulpit, with its great sounding board. The church was erected in 1757 on the site of a former church built in 1751 and destroyed by fire the same year. The building is cruciform and of brick. An unusual feature is the bell tower as a part of the original structure and not a later addition. Three sides of this tower rest on the roof and the fourth is simply an extension of the front wall.

Over the south door may be found the information: "Built A.D. 1751. Destroyed by fire 1751, and Rebuilt A.D. 1757 by Mourning Richards Undertaker. Wm. Copein, Mason." The name "Mourning Richards" would seem particularly appropriate for an undertaker were it not for the fact that the designation in those days corresponded to our modern term of architect.

The aisles of the church are of stone with a marble cross in the center. There is a reredos of four panels on which are the Ten Commandments, Apostles' Creed and Lord's Prayer. The pews are of the old square variety and there is a large gallery. In regular use is a silver communion service of chalice, cup and paten, each piece bearing the inscription, "The gift of Rev. Alex Scott, A.M., late minister of this parish Anno 1739." This service was buried in the ground for safe-keeping during three wars, the Revolutionary War, the War of 1812, and the War Between the States.

The church suffered greatly during this latter conflict. Its churchyard became a camping place for soldiers and at the close of hostilities the building itself was in a dilapidated condition. The plastering commenced to fall from the walls, the pillars to the gallery began to give way and the doors being open, desolation reigned. Happily, however, repairs were speedily made and the building saved and preserved for posterity.

The date usually given for the erection of St. Paul's Church, King George County, is 1766 but it is thought that the church may in fact have been built about sixteen years earlier than this, in 1750. Bishop Meade gives the following description of the building as it existed in 1812:

St. Paul's was then in ruins. The roof was ready to fall, and not a window, door, pew or timber remained below. Nevertheless, notice was given that we would preach there. A rude, temporary pulpit or stand was raised in one angle of the cross, and from that we performed service and addressed the people. On the night before the meeting a heavy rain had fallen, and the water was in small pools here and there where the floor once was, so that it was difficult to find a dry spot on which the attendants might stand.

Not long after this the State Legislature turned over the ruins to the county with permission to convert these into a school. The walls were of such masonry that repairs were easily made and then for some years the building existed as a church and an institution of learning combined. A few years later the building was returned to the original owners and three-quarters of the edifice was set aside for use as a place of worship while the remaining one-fourth, in the rear, separated from the rest by thick walls, was made the abode of the minister.

St. Paul's is a cruciform brick structure and, as of old, three parts of the cross make up the place of worship while the fourth is a spacious vestry room. There is a gallery on three sides of the interior and a lofty pulpit. The windows are of the old many-paned Colonial variety.

Some time between 1740 and 1790 was built the little James City County church known as Hickory Neck Church. No actual record of the date of construction is available, however. Because of its small size it is thought that it may have been erected originally not as a church but for secular use and at any rate architects generally agree that the structure is incomplete or has been considerably altered from its original form. The design of the church is nevertheless pleasing, if unpretentious, and the bricks are laid in the customary Flemish bond, with some glazed headers included in the pattern. The name is apparently derived from that of an adjoining farm. In one record it is referred to as Hickory Nut Church.

George Washington himself was the architect for Pohick Church near Alexandria; however, since the structure is so similar to Christ Church, although smaller, it is now considered probable that Washington had access to the plans of the latter church.

The original Truro Parish Church was a frame structure erected some time near the year of Washington's birth. His connection with it started in 1735 when his father, Augustine, became a vestryman and nominated the first lay reader; from then on the family was very active in the congregation.

It was indeed Washington who decided upon the location of Pohick Church. When a new building was agreed upon, a part of the congregation wished to build it upon the site of the original building. Washington drew a map of the parish which showed where each member lived and then suggested that the building be located in the exact center of population, a recommendation that was carried out. It might be added in passing that in this way the building was located two miles closer to Mount Vernon than before!

The builder was one Daniel French but Washington was very active in overseeing building operations. The structure cost eight hundred and eighty-seven pounds and was ready for occupancy in 1772 when the vestry accepted it and auctioned off the pews, Washington purchasing pew number twenty-eight for his own use, paying the sum of ten pounds, and pew number thirty for the use of the guests who inevitably accompanied him to church, for which he paid thirteen pounds, ten shillings. The old family coach of the Washingtons, with its liveried postilion riders and its four and sometimes six horses, was a familiar sight at Old Pohick.

The church has had many distinguished parishioners in addition to Washington, among these being George Mason the "Author of the Bill of Rights and the Constitution of Virginia" who was also a member of the vestry.

Washington's diaries contain many references to the church and its early rectors who were frequent guests at Mount Vernon. A later rector was the Reverend Mason L. Weems, most generally known as Parson Weems, who it was that first reported the fabulous Washington cherry tree story in his "Life of Washington." His book is very readable but is now generally considered inaccurate.

For many years Pohick Church was deserted and fell into a bad state of repair. During the War Between the States most of the removable woodwork was carried away, including the doors to the pews occupied by George Washington and George Mason, and the building left desolate and alone. No services were held there until 1874 when, through the interest of a wealthy New Yorker, the building was put into good condition and services resumed.

Later a true restoration of the structure was made and the quaint appearance of the church today is most interesting. The old vestry book carried away as a souvenir was located and purchased for twenty dollars. This prized possession, dating from 1732, was deposited at Mount Vernon for safe-keeping. The old baptismal font was lost for many years but was finally discovered in a farmyard where it was being used as a watering trough.

It is the custom of the regents of the Mount Vernon Ladies' Association to attend services once a year in Pohick Church when they gather for their annual meeting.

On Christmas Eve in the old town of Alexandria along about the year 1818 a group of young people, laden with pine and cedar boughs might have been seen trudging through the town in the direction of Old Christ Church. Presently they are inside and start decking the walls and pulpit with the evergreen branches. Perhaps they lay a few in the pew occupied by General George Washington when he was a member of the board of vestrymen and as they do this it is undoubtedly without a thought that there is one now among them whose pew will also be preserved and pointed out to visitors in the years to come; the pew of their serious-eyed young companion who at the moment has not a thought in his head of the future glory that is to surround the name of Robert E. Lee!

Now both the pews of General Washington and General Lee are marked by silver plates and another plate designates the spot where Lee knelt at the rail to be confirmed.

Old Christ Church was commenced in 1767 and the original structure still stands. The durability of the early Colonial church buildings and mansions is not hard to fathom when the specifications covering their erection are studied. We read, for instance, that the specifications for this church required a mortar of "two parts lime and one part sand." The shingles were to be of the best cypress or juniper—juniper was used—and three-quarters of an inch thick!

The architect was one James Wren, said to have been a descendant of Sir Christopher Wren, and the original contractor, James Parsons. The price agreed upon was six hundred pounds sterling. In 1772 the building was still unfinished and James Parsons for some reason refused to continue the work, so his bondsman, Colonel John Carlyle, agreed to complete the structure for a further payment of two hundred and twenty pounds.

The church was finished and accepted by the vestry on February 27, 1773, and the pews sold to the various members of the congregation. George Washington paid thirty-six pounds, ten shillings for his. He also contributed the brass chandelier which still hangs from the ceiling.

Women were held in particularly high esteem in the early days of Christ Church and we learn that one Susannah Edwards was chosen as sexton. It is written that she "preceded the members of the congregation up the aisle, locating each family in their respective pews according to dignity."

So successful was Susannah Edwards in performing her duties that her successor was also a woman, a "Mistress Cook," who was "peculiar in dress and physiognomy" and "had a stately manner of ushering people into their pews and locking the door upon them, and with almost a military air patrolling the aisles, alert to detect and prompt to suppress any violation of order."

Unfortunately many changes have been made in the building, through necessity, for Christ Church is still in use and must meet new conditions. The gallery was added in 1787, the west aisle in 1811. Chimneys were built the following year to provide for stove heat, foot stoves having furnished the only warmth to the worshipers in the early days. The tower is also of more modern construction.

The old high-backed pews were later divided, including the one that Washington occupied, but this pew has since been restored.

In the shaded churchyard is buried Colonel Philip A. Marsteller, one of Washington's pallbearers. His grave is unknown but is supposed to be under the sycamore tree near the west gate. The handsome table stone monument which it is said once marked the spot is thought to have been carried off during the Civil War, probably to be used as a door step. Some of the earliest gravestones in the yard

are marked with formal, precise epitaphs. The following from a
stone dated 1799 is a variation of the verse found on so many
colonial markers and once again issues a solemn warning to the
observer:

> *All you that cums my grave to see,*
> *Prepare yourselves to follow me,*
> *Repent and turn to God in time,*
> *You may be taken in your prime.*

In the following inscription from a gravestone dated seven years
earlier the same verse is paraphrased slightly:

> *Weep not for me my parents dear,*
> *I am not Dead, but sleeping here.*
> *As I am now you all must be;*
> *Prepare yourselves to follow me.*

The oldest stone in the churchyard is that of Mr. Isaac Pierce:
"Born in Boston, son of Mr. Isaac Pierce, Distiller, who departed
this life March 26, 1771, aged 24 years."

Christ Church counts among its most treasured relics "The Family Bible of Gen. Washington used at Mount Vernon," presented
by George Washington Parke Custis, his adopted son, in 1804.

In 1861 Federal troops occupied the town of Alexandria and
while other churches were turned into hospitals, Christ Church
continued on as a church, army chaplains filling the pulpit.

However, during this period the original silver plate marking
Washington's pew as well as the parish register, covering the
period 1765 to 1860, and containing records of births, marriages,
burials and other official acts of the various rectors, disappeared. It
is not known whether these were lost, stolen or destroyed but the
hope is still cherished that they may some day find their way back
home.

The Falls Church, so named after the Little Falls of the Potomac River, Fairfax County, was commenced the same year as
Christ Church in Alexandria but was completed first by some years.
When Truro Parish was divided in 1765 a new parish, called Fairfax, was formed out of it. The Falls Church and Christ Church

formed this new parish, both churches having one rector and one vestry in common.

The contracts were given out for this church and Christ Church at the same time. Both were to cost six hundred pounds and James Parsons was the original builder named in both contracts. In Washington's diary for 1764 is entered a copy of an advertisement for "undertakers to build Fall's Church" thus clearly showing him to have been a member of the original building committee. The year previous he had been a member of the vestry which in regular meeting on March 28, 1763 had decided that a new church was necessary. The name of George Mason is also associated with Falls Church and he was in attendance at the vestry meeting which completed plans for the erection of the new house of worship. The first Falls Church on the present site was built about 1734, enlarged in 1750 and then taken down about 1767.

Although Washington regularly attended Pohick and Christ churches, it was also his custom to visit and worship at the Falls Church at least four times a year. It is said that he always sat in one particular pew which was reserved for him and the location of this pew is still pointed out although the original floor and pews have long since been destroyed.

A portion of Braddock's Army is said to have once camped in the churchyard and during the Revolutionary War the old church served as a company recruiting headquarters of Colonel Charles Broadwater, one of the leading patriots of Fairfax County.

Seldom do we find a church so intimately connected with five wars as Old Falls. Almost from its shadow marched Captain Henry Fairfax with his Fairfax volunteers to the Mexican War, his body later being borne back and laid to rest in the burial ground of this church he loved so well. During the War Between the States many a wounded and dying soldier received attention at the hospital conducted within the walls of this church. Later the Federal troops used the edifice as a stable, the United States Government later appropriating sufficient money to repair the damages done at that time. Then during the Spanish-American War a large portion of the American Army was encamped and trained near-by and many attended services at Old Falls.

Shortly after the Revolutionary War the church was abandoned as a place of worship by the Episcopalians but early in the nineteenth century was repaired and services resumed. Within recent years the Falls Church, wherein the soldiers of five wars have sat, has been faithfully restored to its Colonial appearance. The pews and woodwork are white with chestnut top trimmings. The altar has a very beautiful cross and vases and candlesticks of brass. There is a bust of George Washington near the pulpit and a copy of Stuart's portrait at the rear, near the door. The original baptismal font is there and also a brick taken by a soldier in the conflict of the sixties. Before the church there is a handsome flagstaff from which daily the United States flag flies. A tablet on the highway and another on the church tell of George Washington's connection with Old Falls.

Lambs Creek Church, King George County, was erected in 1769. During the War Between the States the interior of the church was wrecked and the building used as a stable. It has been only partially restored but services are still held there occasionally. In use today is an old "Vinegar Bible" printed in 1716 and a Prayer Book printed in 1739.

The town of Alexandria was largely settled by Scotch and Irish pioneers. One of the last relics of the religious life of these early colonists is The Old Presbyterian Meeting House built in 1774, a fine example of Georgian architecture at its best. The church as it stands today is essentially the structure which was erected in 1774 for although the building was burned in 1835, the walls were left standing and a part of the windows, and when the church was rebuilt these same walls were utilized in the new structure. The present front wall facing on South Fairfax Street and the steeple were, however, added new and were not a part of the original plan.

As is well known, Washington was Worshipful Master in the Alexandria Masonic Lodge and the first religious meeting of the Chapter was held in the old meeting house. Here, too, were held the public memorial services after the funeral of Washington; not in Christ Church as might be supposed. Probably this was because of the fact that the Masons who conducted the funeral were largely members of the Presbyterian Meeting House congregation; however, some members of the two congregations had pews in both churches, which were always on very friendly terms.

The members of the congregation played an important part in the War of the Revolution. The pastor during that time was the Reverend James Muir who was also one of the chaplains of the funeral lodge which buried George Washington. Washington and the Reverend Mr. Muir were warm personal friends and a descendant of the latter is today in possession of a cup and saucer presented by America's First Citizen to the Revolutionary-day pastor of The Old Presbyterian Meeting House.

Many famous citizens of Virginia worshiped in this church, among these being John Carlyle, whose home is also a historic shrine and who, it will be remembered, helped to build Christ Church, and Dr. James Craik, Washington's personal physician.

Unbelievable as it may seem, the old church adhered to the Northern Presbyterian Assembly following the Civil War but as a result of differences arising out of this war was forced to close its doors in 1886 and allowed to fall into a dilapidated condition. In 1925 a national campaign was commenced to rescue it from its forlorn state and this campaign has now been carried to a successful conclusion.

Some of the original pews dating back to 1774, the year the church was erected, may still be seen. Both Chief Justice John Marshall and Francis Scott Key, author of our national anthem, delivered famous orations to members sitting in these old pews. They are hand carved and held together with wooden pegs. The original hand pumped organ is still there and the present lighting system, while modern, is a copy of the old whale oil lamps of Colonial days.

It is in its churchyard that The Old Presbyterian Meeting House perhaps reaches its greatest fame. Here are buried thirty fellow Masons of General Washington. Among these is Colonel Dennis Ramsay, one of Washington's pallbearers and Mayor of Alexandria in 1789. When Washington left the city to assume the Presidency of the United States, Colonel Ramsay delivered a farewell address on behalf of the citizens of the town.

Colonel Philip Marsteller who lies buried in an unmarked grave in the churchyard of Christ Church, was the only pallbearer of General Washington who was not a Mason. His wife lies buried in the churchyard of the old meeting house.

Here also are buried the already mentioned Colonel John Carlyle and Dr. James Craik. Dr. Craik was a very colorful figure and was with Washington in every battle in which he participated from Great Meadows in 1754 on down to the surrender of Cornwallis at Yorktown. When John Custis, Mrs. Washington's son, died at Eltham, after Yorktown, it was Dr. Craik who attended him; he also dressed the wounds of Lafayette at Brandywine and was at the bedsides of both General Washington and Lady Washington when they departed this life.

The old church is also connected with the War of 1812 and Captain Charles McKnight and Robert Allison and Samuel Bowen, all veterans of that war, are buried here, although the graves of the latter two are unmarked. In the War of 1812 Captain McKnight commanded the Alexandria Independent Blues, the last body of troops reviewed by General Washington before his death.

Scores of Revolutionary soldiers of distinction lie buried in the old churchyard and the building has been called a veritable Masonic Westminster Abbey. Most prominent of all is, perhaps, the grave of the "Unknown Soldier of the Revolution" which was marked on February 22, 1928, by the American Legion Post in Alexandria. Assisting the Legion were representatives from the Descendants of the Signers of the Declaration of Independence, the Sons of the Revolution, the Daughters of the American Revolution, the Colonial Dames and other patriotic societies. A permanent monument has since been placed over the grave. The inscription on this monument was written by Wm. Tyler Page and reads as follows:

Here lies a soldier hero of the Revolution whose identity is known but to God.

His was an idealism that recognized a Supreme Being, that planted religious liberty on our shores, that overthrew despotism, that established a people's government, that wrote a Constitution setting metes and bounds of delegated authority, that fixed a standard of value upon men above gold, and that lifted high the torch of civil liberty along the pathway of mankind.

In ourselves his soul exists as part of ours, his Memory's Mansion.

Occasional religious services are still held in the old meeting house. Whenever the Washington Society has any functions they usually are held in this church.

The Monumental Church, Richmond, is, as its name implies, a memorial erected to seventy-two people who perished in the burning of a theatre which formerly stood upon the spot. This fire took place on the night of December 26, 1811, when a large and distinguished audience, including the Governor of the state, George William Smith, had gathered to witness the performance of two new plays: the first called "The Father; or Family Feuds," and the second, "Raymond and Agnes; or The Bleeding Nun."

The whole town was plunged into gloom and the aversion to playgoing became so pronounced that for many years Richmond was a very poor town for theatrical offerings of any kind—in fact the city became proverbial among theatrical managers as one place to be avoided.

Immediately after the fire a mass-meeting of citizens was held in the capitol to decide upon a suitable memorial to those who had perished in the fire and a monumental church, to be built upon the very site of the burned theatre, was the result. It was decided that the church to be erected would be an Episcopal Church; however, members of all creeds were subscribers to the building fund and the new house of worship soon found a place in the hearts of all citizens of Richmond.

"Old Monumental" as the church is affectionately called, has a very unique design, at first glance resembling more a library or museum than a house of worship. The architect, Robert Mills, allowed his imagination full play in designing the structure and since he himself was quite evidently a very original thinker, the church is a masterpiece in its own particular field of design, which might be described as being plain, and dignified, and impressive.

The ashes of those who perished in the theatre fire lie underneath the building and their names are inscribed upon a marble cenotaph to be found on the porch.

Many prominent men of Virginia have been associated with this church and its first rector was Bishop Channing Moore who served at the same time that he was Bishop. On Sunday, October

31, 1824, General Lafayette attended services in "Old Monumental." Chief Justice Marshall was the owner of a pew and Edgar Allan Poe often attended this church in his youth.

While not of colonial origin, St. Paul's Church, Richmond, has had an interesting and varied existence and is closely connected with the Civil War History of Richmond.

The builders of this house of worship made up the bulk of a congregation then worshiping in The Monumental Church. The corner-stone was laid on Tuesday, October 4th, 1844. The architect was Thomas S. Stewart of Philadelphia and the building is of Corinthian style, its classic model being the Choragic Monument of Lysicrates, commonly called the Lanthorn of Demosthenes. Yet on top of this Grecian temple there arose at first a tall spire some two hundred and eight feet high, thereby blending old and new architecture in a not unpleasant manner. After 1845 no print or engraving giving a panoramic view of Richmond failed to show St. Paul's church sending its tall spire high into the sky. In the year 1900 Richmond was visited by a hurricane which partly demolished the spire of one of the churches and following this, the City Fathers advised as a safety measure the removal of all spires and steeples. Naturally this ruling greatly changed the ecclesiastical aspect of Richmond—until then a city of many spires—and St. Paul's lost much of its "pristine beauty." The visitor to Richmond today is immediately struck by the somewhat unusual appearance of some of these spireless churches.

It was in July of 1845 that the building was solemnly consecrated but the large crowd expected on this occasion did not materialize as some one had spread the report that the new arch galleries were unsafe and this kept many people away.

In the fall of 1859 St. Paul's became the scene of the General Triennial Convention of the Episcopal Church of the United States which was for the first time held in Virginia. This was likewise the first meeting of the General Convention ever held in the South. As it happened, it was the last until 1907, and in the interval the entire Southland had suffered its baptism of fire and sword.

Almost exactly a year later occurred another event which was long remembered by the church. This was the visit to Richmond of the Prince of Wales, afterwards King Edward VII, accompanied by Lord Lyons and the Duke of Newcastle. They arrived on October 6th and the next day being Sunday, it was announced that the Prince, traveling as one Baron Renfrew, and his suite, would attend services at St. Paul's. Fully five thousand people gathered in front of the church to greet the royal party as it drove up about eleven o'clock.

On May 29, 1861, Jefferson Davis, President of the Confederacy, arrived in Richmond, thus making the city the capital of the Confederacy. Not only did President Davis and his family attend services at St. Paul's Church but also General Lee and his family and all of the High Command whenever they were in the city on Sunday. Later, when President Davis was incarcerated at Fortress Monroe for many months after the war, Dr. Minnigerode, the Rector of St. Paul's, visited him from time to time and administered Holy Communion to him there. When speaking of these visitations later, Dr. Minnigerode's eyes always flashed with indignation as he recounted how the ever present eye of a sentinel would peer through a small hole in the partition wall while the service was going on. Dr. Minnigerode also baptized little Varina ("Winnie") Davis—afterwards known as "The Daughter of the Confederacy"—in St. Paul's Church in March, 1865, and her funeral took place from there many years afterwards.

One Sunday morning during the war somebody counted fourteen generals worshiping in St. Paul's. The old church witnessed the first troops leaving for the defense of Richmond and the inauguration, just across the square, of Jefferson Davis, the only President of the Confederacy. And at the end it was by St. Paul's that the Federal officers rode up to the capitol to lower forever the flag of the Confederacy and raise that of the Union—it was indeed, as some have said, the "Church of the Confederacy."

The cushions from the backs and seats of St. Paul's pews were donated by the congregation for use in the emergency hospitals of the city. In 1862 the lecture room of the church was itself fitted up as a hospital; all through the war it was crowded with women sewing busily for the soldiers at the front. Oftentimes General Lee tied his horse to a tree in front of the Ninth Street entrance and stepped inside just to give these women a word of commendation or thanks.

St. Paul's most stirring piece of history came on the Sunday morning of April 2, 1865. In the middle of the rector's sermon a military messenger entered the church and walked swiftly up the aisle to where President Davis was sitting. A few whispered words were exchanged; then the President of the Confederacy picked up his hat and walked briskly out of the church. And presently the congregation was to hear the thing it had long dreaded. The messenger was from General Lee and told of the defeat at Petersburg and the order to evacuate Richmond . . . it was like the tolling of the great doomsday bell. This incident is beautifully recorded by Mary Johnston in her novel "Cease Firing."

St. Paul's treasures its traditions of Lee and Davis; today practically everything in the church is a memorial. Mrs. Jefferson Davis, in writing to a friend on one occasion, referred to the church as the "Westminster of the South."

The windows to General Lee rank among the handsomest in America. One of these represents Moses leaving Pharaoh's court to join his lot with his own oppressed people, with the Scriptural significance: "By faith Moses refused to be called the son of Pharaoh's daughter, choosing rather to suffer the affliction with the children of God for he endured as seeing Him who is invisible." This window is located in the eastern wall in line with the pew General Lee always occupied in St. Paul's, No. 111. On the great chieftain's birthday the Confederate flag is appropriately draped across this pew.

Directly above this window is another, also to General Lee. This represents Moses gazing up, in an attitude half of awe and half of worship, at two angels holding a scroll bearing the words, "The eternal God is thy refuge and underneath are the everlasting arms." Below, beneath the wisps of clouds which touch the feet of Moses may be seen the Children of Israel silently awaiting the return of their leader after his vigil with his Maker on the mountain top. The plate opposite this window reads: "Robert Edward Lee, born at Stratford, Westmoreland County, Virginia, 1807, died at Lexington, Virginia, 12th of October, 1870. 'This man died, leaving an example of a noble courage and a memorial of virtue, not only unto young men, but unto all his nation.' II Mac. 6:31."

There are also two memorial windows to President Davis. The lower window represents St. Paul, in chains, before King Agrippa, with the inscription: "This man doeth nothing worthy of death or of bonds. Acts 26:31." The one above represents the Angels of Goodness and Mercy, with this inscription from Job: "Let me be weighed in an even balance, that God may know my integrity. Job 31:6."

One of the first recommendations made by General Robert E. Lee to the Board of Trustees after he became President of Washington College was for the erection of a larger chapel in order to accommodate the increasing number of students. The building of a new chapel was authorized by the Board of Trustees July 16, 1866, and it was completed and dedicated in June, two years later. The building is situated on the campus in front of and facing the main building, and the site was chosen and the plans approved by General Lee.

When Lee died in October, 1870, his remains were interred in a brick vault beneath the floor of the basement of the chapel. In 1883 a mausoleum was erected as an addition to the rear of the chapel. This was especially designed as a burial place for General Lee and the immediate members of his family and as an appropriate resting place for a monument in his memory. The monument, a recumbent figure in white marble which represents Lee lying asleep upon the field of battle, was designed by the distinguished Virginia sculptor, the late Edward V. Valentine, after conferring with Mrs. Lee. An antechamber connects the monument chamber to the chapel and is separated from the former by iron doors. A large arched opening, heavily curtained, leads from the chapel into this antechamber. The monument is so placed and the light so arranged, that when the curtains are drawn and the iron doors opened, the marble figure can be seen from nearly every portion of the floor and galleries of the chapel.

The lower portion of the mausoleum is constructed of coraline limestone to correspond with the basement of the chapel and is a crypt containing cells or receptacles for twenty-eight bodies. These contain the remains of General Lee and members of his family, including those of his father, "Light Horse Harry Lee," which were removed from Cumberland Island in 1913.

Underneath the chapel and adjoining the crypt is the room used by General Lee during the last years of his presidency of Washington College and it is preserved as far as possible just as he left it on the day he was taken ill. On his desk may yet be seen his old palm leaf fan and certain of his books. Every Sunday the students of Washington and Lee University, the residents of Lexington, and many, many visitors worship in the Lee Memorial Chapel.

For many years Washington and Lee University has had in its possession countless priceless relics intimately associated with Robert E. Lee, the Confederacy and the early history of America. In 1927 two other rooms in the basement of the chapel were fitted up to house this collection and this portion of the chapel is now known as the Lee Museum and is open to the public free.

CHAPTER II

OLD CHURCHES OF THE PILGRIM COUNTRY

So long as Boston shall Boston be,
And her bay-tides rise and fall,
Shall freedom stand in the Old South Church
And plead for the rights of all.
—John Greenleaf Whittier

THE only seventeenth century church remaining in Massachusetts, whose old churches we shall next visit, is the Ship Meeting House at Hingham, a quaint wooden structure with a hipped roof in the form of a truncated pyramid, surmounted by a belfry and lookout station. It is this "lookout" station which has given the church its nautical nickname. Surmounting the belfry is a weather vane while the bell rope dangles down in the center aisle to the floor of the church.

Hingham was settled in 1635 by a group of people under the leadership of Peter Hobart, a young minister from Norfolk, England, and the first meeting house was built soon after. The present church is the third erected and was put up in 1681. The church was built by direct taxation on the one hundred and three members of the congregation and cost four hundred and thirty pounds. It is now the oldest building in the United States that has been used continuously for public worship.

According to tradition, the meeting house was constructed by ship's carpenters, and whoever they were, these early builders did their work well, for it is seldom we find a frame structure that is able to withstand the wear and tear of over two centuries and a half in such a splendid manner. Fourteen feet were added to the north side of the original building in 1730 and a quarter of a century later another fourteen feet were added to the south side and it is, of course, the building as it was enlarged in the eighteenth century that exists today.

The first town meeting was held in this church on January 5, 1682. The interior was very plain, the congregation worshiping under bare rafters and there being no heating arrangements. The seats were wooden benches devoid of all ornamentation, hewed by hand and having no backs. Stoves later superseded the old foot warmers and more comfortable seats were put in about 1817. In 1869, when it became necessary to replace the floor timbers, modern seats were installed. The pulpit, built in 1755, is a massive structure reached by a stairway on each side and there is an oddly designed canopy serving as a sounding board. In the early days separate pews were assigned to the elders, deacons, and the widow of the first pastor, and in 1763, to "persons skilled in musick."

For more than a century Old Ship Church was used for all town meetings and village gatherings. Week-days the congregation met to discuss ways and means of preventing Indian depredations and on Sundays came to hear the Reverend Peter Hobart preach for two hours upon the sin of hoop skirts and women's millinery. It was a minister of Hingham who, "once on hearing some others laugh very freely while I supposed he was better busied in his room above, he came down and said, 'Cousins, I wonder how you can be so merry unless you are sure of your salvation.' "

According to tradition the Hingham church was the last to permit the solemnization of marriage by the clergy. Marriage by the clergy was considered a very evil thing by the early Puritans and prayers for the dead were strictly prohibited. At one time Peter Hobart is said to have been sadly taken to task for transgressing this rule by going to Boston to officiate at the marriage of a member of his parish. " 'We were not willing,' said Governor Winthrop, 'to bring in the English custom of ministers performing it.' "

The severe style of architecture of Old Ship Meeting House is rather typical of the taste of the New England colonists; there is nothing especially attractive about the building but its quaint design is very interesting.

In 1930 the "restoration" wave reached Hingham and the old

church was happily returned to its Colonial appearance. Thirty of the original eighty pew doors were acquired from various sources and utilized in the square pews installed in the meeting house.

A wall tablet gives the information that for a period of one hundred and fifty-two years there were only three ministers, one preacher holding office for sixty-five years. "Saint Peter's Keys," a carved bas-relief dating back to the year 1315 may also be found on one of the walls. This was sent to New Hingham from Old Hingham, as a relic of the days when Henry the Eighth ravaged the monasteries of England and despoiled them of their possessions. Two chairs on the platform are also of historic significance, one having belonged to Thomas Lincoln, the ancestor of President Lincoln, who was among the first settlers, and the other having been made from an oak planted by Queen Elizabeth.

Of the thirty-three persons whose names are recorded as contributors to the original building fund of St. Michael's, Marblehead, twenty-nine were sea captains, the majority of whom were probably masters of English vessels trading at this port and who felt the need of the churchly influence they had been accustomed to in England. Among the contributors was General Francis Nicholson, the most distinguished military chieftain in the colonies at that time.

The frame and all the materials used in the construction of the building were brought from England, the reredos being brought entire, in readiness to be placed in position. The pulpit was of the high, wine-glass pattern with a huge sounding board above. Behind the altar was placed the reredos surmounted by the royal coat-of-arms. So important a personage as the Collector of the Port of Bristol, in England, some eighteen years later presented St. Michael's with the handsome brass chandelier which still hangs from the ceiling of the church.

The corner-stone of the quaint little edifice was laid on September 2, 1714, and that same fall General Nicholson sailed for England bearing with him a petition to the "Society for the Propagation of the Gospel in Foreign Parts" asking that a minister might be sent to Marblehead. The earnest efforts of General Nicholson were not without avail and on July 20, 1715, the Reverend Wil-

Old Ship Meeting House, Hingham, Mass. The oldest church remaining in New England.
Photo by Halliday Historic Photograph Co.

Christ Church, Cambridge, Mass., where a special service was once held at the wish of Martha Washington.

Photo by George Brayton.

liam Shaw arrived with full credentials from the Bishop of London to take charge of the new religious organization.

No town in the country had citizens more patriotic than the men of Marblehead and when the controversy between the colonies and the mother country broke out in 1775 no other group of citizens sprang to arms more readily or gave their lives more willingly.

The rector at this troublous time was the Reverend Joshua Wingate Weeks, a pronounced loyalist whose public declarations of fealty to the King increased the hostility of the people. The liturgy, also, was not such as would be likely to meet with a favorable reception. The prayers for the preservation of the royal family were read at every public service, and there were several supplications in the Litany that the enemies of the King might be brought to confusion.

When the news of the Declaration of Independence reached Marblehead there was wild excitement. The bells of the churches were rung for an entire week and every evening fires were lighted on the hilltops in honor of the great event. During this celebration a body of men entered St. Michael's Church, pulled the royal coat of arms from its place above the chancel and rang the bell until it cracked.

For more than a year after this public display of patriotic fervor services were regularly held but the hostility of the citizens daily increased. Finally a law was passed by the Provincial Congress forbidding the use of the liturgy and the rector, with the advice of the wardens and vestrymen, reluctantly closed the church. Services were held in private homes for some time until the Reverend Mr. Weeks could no longer remain in town in safety and was forced to take refuge in Nova Scotia.

Following the war, one by one the families of the communicants died out or removed to other localities. The church became so depleted in 1818 that funds were no longer forthcoming for its support. However, when it was proposed that it be rechartered as a Congregational Meeting House the congregation was aroused and the historic old building saved for the use of future generations who might desire to worship according to its time honored liturgy.

The English bell, which was rung at the announcement of the

Declaration of Independence until it cracked, was recast by Paul Revere in 1818 and still calls the congregation to worship. The old organ from St. Paul's Church, New York City, which was played at Washington's inauguration and later purchased for St. Michael's, in time gave out entirely and was replaced with a new instrument, a portion of the old case, however, being retained in the new.

The first edifice of the Church of England in New England was King's Chapel, Boston, whose organization dates from May 15, 1686, with the coming of the Reverend Robert Ratcliffe, the first minister of the English church who had ever come commissioned to officiate on this soil.

Permission was asked of the three congregations then having houses of worship in Boston to use their churches for services, a request that was promptly refused. Permission was finally given for the use of the library room in the east end of the town house and here the liturgy of the Church of England was for the first time publicly read in Boston. The following year Governor Edmund Andros ordered the trustees of Old South Church to open their building for Episcopal worship.

Because they were backed by the Governor, the Church of England services frequently extended into the afternoon; meantime the people who actually owned the meeting house were walking up and down in the street awaiting a chance to enter. After a time Governor Andros relented and set the liturgical service at such an hour that the rightful owners could have the use of their meeting house before noon; then for a period of about two years the joint occupancy of Old South seems to have settled down into a state of armed truce.

During this time steps were being taken to provide money for the building of a church but here again a difficulty presented itself. No friend of the new religious organization owned any land so situated as to make a suitable site and none of the Congregationalists would sell a foot of land for this purpose at any price. The Governor again intervened and the Council set apart a corner of the burying ground as a place where the new church might be erected. This is where the foundation of the first chapel was laid in 1688 and that is where King's Chapel has been ever since.

In 1710 the small chapel was enlarged to twice its former size to take care of the growing congregation which now represented a considerable part of the wealth and fashion of the town. With the color contributed by uniforms of British officers; the escutcheons, or coats of arms, of knights and baronets connected with the government hanging upon the pillars and the walls; the scarlet draped pulpit; and the full court mode of dressing indulged in by those who belonged to the royal party, the outward appearance of the worshipers must have been nothing short of brilliant. This fact was not overlooked by the Puritan element of Boston who regarded such display with extreme disfavor.

By 1741 the enlarged chapel was once more too small and a committee, with Peter Faneuil as Treasurer, was appointed to raise the necessary funds for a new church. Work was begun in 1749, the corner-stone being laid by the governor of the colony, and completed five years later. The designer was Peter Harrison but because of a lack of funds, a spire which was a part of his original plan was not executed.

The design of the interior especially is very lovely and as is the case with a great many of the Episcopal churches of that day, the reigning King or Queen of England presented certain furnishings to the church from time to time. Queen Anne sent a red silk damask cushion for the pulpit, surplices, and altar linen. In 1696 the Decalogue and Lord's Prayer and Apostles' Creed, now in the chancel, were painted in England and sent to the church. The communion rail also was a gift from England and a clock was presented by "gentlemen of the British Society in Boston." The organ was for many years the best in America and is said to have been purchased through the instrumentality of the great composer Händel. In 1772 King George III presented an additional set of communion silver.

Being a Tory church, King's Chapel suffered no damage during the British occupancy of Boston. But with the coming of the Continental troops, Dr. Canier, the rector in charge, gathered together his possessions and in company with eighteen other clergymen, some thirty families belonging to his congregation and a numerous company of loyalists besides, set sail for Halifax in one of the ships of the British fleet. Dr. Canier took with him most of the record books of the parish and all of the communion silver. The records were afterwards recovered but no sure trace of the silver has ever been found.

When the Continental troops occupied the town the church was closed. In 1777 an invitation was extended to the congregation of Old South Church, whose building was in need of repair, to worship in the chapel, the old quarrel by this time being entirely forgotten. This gracious proposal on the part of the chapel caused the feeling of bitterness against the congregation, on the part of the other denominations, to disappear entirely.

In 1785–87 a colonnade was added around the tower, the crown and miter removed from the organ and the Governor's pew torn out. For a long time after the Revolution the building was not spoken of as King's Chapel but was called merely the "Stone Chapel." In time, however, the old name was resumed and the royal insignia returned to the organ. Since 1790 the interior has seen no changes but the church is no longer Episcopalian, King's Chapel being the first church in the United States to become openly Unitarian. This change dates from 1785 under the leadership of the Reverend James Freeman.

The pulpit in King's Chapel dates from 1717. It stood then against the north wall, with the Governor's pew opposite as it now stands, beautifully restored, in its original location. This pew was certainly occupied by President Washington, on the occasion of the performance of the "Oratorio or concert of Sacred Musick," October 27, 1789. The Reverend Henry Wilder Foote in his "Annals of King's Chapel" notes, "I like to think that Washington was in this church . . . when he came, a survivor of Braddock's rout, to tell Gov. Shirley of his son's death in that disaster, and sat, a young man in his Virginia colonel's uniform in the Governor's pew."

There was a very close union between church and state in the early Massachusetts colony and church membership was a necessary qualification for citizenship. As the colony grew, the number of non-members and dissenters increased yearly so that finally the colony became a sort of religious aristocracy, in place of a landed one, with a large proportion of those living within its bounds disfranchised. Dissatisfaction grew more and more pronounced and in 1662 the General Synod of Massachusetts was convened to decide this matter, the dissenting faction holding that baptism was the only requisite for citizenship. The Synod failed to agree but recommended that church membership be continued as a necessary requirement.

The First Church of Boston accepted this recommendation but twenty-nine of its members, including the most respectable among the residents of the city, seceded and formed the third congregation then in Boston. The First Church, however, refused to give the required permission for this secession and an appeal was made to the Governor. When he likewise refused to permit a new church to be formed the little group then petitioned the Selectmen of Boston, who granted their request.

The first Old South Church was a two-story structure of cedar, with a very modest interior. The site was at that time considered to be in the south portion of the town and the structure early received the name of South Meeting House. At first the wives, mothers and daughters of the twenty-nine male members were not allowed to worship in the new church, being forbidden by the First Church to sever their connection with it under pain of excommunication, a dire possibility in those days. Although the General Council of Massachusetts in 1674 decided that the womenfolk should be permitted to rejoin their families, the bitterness engendered between the two congregations lasted for many years.

The first church structure was erected only after the Governor of the State, a member of the First Church, had unsuccessfully attempted to stop its construction. This building had several points of historic interest. During the days of the notorious witchcraft delusion, the pastor of Old South, the Reverend Samuel Willard, sternly denounced the cruelties of the times and forced Judge Sewall to make public confession of the part he had taken; also Benjamin Franklin was baptized in this church in 1706.

The second church edifice, the present building, was completed in 1730, the designer being Robert Twelves. It is built of brick, laid in the style known as Flemish bond, with a steeple continued in wood to a height of one hundred and eighty feet and with a very plain interior. In 1745, during the French and Indian War, the city of Boston held a mass meeting in Old South Church to pray for divine intervention between them and a French fleet at that time on its way to destroy the city. According to the story told, while the meeting was yet in session a terrific storm arose which completely annihilated the French fleet.

This was the first mass meeting held in the church of which we have any record but as time went on mass meetings in the meeting house became more and more frequent as acts of British oppression increased. Overflow meetings in Faneuil Hall were held in Old South Church and on June 14, 1768, the largest meeting that Boston had ever seen, assembled there. It was this meeting that sent John Hancock as a delegate to the Governor to ask that the Boston port be opened again, and it was after another meeting held in Old South Church, on December 16, 1773, that many of the first citizens of Boston disguised themselves as Indians and staged the famous "Boston Tea Party."

These acts of patriotic ardor were not forgotten when the British troops occupied Boston during the Revolution. The interior furnishings were all torn out and burned and the building was utilized as a riding school for the cavalry. It was Burgoyne's own regiment, the Queen's Light Dragoons, that pursued their exercise in the meeting house. To complete the desecration, one of the old pews, with its silk hangings, was used as a pig sty. When Boston was again in the hands of the patriots, Old South was in a terrible state of disrepair. When King's Chapel offered the congregation accommodations, the offer was speedily accepted and in the house of their one-time enemy the members of Old South worshiped until 1783 when their own meeting house was repaired.

At the beginning of the Civil War a series of public meetings were held in Boston for the purpose of promoting enlistment. One of the first and most enthusiastic of these was held in the yard of Old South and in the following eight weeks over a thousand men volunteered and were examined in the porch of the church. When the news of the surrender at Appomattox reached Boston a service of praise was held in the old meeting house but the happiness felt on this occasion was changed to sorrow the following Sunday when the pulpit was draped in black for President Lincoln, who had been assassinated.

By 1869 it was already apparent that the church as a religious organization would be forced to change its location, the character of the old neighborhood having completely changed with the encroachment of business houses on all sides. In the great fire in Boston in 1872 the church was damaged so as to make it unfit for occupancy. Boston's post-office was destroyed in this fire and for several years the Government leased Old South for use as the city's post-office. The congregation moved to a new and more favorable location and since then no regular services have been held in the church. In 1876 when the building was offered for sale and there was even some talk of demolishing it, the women of Boston purchased the old structure to preserve as a memorial and it now serves as a sort of historical museum.

Probably no two historic churches are better known than Old South and Old North of Boston. The former was, as we have seen, an offshoot of the First Church of Boston and the latter was a daughter of King's Chapel.

There has probably been more confusion concerning the beginnings of Old North than any other religious organization in the United States. Most of this confusion arises from the fact that there were two structures known by that name in Boston: "The Old North Meeting House," which stood in North Square, and the present Christ Church on Salem Street near the summit of Copp's Hill, which was known even in pre-Revolutionary times as "North Church."

The Old North Meeting House was taken down by the British in the winter of 1775–76 and used as firewood. Afterwards "as the Old North Society had lost their meeting house, and the New Brick Society had lost their minister, the two congregations united, and worshiped together," in the building called the New Brick Meeting House. Here a number of writers have been led astray into thinking that the New Brick Meeting House was the structure now known as Old North. As a matter of fact the original

New Brick Meeting House stood on Hanover Street and continued to stand there until 1844 when it was taken down and a new meeting house built by the congregation.

Another point of confusion exists as to whether the signal lanterns of Paul Revere were displayed in the steeple of the present Old North or in the tower of the Old North Meeting House which was torn down.

After examining all evidence it hardly seems possible that there can be any serious doubt that the present Old North is the correct building. Paul Revere's narrative states "that if the British went out by water we would show two lanterns in the North Church steeple and if by land one, as a signal, for we were apprehensive it would be difficult to cross the Charles River or get over Boston Neck." Now Christ Church was referred to as "North Church" as early as 1768 in a pamphlet published in that year and in various correspondence of the day.

Also Paul Revere stated "North Church"—not "North Meeting House." In New England it was generally customary to refer only to Episcopal houses of worship as "churches," the term "meeting houses" being used for the Congregationalists. Another point, and a strong one, is that while Christ Church had a very high tower, or spire, the Old North Meeting House had only a low tower or belfry and being situated in North Square, surrounded by buildings, it seems scarcely possible that it would have been chosen as a signal tower.

Under date of March 15, 1795, a certain Eb. Stiles jotted down on some half dozen leaves of an old folio account book his poetic effort entitled "Story of the Battle of Concord and Lexington, and Revere's Ride, twenty years ago." The verses never achieved publication but the original manuscript is now in the possession of the Massachusetts Historical Society and in view of the foregoing descriptions of the Old North Meeting House and Christ Church, the following lines are very illuminating:

> *He spared neither horse, nor whip, nor spur,*
> *As he galloped through mud and mire;*
> *He thought of naught but liberty,*
> *And the lanterns that hung from the spire.*

In addition to these points, it has always been Christ Church around which the story of the Paul Revere incident has clung and it has likewise ever been a proud tradition of the church that Robert Newman, the sexton of that day, actually hung the lanterns out, following the directions of Captain John Pulling, Jr., the friend referred to in Paul Revere's narrative as having had charge of the assignment. The memorable day on which this historic act took place was the 18th day of April, 1775. On that evening the sexton is said to have waited quietly in his home near-by, presently emerging from an upper window in the rear and climbing down a sloping roof to the yard below where he was joined by Captain Pulling, a member of the vestry. The two then went to the church; Newman entered, and Pulling from the outside locked the church door. The sexton took the lanterns and going up the wooden stairs to the belfry chamber hung them in the "upper window," then made his exit from the church through a back window which is now concealed by a bust of George Washington.

Longfellow has incorporated all these thrilling incidents in his stirring poem, "Paul Revere's Ride."

> *On the opposite shore walked Paul Revere.*
> *Now he patted his horse's side,*
> *Now he gazed at the landscape far and near,*
> *Then, impetuous, stamped the earth,*
> *And turned and tightened his saddle girth;*
> *But mostly he watched with eager search*
> *The belfry tower of the Old North Church,*
> *As it rose above the graves on the hill,*
> *Lonely and spectral and sombre and still.*
> *And lo! as he looks, on the belfry's height*
> *A glimmer, and then a gleam of light!*
> *He springs to the saddle, the bridle he turns,*
> *But lingers and gazes, till full on his sight*
> *A second lamp in the belfry burns.*

Christ Church had its beginning in 1723 when King's Chapel became inadequate to serve the entire city and a new church was planned in the North End. The corner-stone of the present structure was laid by the Reverend Samuel Myles, rector of King's Chapel, in April of that year with the following words: "May the gates of hell never prevail against it."

The church is a substantial brick structure, seventy feet long, fifty-one feet wide and forty-two feet high. The architect was William Price who is thought to have made a study of the work of Sir Christopher Wren before starting to work on his design. The original spire rose to a height of one hundred and ninety-five feet but this blew down in 1804 and when it was rebuilt three years later from drawings by Bulfinch, its height was reduced to the present one hundred and seventy-five feet.

The bell in this spire was cast by Abel Rudhall of Gloucester in England in 1744. It proclaimed the repeal of the Stamp Act on the morning of May 19, 1766, and the surrender of Cornwallis in 1781. A Bible was presented to the church by King George II in 1733, together with fourteen Prayer Books, five of which are still in existence. The Bible, printed by John Baskett at Oxford, England, in 1717, is very large and is one of the famous "Vinegar" Bibles, an error on the part of the compositor causing a portion of the twentieth chapter of St. Luke to read, "The parable of the vinegar," instead of "The parable of the vineyard," thereby making the work much sought after by book collectors. The earliest piece of communion silver dates from 1724.

Commodore Samuel Nicholson, First Commander of the frigate *Constitution,* lies buried beneath the aisle of the church, and a pew bought by a son of Paul Revere in 1808 is still owned by his descendants. At the right of the chancel, in a niche made by the southeast window, is a bust representing George Washington that was presented to the church in 1815 and is reputed to have been modeled from a plaster bust known to have been made by Christian Gülliger of Boston in 1790. When General Lafayette visited the church in 1824 he was asked by the rector if that was a good likeness of General Washington. Lafayette replied, while pointing to the bust, "Yes, that is the man I know, and more like him than any other portrait."

Old North was thoroughly repaired in 1912 and the interior returned to its Colonial appearance. The box pews put in the church at that time retain the doors, hinges and some of the paneling of 1723 and on each pew door the Massachusetts Society of the Colonial Dames has placed the name of the first owner of the pew. The restoration to the ancient plan included also a return to the larger and more harmonious proportions of the original apse, with the large window, hitherto unknown to this generation.

On September 30, 1740, the Reverend George Whitefield, then a young man of twenty-six, was forced to tarry in the town of Newbury because of a blinding snowstorm. A wonderful orator, all of New England had been stirred by his preaching. About five years after Whitefield's visit, following his advice, the Old South Church was organized by a group of people who had heard him preach and had banded together for worship. The church was Presbyterian from the beginning and that form of government was formally adopted in 1802.

At first the members of Old South were frowned upon by the established churches of Newbury and their first pastor was called a dissenting minister. As a result of this disfavor, for many years the town tried to collect double taxes from the congregation and not until 1795 were the rights of the members definitely conceded.

The present place of worship was completed in 1756 and aside from the tower, which was repaired in 1848, the old church has seen few changes through the years. In 1829 the pulpit was changed to its present position and the Dutch Oven Crypt built beneath it, reached by a trap door. In this crypt was placed the body of George Whitefield who had died in Newburyport on Sunday, September 30, 1770, a day on which he had planned to preach in Old South, as he had preached there many times since the church was first organized.

People from all over the world have visited the crypt and viewed the remains of the great evangelist but recently these remains were officially sealed from public view. Among the treasures of the church is the Bible which Whitefield used; another is the bell cast by Paul Revere which still hangs in the tower.

Old South Church has seen much stirring history. On the Sunday after the Battle of Lexington a patriotic sermon was preached by Dr. Jonathan Parsons, the pastor, and following this, Major

Ezra Lunt stepped into the broad middle aisle and enrolled a company of sixty men on the spot. From the doors of Old South in 1789 went forth the Presbytery of the Eastward to greet General Washington on the occasion of his visit to Newburyport.

The Unitarian Church in Cohasset was begun in 1747 and finished about 1755. Cohasset was until 1770 a part of the town of Hingham, where the early inhabitants went to meeting. About 1713 the inhabitants of Cohasset precinct were granted the privilege of building a meeting house, but not until 1721 was the first minister settled.

By 1746 the parish had so outgrown its original home that it was decided to build a new meeting house. Its dimensions when finished were the same as those contained within the four walls of the present edifice but there was no tower and no porch. There were three doors, one where the tower now stands, one opposite, on the south side, while the third faced the pulpit. Upon the roof at the north end was placed the belfry, a modest appendage something like the one on the Old Ship Meeting House. In 1768 a front porch was added and in 1799 the tower and steeple. A number of changes have been made in the interior furnishings and arrangement and the parish is not especially noteworthy in history; this probably being due to the fact that its activity was so vital, deep and fundamental that it was accepted as a matter of course and no special effort made to record it.

Christ Church, Cambridge, erected in 1761, was designed by Peter Harrison of Yorkshire, who had come to Newport, Rhode Island, as the first trained architect in New England. It is built in the same general style as King's Chapel designed by Harrison a few years before, although it is much simpler in design and material. The interior has been considerably altered from time to time and the church was lengthened by two bays in 1857.

The organ loft is the finest original feature remaining. During the Revolution the metal pipes of the first organ were mostly melted into bullets but a few fragments of this ancient instrument are still preserved as historic relics of the past.

With the coming of the Revolution the congregation was all but completely broken up. Nearly all the parishioners followed the

British Army to Halifax, at the Evacuation of Boston, and many, including the second rector, the Reverend Winwood Serjeant, went to England, never to return.

When, after the Battle of Lexington in 1775, Cambridge was filled with the hastily gathered army of revolutionists, the unused Tory church was seized to shelter some of the troops. At the date of the Battle of Bunker Hill it was occupied by the company of the renowned Captain Chester of Wethersfield, Connecticut; later by some of the Maryland riflemen, "painted like Indians, in hunting shirts and moccasins."

When Mrs. Washington joined her husband at headquarters in December of 1775 she seems to have taken much interest in the church and it is known that at her request, at least one service was held there—on Sunday, December 31, 1775—at which "there was present the General and lady, Mrs. Gates, Mrs. Custis and a number of others." Since there was no available clergyman, Colonel Palfrey, commemorated today by a tablet on the east wall, read the prayers, including one of his own composition which has been carefully preserved.

When the British army, captured at Saratoga, were prisoners at Cambridge, the church was again opened—June 20, 1778—for the funeral of one of the officers, Lieutenant Browne. It is thought probable that he is buried in one of the tombs beneath the old building.

On this occasion the townsfolk swarmed into the church and wrecked the interior completely. The scar of a musket ball is to be seen today in the porch, at the right of the main door frame. The parish did not recover from the effects of the war until many years afterwards.

Among the objects of interest to be found in Christ Church is the communion plate originally given to King's Chapel by the English sovereigns William and Mary in 1694 and transferred to Christ Church by the royal governor, Hutchinson, in 1772. It is now used only at Christmas and Easter. The "Baskett" Bible, published in 1753, and the folio Prayer Book of 1757, with the prayers for the King struck out, are still in good condition, as is a Prayer Book from King's Chapel bearing the date 1766 and the royal cipher "G. R." (*Georgius Rex*) surmounted by a crown.

The first meeting house at Dedham was completed in 1638 and was a plain structure thirty-six feet long and twenty feet wide. The interior consisted of a single room twelve feet high and unceiled. This original building was improved and enlarged from time to time to accommodate the slowly increasing community but in 1672 was torn down and the following year a new meeting house was put up. This new church lasted considerably longer and did not give way to the present structure until almost a century later, in 1762. The expense of erection was borne by the sale of pews, the wealthiest man in town having first choice, the next wealthiest second choice and so on, the wealth of each individual being determined by the amount of taxes he paid.

The meeting house was extensively repaired in 1819–20, the roof turned from its position, then north and south, to its present position, east and west. The steeple on the northerly end was at this time taken down and the present steeple put up at the east end. Despite these major changes the outward appearance of the church was not greatly altered and the structure as it now stands has served as a model for many churches in the vicinity. For this reason it is interesting to note that the building itself is without and designer of record. Its dimensions were laid out by the building committee, and the contractor was directed to follow them and, according to tradition, for design to look to one of the London churches that the committee admired. There is, however, no London church which bears any resemblance to this one so either the tradition is untrue or else the builder failed to follow the wishes of the building committee.

The discipline administered by the church in the early days was very strict indeed. Until as late as 1771 public confession had to be made by the "offending party or parties standing in the broad aisle, and before the whole congregation," and it was not until 1800 that the latter condition was dispensed with.

Many of the large square pews in the early meeting houses were equipped with hinged seats and when the congregation arose for prayer these were put up, an operation which sometimes caused a considerable clatter. The amusing story is told of an out-of-town visitor who was present at this proceeding for the first time in one of the New England churches, became panic-stricken and, thinking the gallery was falling, leaped into the aisle for safety. The meeting house at Dedham also had these hinged seats and so much energy was employed in raising them that the minister was forced to register a protest.

In the early days a drum was used to call the congregation to worship and many important town meetings were held in the building during the week.

The First Church of Christ, Longmeadow, has been remodeled so many times that only the frame of the original building remains. This was put up in 1767 and for more than fifty years remained in its original state. In 1828 the pulpit was placed in the east end and the gallery rebuilt on the three remaining sides of the church. At this time also, slip pews were substituted for the old square variety and the outside porches removed. In 1874 the building was moved from its original location on the village green to its present location, and extensive repairs were made.

With the large increase in church and affiliated membership, the old Longmeadow Meeting House became too small to continue to serve its growing congregation and the question of whether to remodel the building or to build an entirely new one arose. It was finally decided to keep to the old structure but the repairs decided upon amounted almost to a complete rebuilding. The foundations, side walls and roof were left standing. A new front and steeple were added and the rear end enlarged and rebuilt. The interior of the building was completely remodeled and the present white, pure colonial decorations are in vivid contrast to the gray walls and black walnut pews that were there before.

The first meeting house in Longmeadow was erected in 1714 and for many years the beating of a drum called the congregation to worship. This custom of drumming up the congregation still exists even today in Holland and certain other countries of Europe. The first bell was purchased about 1744. A new bell was secured in 1808. This bell, cast by Paul Revere and Sons, was rung so violently to express the joy of the inhabitants over the declaration of peace with Great Britain in 1815 that it cracked and had to be recast.

The old Church on the Green at Longmeadow has its halo of romance in the remarkable story of the Reverend Eleazer Williams, believed by many to have been Louis XVII of France. The theory advanced is that the Dauphin Louis XVII did not die in the Temple but was secretly brought to America and it is now generally conceded by even cautious students of history that there exists some evidence in favor of the first part of this theory at least. According to the story here told he was later left in charge of an Iroquois chief, a half-breed named Thomas Williams, whose grandmother was the Eunice Williams of the famed Deerfield raid, and a sister of the Reverend Stephen Williams of Longmeadow.

In 1800 Thomas Williams brought to Longmeadow his two boys, Eleazer and John, to be educated under the care of Deacon Nathaniel Ely who had married the grandniece of Eunice Williams. One local tradition tells that from the first the Longmeadow fold noted the curious difference both in appearance and in mental aptitude between these two boys; another seems to refute this; indeed so much has been written, and with such decided prejudice one way or the other, that it is difficult to weed out fancy from fact. At any rate there was from the first some mystery in connection with Eleazer's birth and the deacon is said to have remarked on many occasions that the boy was born to be a great man, and that he intended to give him an education to prepare him for his rightful station.

Eleazer Williams was converted in the old Longmeadow Meeting House under the preaching of the Reverend Mr. Storrs but later he joined the ministry of the Protestant Episcopal Church and engaged in missionary labors among the Indians at Green Bay, Wisconsin, where in 1841 he is said to have received a mysterious visit from Prince de Joinville, eldest son of King Louis Philippe, at which the secret of his birth is said to have been revealed to him for the first time.

His story gradually spread, exciting occasional discussion but

First Church of Christ, Longmeadow, Mass., with which is associated the romantic story of Eleazer Williams, believed by many to have been Louis XVII of France. *Photo by The Harts.*

Interior Touro Synagogue, Newport, R. I. The oldest Jewish place of worship in the United States. *Photo by John Rugen.*

not creating general interest until 1853 when the publication of an article "Have We a Bourbon Among Us?" in the February number of *Putnam's Magazine,* written by the Reverend John Hanson, also an Episcopal clergyman, created immediate and widespread interest among readers on both sides of the water. A marked copy being sent to the Prince de Joinville, he promptly denied the whole story, declared that he had not sought out the Reverend Eleazer Williams; that he had met him only by chance and stated further that whatever conversation he had had with him was devoted altogether to Indian matters.

Many books and articles have been written about Marie Antoinette's little son. That he did actually perish in the Temple now seems improbable but as to identifying the real Dauphin from among the many claimants for the honor, that is something else again. Each fascinating theory has its own group of followers and among these is the one centering about the Indian missionary who in his youth was "converted" in the old Longmeadow Meeting House.

The church at Chestnut Hill was organized in 1768 as the Third Parish in Mendon and the present meeting house was finished the following year. The general custom of the various Massachusetts towns during the seventeenth and eighteenth centuries was to build a single town church of the Congregational order, to be maintained by public taxation voted in town meetings—for this reason the opinion sometimes held that whereas the church of Virginia was a state church while the church in New England was free, seems incorrect. Where sufficient population existed at considerable distance from the meeting house, it could be set off as a separate parish within the town and it was then required by state law to provide a new meeting house and settle a minister. It was in this way that the Chestnut Hill Meeting House was organized and built but the first minister was the only one ever "settled" formally and as it happened he left the community by night a few years later as the result of a dispute with his congregation over wood to be provided and other salary matters.

Until about the beginning of the Civil War services were held in the old church on Sunday afternoons by the minister of the first parish in Mendon Center. The building gradually fell into disrepair but at a centennial celebration in 1869 repairs were made and later a corporation was formed to hold the property and care for its upkeep. There have been almost no changes in the structure except that a wooden ceiling was installed and plans are now under way to remove this and return the meeting house to its original appearance.

The interior is simple and unadorned and the exterior barnlike in appearance, some forty feet square and clapboarded. There are three entrances and two rows of windows. There is a high pulpit with sounding board above and deacons' seats below; also a shelf that can be raised and used for a communion table. The pews are square with the usual uncushioned seats. There is a gallery on three sides, with large hewn planks for benches. One side was for unmarried girls and the other for the boys, while the choir occupied the section at the rear.

The building is still used for occasional services. The territory it serves was taken from Mendon about 1845 as the town of Blackstone and much later made the separate town of Millville. In this manner the old meeting house has achieved the unusual feat of having been in three different towns. Probably the most exciting incident in its history was the assembly held within its walls, at which it was voted to secede from the mother town of Mendon and establish the town of Blackstone.

The Congregational Church at Enfield was erected in 1787 and it is notable that there has been in the entire history of the congregation only this one meeting house. The building is on its original site although the structure was turned quarter way around in 1814 and a steeple and belfry added to make possible the securing of a bell promised by one of the members. This bell has not only served the community in its call to worship but until the installation of the town clock, rang at noon daily, and at nine in the evening sounded the curfew hour. For many years, also, it directed the attention of the living to the passing of some soul into the beyond, one stroke for a man, two strokes for a woman and three for a child.

An interesting item dug up out of the dusty past records that it was "Voted April 1, 1816 that Ebenezer Winslow sweep the meeting house for one dollar and fifty cents per year, to sweep it six times a year and after every town meeting." Another item records that women were allowed to vote in the business meetings for the first time on January 12, 1870.

A fine example of an old New England meeting house is to be found in the village of Southampton.

The close connection between the building of the meeting house and the organization of the national government has been carefully pointed out. "In 1785, when George Washington was formulating plans for a closer federation of the original states, the town of Southampton voted 'that the town shall be in preparation this fall and next spring to set up a new meeting house next spring or summer.' The steps toward the building of the federal constitution and of the church in Southampton went forward concurrently, until both enterprises came to completion almost simultaneously. A sufficient number of states to establish the new form of government had ratified the Constitution of the United States by the summer of 1788, and in September of that year the present church building in Southampton was dedicated." After the church had been in use for eight months George Washington was inaugurated as First President of the United States and in the then new meeting house the Reverend Jonathan Judd led his congregation in petitions for God's blessing upon the new President and all associated with him in authority.

It was this minister who had come as a young man to minister to a few struggling families in the wilderness. With them he had organized a church in 1743; had seen the first meeting house built; had lifted up the hearts of his people through pioneer hardships in the new settlement; had fortified his home as their refuge against marauding savages; had sent their sons to most of the battlefields of three wars and now his labors were crowned with this new meeting house so long under construction—in which all now gathered to give thanks to God and to take new courage for the future.

The church was built sidewise to the road and faced north. In 1822 a steeple and porch were added and a new covering placed on the roof. As soon as the steeple was finished a bell was secured but "Poor bell!" wrote the Reverend John P. Richardson, historian of the 150th Anniversary Celebration of Southampton, held July 23, 1891, "It came to a violent end. Because it seemed a little too quiet its tongue was taken out and a greater one substituted. This cracked the bell, so that there was no further use for it. The moral is: Beware of having too great a tongue."

A new bell soon took the place of the old and in addition to pealing the hours of worship, also rang at twelve o'clock, noon, and at nine o'clock in the evening. People set their clocks by these peals which were the forerunners of the present radio time signals. The bell likewise tolled the death of each resident of the town and marked the passing of a funeral cortege by the church. It also served as a fire bell and rang forth in all national and state rejoicing.

In 1840 the church was swung into its present position, facing east, and extensively repaired. It was at this time that slip pews took the place of the old square ones. Some fifteen years later the interior of the meeting house was modernized to provide for parish activities. An auditorium was built on a level with the gallery floors and the ceiling raised to take in part of the area under the roof. The doors of the old pews were used for a wainscoting in the new audience room.

Until 1831 the church building served as the meeting place of the citizens for both spiritual and secular affairs. So long as the whole town was the church parish, the need of a separate town hall was not imperative but with the installation of a new parish system the old plan was discarded and the town erected a house of its own.

Colonel Elisha Austin Edwards, President of the Day at the 150th Anniversary Celebration of the town, spoke with deep feeling when he referred to the old church, under whose shadow the gathering was held:

"To the ancient church of our fathers, with all its hallowed memories, we bid you welcome. Within its walls, our first pastor, Jonathan Judd, has stood, and from it he was carried to his burial. Reverend Enoch Hale of Westhampton, brother of the martyred spy (Note: And grandfather of Edward Everett Hale) preached the funeral sermon. Here was ordained his colleague and successor, Reverend Vinson Gould, and here Father Williston of Easthampton pronounced his funeral discourse. Their united pastorates covered nearly a century. Their words and works still live."

The "White Church," as the Congregational Church of West Springfield is called, was commenced in 1799 and finished the following year. The building was the gift of Mr. John Ashley who contributed thirteen hundred pounds on the condition that a meeting house be erected on a site to be selected by him. Captain Timothy Billings was the builder and, it is presumed, the architect as well although this is just supposition, the designer's name not being preserved in the records. The building was remodeled in 1871 and used as a place of worship until 1909. It is now owned and used by the Masonic Fraternity for lodge meetings. The steeple has a Paul Revere bell and is surmounted by a quaint old weather vane resembling a sturgeon. A clock for the tower was donated in 1902 by a descendant of John Ashley.

The church history of Maine is not so well preserved as that of the other New England states and only glimpses from town histories may be caught here and there. One reason for this is that although a number of old buildings remain, the communities have changed and the religious organizations which once flourished in connection with these old meeting houses are no longer in existence.

There is an old church in Harpswell built in 1757 and now used as a town house for many years. It has been kept in good repair, and although the old pews have been removed from the center of the building, the original seats have been left on the sides and in the gallery. The high pulpit with its sounding board has likewise never been changed. The original plaster is still smooth and uncracked and everything is kept as nearly as possible as it was when the church was first built.

The parish organization of the First Congregational Church, Unitarian, of Kennebunk had its beginning on May 30, 1750, when a petition to organize was made to the Lieutenant Governor of Massachusetts, his Majesty's Council and House of Representatives of the Bay Province. The first meeting house had been erected the previous year. In 1767 it was voted to build a new church on the country road a mile westward from the first site. There were to be forty-five pews on the floor and twenty-four in the gallery and the timber frame, windows, window frames and inside and outside finish work of the old church were to be used in the construction of the new building.

In 1803 it was voted to enlarge the building by sawing it in two, moving the rear portion back and filling in the space between as was done in the case of Trinity Church at Newport, Rhode Island, many years before. The tower was built as far as the belfry floor and the following year the steeple was completed and the bell hung. Cast on the bell is the information "Revere and Son, 1803."

Again in 1830 the building was changed by carrying across the gallery floors, thereby providing lower rooms for the library, Sunday School room, kitchen and parlor. These rooms were used for town meetings and for work during the World War.

The old German Church at Waldoboro is a relic of an early German settlement and the building almost died aborning. The church is thought to have been first commenced about 1770. As originally constructed it had no windows and the only seats were rude benches; therefore services could only be held in summer. The members were very poor and before the building could be finished, some fifteen families took their departure for North Carolina. After this disaster a number of years went by before efforts were finally put forth to complete the church. During this time adverse claims to land titles on the western side of the river had been settled, and this probably was the chief inducement which prompted the early settlers to move the building to another location.

Accordingly the church was taken down in the winter of 1795 and moved across the river on the ice, to its present location. The last town meeting held on the east side was in 1794 and a map executed in Boston in 1795 shows the meeting house on the west side as at present.

The old church is thirty-six feet wide by forty-five feet deep with a large enclosed porch at one end. The structure is not unlike that of the meeting house to be found at Alna, Maine, except that the enclosed porch is located at one end instead of on the side. A gallery runs around three walls and the supporting beams are about ten inches square. The front of the gallery and the pulpit are painted but the pews, which are four feet square, with seats on three sides, never received this treatment. The desk of the pulpit is nine feet from the floor. The communion table and collection baskets are home-made, antique affairs.

There has been no regular pastor since 1854 and services are held only once or twice each year, in the summer. The "German Protestant Society," organized in 1800, is still in existence, however, and the credit for the careful preservation of the old meeting house is largely due to this society. Several years ago interested parties began the collection of the old German books and other articles which now attract attention in the meeting house.

Walpole Church, Bristol, was built in 1772 and today remains almost exactly as when first built. The structure is also not greatly unlike the meeting house at Alna. It still retains its original square pews, high pulpit with its sounding board, and there is a gallery on three sides. Meetings are held there quite often in the summer.

The old meeting house at Alna, already referred to, was erected in 1789 and is called one of "the finest existing specimens of the earliest form of New England meeting house." The building is rather severe in its plainness and aside from the enclosed porch is not unlike a dwelling house of comfortable proportions.

It was erected under the direction of Joseph Carleton, and Jonathan Scott was the first preacher. A definite religious organization was not formed until September 27, 1796. Reverend Jonathan Ward was the pastor from then until 1818. He was a native of Plymouth, New Hampshire, and a graduate of Dartmouth College and aside from his work in building up the Alna—or New Millford as it was first known—church to a position of importance in Congregational circles, he is perhaps best remembered for his long resistance to the use of the "bass viol" in his choir as an unholy intrusion, presumably because this instrument was associated with dancing and dancing in those days was considered an invention of the devil. Finally, grown weary with the struggle and at last overruled, he yielded, but as a punishment instructed the choir to sing the 119th Psalm, the longest in the Bible, and to "fiddle it to their hearts' content."

The meeting house is today preserved in the essential design in which it came from the hands of its builders. There has been no regular pastor for many years and the structure is now kept in repair by the town of Alna. Visiting pastors speak there on Sunday afternoons during July and August and hundreds of people from all parts of the country, in Maine for the summer, visit and worship in this "relic of church services of former days."

CHAPTER III

CHURCHES OF THE CONNECTICUT VALLEY

For freedom of conscience the town was first planted.
Persuasion, not force, was used by the people:
This Church is the eldest, and has not recanted,
Enjoying and granting bell, temple and steeple.

THE efforts put forth by the members of the Church of England residing in the Narragansett country for a suitable house of worship were crowned with success in 1707 with the arrival of the Reverend Christopher Bridge and under his supervision a church was quickly erected and dedicated to St. Paul in the same year. This was located some five miles south of the present town of Wickford, Rhode Island. Queen Anne presented the new parish with silver communion vessels and a baptismal bowl. The chalice and paten are still used on special occasions and the silver of the baptismal bowl remains, though it was, in the year 1851, melted and re-formed as a larger paten.

The nearly square form of the church and its two storied exterior suggest the general model of the New England Puritan meeting house of the day, far removed, intentionally perhaps, from the early English and Gothic styles of the old country. At the time of its erection the church was not only the largest public building of southern Rhode Island but easily the handsomest. On the interior there was a large and spacious gallery for the accommodation of the negroes and Indians, the early records of the church showing that strong and persistent efforts were put forth to Christianize the Indians and negroes, most of the latter then being slaves.

By the latter part of 1774 feeling ran so high in the Narragansett country that a majority of the parishioners of St. Paul's strongly objected to the continuance of the prayers for the King and royal family of England. The rector felt it his duty to use them and declined to omit them from the liturgy; the church was consequently closed.

During the war which followed "the old church was used as a barrack for the American Soldiery." According to tradition, there was no wanton or malicious profanation of the sanctuary—it was simply that a shelter had to be provided for the patriotic soldiers and the unused church offered this refuge. Except for this temporary occupation it stood empty and deserted.

In 1784 St. Paul's was reopened but fifteen years later, in 1799, it was decided to move the church to Wickford. Previous to the Revolutionary War the parish had been helped along by the grants of the Society for the Propagation of the Gospel in Foreign Parts, of London, generally referred to as the S. P. G., now this aid was naturally withdrawn and there had been much difficulty in raising money for the rector's salary. The character of the neighborhood had also changed considerably. At the time the church was first erected the road upon which it faced was expected to be the main line of travel from Boston to New York. With the years traffic on this road diminished. It has never revived, even to this day.

The removal of the church took place in 1800 and on May 6, 1819, the building was for the first time consecrated, at the same time being put in thorough repair and supplied with a bell.

A new parish church was erected in Wickford in 1847 and old St. Paul's was again deserted. By 1869 the windows were all broken out, the roof leaking and the interior much damaged, but in the following year funds were raised to repair the little edifice. A new shingle roof was put on, new glass panes fitted into the windows and the inside thoroughly cleaned. Since that time the interior has been completely restored to its colonial appearance and the building is used occasionally for special services of historic and religious importance.

Trinity Church, Newport, was organized in 1698 by Sir Francis Nicholson, a Lieutenant Governor of New York, with the permission of Governor Andros of Massachusetts; however, there was no church structure until 1702 and no rector in charge until that time. In 1709 the Lord Bishop of London presented the congregation with a bell for the tower and in 1726 the present church was erected. This is an exceedingly well-proportioned building and there has been much conjecture as to the identity of the architect but at this late date this would seem to be a point that will never be definitely settled.

In 1729 the Reverend George Berkeley, afterwards Lord Bishop of Cloyne, and author of the verse beginning, "Westward the course of empire takes its way," made a trip to the Bermudas in the interest of education and while on his way there his ship encountered a severe storm and was driven into Newport Harbor on a Sunday morning. The rector of Trinity, learning of his arrival, went with his congregation in a body to meet the distinguished clergyman. In appreciation of this reception the Lord Bishop of Cloyne presented the church with a fine organ which must have caused much rejoicing among the members.

When Newport was held by the British the "rebel" parishioners left the town and with the return of the Continentals, those whose sympathies were with Great Britain fled for the country. It was during these stirring times that Trinity Church was entered and the insignia of the royal family of England torn from the wall and used as a target in gun practice until it was demolished. Happily the crowns upon the weather vane and the organ were overlooked and therefore escaped destruction. The pipes of this organ were long since so worn as to make it necessary to replace them but the case of English oak, beautiful in design and as beautifully made, remains as of old.

In 1762 the church was enlarged by sawing the body of the building in two, moving back the rear portion and filling in the space in conformity with the architectural lines of the original structure. Aside from this the edifice today is very much the same as when first built. The pulpit canopy always evokes comment as well as do the candelabra and the old square pews.

The present Cathedral of St. John, Providence, was originally known as King's Chapel. The first little mission church was built in 1722 and replaced in 1811 by the present structure. Beneath the clock tower of St. John's lies buried Gabriel Bernon, French

Huguenot refugee from La Rochelle, France, who was foremost in establishing the three Rhode Island Episcopal churches we have been visiting. Just this year the Alliance Francaise Group of Providence joined with the Gabriel Bernon Family Society in restoring the old clock in St. John's tower and in providing a suitable doorway for Gabriel Bernon's tomb.

At the rear of the main building of the Newport Historical Society stands a small building that has been called by some "the best and earliest example of the pitch-roof meeting house without tower." This is the old place of worship of the Seventh Day Baptists in Newport, owned by the historical society for many years now and carefully preserved by them, even to the extent of a brick facing, a slate roof and iron shutters, encasing, as it were, "a precious stone in a plain setting."

The meeting house was first erected in 1729. Mrs. R. Sherman Elliott, in a paper read before the Newport Historical Society on November 18, 1929, gives the following interesting picture of the building of the meeting house and its early appearance:

After the raising, which was usually attended with great ceremony and a large dinner with plenty of rum, came the boarding up, window casings were fitted, the flooring put down, the pews built, the pulpit and beautiful little staircase put in place, and finally the plastering. Of the pews, we believe there were fourteen on the lower floor. Four in the center, four on the west side, three on the east side, one to the right of the pulpit as we look at it and one each side of the entrance, the one on the right being reserved for strangers. The stairway leading to the gallery at that time was slightly different; one reached it by going to the east of the strangers' pew. There were two landings instead of one, as now. The gallery contained ten pews which no doubt were occupied by the servants of the more prosperous parishioners. Long and tedious must have been the sermons in former years, for even today may be plainly seen initials carved in the railing. This was not because the pastor lacked knowledge of the fleeting hours, for there before his very eyes hung the clock made by William Claggett, a worthy member of the Sabbatarian Congregation in 1731 and an excellent clock maker of that period.

Originally there was no paneling on the side walls as now, from the window sills down. The walls were plastered from the ceiling down to the frieze paneling, about 18 inches above the window sills; below this was plain wainscoting of three boards laid horizontally, perhaps finished off at the floor with a mopboard about four inches high. The whole may have been painted in the conventional grey or white of that period . . . the outside door was extremely plain without ornamentation.

Although the old meeting house was not abused during the Revolutionary War, the church never recovered from the ill effects of that struggle. The congregation was scattered and the church never regained its prestige, which before the war had been very great.

The records of the church terminate in 1839 and the doors of the meeting house were closed a few years later. From 1864 to 1869 the building was occupied by the Shiloh Baptist Church (colored). At this time supports were placed under the balcony and "to those of you who have attended a New Year's Eve revival meeting of an animated Ethiopian congregation," suggests Mrs. Elliott, "there is no need to explain the need of extra supports."

In 1884 the Newport Historical Society was looking for a suitable place in which to hold its meetings and exhibit what few valuable relics it already possessed and the remaining members of the old congregation, feeling that in its hands the building would best be preserved, conveyed the meeting house to the historical society, its present owner.

The building was then in a terrible state of disrepair and it was necessary to put in an entirely new sill and floor. The pews were taken out and fastened to the wainscoting around the room, thereby preserving what remained of the original pews in the present paneling. The roof was much rotted and had to be replaced, the old oaken frame of the ceiling and the heavy oaken trusses that support it, alone being saved.

In its original location the old meeting house was, by reason of its close proximity to inflammable buildings, ever in danger of being destroyed by fire but in 1886 the society purchased the lot adjoining the Jewish Synagogue on Touro Street and the building was moved there, standing in the exact center of the lot. In 1902 a new building was needed for the housing of the collection of the historical society and a structure of red brick was erected in front of the meeting house. In 1915 an addition was built to this structure and in order to do this the old meeting house had to be moved once more, this time to the rear of the lot, and it was at this time that the brick facing, slate roof and iron shutters were added.

A very perfect example of an early house of worship, the little meeting house of the Seventh Day Baptists has now safely passed its 200th anniversary and stands as a valuable relic of the past.

Among the earliest of the colonists who came to America were those of the Jewish faith who left Spain and Portugal during the inquisition. The congregation of Jeshuat Israel, Newport, is one of the oldest in the land, dating from the first Jewish settlement in 1658, and the present synagogue, erected in 1759, is the oldest Jewish house of worship still existing in this country.

It was designed by Peter Harrison, the same Peter who designed King's Chapel, Boston, and Christ Church, Cambridge, and the synagogue, especially the interior, is considered a very fine example of Colonial architecture. This interior is in the Corinthian style, which at once gives the visitor a feeling of awe and reverence. On the ground floor are twelve graceful columns which support the gallery. These columns represent the twelve tribes of Israel which are the parent stock from whom all Israelites spring. Facing the east is the sacred ark, where are deposited the scrolls of the law. One of these scrolls is over three hundred and fifty years old, having been taken out of Spain during the inquisition. Before the ark hangs the perpetual lamp. In the center of the building are five massive, hand-wrought bronze candelabra, gifts of early members of the congregation.

Reverend Isaac Touro was rabbi to the congregation at the time the building was dedicated and continued to serve until the synagogue was closed at the outbreak of hostilities between the colonies and the mother country, many of the public buildings in Newport being closed at this time.

In March, 1781, the General Assembly directed the Sheriff of the colony to place benches within the synagogue for the holding of the session of the assembly and after the Revolution the courts of the colony met within the building. In 1790 George Washington, then President of the United States, visited the synagogue where he was warmly received on behalf of the congregation by Moses Seixas, the warden.

Many men of the Jewish faith, prominent in the colonial affairs of Newport and of the colony of Rhode Island, lie buried in the old cemetery which was established in 1677, almost over three quarters of a century before the erection of the present synagogue. Here are buried the first rabbi, the Reverend Isaac Touro, and Moses Seixas, the warden who welcomed Washington. The cemetery with its beautiful foliage and flower beds inspired Long-fellow to write the poem "The Jewish Cemetery at Newport," which pays homage to those who have gone to the far beyond, the everlasting life.

How strange it seems! These Hebrews in their graves,
Close by the street of this fair seaport town,
Silent beside the never-silent waves,
At rest in all this moving up and down!

The trees are white with dust, that o'er their sleep
Wave their broad curtains in the southwind's breath,
While underneath these leafy tents they keep
The long, mysterious Exodus of Death.

And these sepulchral stones, so old and brown,
That pave with level flags their burial-place,
Seem like the tablets of the Law, thrown down
And broken by Moses at the mountain's base.

At a patriotic celebration held in the city of Newport on July 4, 1876, the Honorable William Payne Sheffield delivered an address in which he said:

Let no Vandal hand of desecration ever be laid upon that synagogue or that graveyard, but let them remain, and keep preserved for ever, as venerated memorials of a frugal and useful people, who in their day and generation contributed to the prosperity and renown of Newport.

The quaint little structure known as the Elder Ballou Meeting House, in Cumberland, near Woonsocket, Rhode Island, was built probably about 1740 and certainly no later than 1749. The section was an utter wilderness when first settled by the Ballou family and others in 1713.

The "Six Principle Baptists" who built this church were organized in Rhode Island about 1732. The structure derives its name from Elder Abner Ballou who served the congregation from 1775 to his death in 1806, after which time the Society declined rapidly. Although regular services are no longer held there, the little house still stands, a precious relic of its time and a splendid example of the primitive type of meeting house which had very little that was churchly about it.

The building is approximately twenty-five feet by thirty feet. The sides are shingled and there are narrow sash windows and a door at the south and east. On the interior there are two side aisles with six long benches in the middle of the house, divided by a rail which served to separate the men from the women. The benches, incidentally, are about as uncomfortable as one could imagine, the top rail of the backboards projecting and striking the sitter squarely in the back.

The First Baptist Church, Providence, Rhode Island, is the oldest Baptist organization in America; it is also the oldest religious organization in the State of Rhode Island.

When Roger Williams was ordered to leave the Plymouth Colony he and six others embarked in canoes in search of a new location. When this was found, a new settlement was made, on land purchased from the Indians, and named Providence, in recognition of God's care over the little party in search of a new home.

Two years later, in 1638, the new religious convictions of the Providence settlers were sufficiently matured to demand organized expression in church-fellowship. In the absence of any scripturally baptized person in this new world, Ezekiel Holliman, one of their number, was deputized to baptize Roger Williams, and then he in turn baptized Mr. Holliman and "some ten more." These twelve or more persons constituted the first Baptist Church in America with Roger Williams as the first pastor. Mr. Williams, however, withdrew before the close of the year in which the church was organized and during the rest of his life remained in Providence as a missionary among the Indians. The founders adopted no articles of faith and the church has remained to this day without formal creed or covenant.

The first meeting house in Providence was not erected until 1700, more than sixty years after the church was organized. Before this, services were held in the homes of members or under the trees. The second meeting house was erected in 1726 and the present structure begun in 1775. It is built upon the site of the former churches and stands "midway between the battles of Lexington and Bunker Hill."

When it came time to build the church the congregation sent Joseph Brown and Jonathan Hammond to Boston "to view the different churches and meeting houses there, and to make a memorandum of their several dimensions and forms of architecture"; then in the beginning of March, 1774, "John Brown, Jonathan Hammond and Comfort Wheaton" were appointed a committee "to make a Draught of a House 90 by 70 feet together with a Tower and Steeple."

Mr. Brown possessed a copy of James Gibbs' "Book of Architecture" published in 1728, which contained many drawings of St. Martin's-in-the-Fields put up two years earlier, and of other churches also. The Providence meeting house shows the influence of several of these designs and its tower was entirely due to Gibbs. When St. Martin's-in-the-Fields was built, the architect made four designs for the spire. One was selected by the vestry and built; the other three Gibbs published in his book. One of these was picked by Mr. Brown for the Providence church. The only change is in the last window stage. Gibbs made this cylindrical; in the Providence steeple this stage is octagonal, probably because this was cheaper.

The church has very graceful lines, the tower being considered especially fine. The bell weighing twenty-five hundred pounds was made in London, and bore at first the quaint inscription quoted at the head of this chapter. It has been cracked three times in the ringing, and recast each time in this country. It now bears the date of the origin of the church and the name of its founder, together with the information, "it was the first church in Rhode Island, and the First Baptist Church in America." The gallery reserved for the slaves and freedmen is gone and in its place is a square loft. The square pews have likewise been replaced by modern benches and the old-fashioned pulpit with its sounding board is also missing; however, hanging from the center of the ceiling there yet remains a beautiful cut-glass chandelier, brought over from England in 1792, one of the most handsome pieces of Colonial light fixtures to be found in America today.

Rhode Island was the first state to declare for Independence and many members of the Providence Church took an active part in the Revolutionary War. Pastor and flock were as one in their support of the colonies and the congregation furnished many volunteers to the army.

The Congregational Church at Wethersfield, Connecticut, was begun in 1761 and was the third meeting house erected by the congregation. Old South, of Boston, was used as a model, a circumstance easily discernible today in the great resemblance between the two buildings when the different kinds of materials are taken into consideration.

The exterior of the church has seen few changes. A lightning rod was attached in 1771; the south porch added in 1838. At first the windows were filled with small panes of glass and not until many years later were large panes substituted.

Inside, many changes have been made. In 1838 the front gallery was moved back eight feet, new pews put in and an elevated square pulpit installed. In 1882 the interior was again remodeled and a vestibule and porch took the place of the small open porch on the south end. New stairs were built in the tower and the north alcove added for the accommodation of the organ and choir. At the same time the south gallery was removed and the side galleries narrowed.

In the days preceding the Revolutionary War many important political meetings were held in the old meeting house. At the very beginning of that contest there was organized that famous company of a hundred men, who were addressed by the pastor on a Sunday morning, upon the tidings of the Battle of Lexington, and dispersed in the afternoon to make the needed preparations, meeting that evening upon the green in front of the church, commended to God in prayer, and at once starting out for Boston, escorted by the pastor and others to a point beyond the river. The company

First Baptist Church, Providence, R. I. The oldest Baptist congregation in America. *Photo by Norman S. Watson.*

Old Rockingham Church, Rockingham, Vt. The oldest church in the State of Vermont.
Photo courtesy L. S. Hayes.

returned not long afterward to report that their services were not yet needed, but soon set out again to take part in the Battle of Bunker Hill.

During the war George Washington attended "Divine Service in this church" on May 20, 1781, when he was in Wethersfield for a conference with Rochambeau and others. It is said that plans were formulated at this time for the siege of Yorktown which ended the war. According to tradition there were one hundred and fifty in the choir the day Washington attended services.

Old Trinity Church, Brooklyn, is the oldest Episcopal Church now standing in Connecticut and it is the only church in the diocese built before the Revolution. A great many of the now existing parishes were organized before this one but Providence decreed that Old Trinity alone should remain preserved in its original form.

Trinity Church had a curious beginning and its very existence is attributable to one man "and the work was, he confesses, undertaken by him, not from a religious motive only, but primarily as a means of saving himself from unjust and unreasonable exactions."

That man was Godfrey Malbone, a stanch churchman who, nevertheless, in order that he might live at peace with his neighbors paid regularly the yearly tax of nine or ten pounds levied upon his property for the support of their minister. In 1769 the Ecclesiastical Society of Brooklyn decided to tear down their meeting house and build a new one. As his proportionate share of the expense of erecting a new house, to whose congregation he did not belong, Colonel Malbone was to be assessed about two hundred pounds, more than one-eighth of the entire cost.

An appeal to His Majesty in Council was uncertain and meant long delay so Colonel Malbone decided upon another course; this was the erection of a Church of England structure. Once this was done a Colonial law would permit him to pay his society taxes for the support of services in this church.

Others in the community joined him in this enterprise; all signing a declaration of conformity to the Church of England and one of the number donating the land upon which the church structure still stands.

· 85 ·

Old Trinity was designed by Colonel Malbone, as he says, "from a recollection of other edifices of this kind," and is a plain but neat building, forty-six feet by thirty feet. The frame of this little structure was raised in June, 1770, and the work then went speedily forward, the main burden of the expense and all the responsibility resting upon Colonel Malbone. In the meantime the Ecclesiastical Society of Brooklyn had definitely decided to build a new meeting house and work was in fact progressing rapidly. It was planned to finish the structure before Malbone's Church, as it was called, could be completed; in this way the Colonel's assessment could still be secured.

But that gentleman thereupon petitioned the Assembly for the relief of himself and his associates from these assessments which would work a double hardship on them. The petition was allowed in the case of Colonel Malbone as he had always been known as a churchman, but rejected in the case of his associates since it was likewise known that many of them had simply made churchmanship a plea for evading the society's taxes.

Services were at first conducted by Colonel Malbone himself and such missionaries as came that way, and usually consisted of the regular reading of the church service and a sermon. Relations between the new Church of England and the old Ecclesiastical Society were strained for a number of years but presently this feeling died down and the two congregations got along in perfect harmony.

The first official rector in charge of the church was the Reverend Daniel Fogg who took up his duties in April, 1772, and served during the difficult period of the American Revolution. While no flaming royalist, Mr. Fogg did feel it his duty as a churchman to read the prayers for the royal family in the liturgy. Since public reading of these could not be allowed, the doors of Old Trinity remained closed during the war but services were regularly conducted in Colonel Malbone's home. Mr. Fogg's actions during these exciting years are best judged by the attitude of the selectmen of the town who, near the end of the war, in 1782, said of him that he had "conducted himself in a quiet and peaceful manner since the contest began with Great Britain."

Following the war Mr. Fogg was one of the ten clergymen who in April, 1783, chose Samuel Seabury to the episcopate. "We clergy," wrote Mr. Fogg, "have even gone so far as to instruct Dr. Seabury—if none of the regular Bishops of the Church of England will ordain him—to go down to Scotland and receive ordination from a nonjuring Bishop," which explanation disposes of the statement sometimes made that the suggestion of Dr. Seabury's final resort to Scotland for ordination was made in England.

Various changes were made in the interior of the church in 1828, the old altar, desk and pulpit being removed at that time. In 1865 the corner-stone of a new house of worship was laid and since Easter, 1866, regular services have not been held in Old Trinity. Once a year, however, on All Saints' day, the parishes of Brooklyn and Danielson hold a combined service in the old edifice. It is also used for funerals as the burial ground is there.

The First Church of Christ, Farmington, Connecticut, has been much admired by architects. It was built in 1771 after plans contributed by Captain Judah Woodruff, a descendant of one of the eighty-four original proprietors of the town. Captain Woodruff served as First Lieutenant during the French War and later as a captain in the Continental Army. It is said that he drew his plans for the Farmington meeting house after making a trip over New England, spent in studying the old church structures and the result is a building not unlike the Wethersfield meeting house erected some ten years earlier; also it possesses traces of Old South Church, Boston, thereby strengthening the impression that Old South served as a model for the Wethersfield structure.

The selection of all materials was done with painstaking care, Captain Woodruff picking out much of the wood himself as well as carving the letters on the original pulpit and the elaborate leafy designs on the sounding board. So well was the work done that not until 1899, one hundred and twenty-eight years after the church's erection, was it necessary to replace the original white cedar shingles of the roof, while the frame of heavy white oak timber is still entirely sound.

The congregation at Farmington is an old one, the first house of worship being erected in 1709. This was a rude log structure, half church, half block-house, or fort. The second church was thought to have been in appearance not unlike the Old Ship Meeting House at Hingham, Massachusetts. It was, at any rate, square in form and adorned with a cupola, or turret, in the center of the roof.

In the early days a drum was used to call the congregation to worship but in 1731 a bell was purchased. At the one hundred and fiftieth anniversary of the building of the church, celebrated in Farmington on October 19, 1922, the choir and guards were attired in appropriate Colonial costume and the congregation was again called to worship by drumbeat. For his services on this occasion the drummer was paid the old yearly rate of one pound, ten shillings.

The meeting house in the early Puritan settlements, while primarily utilized as a place of worship, was generally employed also to serve the educational and political needs of the community. The Farmington meeting house has witnessed many a stormy town meeting. These meetings were always opened by prayer and not infrequently a sermon was included for good measure. The men attending these meetings did not remove their hats or make any effort to modulate their voices or modify their demeanor for the "Puritan did not reverence the meeting house as a structure, though he was punctilious in honoring it when it was used for the worship of his God."

The First Church of Christ, East Haddam, Connecticut, was built in 1794 and is a beautiful example of early Colonial architecture. It is the third house of worship used by the society. The first was a log structure built in 1705 and the second was a more elaborate meeting house built in 1728. The present building is located a considerable distance from that of the first edifice and the change of location was the subject of a violent church quarrel which resulted in the formation of an Episcopal Church.

According to tradition, the present meeting house is built upon the same plans substantially as a church built only a short time before in Stanstead, a Canadian town located just north of the Vermont boundary line. A member of the building committee is thought to have gone to Stanstead, viewed the church there and obtained the plans. Unfortunately the name of the architect has not been preserved in the church records; the master builder is likewise unknown.

The oldest church in the State of Vermont is the Old Rockingham Church built in 1787; this is likewise the only ecclesiastical structure in Vermont dating back to colonial days which retains its original appearance, both in its interior and its exterior as well.

Rockingham was first settled as a town in 1752 and in 1772 the first meeting house was built. Twelve years later this gave way to the present church, erected on the same site. In building it the general custom of the day of locating a house of worship always upon a hill in the midst of the town, was followed. The building is a plain rectangular structure with the exception of an enclosed two story "porch" at the end, from which the stairs ascend to the gallery. Inside, the pulpit has been lowered a few feet—originally it was reached by a winding stairway—otherwise the appearance of the interior today is very much the same as when the meeting house was first put up. The pews are of the old square variety, with high backs. There are many, many windows and each contains forty panes.

It is interesting to note that the meeting house was built by the town itself, the money for its construction being paid directly from the public treasury, and it was the only public building owned by the town for just exactly one hundred years. The church was used for all town meetings but after 1839 only occasionally for religious services, a regular congregation ceasing to exist after that date.

Between 1869 and 1906 the structure gradually fell into a half-dilapidated condition and some of its furnishings were destroyed and some carried away as souvenirs. It was at this time that public-spirited citizens raised a fund, which was supplemented by town funds, and the building thoroughly renovated and restored. Since then an annual pilgrimage has been made to the shrine each summer, usually on the first Sunday in August so as to accommodate the summer visitors in the surrounding community.

For many years notices of all important town meetings were posted on the front door of the old church. All matrimonial banns and intentions of marriage were likewise posted there and no doubt the following unusual announcement which appeared on March 15, 1804, must have created something of a sensation:

Notice,—John Parks Finney and Lydia Archer, of Rockingham, came to my house, and having been published agreeably to law,—but he being a minor and not having his father's consent, I refused to marry them. They, however, declared that they took each other as husband and wife, meaning to live and do for each other accordingly.

Samuel Whiting, Minister.

Thetford Hill Church, Thetford, Vermont, was built in 1787, replacing a log meeting house which had been erected in 1780. The church organization, however, dates from 1773. The first pastor was the Reverend Clement Sumner who was forced to leave his post rather suddenly because of his pronounced Tory sentiments, to be succeeded by Dr. Asa Burton who achieved the remarkable record of having served the parish for some fifty-seven years.

When the time came to replace the first temporary structure with a permanent church building, a somewhat spirited discussion took place as to where it should be located. The argument grew so heated that finally the County Court was called upon to decide the matter. The court ruled that the meeting house should be placed on a highland between two valleys, the settlers of these two valleys being the parties in dispute, each side wanting the church.

The main building expense was met by the levying of a tax consisting of "two pence upon each acre of the town." The new house of worship was a square, plain barn like structure built from the white pine which grew to great size in this region. There was a high pulpit with sounding board and the usual high-backed square pews.

In 1830 the building was sold by the town to the society for one hundred and twenty-eight dollars. The same year it was moved from its original location to the more convenient spot that it now occupies on a near-by street. The tower and vestibule were then added but the old square pews were removed. Even so the interior of the church today is interesting and seems to retain something of its old atmosphere. The walls are a deep cream and the wood paneling white. Only recently a new hardwood floor was put in.

Today the "Hill" is largely occupied by summer residents drawn there by the scenery and summer climate. The old church, however, continues to serve a wider area of permanent residents. It is now the oldest structure in Vermont which has been used continuously as a place of worship.

The Old First Church of Bennington, Vermont, was organized December 3, 1762, fifteen years before the Independent Republic of Vermont came into existence. Vermont was an Independent Republic from January 17, 1777, until its admission into the Union, March 4, 1791.

The first meeting house, erected in 1763–65, stood on the village green and was a plain barn like structure, forty feet wide and fifty-five feet long. There was no steeple but there was an annex on the east end which was called a porch. Many historic scenes were enacted in this quaint little structure. Here the first settlers prayed for relief from the oppressive powers of Great Britain and here thanksgiving services were held after the capture of Ticonderoga, the Battle of Bennington and the final surrender of Burgoyne. Here also were brought the seven hundred prisoners captured at the Battle of Bennington, August 16, 1777. The first legislature in the history of Vermont, elected in 1778, held its June session in the old meeting house and here, later, met the convention which ratified the Constitution of the United States, January 10, 1791, making Vermont the first state to come in after the original thirteen.

The old meeting house served for forty years and in 1806 was replaced by the present structure which was considered to be one of the most perfect examples of colonial architecture in New England, constructed, as it was, at a time when the Georgian period had reached its flood and was about to recede. The plan is thought to have had its basis in one of the drawings contained in a book by Asher Benjamin entitled "The Country Builder's Assistant." There are deviations from the plan, proving that the carpenters of Bennington were men skilled in their craft and quite capable of exercising their own originality in improving upon a standard design.

Unfortunately the structure, an architectural jewel as it came from the hands of the builders, was not allowed to remain in that state. In 1832 the forty-eight original box-pews were taken out and replaced by seventy-seven so-called "slips." The handsome Asher Benjamin pulpit, which rested on four graceful columns, was likewise removed to make room for more "slips."

Then in 1865, a period which has been called "the most uninformed, and consequently the most deplorable, period of American architecture," a whole year was spent in "modernizing" the building. A large apse was built into the east wall to house a massive pulpit. A Sunday School room was added at the rear, necessitating the elimination of four windows. A portico-entrance was built at the southwest corner of the meeting house, eliminating another window and along with it the beautiful staircase going up to the gallery. Inferior colored glass was substituted for the panes in the east and west Palladian windows and all the windows were provided with shutters.

Nor were the "modernizers" yet content. In 1903 an organ was placed in the choir loft, blotting out the west Palladian window completely, and modern doors were added to the façade. Fortunately, at the present time, plans are under way for the removal of all these so-called "modernizing" effects and the structure is to be returned to its ancient appearance—"one of the most perfect examples of Georgian ecclesiastical architecture in New England."

The minister at the time of the Revolution was the Reverend Jedediah Dewey an ancestor of Admiral George Dewey of Manila fame. Ethan Allen was a member of the congregation and following the capture of Ticonderoga he attended the thanksgiving services held in the old meeting house. It was during the course of the Reverend Mr. Dewey's long prayer giving the entire credit for the victory to God, that Ethan Allen is said to have called out, "Parson Dewey, Parson Dewey, Parson Dewey," and after the third count when the parson paused and lifted his eyes, "Please mention to the Lord about my being there!"

The Old First Church stands on the southwest corner of Bennington's burial ground, mounting guard over the graves of many of the famous Green Mountain Boys, seventy-five Revolutionary soldiers, the author of Vermont's Declaration of Independence, the men who fell at the Battle of Bennington, the Hessian prisoners who died of their wounds in the meeting house, converted as it was into a temporary hospital, as well as Parson Dewey, first minister to the congregation.

The oldest church structure still standing in New Hampshire is apparently the meeting house at Danville, originally a Congregational Church but now used only for annual services held generally late in August. The town of Danville, once known as Hawke after an old English admiral, was originally a part of Kingston, not entering upon its career as an independent township until 1760.

From the early records it is evident that the meeting house was partially erected in 1759 and the first meeting of the parish was held in the unfinished building on March 10, 1760. It was put up by twenty-eight citizens who conveyed it to the parish free of charge. The first minister was the Reverend John Page of New Salem who was also a physician and therefore able to minister unto his parishioners physically as well as spiritually.

The pulpit in the old Danville meeting house is on the side as at first. Seven steps, with a nicely carved rail, lead up to it and a window behind it allows the preacher light to read his notes. Over the high pulpit is an old-fashioned sounding board while just below and in front of the pulpit is the old communion table and two built-in seats for the deacons. The rough, hand-hewn beams put together with wooden pegs may yet be seen. The box-pews were removed to the balcony some years ago in order that the floor might be used for dancing, due to the fact that the building served as a town hall as well as an occasional place of worship! Little repair work has been done inside for years but the outside has been kept in good condition.

The Congregational Church at Westmoreland, New Hampshire, stands on what is now known as Park Hill but was formerly known as Federal Hill in honor of the men of Westmoreland who served in the Revolutionary War. It seems too bad that the more prosaic designation has come to be the popular one.

The church has not always been located there. When first erected in 1762 it stood on another hill in the north cemetery. It was at first a plain structure, without belfry or any ornamentation but suitable for the needs of the community. For many years it served as a school building during the week.

The first minister was the Reverend William Goddard who served until his dismissal on August 7, 1775, for reasons which remain a mystery to this day. Public feeling ran high against him but the records show no fault was found with his theology or moral character and he was given a recommendation when he left the town.

In 1779 the church was moved to another hill, more centrally located, and about a hundred feet south of its present location. The last resting place, high on a ledge out of reach of floods, did not come until 1827. Twenty feet were added to the front after the move was made, a steeple erected and a Paul Revere bell installed. This bell still hangs in the belfry although it became cracked in 1847 and had to be recast. Town meetings were held in the vestry of the church until the early fifties, when a town hall was built.

Few meeting houses in the United States remain in such a completely unaltered state as the one which, after a period of over a century and a half, still stands in the exact geographical center of the town of Sandown, New Hampshire. This structure, begun in 1773 and completed the following year, thereby being a pre-Revolutionary building, is two and a half stories high, and is almost square in shape with no belfry or spire to break its plain lines. There are three massive doors and some thirty-eight windows, each containing twenty-eight small panes of glass.

According to the story always told, a large barrel of old Newburyport rum played a big part in the erection of the meeting house, this liquid refreshment being obtained to stimulate the brain and quicken the muscles of the sturdy pioneer builders who, whether due to its influence or otherwise, did their work so well. Tradition further relates that just before the roof was finished the supply of Newburyport rum became exhausted; work was therefore suspended until a fresh supply could be obtained. This fresh supply did the trick and the building was then finished with no further interruption.

The old meeting house is forty-four by fifty feet in size, and twenty-four feet high and there is a comfortable attic above the ceiling of the auditorium. The pulpit is of the goblet style and stands eleven feet above the floor. Over this pulpit a large sounding board is suspended, this being nineteen feet above the floor; while directly beneath the pulpit is a small enclosure which was reserved for the deacons. The pulpit and the wainscoting on the front of the gallery are stained cherry but the remainder of the interior is entirely unpainted. Two staircases run from corners in the interior to the gallery. An interesting feature of the gallery is the enclosure reserved for the slaves, who accompanied their owners to meeting, twenty box-pews and two rows of benches.

The erection of the meeting house, incidentally, was the subject of much discussion and a violent quarrel arose as to its location. This was finally adjusted by deciding at a town meeting to locate it at the geographical center of the town. Practically the only change that has taken place since the beginning has been the introduction of stoves for giving heat. Before this the only means of heating the meeting house was afforded by warming pans which the early worshipers carried along to church with them.

In the old meeting house the Congregational Society held its services until it was dissolved in 1834 and here the town meetings were held from 1778 to 1929. During the years in which the meeting house was in the hands of the town, it gradually fell into disrepair. Some years ago the Sandown Old Meeting House Historical Association was formed to assist the town in keeping the old structure in repair, the incentive being the report that an agent of a certain wealthy manufacturer had intimated that he would not hesitate to part with forty thousand dollars for the building, which he then proposed to move out of the state, and the desire to save it for Sandown and for New Hampshire. The association has supervised the repair of the building and is now responsible for its preservation.

Union Episcopal Church at West Claremont is another pre-Revolutionary structure and the oldest Episcopal church building in New Hampshire. Work on the little edifice was commenced in 1773, the plan of the building being furnished by Governor John

Wentworth who promised to give the parish whatever nails and glass they might need; also a bell and an organ; however, due to causes beyond his control, these promises were not kept. The frame was put up and enclosed, however, and a floor laid. A desk and deacon's seat were installed and in this condition the building was used for Divine worship during the summer months, until 1789–1790 at which time the interior of the church was finished and the pews sold to cover the cost.

Like a great many other Church of England congregations, Union Church saw stormy days during the War of the Revolution. The rector refused to bear arms against the King—likewise refusing to fight or plot against the colonists—and in 1785 was forced to leave Claremont as his life was in danger, Revolutionary ardor running very high in the little town.

Yet in spite of the hardships of these trying days, the church prospered and actually had more members at the close of the war than at the beginning, a situation somewhat difficult to understand.

The original little building erected in 1773 has seen many changes, which make it seem of more modern construction than it actually is. The belfry was not added until 1801. In 1820 an addition of twenty-five feet was added to the east end to accommodate the increasing congregation, the organ removed from the gallery at the west end to the chancel, and the gallery then torn out. The old enclosed pews still remain however and suggest to the visitor thoughts of other days.

The first Episcopal Church in Portsmouth, New Hampshire, took the form of a parsonage house, with a chapel attached thereto, built on glebe lands granted in 1640. Sir Richard Gibson is recorded as the first minister but his stay in Portsmouth was but fleeting and there is no record of any Episcopal worship in the town for ninety years after his departure.

In 1732 there was erected a church under the auspices of the English Society for the Propagation of the Gospel in Foreign Parts, on the site now occupied by St. John's Church. This was called Queen's Chapel in honor of Caroline, consort of George II. Queen Caroline presented the little church with two chairs, a Bible, Prayer Books and a silver communion service. The latter, bearing the royal arms, is even now in regular use. The Bible is also a prized possession of the church. It is another of that edition published by John Baskett of Oxford in 1717 and one of the exceedingly few so-called "Vinegar Bibles" known to be in existence today.

In the first Prayer Book used from the chapel pulpit, also the handiwork of John Baskett, may be seen the changes made when the old prayer for the British sovereigns became obnoxious to the patriotic members of the parish. Like a number of other churches, no regular services were held in Queen's Chapel during the troublous times of the Revolution.

In 1789, just after his inauguration, General Washington visited Portsmouth. On Sunday, November 1st, President Washington, dressed in an elegant suit of black silk adorned with brilliant buckles, was escorted to Queen's Chapel. There he occupied the old governor's pew, which was draped with plush curtains with a heavy wooden canopy overhead bearing the royal arms. The two chairs given by Queen Caroline were in place in this pew and one of these was occupied by Washington.

It was a sad day for all Portsmouth when Queen's Chapel was destroyed in the great fire which swept over the town the early morning of December 24, 1806. Among the few pieces saved was one of the two Queen Caroline chairs from the governor's pew. Tradition says that this was the one in which Washington sat when in the chapel, but since an exact copy of it was made at once and the two, unmarked in any way, have since stood in the chancel of St. John's, the visitor who would be sure of sitting in the right one must try them both!

Following the fire the parish at once set to work to build a new church and in the following year the present St. John's Church was erected on the site of old Queen's Chapel. At first the new church had the old style box-pews but later modern benches were installed. The style of the original pews may yet be seen in one of the galleries of the church where they are still preserved.

The early history of Queen's Chapel was not without its share of romance. On March 15, 1760, the rector, the Reverend Arthur Brown, much against his will, married Governor Benning Wentworth to Martha Hilton, the aged magistrate's pretty house-keeper. Longfellow has immortalized this bit of romance in one of his "Tales of a Wayside Inn." Young Martha Hilton, idling along the street, ragged and barefooted, is one day sharply rebuked by the mistress of Stavers Tavern, who says:

> 'O Martha Hilton! Fie! how dare you go
> About the town half dressed, and looking so!'
> At which the gypsy laughed, and straight replied:
> 'No matter how I look; I yet shall ride
> In my own chariot, ma'am.'

Not long after this Martha's prophecy showed signs of coming true, for upon the death of the Governor's first wife, Martha went to the executive mansion as his housekeeper. Presently the Governor had a birthday, his sixtieth, which he celebrated by giving a dinner. In the midst of all the feasting Martha Hilton was called in and:

> How ladylike, how queenlike she appears;
>
>   *   *   *   *   *
>
> Yet scarce a guest perceived that she was there,
> Until the Governor, rising from his chair,
> Played slightly with his ruffles, then looked down,
> And said unto the Reverend Arthur Brown:
> 'This is my birthday: it shall likewise be
> My wedding-day; and you shall marry me!'
>
>   *   *   *   *   *
>
> 'This is the lady; do you hesitate?
> Then I command you as Chief Magistrate.'

Governor Wentworth lived but a short time after his very romantic marriage and not long after his death the old parish register recorded the remarriage of his widow, for in what appeared to many a most unseeming haste, Martha married the Governor's brother, Michael Wentworth!

One of the unfortunate results of the fire of 1806 was the cracking of the historic bell hanging in the steeple of Queen's Chapel. This bell had begun its career by ringing out its peals from a French Catholic Cathedral in Louisburg and had been brought to Portsmouth by Colonel Pepperell, of Kittery, just across the river, after his triumphant capture of the defiant French fortress. After the fire the bell was sent to Boston and recast by Paul Revere. In 1896 the old relic became so worn as to crack and this time the Blake Bell Company, successors to the Paul Revere company, recast the historic metal into a new bell which continues to ring forth its summoning tones to rich and poor alike, on sad and gay occasions. . . .

The credence table in St. John's is interesting, being made of wood from the U. S. frigate *Hartford*, the flagship of Admiral Farragut at the capture of New Orleans, April 24, 1862. Admiral Farragut died at the Kittery Navy Yard opposite Portsmouth. His funeral services were held at St. John's Church and his body interred in the churchyard, although later the remains were taken to Arlington Cemetery in Washington.

Another object of great historic interest is the old Brattle Organ. This was originally the property of Mr. Thomas Brattle who imported it from London in 1713. At his death it was left by will to the Brattle Street Church, Boston, provided that "they shall accept thereof and within a year after . . . procure a sober person that can play skillfully thereon with a loud noise." His will further provided that if the organ were not accepted according to the provisions of his will it should go to King's Chapel. To the early Puritan minds there was something peculiarly devilish in instrumental music and it did not take the Brattle Street people anything like a year to make up their minds. Mr. Brattle died in May. His brother informed the church by letter of the gift and in the following July the church voted that, "with respect," they did "not think it proper to use the same in the public worship of God." The organ therefore went to King's Chapel.

After remaining unpacked in the tower for some eight months, the organ was used by King's Chapel until 1756. Then it was sold to St. Paul's Church, Newburyport, Massachusetts, where it remained in constant use for eighty years. In 1836 it was purchased for St. John's Church by Doctor Charles Burroughs, the first settled minister after the rebuilding of the church, and is still usable. The case is new but the old wind chest and most of the pipes of the original organ remain. It was, according to the Annals of King's Chapel, "the first organ that ever pealed to the glory of God in this country."

The oldest object in St. John's Church is undoubtedly the baptismal font. It is made of porphyritic marble of dull brownish gray, finely veined. It was taken by Colonel John Mason from the French in 1758 at the capture of Senegal. According to tradition it had been originally taken by the French from a heathen African temple and was very old at the time of its capture. Colonel Mason's daughters presented it to Queen's Chapel in 1761.

No account of St. John's would be complete without mention of the custom made possible in this church by the elder Colonel Theodore's legacy which provided for doling out a portion of bread each Sunday to the poor of the parish. This custom is still maintained, the bread always being placed in the ancient baptismal font, at the right of the chancel, and covered with "a fair linen napkin."

Old Meeting House, Sandown, N. H., in whose history a large barrel of old Newburyport Rum played an important part. *Photo by Halliday Historic Photograph Co.*

St. Paul's Church, Kent County, Md. The oldest Episcopal Church in Maryland used continuously as a place of worship. *Photo by Dr. H. Benge Simmons.*

Chapter IV

RELIGIOUS FREEDOM IN THE NEW LAND

Lord Baltimore and his colonists sought in their charter liberty not alone for the members of the expedition but for all later comers as well. It is a good thing to demand liberty for ourselves and for those who agree with us, but it is a better thing and a rarer thing to give liberty to others who do not agree with us.
— Franklin Delano Roosevelt

THE first Catholic religious settlement in British North America began in March 1634, when Father Andrew White, known today as the Apostle of Maryland, landed on St. Clement's Island in the historic Potomac River, with Governor Leonard Calvert and others of Lord Baltimore's colony. Maryland celebrated her three hundredth anniversary in 1934 and this event also commemorated the founding of the Catholic Church in the colonies and the first establishment of religious freedom in the new world.

The ships the *Ark* and the *Dove* which bore the Maryland pilgrims to their new home, brought a people who not only sought religious freedom for themselves but offered it to others as well, and whose kindly and just treatment of the Indians insured their homes against the attacks and depredations committed in other colonies.

Father White's first church was an Indian cabin but the old records state that soon there was a "new chappell at St. Maries." This was erected some time between 1638 and 1643, the exact date being unknown. Father White was a great evangelist and soon set out to convert the Patuxent Indians twenty miles to the east, on the shores of the Chesapeake, and later the Piscataways, sixty miles north on the Potomac. His "Account of Journey to Maryland" was really the first history of the state to be written and later he composed a dictionary, grammar and catechism in the Indian language.

The religious freedom established by the Calverts did not last long and ten years later Father White's labors were cut short when he was taken prisoner to England in the first Claiborne Revolution. There he was tried for his life on the charge of entering the kingdom as a priest. Although subsequently acquitted, Father White was forced to remain in prison for a long time and later his advanced years and broken health made his return to Maryland, which he so desired, impossible.

In 1694 the state capital was moved from St. Mary's City to Annapolis and in 1704 the Catholic Chapel at St. Mary's was closed by order of Governor Seymour. The structure remained standing until at least 1729 and very likely to a much later date. The buried foundations of this chapel, the first church erected in Maryland, were discovered by the Reverend John La Farge, S. J., in September, 1931, and some of its bricks may yet be seen.

The laws enacted by the Maryland Legislature in 1704 "to prevent the growth of popery in this province," were so harsh that an appeal was made to Queen Anne to extend her royal protection to her menaced Catholic subjects in America. Queen Anne's name is linked with a great many churches. Naturally she favored the Church of England and she personally perhaps did more to advance the cause of that church in the colonies than anyone else, her name being gratefully remembered to this day by many Episcopal churches possessed of Queen Anne communion sets and altar cloths, but it seems well to record here, as others have recorded elsewhere, that in Maryland she won just as enduring a claim to the gratitude of Catholics because of the kindly protection she extended to them. Under her orders the harsh laws were somewhat relaxed and the offices of the church at least allowed to be performed in the dwellings of private families, a great concession for those days.

When the Catholic Fathers were excluded from St. Mary's they retired to St. Inigoes Manor, a grant of three thousand acres deeded to the pioneer priests by Governor Leonard Calvert, not for the support of religion but because of the contributions in men and money which, according to the original "Conditions of Plantation," the Society of Jesus, in England, had made to Lord Baltimore's venture.

In 1705 a residence was built at St. Inigoes, on what is now known as Priest's Point, and in this building religious services were held for the grandchildren of the original founders of the colony, to whom public worship was then forbidden. This spacious manor house was destroyed by fire in 1872 but its remains may still be seen near the present Church of St. Ignatius.

The first Church of St. Ignatius was built about the year 1745; the present church, with its quaint boxlike pews and slave galleries, was begun in 1785. It is a brick structure twenty by forty feet, originally with a high longitudinal sloping roof, all done in the true Colonial style of straight lines and strong materials.

About 1816 a sacristy, twenty by fifteen feet, was attached and at this time the roof was arched. Later the plain beauty of the bricks was hidden by a coat of yellow paint and the bell tower added. These two latter features especially are out of harmony with the rest of the building—the unrelieved severity of the bell tower added to its unsubstantial material makes it unsightly—and it is to be hoped that in time both will be removed, the paint and the tower, and the little Church of St. Ignatius returned to its true Colonial form.

On the interior the altar rail encloses the sanctuary on three sides. The pews run right to the front wall, becoming lateral-like choir stalls when they reach the line of the altar rail. The pews are stall-like and have solid wooden doorlets. The galleries, about eight feet wide, run along the side walls up to the sanctuary. The ceiling is decorated with stenciled architectural lines, and each corner is marked by dates which connect the history of Maryland with the history of the Society of Jesus. Thus we find 1534, the date of Papal approbation of the society, and 1634, the date of the landing of the colony.

The historian John Gilmary Shea records an interesting incident in the history of St. Ignatius Church, St. Inigoes, and the old Church of St. Francis Xavier at Newtown:

In October 1814 the English vessels were committing such depredations along the Potomac that services were suspended at Newtown. On the Eve of All Saints, a barge from the British sloop-of-war *Saracen,* landed a pillaging party at St. Inigoes, who not only stripped the residence of kitchen and bedroom furniture carrying off all the clothing of the clergymen but they extended their sacrilegious hands to the church, seizing all the sacred vessels of the altar, even the ciborium, with the Blessed Sacrament. The Commander of the fleet, however, when an appeal was made to him, ordered all the property should be restored, and much in fact was given up under a flag of truce on the 18th of November.

A somewhat more detailed account of this incident is given in a letter quoted in Scharf's "History of Maryland":

They advanced to the house; immediately four or five of them ran into the private chapel, when, painful to relate! the sacred vestments were thrown here and there, the vessels consecrated to the service of God, profaned, the holy altar stript naked, the tabernacle carried off, and the Blessed Sacrament of the altar borne away in the hands of those sacrilegious wretches.

The captain was entreated, over and over again, to protect the church and have all things returned; he promised he would; he ran to the barge and ordered the men to restore the sacred vessels and vestments; they handed one chalice out of the barge, when the captain said he could not command them, they were a set of ruffians. The reverend gentleman who resides there, also joined in entreating them to return the sacred vessels, vestments and other articles for the use of the altar. The captain answered he would, seated himself in the barge and ordered his men to move off, without taking any more notice of the entreaties. An old lady, who lived on the place, prevailed on them in the meantime to return the tabernacle, which they did, also a part of the vestments.

On returning to the house it was pitiful to view the different rooms they had ransacked, particularly the chapel; they left the crucifix on the altar; broke the cruets and scattered the pieces over the floor, they carried off six feather beds, sheets, blankets and pillows—bed curtains, an alarm clock, silver spoons, knives and forks, glass, the reverend gentleman's watch, the candlesticks belonging to the altar, kitchen furniture, and almost all the clothing belonging to the persons who reside in the house, two trunks with clothing, books and medicine, several pair of new shoes, made for the people, and a quantity of leather; even the linens which were at the wash, and many other articles not yet known. The loss of that house, on this and a former occasion, cannot be much less than $1200.00.

Religious Freedom in the New Land

On the 18th of November, 1814, Captain Alexander Dixie, Commander of the *Saracen*, sent an officer, with a flag of truce, and a letter of apology to the priests in charge of the church, and other inhabitants of St. Inigoes, acknowledging the robbery, declaring the proceedings unauthorized, and restoring some of the articles taken, "hoping this justice will efface prejudicial sentiments toward the British." A frank confession, but poor atonement for the common rapine practised by the British navy in Maryland waters.

When the early settlers of Maryland began to take up grants of land outside of St. Mary's City and its immediate neighborhood, several prominent Catholic families settled around St. Clement's Bay, and it is thought that the first Jesuit priests, Fathers White, Altham and Copley, must have visited them on their missionary excursions. The Newtown Manor estate on St. Clement's Bay was acquired by the Jesuits in 1668 and has remained in possession of the church until this day. The property was purchased, the old records indicating that "Mr. William Britton and Temperance his wife conveyed the two tracts of land containing in all eight hundred and fifty acres, and constituting Newtown Manor, to Father Henry Warren in 1668," the consideration being "40,000 pounds of tobacco," a fair price for the times. The land came down by a line of descent through testamentary devise until the incorporation of the Roman Catholic clergy of Maryland in 1793; since then it has formed part of the property held by that corporation.

For more than two hundred years Newtown was an important residence of the Jesuit Fathers and a center of missionary activity for all the districts of St. Mary's County which were not dependent upon St. Inigoes. For more than two centuries all of the territory embracing the northern and western portion of old St. Mary's County depended for spiritual ministrations upon the old residence of Newtown.

The first chapel erected upon the manor estate must have been a modest structure; its location is unknown and its existence was of short duration. Very probably it was seized and closed during the Puritan domination. A larger church under the title of St. Ignatius Patron of Maryland was provided in 1662 but some old bricks covered with mortar are the only remaining relics of this chapel.

The present Newtown residence, built about 1740, with the Church of St. Francis Xavier adjoining it, is situated on as charming a spot as is to be found in this country, a neck of land bounded by the historic Potomac River on the south, and by Britton's Bay and St. Clement's Bay on the east and west. In the distance is St. Clement's Island where the Maryland pilgrim's first landed in 1634. . . .

The Church of St. Francis Xavier at Newtown is not only the oldest in origin of all Catholic churches in that section of St. Mary's County, but it is also today the oldest Catholic church standing in Maryland and is one of the oldest English-speaking Catholic churches which is actually standing in the United States. St. Francis Xavier's was rebuilt by Father James Ashby some time prior to 1767; frequently repaired and restored it still remains a simple frame structure with its sacristy, square bell tower and cross. The bell is quite old and bears the inscription "1691. S. T. Joannes Ardren." In olden times this hung in the crotch of a tree.

The center section of the church is the orginal structure. The small vestibule and the sacristy are of brick and were added later. About five years ago the roof became so bad it had to be replaced; the present roof has an air of newness out of keeping with the ancient building.

Originally there was a gallery extending around three sides of the church. The two side sections were reserved for the slaves while the end section served as a choir loft. The interior ceiling consists of a triple vaulted effect in Colonial style and there are three rows of pews and two aisles. The wall above the altar has an old painting of St. Francis Xavier that is very well preserved. This painting is flanked by flat pillars, something on the Doric order. The whole interior is characterized by a quaint doll-house appearance that accentuates rather than detracts from its devotional atmosphere.

St. Ignatius Church, St. Thomas' Manor, Chapel Point, is another eighteenth-century Catholic church but only by a slight margin for the present structure was not started until 1798. The brick of this church is laid in the Flemish bond, so distinctive of early Colonial buildings, that is, one length of brick is followed by the end of another and so on.

Attached to the church is the old manor house erected in 1741. St. Ignatius was originally built as a private chapel of the manor house since, as we have already seen, the penal laws of Maryland did not permit Catholics to have church buildings for public worship. The original little chapel of the manor house now serves as the sacristy of the present church, in this way connecting up the new with the old.

A short ride up the creek from St. Thomas' will be found the deserted village of Port Tobacco. This was the original county seat of Charles County and was started as a mission tended from St. Mary's City very shortly after the arrival of the first settlers. The Indian name for the spot was Pawtopaco and this was Anglicized in an ingenious manner by the early settlers who actually did ship their tobacco from the spot.

Although we have seen that St. Mary's County was settled by Catholics and St. Francis Xavier's is the oldest Catholic church to be found in this county and in the state, this little chapel is not in fact the oldest church building now standing in the county, this honor going to Christ Episcopal Church, better known as Chaptico Church, which was built by an act of assembly in 1736 and finished the following year. Philip Key, high sheriff of the colony, who came over in 1720, was in charge of building operations and it was he who built the family vault on the south side of the chancel.

Chaptico Church is a very fine example of Georgian architecture. There is an apsidal or semi-circular chancel and a high arched ceiling over the nave, supported on composite pillars, carved in wood—a somewhat rare feature in Colonial architecture, owing to the intricacy of the carving. The church is of brick with round-headed windows and doors. The high box-pews were removed in 1839 and the present pine benches substituted, but the gallery ones are happily intact. The communion silver, a chalice and paten, was purchased in 1770. The old Bible and Prayer Book, with alterations made in the prayer for the King after the Revolution, still remain. Both were bought at the same time as the silver, a marble font also being purchased at this time.

In 1773 a pipe organ was installed and "5 pounds of tobacco per poll" assessed to pay the organist. This organ was destroyed in 1813 by the British who are said to have stabled horses in the church.

The church, incidentally, was twice consecrated, first as Chaptico Church by Bishop Kemp in 1817, and the second time in 1840 as Christ Church by Bishop Whittingham, the earlier consecration apparently having been forgotten by this time.

There was originally a belfry on the roof but this became insecure and finally had to be taken down. For a number of years a low wooden frame in the yard carried the church bell but in 1913 the present attractive tower, which so adds to and completes the church, was erected. In 1875 Gothic windows took the place of the Colonial chancel window but in 1909 this latter window was happily restored.

In the churchyard is buried Captain Gilbert Ireland, a high sheriff of the colony. His gravestone, which disappeared some years ago, recited that he wished to be buried standing up and this was carried out and he was placed at rest in this manner.

Like Virginia, Maryland is especially rich in old brick Episcopal churches. By some authorities the sturdy brick walls of Trinity Church, located in Dorchester County in a picturesque spot on the Little Choptank River and on the narrow creek to which it has given its name, are attributed to the year 1680 but so vague is the exact information on this point that the time most generally given is "some time prior to 1690." It is known that the structure was standing for several years, at least, prior to the establishment of the Church of England as the state church of Maryland in 1692. Until the middle of the nineteenth century it was always known as "The Church in Dorchester Parish," and it is today familiarly known as "The Old Church."

The exterior has been fairly well preserved except for some changes made about 1850, when, after a long period of disuse, it was so dilapidated as to be considered unsafe when services were to be resumed. At this time an effort was made to "improve" the interior appearance. This "effort" ran along the usual lines: the high-backed box-pews with doors, the high pulpit with sounding board, the gallery with steps leading up from the outside, and the hand-carved wainscoting which is said to have formed a part of the original interior, all being removed. The church was then reconsecrated and named Trinity for the first time.

Several times has the old edifice fallen into periods of neglect, due to changing conditions in the life of the community. At one time it is recorded that the building was used only as a sheep-fold. In 1897 one wall showed signs of bulging and was braced with bricks from the outside. By 1914 the church had again fallen into such a terrible state of disrepair that its rescue at this time undoubtedly saved it from utter annihilation. It is too bad that more is not known concerning the early history of Old Trinity. It is the oldest Episcopal Church structure in the state, although not the oldest in continuous use, that honor being reserved for St. Paul's in Kent County.

As a result of its several periods of depression, many valuable possessions of the church have been lost but there remain two objects of particular interest. One is an old cushion which according to tradition was presented to the church by Queen Anne and upon which she is even said to have knelt when crowned! As to the truth or falsity of this tradition no one can say. The cushion, at any rate, is of royal purple lined with white kid and is brought out only upon special occasions. It was part of the Maryland Historical Exhibit at the Chicago Columbian Exposition and also at the Jamestown Exposition. The other object referred to is the chalice of a communion service, also reputed to be the gift of the Queen and bearing the inscription "To The Church in Dorchester Parish." This piece alone was saved when the silver was stolen from the church. The hall-marks, however, indicate a period later than Queen Anne's reign.

An interesting grave in the old churchyard is that known as the "Miller's Grave," which is appropriately marked by two solid millstones.

Built in 1713, St. Paul's Church, Kent County, today enjoys the distinction of being the oldest Episcopal Church in the state used continuously as a place of worship. The parish was organized in 1692, and on January 30, 1693, at "their majesties order," the first vestry was elected. As early as 1650 there was in existence a church called St. Peter's several miles from where the present Church of St. Paul is located. When the latter church was built on its present spot in 1713, it was to replace another church which had stood there ever since the "Establishment" and perhaps even longer than that. Several years ago, while excavating a grave, a portion of the foundations of this former church was found.

From a description recorded when the church was first built we learn that the structure was forty feet long by thirty feet wide and sixteen feet high. The walls were two and a half bricks thick, and there was "a circle at the east end." The structure stands today just as it did then with the exception of one wing which was torn down, thereby destroying the cruciform plan.

In 1776 the vestry house was built for twenty thousand pounds of tobacco, the date of its erection being worked in the bricks of the gable. The cost of the church was one hundred and forty thousand pounds of the same product.

During the War of 1812 old St. Paul's Church was used as a barracks for the troops and not until some thirty-one years later were the damages sustained during this period fully repaired. The silver communion service that is in regular use was presented by Thomas Smyth in 1699. There is also in the possession of the congregation a silver wine flagon presented by Queen Anne. This, however, has not been in regular use for some time.

Shaded by giant oaks and sycamores the old cemetery of St. Paul's Church is at once a peaceful and restful retreat. There are hosts of evergreen trees to enrich the air with their spicy odor and ancient boxwood and flowers in abundance contribute to the charm of the spot. The oldest gravestone is that of Daniel Doley who "departed this life Oct. Ye 20, 1729" and on the stone marker is carved the familiar old epitaph:

> *Behold & see now here I lye,*
> *As you are now so once was I,*
> *As I am now so must you be,*
> *Therefore prepare to follow me:*

Over the doorway of St. Paul's Episcopal Church at Baden is to be found the only sundial adorning a church in America. This was installed in 1753 and served as the community's first public time piece. The oldest portion of the church is thought by one of the church's historians to have been erected prior to 1692 and the south portion of the building added in 1793; however, the year 1733 is given as the correct date of erection by Percy G. Skirven in his "The First Parishes of the Province of Maryland." Among the treasures in the possession of the parish might be mentioned the communion vessels of the period of King George the First and the old Bible brought from England in 1739.

Old Wye Church, Wye Mills, was built in 1717 and today presents much the appearance of two hundred years ago. The interior was completely repaired in 1923 and is also in keeping with its original condition, with the exception of the large square pews which are missing.

During the first half of the nineteenth century the building became so dilapidated that services had to be discontinued. Later it was used as a stable, seemingly the traditional fate of a neglected house of worship. Bishop Whittingham and three friends, happening to be in the vicinity, paid a visit to the old church, drove out the cattle and after saying some prayers barred the entrance door with fence rails. From this visit grew the movement to restore the old church and on July 20, 1854, this was finally accomplished. Since that time it has been known as St. Luke's, Wye.

Old St. John's, Broad Creek, King George's Parish, was built in 1723 on the Maryland shore diagonally opposite Mount Vernon. As might be expected from such a location, George Washington, and members of his family, on numerous occasions rowed across the Potomac in an eight-oared barge, manned by husky slaves, to worship in Old Broad Creek Church as it was then called. After services were completed it is said that the General invariably lingered awhile, chatting pleasantly with the rector and members of the congregation before starting back home, thereby shattering the opinion held by some that George Washington was a cold and reserved individual, and making him appear, instead, as a friendly neighborly sort of man.

The church lies in what was originally called Piscataway Parish, named after the tribe of Indians whose home was close by. Their chief was called Emperor of Piscataway and held sway over all the tribes along the Potomac. According to tradition the last skirmish between the Indians and the white newcomers was fought in the very vicinity of the present church, perhaps even on the very ground on which St. John's now rests.

The first church erected there was a frame structure. In 1713 this was torn down and a larger church, also frame, substituted. This second frame church gave way to the present brick structure in 1723, just nine years before Washington's birth.

Old Durham Church, Charles County, was built in 1732; however the structure was almost completely rebuilt in 1793. The side walls were raised at this time, the second story windows added and galleries with pews were placed along the south side and at the ends. There was a new roof, new floor and window frames, and the whole building restored throughout. Again about 1843 the whole interior was reconstructed, the south and east galleries being removed along with the old pews. Plans now under way call for returning the church to its original Colonial appearance, including a beautifully-landscaped churchyard which will give it a proper setting.

Old Durham is among those churches which are said to have been honored by a visit from George Washington, he having been there in June 1771. From 1775 to 1791 it was honored by having as a member of its board of vestry William Smallwood, Maryland's most famous general.

Above the little village of White Haven is old St. Bartholomew's, known as Green Hill Church. It was built in 1733 to replace an earlier wooden church erected soon after the province was laid out into thirty parishes, in 1692, among these being Stepney Parish, in which this church is located.

The walls of Green Hill Church are eighteen inches thick, of alternate red and dark gray bricks. It has box-like, high-backed family pews with seats around three sides and a door at the entrance. The wood for their construction was hand-hewn from former companions of the old pines that face the church along the wide and beautiful banks of the Wicomico River. Several of these pews have on their sides the initials of their former owners. On one is "No. 35. G.D.S." Shortly after the Revolution the owner of this seat locked it up because the prayer for the King of England had been changed to the prayer for the President of the United States. He declared no one should pray that prayer in his pew while he was alive!

The floor of the church is made of the same brick as the walls. Halfway down the south wall, high up, is the pulpit with its quaint canopy, and under it, the clerk's desk where morning and evening prayers were read. Among the chief treasures of the parish, still in use, is a massive silver communion service presented by the rector in 1752. On the silver service presented by the State of Maryland to the United States battleship *Maryland* appear both Old Green Hill Church and its rectory which was erected the same year.

The date 1733 is outlined in dark brick under the eaves of the east wall. In the churchyard are a number of old tombstones, some nearly two hundred years old. On one of them is this curious inscription:

> *This world is like a mighty city full of crooked streets,*
> *And death is the market place, where all men meet;*
> *If life were merchandise that men could buy,*
> *The rich would live always—the poor would die.*

Old St. George's, Poplar Hill Church, St. Mary's County, was built about 1740, or possibly a little later, with the bricks, so it is said, of an earlier church erected on the same spot over a century before. The building is a quaint, snug little structure but with a tower that is an addition of recent years and is said to be out of keeping with the old English countryside type of church. The interior has suffered many changes. The old gallery and wine-stem pulpit have been missing for over half a century; the doors of the pews have been gone for a like period.

In the old and peaceful churchyard are many very ancient and interesting tombs and graves covered with the running box or periwinkle brought from England. There is also the English ivy.

Many interesting anecdotes of the Reverend Mr. Stanley, who was rector of Poplar Hill around 1840, have been preserved and handed down. He was considered by the congregation a man of splendid mind, and quite able to handle his vestry, which at one time seriously objected to his plans for burying his slave, Charity, near the church and not with the colored folks on the other side of the ravine. Reverend Mr. Stanley, however, insisted on burying her right back of the chancel as close to the church as he could get her and there she lies to this day. No doubt old Charity would have been greatly puzzled if she could have foreseen the discussion her burial was going to cause.

St. Mary's Church, North East, was erected in 1742, but services were held as early as 1706 in an old building on the site of the present church. At an early date a petition was sent to England for the services of a regular minister and a gift of books for the use of the parish. In response to this petition Queen Anne presented the vestry with the large Bible which is still in the possession of the congregation and which is one of those printed in Oxford, England, in 1716 by John Baskett, printer to the King and to the university. With this was sent a large Prayer Book which is also still owned by the congregation. The communion service likewise came from England. It is of solid silver and made by Folkingham, London, 1717.

St. Mary's Church has seen a number of changes. The original tower was of wood but in 1904 this was removed and a brick tower built. About the middle of the last century the interior was modernized, the old pulpit removed and the altar enlarged.

St. Thomas' Church, Garrison Forest, went up in 1743. After fighting Indians all week, it was pointed out that it was perhaps too much to expect the "forest inhabitants" to ride or trudge all the way into Baltimore Town to attend St. Paul's of a Sabbath. Hence the little brick church on the oak-crowned hill, which stands there to this day.

And the church was not completed long until time and the arrows of hostile Indians started to fill the graves which crowd its yard. Among the first was the famous Ellen North, first white woman to be born in Baltimore Town. On one rain-smoothed slab these words may still be traced:

Young & old as you pass by,
As you are now so once was I;
And as I am so you must be,
So prepare for death & Eternity.

And not far away may be found these quaint lines:

Afflictions sore long time I bore,
Physicians were in vain,
Till God did please,
& Death did cease,
To ease me of my pain.

In 1692, in the reign of William and Mary, when Maryland had become a royal province and Lord Baltimore had been succeeded by a royal governor, the Church of England was established in the colony and the five counties of its eastern shore were subdivided into thirty parishes.

In 1742 the Parish of Snow Hill, or, as it was first called, All Hallows, was erected into a separate county, Worcester, and in 1744 the northern part of it became a separate parish of the same name. Here, near St. Martin's River, stood St. Martin's Chapel, the first St. Martin's, of which seemingly there is no record until we read of the plans for its replacement in 1756 by a proper parish church, the familiar old St. Martin's of today.

During all the turmoil of the Revolution services were apparently continued at St. Martin's despite the fact that in 1776 the rector, the Reverend John Bowie, was sent to Annapolis and imprisoned as a royalist by the Whigs.

During the nineteenth century, however, St. Martin's fell into a state of disrepair; the windows were broken, the plaster torn in places and the enclosures, even those about the graves in the yard, carried off. About 1844–45 the building was partially repaired and put into condition for use at least in the summer season. The structure today is somewhat dilapidated; the walls are as sturdy as in the past but the woodwork and other perishable portions are in need of restoration.

The building is popularly reputed to be haunted but apparently the only unwelcome visitors are those who from time to time take advantage of the building's isolation to break open its barnlike doors or its roughly shuttered windows, in which it has been found impossible to keep glass. Most of the visiting vandals boldly leave their names upon the woodwork of the antique pews. Upon one occasion a pew was destroyed; upon another the charred embers of a fire were discovered on the brick of the aisle. . . .

The year 1756 is also the date usually assigned for the erection of All Hallows Church, Snow Hill, and until 1872 the building appears to have remained substantially as first built. At that time, however, the box-pews were torn out and the old gallery removed. Later the present chancel was built and modern windows were substituted for the old. Originally there was a small belfry at the western end of the building but weakening timbers forced the removal, within recent years, of both bell and belfry. The former now hangs on a stout beam suspended between two pine trees which grow close by.

An English ivy spreads a protecting mantle over the walls of the church, the shoots of which were brought many years ago from the mother country. Although the modern note is now very evident within, touches of older days are still evident—notably in the memorial tablets upon the western wall, and in far greater measure in the Bible which Queen Anne presented to the parish, which is carefully preserved in a glass case near the church door.

In the churchyard of St. James, Herring Creek Church, in Anne Arundel County, will be found the oldest gravestone in Maryland. This is the stone erected in 1665 to mark the grave of Anne Brickhead. The curious epitaph on this monument reads:

This Register is for her bones,
Her fame is more perpetual than ye stones,
And still her virtues, though her life be gone,
Shall live when earthy monuments are none.
Who reading this can choose but drop a tear,
For such a wife & such a Mother deare.
She ran her race & now is laid to rest,
& Allaleguis singes among the blest.

The age of Herring Creek Church, like that of a certain lady, is somewhat uncertain but it is known that there was already a church in existence when the parish was formally laid out in 1694. In 1706 a bell was given, according to the records, by Queen Anne and a silver alms basin in 1724 through the generosity of the widow of an early rector, the Reverend Henry Hall.

This Reverend Hall once had quite a controversy with the Quakers, who were very numerous in the parish. They refused to pay tithes and Mr. Hall went down to their meeting house and threatened to horsewhip every one of them unless they complied with the law. Apparently this settled the matter; at least we do not hear that he had any more trouble with them.

On June 22, 1762 the vestry advertised for bids for a new church to be built of brick, sixty feet long and forty feet wide, the bids to be in by July 3rd. Mr. John Weem's bid of fourteen hundred pounds sterling was the successful one. The completed church was turned over to the vestry in December 1765 and this is the building in use today.

Old St. Andrew's Church, below Leonardtown, St. Mary's County, is one of the most picturesque churches in Maryland. The present building was erected in 1766 and stands in a wonderful state of preservation. The aisles are made up of stones. The pews still have the old doors attached and there is a silver communion service which tradition insists was given by Queen Anne.

Being in a thickly wooded section, many bootleggers are said to have sought shelter within the church—a somewhat unique and modern misuse of a house of worship, if true—and it has been found almost impossible to keep the front doors locked on account of chance visitors. Surrounding the old church is the graveyard in which are buried many notables in Colonial history, including the Colonial governor, George Platter.

St. Andrew's, Princess Anne, Somerset County, built in 1771 as a chapel of ease of Somerset Parish, is now the main church of the parish. Incidentally, in English ecclesiastical law a chapel of ease is a chapel built by a mother church for the ease and convenience of her parishioners. From time to time since the erection of this little chapel of ease in Princess Anne Town there have been modifications and marked changes in both the exterior and interior of the building until today the only remaining parts of the original structure are the north, south and west walls.

St. Barnabas' Church, Leeland, Prince George's County, was built in 1772. The rector at that time was the Reverend Jonathan Boucher, an intimate friend of George Washington and tutor to John Parke Custis, son of Martha Washington. It was just after Dr. Boucher was installed, on August 4, 1772, that George Washington and his family paid him a social visit of several days. This incidentally gave Mrs. Washington a chance to visit her son who lived with his tutor. At the same time Governor Eden, the last Colonial governor of Maryland, was also a guest. On Sunday the whole party went to church, as Washington records in his diary, in the Governor's phaeton. On other occasions Washington stopped with Dr. Boucher on his way from Mount Vernon to Annapolis.

The old church was pulled down late in 1772 and work on the new one was promptly commenced. The contract states that Christopher Lowndes is "to make, erect, build, and set up a new Brick Church near the place where the old Brick Church in said Parish now stands, to contain sixty feet in length and forty-six feet in width."

Dr. Boucher became very unpopular during the Revolution. He was a pronounced Tory and refused to retreat one step from his position. Not only did he refuse to compromise his views but he further insisted that others should know his feelings as well. He wrote during this period: "For more than six months, I preached (when I did preach), with a pair of loaded pistols lying on the cushion, having given notice that if any man or men were so lost to all sense of decency as to drag me out of my pulpit, I should think myself justified before God in repelling violence."

In the sermons preached in the new unfinished church politics crept in from time to time and members of the congregation grew more and more incensed. The climax came when on one occasion Reverend Mr. Boucher was by force prevented from entering the pulpit. Finally, still fighting and clinging to his convictions, his property was confiscated and he was forced to leave the country. The last ship to sail from Annapolis before the commencement of hostilities carried Dr. Boucher and his American wife to England.

St. Barnabas' Church is very interesting from an architectural standpoint. It is one of the exceedingly few Colonial buildings of any size to have a hipped roof. The real charm of the building lies in its simplicity, due, no doubt, to the uncertain times in which it was built, for, under ordinary circumstances, the wealth of the congregation would have demanded a more ornate and costly building. The windows and walls of the church are filled with memorials to vestrymen, members of prominent families who once lived near it and other people of note. "The trusses that hold the vaulted roof have been ceiled," writes Percy G. Skirven, "hiding the beauty of the timber work."

Among the other old brick Episcopal churches of Maryland, still standing, and their dates of erection, might be mentioned: All Hallows, South River, Anne Arundel County, about 1727; St. Luke's, Church Hill, Queen Anne's County, 1730; Christ Church, Port Republic, Calvert County, 1772, and its chapel of ease, Middleham Chapel, Calvert County, 1748; and All Faith, St. Mary's County, 1765. This completes the list known to the writer. There may be others but information on them is lacking and even on some of these covered it has been very hard to obtain, nothing being available in printed form; simply the old records and traditions of the neighborhood which are very hard to run down. If it had not been for the splendid cooperation on the part of the clergy and laymen who so kindly helped in the work, my story of the old Maryland churches would have been very meager indeed.

The oldest building for public worship now standing in Maryland is strangely enough not an old brick church at all but a wooden structure, the Friends' Meeting House near Easton, Talbot County. This building, constructed in 1684 of massive timbers, boarded and shingled, is one of the most ancient in the country and although repaired and enlarged from time to time, still retains much of its original appearance. Over two years were required in its erection for the timbers had to be hewed and dressed with a broad-axe and such other tools as were used in that day.

The Quakers settled early in Talbot County and their first house of worship, "primitive in the extreme," since they did not believe in any outward display of grandeur, was erected soon after 1657. Prominent among the early members in attendance at this meeting house was Wenlock Christison, a man several times mentioned in Massachusetts State History and at whose home was held the very first meeting of Friends, *of which there is any official record*, in the State of Maryland and perhaps even in the United States.

In 1673 George Fox, the founder of the Society of Friends, was in the vicinity and attended services at the old meeting house. When he returned to England he sent a parcel of books to the church, laying the foundation for probably the first library in the province. Some of these books are still in existence and are even yet a part of the church library.

In 1682 the earlier building having become too small, a meeting was held and a new structure decided upon, together with its present location at the head of the Third Haven, or Tred Avon, River. The church prospered and it was here that William Penn preached in 1700 and in attendance were Lord and Lady Baltimore and their train of attendants.

Getting married in the Friends' Meeting House in the early days was a slightly more complicated procedure than it is now. Marriage intentions had to be announced on two separate occasions, in both men's and women's meetings, and thirdly, in a written form; consequently three months had to elapse before the ceremony was finished. In addition to this, when the young couple was under age, the written consent of the parents of both was necessary. The quaint old-fashioned wording of the first marriage intention on the meeting house records is interesting enough to be quoted in full:

William Southbee, of Talbot County, in the province of Maryland, the 29 day of the First Month (O.S.) and in the year 1668, in an Assembly of the People of God, called Quakers, at their meeting, at the house of Isaac Abrahams, solemnly in the fear of God, took Elizabeth Read of the aforesaid county and province, spinster, to be his wife; and she, the said Elizabeth Read, did then and there, in the like manner, take the said William Southbee to be her husband, each of them promising to be faithful to each other. To which the meeting now witnesseth, by signature.

Quaker Meeting House, Easton, Md. The oldest building for public worship now standing in Maryland. *Photo courtesy James Dixon.*

"Where Lincoln prayed." The Lincoln Pew in the New York Avenue Presbyterian Church. *Photo by Buckingham Studio, Inc.*

So indifferent were the early worshipers to the ordinary comforts of life that when a stove was proposed for heating the building there was objection on the ground that religious zeal should afford sufficient warmth! Even when the stove was at last installed, one of the members was so unyielding that he voiced his disapproval in no uncertain terms, calling the stove a "dumb idol" and made it an object on which to hang his overcoat. Happily there was no fire that day and no damage was done; not so the following Sunday when after a similar performance the odor arising from the smoking garment caused the obstinate Friend to rush to its rescue, much to the amusement of the witnesses, especially the children. After this there is no further record of this particular member ever again referring to the new stove as a "dumb idol" or any similar endearing term.

There is in existence a continuous record of the business transactions of the society from 1676 to the present time and so valuable are these papers that the county has provided a special safe for them within the fireproof vault at the county court house.

Today the meeting house stands in a very good state of preservation. Twice was the old structure saved from fire; the last time in about 1810 when, through the quick-wittedness of one Sarah Berry the flame was extinguished by rubbing it with a stick, there being no time to obtain water or give an alarm. The interior is plain and undecorated; the benches unpainted; the ceiling low. The whole structure, inside and out, is unassuming in the extreme yet crowded to the fill with memories of the early days of Maryland and of the nation.

The home of Colonel William Stevens on the banks of the Pocomoke River was known as Rehoboth Plantation, the name having been chosen from Genesis 26:22, "And he called the name of it Rehoboth; and he said, For now the Lord hath made room for us, and we shall be fruitful in the land."

Many followed Colonel Stevens to his new home, in search of religious freedom, and preaching was held at the Rehoboth plantation. In 1672 the Reverend Robert Maddux preached there and the next year came the Quaker, George Fox. By 1680 the number of Presbyterians in the vicinity had increased to such an extent that a request was forwarded to the Presbytery of Laggan in Ireland for a minister to form the band of religious exiles into a church. As a result of this request Francis Makemie was sent over. He was born of Scotch lineage in County Donegal and was a graduate of the University of Glasgow.

Makemie, considered the father of the Presbyterian Church in America, arrived on the banks of the Pocomoke in 1683 and Rehoboth Church was soon organized and a church building erected. The exact date of the beginning of the church is not definitely known but the date of 1683 is most probably correct. Tradition has it that the first church was a cypress log structure built quite close to the banks of the Pocomoke River. This was the first Presbyterian Church in America.

During the years that followed, Makemie journeyed from place to place, preaching and organizing churches. A great pioneer, he traveled all the water courses of Chesapeake Bay and in 1706 succeeded in forming the first presbytery of the Presbyterian Church in America, in Philadelphia.

When it became necessary to erect a new church at Rehoboth, Makemie had this built on his own land as a protection against certain laws in effect in Maryland at this time. When he died he willed this land and the "present church" to the congregation.

It is claimed by some that the church referred to in his will is the building still in use today, the term "present church" quite evidently implying a former structure, presumably the cypress log structure, and while this cannot be definitely proved, it seems fairly certain the now existing structure was built some time during that period, say from 1706 to 1710, and most probably it was, in fact, built in 1706. This is a well constructed brick structure, evidently patterned after the church in Ireland where Makemie was ordained, as the building is identical in design with a picture of the older church.

Originally the building adhered to the old Scotch idea of having the doors face south and the pulpit on the north side but a number of years ago both front doors were converted into windows and an entrance made at the west end. A lower ceiling was also built in at about the same time to take the place of the high arched one which had been in use since the church was first erected. All of these repairs were made to increase the heating possibilities of the building, evidently not an important point to the early church fathers.

The old pulpit in which Makemie preached is no longer there but the box-pews now in use are very old and in a remarkable state of preservation. At one end is a balcony, one of the three original balconies thought to have been built in Makemie's time but for many years sealed in the wall.

Makemie's name will always be associated with the struggle for religious liberty in America and he was forced to undergo many hardships in this connection. After his success in forming the first Presbytery at Philadelphia, he started to Boston, stopping on the way in New York where he preached, and baptized a child. Although there was no established church in the colony, the corrupt governor had him arrested and prosecuted for preaching without a license. Makemie defended himself and won one of the first victories for religious liberty in America but the trying experiences he was forced to undergo hastened his death the following year.

Francis Makemie was one of the great intellects of his day. He had one of the largest libraries in America. In 1708 the Reverend John Hampton was ordained at Snow Hill Church, the first minister ordained in the Presbyterian Church in America. The Snow Hill Church was founded by Makemie.

Some thirty or so years ago the Reverend L. P. Bowen, Makemie's only biographer, found his bones at rest in a neglected and poorly kept spot. He was so incensed that the founder of the Presbyterian Church in America had been allowed to undergo such treatment that he aroused the church body to do something and as a result of Dr. Bowen's crusade six thousand dollars was raised, the grave rescued from desecration and a handsome monument erected. This monument, a granite statue with one hand raised in benediction, is located some ten miles south of Rehoboth Church, in Accomac County, Virginia.

The first cathedral in the United States, built as such, is happily still standing. This is the well-known Cathedral of the Assumption, Baltimore, designed by Benjamin H. Latrobe who was engaged at the same time in building the National Capitol. Although members of different faiths, Mr. Latrobe and Archbishop Carroll of Baltimore were close friends and the architect very generously gave his services gratis and faithfully supervised the erection of the edifice.

The site chosen for the new church was itself historic. In 1782 Count Rochambeau, returning with his army from Yorktown, halted in Baltimore and the ground upon which some of his men encamped is that occupied by the present cathedral. The cornerstone was laid July 7, 1806, by Bishop Carroll—he did not become Archbishop until 1808—and although work had to be suspended during the War of 1812, it was afterwards speedily resumed and the cathedral opened for worship four years later.

The plan was a Latin cross, vaulted throughout and with a majestic dome over the crossing, supported by impressive pillars of corresponding size and form. The towers were completed later while the imposing portico was not added until about 1863 but the turnip-shaped roofs were placed on the belfries quite early, sometime before 1832. These are said by some authorities to be the only incongruous feature of an otherwise almost perfect design and were not a part of Latrobe's original plan.

The church has been twice lengthened. The rear wall was originally straight; this end was extended twenty-four feet and a twelve foot circular sanctuary added, this addition merely supplementing and enhancing the original design which remains unchanged. The building was constructed of porphyritic granite, hauled from near Elicott City on wagons drawn by oxen. It now measures almost two hundred and twenty-seven feet from the rear wall of the sanctuary to the front of the portico, while its width, including the arms of the cross, is one hundred and seventy-seven feet.

The final design chosen for the cathedral was the seventh submitted by Mr. Latrobe. When, after the work was started, certain of the building committee wished to make changes in the plan, Mr. Latrobe appealed to Bishop Carroll who backed him up and insisted that the original plans be adhered to. Thus, aside from a few minor changes made at the start, the cathedral exists almost exactly as its creator would have wished it. Mr. Latrobe's other famous church, St. John's in Washington, has been extended and enlarged and altered so many times that its original design, that of a Greek cross, has, unfortunately, been lost.

The high altar of the cathedral was a gift to Archbishop Maréchal from his pupils in Marseilles. There are a number of noted paintings to be found in the cathedral and rectory including the two presented by Charles X and Louis XVIII of France: "St. Louis Burying His Dead Soldiers" and "The Descent from the Cross." The former, painted by Steuben, hangs in the baptistry and the latter, the work of Guerin, hangs on the west wall of the main entrance. Among the sacred vessels is an old missionary chalice which tradition says belonged to Archbishop Carroll.

During the great fire of 1873 the cathedral was in imminent danger of being destroyed and was saved only through the bravery of a number of persons who at great personal risk ascended to the great dome and protected the roof with wet blankets.

"There are few edifices in the United States as rich in historical memories as the Baltimore Cathedral," says the "Catholic Encyclopedia." Three plenary councils were held within its walls and hundreds of priests received their ordination there; then went forth to connect the history of the old building with that of other sections of the land. Among the many distinguished pewholders in the church's long history might be mentioned Chief Justice Roger B. Taney and Charles Carroll of Carrollton, who lived to be the last surviving Signer of the Declaration of Independence. The remains of Archbishop Carroll, under whose jurisdiction the cathedral was first planned and started, today lie beneath the high altar of a chapel built by Cardinal Gibbons.

"Thus, although a hundred years have passed since its building," wrote Fiske Kimball in 1918, "the patriarchal cathedral still remains without question the finest classical church in America," and Thomas Eddy Tallmadge reiterated this opinion in 1927 in his book "The Story of Architecture in America."

CHAPTER V

IN THE NATION'S CAPITAL

Where Lincoln prayed! Such worshipers as he
Make thin ranks down the ages.
                    —Lyman Whitney Allen

THE corner-stone of St. John's Church, "The Church of the Presidents," was laid on September 4, 1815. The architect was Benjamin H. Latrobe and the building was erected under his supervision. Mr. Latrobe declined to receive any compensation for his services, just as in the case of the Baltimore Cathedral, and even refused the offer of a pew free of rent, expressing his preference for some token that he might hand down to his children so the testimonial voted by the church took the form of a plate.

St. John's Church as it came from the hands of its builders took the form of a Greek cross, the equal transepts perfectly proportioned to the nave. At the crossing stood massive pillars which upheld the beautiful cupola and lantern. The building has undergone many changes with the years. In 1820 the west transept was extended to the building line of 16th Street, according to Mr. Latrobe's supplemental plan, and a gallery placed over the whole of this extension. The portico and steeple were also added at this time, the building now taking the form of a Latin cross. Later the box and high-backed pews were removed and the wine-glass pulpit replaced. In 1883 still more extensive repairs were made; the chancel was considerably enlarged and the wnidows filled with stained glass, dedicated, for the most part, to deceased members of the congregation.

Situated as it was, just across Lafayette Square from the White House, St. John's was known from the beginning as "The President's Church. James Madison was the first Chief Executive to attend services there. In December 1816 the committee appointed

New York Avenue Presbyterian Church, Washington, D. C., where Abraham Lincoln worshiped. *Photo by Buckingham Studio, Inc.*

Friends' Meeting House, Flushing, N. Y., where was held the first public meeting in New York to agitate the abolition of slavery. *Photo by C. Manley De Bevoise.*

to wait on President Madison and offer him his choice of a pew in the church free of purchase, reported that the President desired that the choice should be made by the committee, which accordingly selected one among the large pews of the first class.

Mr. Monroe and his family next became occupants of the President's pew and when John Quincy Adams was president he occasionally occupied one of the large pews which had previously been taken by Henry Clay. General Andrew Jackson, although not a member of the Episcopal faith, while in Washington sometimes occupied one of the four large pews at St. John's; likewise in attendance were Martin Van Buren, General Harrison, John Tyler, Zachary Taylor, Millard Fillmore and Chester A. Arthur. James Buchanan and Theodore Roosevelt also came to this church upon occasion and William Howard Taft and his family often worshiped there. Many men prominent in public and private life regularly attended St. John's; in fact, a list of its parishioners reads almost like a roster of Washington's officialdom.

The church today contains many beautiful memorials dedicated to deceased members of the congregation. Over the altar is a brass cross commemorating President Arthur. The chancel window is in memory of Mrs. Arthur. In the west wall is a window in memory of Presidents Tyler, Harrison and Taylor. Over the south gallery is one to General Winfield Scott. These are only a few of the many interesting memorials to be found there—it has, in fact, been said that "the eye cannot glance in any direction without seeing some memorial."

St. John's is upholding the best traditions of historic churches by continuing to make history. On March 4, 1933, a private service for the President-elect and Mrs. Roosevelt, members of the new cabinet and their guests, was held there in the morning before Mr. Roosevelt went to the Capitol for the inauguration. This service lasted for twenty minutes and consisted of prayers by the clergy for the new President and others in authority and for the country, and of music by a choir of men and boys. The prayer for the President was as follows:

O Lord, our Heavenly Father, the high and mighty ruler of the universe, Who dost from Thy throne behold all the dwellers upon earth;

most heartily we beseech Thee, with Thy favor to behold and bless Thy Servant, Franklin, chosen to be the President of the United States, and all others in authority; and so replenish them with the grace of Thy holy spirit, that they may always incline to Thy will, and walk in Thy way. Endue them plenteously with heavenly gifts; grant them in health and prosperity long to live; and finally, after this life, to attain everlasting joy and felicity; through Jesus Christ our Lord. Amen.

During this service Mr. and Mrs. Roosevelt sat in the President's pew, always reserved for the Chief Executive, and which had, until recently, been occupied by Mrs. William Howard Taft.

The New York Avenue Presbyterian Church has also often been called "The Presidents' Church" because of the many Chief Executives who have worshiped there. John Quincy Adams was a regular attendant and it was from its pulpit that he delivered his farewell address. Here also attended Andrew Jackson, William Henry Harrison, Franklin Pierce, James Buchanan, and Andrew Johnson. Millard Fillmore worshiped here frequently, as did also Benjamin Harrison, Grover Cleveland, Theodore Roosevelt, and, on occasion, Woodrow Wilson. But most of all this church is associated with Abraham Lincoln, for it was here that he worshiped while President of the country.

One Sunday during the Civil War the pastor announced, no doubt with deep regret, that the church would be closed indefinitely because of the fact that hospital accommodations were not adequate to care for the wounded soldiers, and word had gone out from army headquarters that all churches in Washington were to be turned over to the military for hospital purposes. Lincoln was in the church that Sunday and appeared greatly surprised. When the minister had finished his announcement the Civil War President arose in his pew and said simply, "This church shall not be closed. We need it too much. I shall countermand the order."

The pew in which Lincoln always sat is visited by thousands each year and has become, so to speak, "A shrine within a shrine." It is not, however, the only Lincoln relic possessed by the church. There is also a room on the first floor where he came to attend the midweek prayer service, a small room adjoining the main lecture room where the services were held. Here Lincoln sat with the door partially ajar, praying with the rest of the congregation for Divine guidance. Only the minister of the church and the secret service men were aware of this and it was not until the close of Lincoln's life that this fact became known to all. One day, however, two young men desiring to know who the strangers were leaving the little room, traced the President by the large footprints made in the freshly fallen snow to the White House. The pastor at that time was the Reverend Dr. Gurley and when they told him their discovery he exacted from them a promise of honor to tell no one and they kept their word.

The New York Avenue Presbyterian Church was organized in 1803, during the Jefferson administration, when a group of Scotch-Irish Americans who had fought in the Revolution came to Washington with the planting of the government there. The first meetings were held in the Treasury Building and the first minister of the church was the sainted Dr. James Laurie, who was for many years also a clerk in the Treasury Department, since the salary he received from his small congregation was not sufficient to care for his practical needs. It was not long though until Dr. Laurie had sufficient funds with which to build the first little brick church, later called Willard Hall. The donors of these funds were from as far north as Boston and as far south as Savannah. This church stood on ground now occupied by the New Willard Hotel.

An interesting fact is that the wife of Dr. Laurie, the first minister, was the cousin of Sir Walter Scott who presented to her, at the occasion of her wedding, the manuscript of one of his novels. Another interesting historical association is the fact that the farewell service to General Lafayette on the occasion of his departure from the country at the close of his last visit, was held in this church; that is, in the present building, whose corner-stone was laid on July 29, 1820.

In 1903 the church celebrated its centennial anniversary. Theodore Roosevelt, then President, standing in the Lincoln pew, delivered an address on this occasion. Only a few years ago the Great Commoner, William Jennings Bryan, was buried from this church. While the congregation has a history running back one hundred and thirty years, it has had only seven ministers during this time, the present incumbent being the seventh.

One day a rather distinguished American writer, Lyman Whitney Allen, attended service in the church and was granted the privilege of sitting in the Lincoln Pew. From this experience, which moved him deeply, came his beautiful poem, "The Lincoln Pew," which begins:

> *Within the historic church both eye and soul*
> *Perceived it. 'Twas the pew where Lincoln sat—*
> *The only Lincoln God hath given to men—*
> *Olden among the modern seats of prayer,*
> *Dark like the 'sixties, place and past akin.*
> *All else has changed, but this remains the same,*
> *A sanctuary in a sanctuary.*

On the occasion of its one hundred and twenty-fifth anniversary, the family of Robert Todd Lincoln presented to the church a memorial gift in memory of Lincoln—the beautiful memorial tower with chimes. This tower is of Sir Christopher Wren design while the chimes were made by a firm which traces its enterprise to the family of Nancy Hanks, the mother of Abraham Lincoln, whose people were among the first makers of bells in the United States.

We know today that Lincoln is not really dead. As the present minister of the New York Avenue Presbyterian Church, the Reverend Joseph Richard Sizoo, D.D., so impressively puts it: "His soul goes marching on. In this new day, with its new deliverances from injustice, tyranny, intolerance and inhumanity, the spirit of the martyred liberator still lives. Hallelujah! I bless God for Abraham Lincoln and that I am counted worthy to minister in that church where stands his pew, a shrine within a shrine, hallowed by his hours of worship."

Chapter VI

PATROONS AND PATRIOTS IN NEW YORK AND NEW JERSEY

I never weary of great churches. It is my favourite kind of mountain scenery. Mankind was never so happily inspired as when it made a cathedral.
                                        —Robert Louis Stevenson

CLOSELY entwined with the early Colonial history of Tarrytown, New York, and possessing in addition a quaint architectural interest, the old Sleepy Hollow Dutch Reformed Church is one of the most interesting ecclesiastical structures still standing in the country. In its modest little graveyard lies buried Washington Irving whose writings brought the church and the surrounding community their greatest fame.

"It stands on a knoll surrounded by locust trees and lofty elms," wrote Irving these many years ago, "from among which its whitewashed walls shine modestly forth, like christian purity beaming through the shades of retirement. A gentle slope descends from it to a silver sheet of water bordered by high trees, between which, peeps may be caught at the blue hills of the Hudson. To look upon its grass-grown yard, where the sunbeams seem to sleep so quietly, one would think that there at least the dead might rest in peace."

Down the hill, about a stone's throw south of the church, is the bridge, or rather the place where it once was for a new one has superseded it, over which Ichabod Crane and the headless horseman dashed in their mad midnight ride as related in "The Legend of Sleepy Hollow." Ichabod Crane was one member, who in fiction at least, did not find the churchyard conducive to peace and quiet. It might not be amiss to add that, according to Irving, Mr. Crane was the leader of the music in the old church.

Old Sleepy Hollow Church owes its origin to the generosity of one Vredryck Flypse, a carpenter who came to be known as the "Dutch Millionaire" when he abandoned carpentry for fur trading and became very wealthy. In 1680 this prosperous citizen obtained a grant of land along the Pocantico River and during the next few years erected a manor house, a mill, and the little church that is still in existence.

There is some confusion as to when this church was built. A tablet set in the west wall gives the information: "Built in 1699," which probably means that it was completed in that year. If this is correct, then no doubt the building was started some years before and is entitled to an earlier date. The old bell brought over from Holland is inscribed "Amsterdam 1685"; from this and other information at hand, some have concluded that there was an earlier church edifice which in 1699, or thereabouts, gave way to the present church. There is no suggestion, however, but that the present Old Dutch Church is entitled to a seventeenth century beginning and the structure therefore takes its place in the small group of these buildings yet remaining.

The walls of the old church are thirty inches thick and the windows as constructed originally were elevated seven feet above the ground and had iron bars to serve as protection against a possible attack by the Indians. The seats provided for the early congregation were simply rude benches with no backs, except those pews arranged on either side of the pulpit which were for the special use of the occupants of the Flypse manor house and their guests. There was a huge pulpit and sounding board while a gallery provided accommodations for slaves and "redemptioners" as those unfortunate settlers who had sold their services to pay the cost of their passage from the old world, were called. The small yellow brick surrounding the windows and bordering the doorway were brought from Holland.

During the Revolutionary War the church was closed and in a spirit of democratic fervor the decorations distinguishing the Flypse pews were torn out and burned. After the war these pews were appropriated by the elders and deacons of the church.

Old Sleepy Hollow Church did not escape mutilation during

the nineteenth century. In 1837 drastic changes were made in the building. The pulpit was taken out and the windows cut down to within three feet of the floor. At this time a vestibule was also built. The entrance was changed from the south side to the west side and the roof beams hidden by a ceiling, while pews with backs were installed. The iron bars were likewise removed from the windows. In 1897 the building was at least partially restored to its early condition. The old pulpit and sounding board were gone but the Reformed Church in Albany had made a copy of the Sleepy Hollow pulpit some time around 1800; from this a replica of the old-style pulpit was made for the Tarrytown church.

At present the structure is in a good state of repair and is used for afternoon services during the months of September and October. The weather vane on which are cut the initials V. F.—Vredryck Flypse—yet remains. The beams and walls are the same as at first. The old bell has never been moved and is still used; inscribed on this bell is the motto of the church "Si Deus Pro Nobis Quis Contra Nos"—"If God be for us, who can be against us?"

In the old Sleepy Hollow Cemetery will be found the tombstone of one John Buckhout which carries the rather remarkable information: "Died April 10, 1785, Age 103, I left behind 240 children and grandchildren."

The Friends were early settlers in Flushing, New York, but for some years they had no house of worship, services being conducted in private homes. By 1692 sufficient funds were obtained to purchase land and in the fall of the following year they began cutting timber for their meeting house and the work of construction was actually begun. The first meeting recorded as having been held in the new house was the Quarterly Meeting of November, 1694.

The building, as completed, was exceedingly plain; there was no floor and no means of heating, but, even so, no doubt the early members were very grateful for having it. In 1704 the little structure was shingled, plastered and repaired but in 1716 it was decided to build a new meeting house and orders were issued accordingly. Work on this was completed in 1719 and this, apparently, is the house still standing today. Various repairs have been made from time to time and about 1763 the gallery was taken down and a chamber floor laid, thus making the house one and a half stories in height. Small windows with shutters (and some without glass) were inserted in the upper story, which was partitioned into two rooms, in one of which a school was kept for many years.

This is the story of the meeting house as set forth in Henry Onderdonk, Jr.'s "Friends on Long Island and in New York," an authoritative work; however the Friends themselves have always regarded 1694 as the correct date and in 1894 celebrated the two hundredth anniversary of the building of their meeting house. The minutes, while not conclusive in themselves, at least seem to suggest the correctness of Onderdonk's account. On the other hand, John Cox, Jr., Chairman of the Committee on Records of the Religious Society of Friends, after studying the minutes and examining the meeting house itself, offers the following suggestion:

> The entire evidence as set forth in the records and in the building itself appears to me to prove that the first house was built and occupied in 1694, but unplastered, and the frame covered by boarding; that in 1699 additional work was done, perhaps the benches added among other things; that in 1705, owing to the growth of the society, and to provide for both men's and women's business meetings it was decided to build a new house, but common sense later led the committee to add to the old one.

During the Revolutionary War the old meeting house was used as a prison, a hospital, a barracks and as a storage place for feed. When the British officers came to take possession in 1776 religious services were being held. It is said that the officers were so impressed with the fervor of the worshipers that they waited until services were completed before seizing the building for their use. During this period the army utilized the fence around the grounds as firewood.

Like their brethren elsewhere, many of the Friends of Flushing suffered fines from both sides during the war because they would not contribute funds for the support of the two armies. In 1783, after the close of the war, the meeting house was repaired and restored to its original use; since then there has been no interruption in services.

The first public meeting in New York to agitate the abolition of slavery was held in the Flushing meeting house. This was in 1716 and the subject occupied the attention of the Friends for four subsequent yearly meetings. The first anti-slavery publication ever issued in this country appears to have been the reprint of an address by William Burling made before the Annual Meeting of Friends in the Flushing meeting house in 1718. The Friends in Flushing had not always opposed slavery, however, and in 1684 the meeting even came to the aid of a poor Friend and raised money to enable him to buy a slave.

It seems that one John Adams purchased a negro but was not able to pay for him. His "necessity" was laid before the meeting on the 14th of the 8th month and "The meeting did appoint and desire John Browne of fflushing and William Richardson of West Chester to take ye charge in behalf of ye meeting to procure the sum of money . . . the meeting doeth promise and Engage to ReImburse and pay the said sumb soe procured."

Setauket, formerly called Brookhaven, the name now reserved for the township as a whole, was settled in 1655 by colonists from the vicinity of Boston. The Puritan element formed the dominant type although there was even at first a little sprinkling of members of the Church of England.

At a meeting of the clergy in 1704, the rector of Trinity Church, New York City, called attention to the fact that the churchmen and women planted in the midst of Puritans on the east end of Long Island had "neither Church of England minister, nor any provision made for one by law," and suggested that the Society for the Propagation of the Gospel in Foreign Parts send missionaries to them. From the early records it appears, however, that for nearly twenty years this east end of Long Island was visited by but one clergyman, the Reverend John Sharpe, chaplain of the forces in New York, who accompanied the colonial governor, Lord Cornbury, on a tour of inspection not later than 1708.

The organization of the first Church of England Parish on Long Island was not accomplished until about August, 1723. Services were first held in the town meeting house used by the Presbyterians but by 1729 the little band of communicants was able to erect the little church that is still standing, although it has undergone many changes from then until now. The nave was fixed from the start at its present size of about thirty by forty-six feet, with a low broad roof. Probably as old is the square tower which carries the steeple, formerly fifteen feet higher than at present. On the interior, the roof was open to the rafters and in the eastern end, as now, probably stood the altar and over it a triple-lighted window. The gallery at the rear was added about 1744 and furnished a seating place for the slaves. In 1814 the roof was rebuilt and ceiled and later was added the stained glass which decorates the windows today.

The little Long Island mission was originally called Christ Church but when Queen Caroline, the wife of George II, graciously sent over a silver communion service and embroidered altar cloths, the edifice was renamed Caroline Church in her honor, a designation it bears to this day.

After the Battle of Brooklyn, late in August, 1776, all Long Island fell under British occupation and so remained for seven years. Under the walls of Caroline Church was fought the "Battle of Setauket" on August 22, 1777. Following this engagement it is said that some of the wounded were cared for in the church, hastily turned into a temporary hospital for the occasion. During the British occupancy, no doubt services at Caroline must have been officially favored but at some time during the war there are reasons for believing that the little building was used for barracks and damaged by the British themselves.

Following the war Caroline Parish found itself in an impoverished state. Many of its wealthiest and most cultured members, who had remained faithful to the crown, were driven from their estates and fled to Canada to begin life over again there. Even the American sympathizers on Long Island who had been compelled to inactivity were heavily amerced by the state legislature.

But the little band of survivors struggled on and finally they were able to repair their house of worship and once more the parish began to prosper.

The First Dutch Reformed Church, Fishkill, New York, was erected in 1731, a building of unusually liberal proportions for that time and place. Previously there had been a log structure and even before this services had been held in the homes of the members so that the builders must have been exceedingly proud of their comfortable stone house of worship when it was finished. There was a tower at the front with a belfry and steeple while inside there was a gallery built around three sides.

When the Revolutionary War broke out, many recruits were obtained from among the congregation, the members being as one in their loyalty to the American cause. The church building was offered as a meeting place for the representatives of the Thirteen Colonies and in 1776 the Provincial Convention was held there.

After hostilities had assumed major proportions every available building throughout almost the entire valley was utilized for the housing of prisoners and for the care of the wounded. The Dutch Reformed Church, being the most spacious, served the Continental Army as a military prison for captured soldiers. Bars were placed across the windows, remaining there for a great many years afterwards.

It was in this historic building that the celebrated spy, Enoch Crosby, the man from whom James Fenimore Cooper drew his character of Harvey Birch, was imprisoned by the Committee of Safety and from which he managed to escape by climbing through the upper portion of a window and springing from the window sill into the branches of a tree that grew close by. The church is located in a section of the country made famous by the great American novelist.

Shortly after the close of the Revolutionary struggle the building was restored to its original condition and enlarged to increase the seating capacity. Four times since then, in 1806, 1820, 1854 and 1882, alterations have been made in the interior design and furnishings. The old church is still in active use after over two centuries of service and in its churchyard are tombs almost as ancient as the building itself.

The Fort Herkimer, or "German Flatts," Dutch Reformed Church, Fort Herkimer, New York, was begun some time near 1740, the exact date being unknown. During the French and Indian War the construction of the church edifice had progressed sufficiently to allow it to be used as a place of refuge after being palisaded, and in 1767 the building was finally finished. The span between 1740 and 1767 is a long one and there was either some unusual interruption not mentioned in the records, or else the date 1740 is too early.

The old pulpit now in the church always attracts attention because of its extreme height. It is perched on a pedestal and reached by a steep and winding stairway; once having achieved the top safely the minister could gaze straight down upon his flock and none could escape his piercing glance. The walls of the church are three feet thick and the corners are buttressed. It is evident that the early builders intended their house of worship to last a long time; these extra precautions were also taken so that the building could serve as a protection against Indian attacks.

Radical changes were made in 1812 at which time the building was "heightened" about eight feet, the roof taken off and put back on again, thus providing a second story, and the interior rearranged.

The old church has witnessed many an Indian attack in both the Indian wars and in the Revolution. There was a terrible Indian massacre in 1757 and the Reverend Rosencrantz and about a hundred others who were able to escape, took refuge in the unfinished church. In 1783 George Washington was at Fort Herkimer and while there is said to have visited the old stone church, although this is just a tradition.

When the English took possession of Manhattan Island the Church of England to a great extent superseded the Dutch Reformed Church. Services were held in the little chapel within the fort, known as King's Chapel, until the erection of Trinity Church in 1696. The first Trinity was a small square building standing on the west side of Broadway, with a green lawn sloping down to the Hudson River. This church was enlarged in 1737 and burned in 1776 by a fire which for a time threatened the entire town, four days after the British, under General Howe, took possession of the city. In 1778 a new church of much smaller dimensions was built and the present Trinity Church—the well-known Gothic structure designed by Upjohn—was not erected until 1841.

Historically, Trinity is now chiefly distinguished for its church-yard where, in the midst of New York's hurly-burly financial section, lie buried Alexander Hamilton, Robert Fulton and others whose names recall exciting moments in our history. As a matter of fact though, a child of Trinity is now older than its mother, St. Paul's, which was established as a chapel of ease of the mother church, Trinity, in 1756.

The architect was Thomas McBean, a Scotchman, and the chapel was modeled after St. Martin's-in-the-Fields in London. At the time of its erection St. Paul's Chapel was in the outskirts of the city and there was some criticism directed at the vestry for putting up "so large and ornate a building in a place so remote and sequestered, so difficult of access, and to which the population could never extend." The large churchyard was once a wheat field but in time this was transformed into a beautiful lawn which extended down to the river.

St. Paul's is the sole surviving ecclesiastical relic of New York City's Colonial era. The noise and clamor of the city have closed in about it—the church today basks in the shadow of modern sky-scrapers—but the old chapel still stands on its original site, a magnificent example of Georgian architecture. The Prince of Wales' feathers over the pulpit are a reminder of its British establishment and the fourteen crystal chandeliers are as fine a collection as is to be found in the country. They have all been restored to their original places and the old clerk's desk replaced. A fact not generally known is that the "Glory" over the altar, and some details of carving, were executed by Major l'Enfant, who laid out the city of Washington. Under the altar is buried General Montgomery, killed at Quebec in 1775 and later brought to New York and interred at St. Paul's by Act of Congress. The memorial to General Montgomery, which is found in the portico of the church, was selected in France by Benjamin Franklin.

During the early days of the Revolution St. Paul's was for a time closed but when the British occupied New York, it became the church of the officers, and Lord Howe, Major André and Sir Guy Carleton worshiped there. The Governor of the colony had his pew at St. Paul's and special seats were allotted to the legislature and common council. When New York became the nation's capital a pew was likewise set aside for the Chief Executive and here President and Mrs. Washington attended services regularly. After his inauguration on April 30, 1789, George Washington, together with his entire party, repaired to St. Paul's for special thanks-giving services.

The annual commencement of Columbia College was held in St. Paul's on May 6, 1789, and on this gala occasion there were present President Washington, Vice-President Adams, members of the Senate and House of Representatives of the United States, and the Governor and public officials of the State of New York.

The pews of Washington and General Clinton are still preserved and marked by appropriate wall tablets. Originally Washington's pew had an emergency entrance through the north wall, so that he could easily be reached in case a courier should ride up with an important message.

On September 9, 1824, a grand oratorio was given by the New York Choral Society in St. Paul's Chapel with General Lafayette the guest of honor and on the 7th day of July, 1831, James Mon-roe, fifth President of the United States, was buried from the church.

The Reverend Thomas Barclay was formally commissioned chaplain of the garrison in the fort at Albany, New York, on June 9, 1708. At Schenectady there were at that time "a garrison of forty soldiers, besides sixteen English and about one hundred Dutch families," and the Reverend Barclay preached there once a month, being granted the free use of the Dutch Church. It was from such a humble beginning as this that the present congrega-tion of St. George's Church grew.

The organization took form slowly and it was not until 1759 that ground was broken for the erection of a house of worship. There were many interruptions but finally in 1767 an effort was made to raise funds "for the final finishing off of the church." The year previous the parish had received its present designation by Governor Moore, who also contributed thirty pounds toward the building fund.

The original church completed in 1769 was thirty-six feet wide

St. Paul's Chapel, New York City. The sole surviving religious relic of New York City's Colonial era. *Photo by Wurts Bros.*

Tennent Church, Tennent, N. J. A Revolutionary soldier's blood may yet be seen on one of its pews. *Photo by Ph. B. Wallace.*

by fifty-six feet deep. The walls were of undressed blue stone, thirty inches in thickness. There were two doors, one at the front, or west end, and the other on the south side. Within, the building was divided into nave and aisles by two rows of wooden columns of the Tuscan order. Mr. Willis T. Hanson, Jr., the historian of St. George's Church, has very carefully designated those portions of the old church which are yet a part of the new: "The present front wall (within the one supporting the tower) is undoubtedly now as in the original church. The original side walls form the walls of the present church for a distance of about thirty feet from the original front wall, and can be easily distinguished from the difference in the way the stones are laid. . . . Fortunately later alterations did not change the general scheme of the interior."

At the beginning of the Revolutionary War the rector of St. George's, although born and educated in the colonies, decided to cast his lot with the King. After the Declaration of Independence he was arrested and held in jail for a time in Albany, finally retiring, following General Burgoyne's surrender, with his family to Canada.

The end of the war found the parish in a destitute condition. Desolation prevailed and the building had become so dilapidated, with windows broken out, that it "had become the resort of the swine that roamed at will through the narrow streets of the old Dutch town." To the few parishioners who remained was assigned the task of restoring the little edifice and renewing parish activities. This they accomplished in spite of all difficulties and by 1798 the church was once more functioning in all its phases.

St. Paul's, Eastchester, Mount Vernon, New York, was built in 1763 and the parish at that early date was already nearly a century old. Today the ivy-covered gray granite face of the church presents a perfect picture of peace and quiet but in its early days this little building saw much of the excitement of war.

On September 20, 1775, a military company was organized at Eastchester to fight for the cause of the colonies. All of the officers were members of St. Paul's and today all lie buried in the old churchyard.

Following the Battle of Pell's Point, the church was seized by the Hessian troops under Baron Knyphausen and converted into a barracks and hospital. Ninety men died there the first night and were buried in the adjoining cemetery. In 1910 remains of their bodies were found and the spot marked with a stone tablet which is now pointed out to the visitor.

Before the arrival of the Hessians, the bell, altar chalices, flagons, patens, prayer books and records were buried in a near-by swamp for safety. To make the building more comfortable the Hessians cut large trees and used them as benches. Later, when the Americans returned, these logs served as beams to which the present flooring of fourteen-inch planks was then nailed.

The Battle of White Plains on October 28, 1776, ended the British occupancy of the country, although nearly three years later a company of English soldiers encamped at Eastchester. In 1787 the church was used during the week as a courthouse. Aaron Burr tried many of his cases there and the congregation is in possession of a subpoena dated May 28, 1787, written and signed "Burr for the defense."

When Mrs. John Quincy Adams was First Lady, her son, George Washington Adams, visited relatives in Eastchester. He was drowned while swimming in the Sound and his body recovered by a member of St. Paul's Church. Mrs. Adams so appreciated the kindness displayed by members of the congregation that she presented the church with a silver chalice which is preserved among its choicest treasures today. On the left of the altar stands an oak chair, which is one of the oldest Bishop's chairs in the United States, dating from 1639 and recalling to mind some of the rectors who have served the parish.

Among these is Dr. Samuel Seabury, who became rector in 1766. In 1783 Dr. Seabury was elected Bishop of Connecticut. He set out for England, seeking consecration at the hands of his Anglican brethren in England. As he was unable to take the oath of allegiance to the King, which the English ceremony demanded, he went to Scotland where he was consecrated by three Scottish bishops who had themselves never taken the oath. This act was officially recognized in 1789 and marked the formal recognition of the American Episcopal Church.

There is at present a well-planned restoration program under way at St. Paul's. This program calls for a reproduction of the original interior design of the church, with box-pews, small paned windows of the eighteenth century type, and a pulpit of pure Colonial design. One important change, also, is planned; that is, to remove the present reredos, cut through the wall and create a real chancel. This the building has never had, having been built by non-conformists. A new altar and reredos in the Colonial manner will then be installed. The plans under way extend also to the cemetery and the restoration of that portion of the village green of Eastchester which is now a part of the churchyard. This latter will be equipped with hand-wrought iron gates, a stone and brick wall and reproductions of the stocks and whipping post that were there in Colonial times.

Trinity Church, Fishkill, New York, was organized in 1756 but for some years the congregation had no house of worship. Services were held in homes, barns, out-of-doors, or on special occasions, by invitation, in the Dutch Reformed Church of Fishkill.

A frame church edifice was first constructed and work on the present structure started in 1769. The building originally had a spire a little over one hundred feet in height but being considered unsafe, this was almost entirely eliminated in 1810. The original construction of the church proceeded very slowly, the congregation being hindered by a lack of funds, shortage of help and other causes and even as late as the second year of the Revolution no pews were available.

In September of that year when the Provincial Congress, later known as the Constitutional Convention, met in Fishkill to continue the work of organizing the state government, the members were called to order within the walls of Trinity Church and then adjourned to resume their session in the Dutch Church a short distance down the street.

The rector during the Revolution was the Reverend John Beardsley, a conscientious Royalist, who, when forbidden to pray for the King, closed the Fishkill Church as well as the church at Poughkeepsie which he likewise served. The two parishes were more or less closely connected, both having been organized in the same year. In December of 1777 the "Committee of Safety" voted Reverend Mr. Beardsley's banishment and in the following May he and his family with all their household goods, including "one negro wench," were sent down the river by sloop to New York.

For many years Trinity Church was without a regular pastor and during the war was used almost continuously as a Continental hospital. Many men prominent in Colonial affairs, as well as many brave patriots who died in the church during its service as a hospital, lie buried in the surrounding yard but most of their graves are unmarked and unknown. On November 21, 1789, the little edifice enjoyed added distinction in having been the scene of the signing of the ratification of the Constitution of the United States by New York in state convention.

Nowhere was more patriotic ardor displayed during the Revolution than among the Palatine settlers of the Mohawk Valley. It was here, according to a local historian, that the first striped flag, made from the petticoats of the wives of Fort Stanwix, is said to have received its baptism of fire, and here also, the same historian records, that one of the last battles of the Revolution was fought, on October 25, 1781, six days after the surrender of Cornwallis at Yorktown.

During the war much fighting took place around the old Palatine Church and only the restraining hand of a British soldier prevented an Indian savage from directing a flaming arrow at the old structure. The story goes that before leaving Canada this officer had promised a friend of his, a former resident of the Valley, that the little structure would not be harmed.

The Palatine Lutheran Church was built in 1770, of selected native limestone. It is a small structure with a gambrel or "Dutch" roof, and is wholly different from other churches of the time which have survived. Surmounting the weather vane on the spire is a bronze rooster which has perched there for over a hundred and sixty years now and has in his time observed many changes. The rooster weather vane is found on many early churches. One explanation given is that the cock was the bird that called Peter to repentance; it therefore became about the ninth century a symbol of clerical vigilance. Another significance is that on ancient pagan and early Christian tombs two fighting cocks were often carved, one of which was shown as having succumbed and was probably intended to mean the battle of life. And, again, as the cock, "when it finds anything, does not eat it but calls the hens together and divides it among them; in like manner the preacher should divide among his flock."

The Palatine Church remained as originally built for a century; then in preparation for the centennial services in 1870 the interior was remodeled; the high pulpit with its sounding board, the balcony and the old-fashioned pews, all removed.

The first Church of St. Andrew, Richmond, Staten Island, was commenced in 1709. The Reverend Aeneas Mackenzie came to Staten Island in 1705 as a missionary for the Society for the Propagation of the Gospel in Foreign Parts. He first preached in the French, or Huguenot, Church on Sunday afternoons but four years after his arrival was able to commence the erection of an English place of worship. The little edifice was completed in 1712 and the following year Mr. Mackenzie secured from Queen Anne a charter granting to the new religious organization a corporate existence. Queen Anne also contributed "a Bible, Prayer Books, flagon, two chalices, a paten, a communion cover and a bell." Only the chalice and paten remain of the Queen's gift, and both are on display in the Metropolitan Museum of Art. On the chalice is engraved the inscription "Anna Regina."

St. Andrew's Church has been enlarged and remodeled many, many times—in 1743, in 1770 and again in 1831. In 1822 the steeple was blown down and replaced, to be struck by lightning and again replaced. The structure was twice burned—in 1867 and 1872—but each time the original walls were left standing and were utilized when the church was repaired.

The original church was forty by twenty-five feet. According to the vestry records the enlargement of 1743 was in reality a rebuilding. The present size of the main part of the building—forty by eighty feet—was set in the enlargement of 1770 and this is taken by the writer as the year of erection of the oldest part of the church as it now exists; and, however, some portion of the walls as built originally in 1743, and perhaps even in 1709, may possibly yet stand as a part of the modern church.

During the Revolution two skirmishes were fought at St. Andrew's. On October 17, 1776, American forces under Colonel Griffin planned an attack upon British entrenchments at Richmond. They reached the place before daylight, killed two or three, wounded others, and carried off seventeen prisoners. Damage to the church was but slight; however, on August 8, 1777, a party of Americans approached Richmond from the north shore, drove the British they met into the church, broke its windows by firing at the enemy seeking refuge within its walls. British reinforcements compelled the Americans to retreat but the damage to the church was done.

The first settlement at Flatbush, now a portion of the borough of Brooklyn, was as early as 1634, but the first account we have of the erection of a church there is not until twenty years later. The directions were given by Governor Peter Stuyvesant and the Council of New Amsterdam on December 15th of that year, and the site selected was the ground on which the present Flatbush Reformed Dutch Church now stands. This first place of worship was built in the form of a cross, with the rear reserved for the minister's dwelling. The dedication is thought to have taken place in 1665.

The first church lasted until about 1697 at which time a new building was commenced, and finished two years later. This was a stone church of rather unusual design, having a "double door in the center, a steep, four-sided roof, on which was erected a small steeple. The building was wider in front than in depth, sixty-five feet from north to south, fifty feet from east to west."

This little edifice was still standing at the time of the Revolution. Since the steeple rose from the center of the building, the bell rope was allowed to hang down to the middle of the floor, as in the case of the Old Ship Church at Hingham, Massachusetts. When the British landed, this bell gave the first warning note of their approach and after the Battle of Long Island the church temporarily became a hospital. Afterwards the British troops took possession of the building, some of the artillerymen even stabling their horses in the pews and feeding them there.

The work of erecting the present Flatbush Dutch Reformed Church was begun in 1793 and completed some three years later. The stones forming the foundation of the old church were used for the foundation of the new while the stones for the walls were quarried at Hurlgate. The brownstone of the three upper courses was broken out of the Brooklyn woods but it is said that the brick around the doors and windows came from Holland, they having served as ballast in one of the ships of the Honorable John Vanderbilt.

The old church has seen many changes since its dedication in January, 1797. In 1836 the pews were remodeled and a gallery added at the east end. In 1862 the high-back pews were taken out and replaced by the pews now in use and an open platform substituted for the old-fashioned pulpit. Again in 1887 more radical repairs were made, an extension at the rear of the church added, the organ transferred to the front and the walls redecorated.

Visitors climbing the ladder to the belfry may see the old bell given by John Vanderbilt in 1796, the same John Vanderbilt whose ships are said to have furnished the brick around the windows and doors. The inscription on this bell reads: "John Vanderbilte gave this bell to the Reformed Dutch Church in Flatbush Anno Domini 1796." This bell came from Holland and the vessel on which it was shipped was captured by the British and the bell carried to Halifax but was afterwards recovered by a son-in-law of the donor who went to Holland and testified that the purchaser was a United States citizen.

The church of St. Mark's in-the-Bouwerie had its origin in a chapel erected on the site by Governor Stuyvesant in 1660. The land was then a part of the Stuyvesant estate and the building was a small one built for the accommodation of his own household and the settlement which had grown up around it, known as the Bouwerie. The Governor's body was interred here in 1672 in a vault which is still maintained as a part of the modern church. In 1687 Governor Stuyvesant's widow bequeathed the chapel to the Dutch Reformed Church.

The Stuyvesant family afterwards joined the English church and in 1793 Petrus Stuyvesant, great-grandson of the Governor, proposed to the vestry of Trinity Church that an Episcopal church be erected on the land to replace the chapel, he agreeing to donate eight hundred pounds and a plot of ground one hundred and fifty by one hundred and ninety feet. This proposal met with favor and in 1795 the corner-stone of St. Mark's was laid by Bishop Provoost. The vestry of Trinity contributed five thousand pounds toward the erection of the building.

Since Trinity Church by the charter of 1679, and subsequent legislation, had been made the "sole and only parish church in the City of New York," there was some question as to whether St. Mark's could be an independent parish as some proposed. The problem was submitted to Richard Harison and Alexander Hamilton and their opinions being favorable, the parish of St. Mark's came into existence in 1799, the year of its consecration.

The body of the church remains the same but the tower and the porch, its two most distinctive features, were later additions, the former in 1826 and the latter just ten years later.

For the visitor, St. Mark's has a number of interesting things to see, including the vault of Peter Stuyvesant, first Governor of New York, the bronze bust presented by Wilhelmina, Queen of Holland, and the beautiful churchyard which records the names of some of New York's most distinguished citizens. Entrance to the Stuyvesant vault is marked by a stone tablet in the east wall of the church and near by are the vaults of Governor Sloughter and Daniel Tomkins, likewise a governor of New York and later Vice-President of the United States. The interesting fact is frequently pointed out that these three men represent the Dutch, English and American periods of the state, each having served under a different government.

In 1878 Alexander T. Stewart, the richest merchant of his day, was laid to rest in St. Mark's burial ground. Some months later an attempt was made to steal his body. The family, realizing that a further attempt might be made, with the object in mind of holding the remains for ransom, had the coffin removed to another part of the cemetery. Only two or three trusted persons knew the exact location of the new grave but despite this and other precautions, ghouls entered the cemetery on a dark stormy night in November of 1878, broke open the casket and stole away with its ghastly contents.

In this way the church found itself involved in one of America's most puzzling mysteries. Newspapers published many pages of theories and the entire nation was aroused. Mrs. Stewart offered a reward of twenty-five thousand dollars for the recovery of the body but the thieves demanded a quarter of a million dollars. Two years slipped away before the family consented to make terms with the kidnapers. A payment of twenty thousand dollars was made and return of the remains was effected. The topic continued to be a much discussed one, however, for many years, and numerous indeed were the theories advanced as to how the robbery was perpetrated.

In 1701, Governor Lewis Morris of New Jersey drew up and presented to the newly formed Society for the Propagation of the Gospel in Foreign Parts a petition praying them to send a minister to Shrewsbury. This petition was presented on September 19th and the Reverend George Keith was at once appointed missionary. On the trip across, the ship's chaplain, the Reverend John Talbot, became so impressed by Mr. Keith's earnestness that he left the boat and joined him in his work, finally settling as missionary in the town of Burlington.

George Keith and John Talbot first conducted services at Burlington on November 1, 1702. The latter returned in February of the following year and the corner-stone for St. Mary's Church was laid March 25, 1703, the Feast of the Annunciation of the Blessed Virgin, in the presence of Governor Nicholson and other notables. The Reverend John Talbot wrote on this occasion, "We called this church St. Mary's, it being upon her day." Although not quite completed, first services were held in the building on August 22, 1703, "before my Lord Cornbury," the new Governor of the Province. Mr. Talbot was appointed rector, not however beginning his charge until November, 1705.

Despite the Reverend Mr. Talbot's clear-cut statement there is some confusion in regard to the early name of the church for in the oldest records it is referred to as St. Anne's. It is likewise so mentioned in various wills leaving legacies to the church and in 1704 Lord Cornbury called it by that name. The suggestion has been advanced that Mr. Talbot called the church St. Mary's "being doubtless unwilling to participate in the ceremonies of a cornerstone laying which would establish even the name of Queen Anne, who was then filling the throne of the rightful, but exiled, Stuart."

When King George I came to the throne following the death of Queen Anne, those who held office were required to take an oath of allegiance anew but Mr. Talbot refused. When he was charged by Governor Hunter with being a Jacobite, he replied, "God has been my succour, and I doubt not but that he will deliver me from the snare of the Hunter." Later, on a visit to England, Reverend Mr. Talbot was consecrated Bishop but this was not done in entire accordance with the canons of the church and was the subject of much discussion afterwards and the Reverend John Talbot called a non-juring Bishop. In St. Mary's Church today there is a memorial tablet to him, on which is shown the signet of Bishop Talbot, a miter with flowing ribbons, and the words "Early facsimile of the seal of John Talbot, Founder of this church 1703. A Bishop of non juror consecration, 1722."

The Friends at first were predominant in Burlington and the rector of St. Mary's once complained to the Society for the Propagation of the Gospel that "some course must be taken with these anti Christians who are worse than the Turks." Another time he wrote, "Since I came to be acquainted with the Quakers I have much worse opinion of them than ever I had." In a letter from Mr. Talbot written to Mr. Keith in 1705 is the following quaint statement which gives some idea of the somewhat antagonistic attitude which existed between the two religious organizations:

My horse you know dyed at Burlington and yᵉ Quakers recorded it as a judgment upon me.

In 1763 when St. Mary's Church was laying plans for a church steeple, which incidentally was never built, a smaller belfry being substituted, the records of the Friends warn against the dangerous attractions of the "steeple house." As a further example of the firmness of the Friends of Burlington in their religious beliefs might be mentioned the message sent out from the meeting in 1775, recommending adherence to the principles of Quakerism "in the time of commotion."

Relations between the two ecclesiastical organizations were for many years anything but cordial but most of this ill feeling appears to have been confined to paper. In the case of Mr. Talbot, he was undoubtedly a very pious and devoted minister but as a strict Church of England clergyman he naturally looked upon all dissenters with an unfavorable eye.

During the Revolutionary War Washington and a number of his officers were in Burlington on various occasions, the settlement being at that time an important center of Colonial life, and at least one of these visits is duly mentioned in the church records. Among the famous men who have attended the little church are Captain James Lawrence, remembered for his stirring message to his crew, "Don't give up the ship," and James Fenimore Cooper, the novelist.

The church, built in Colonial style, was so well constructed that it stands today in splendid state of repair and although no longer used for regular services, serves as a Sunday School and choir practice room and for services on special occasions. The structure is of brick and has been enlarged at least three times, the last time in 1834, and in about 1870 the interior was altered beyond recognition. The original side walls still stand, also the east end wall, but the apse is new. Some of the original leaded glass windows presented by Queen Anne in 1708 are still retained and the parish likewise has in its possession the silver communion service and brocade altar cloth given by her at the same time.

The present Friends' Meeting House in Burlington is the structure erected in 1784 near the site of an earlier octagonal building put up in 1682. In the old graveyard, according to tradition, are buried the Indian Chief Ockanickon and Samuel Smith, the historian, as well as many other noted pioneers of New Jersey.

While the Reverend Mr. Talbot was so busily engaged at Burlington, the Reverend George Keith was no less active in Shrewsbury. The first church there was built between 1703 and 1705 and in 1708 Queen Anne presented the communion service still in use. It was not until 1769, however, that the present church was erected, succeeding another put up in 1738 which had become too small for the congregation.

The exterior of the church remains the same as when first built; even to the modest steeple bearing the English crown. During the Revolution this steeple, with its royal decoration, was a source of constant irritation to the patriots of Shrewsbury and various unsuccessful attempts were made to shoot it down. Traces of bullet marks are plainly visible in the ball under the crown. The rector at the outbreak of the war was the Reverend Samuel Cook. His pronounced Tory sympathies made him exceedingly unpopular and he was finally forced to flee the town.

The interior of the building has been somewhat modernized. A recess chancel was added in 1844 and the tower entrance in 1874. The congregation has in its possession one of the old Bibles printed at Oxford, England, by John Baskett in 1717, given by Robert Elliston, Gentleman Controller of His Majesty's Customs at New York in 1752. Another treasure is a Prayer Book printed at Cambridge, England, in 1760 and presented in 1767 by the Hon. William Franklin, son of Benjamin Franklin and the last Royal Governor of New Jersey.

The present Christ Church stands a little to the south of the building preceding it and, therefore, covers several graves; just how many is not known, but the stones covering three of them have been preserved in the floor of the north and south aisles and in the step of the chancel platform. The stone in the south aisle is that of Theodosius Bartow, a young lawyer of Shrewsbury before the Revolution and the father of Aaron Burr's first wife.

The one hundredth anniversary of the present little edifice was held in 1869. These services were attended by General Ulysses S. Grant, then President of the United States and a personal friend of the rector at the time, the Reverend William B. Otis.

Ye Olde Yellow Meeting House, Imlaystown, is another pre-Revolutionary New Jersey church which has passed through many history making years. This quaint little building is now more than two centuries old and countless of its members have played an important part in the making of our nation.

The movement which finally led to the erection of Ye Olde Yellow Meeting House actually began in New England. Here men who had found belief and comfort in the teachings of the Baptist faith desired to affiliate with that body. This the Puritans would not allow and indeed several who suggested such a thing were publicly lashed and fined. As a result of this many Baptists left their homes to follow in the footsteps of the Quakers who, when driven out in the same cruel manner, had sought a haven in the province of New Jersey where the laws were more liberal.

Ye Olde Yellow Meeting House was a direct result of this emigration from New England and the first meeting house at Imlaystown was built about 1720. Some years later this building was destroyed by fire and the present little structure erected in 1731. The building is thirty by fifty feet and is plain in the extreme. A pulpit stands at one end of the interior while at the other a gallery extends across the width of the house. The benches are the old-fashioned white type, with high, stiff backs, topped with mahogany trimmings. The pulpit is likewise old style, elevated five feet and with steps upon each side.

Many men and women now prominent in the social, political and business life of New Jersey are descendants of the original founders of Ye Olde Yellow Meeting House. Former Governor James M. Cox, of Ohio, Democratic candidate for the Presidency in 1920, is descended from the Coxes who helped to build this old house of worship. The already mentioned Captain James Lawrence was likewise descended from an early member.

Old Tennent Church, Tennent, New Jersey, has one of the oldest Presbyterian congregations in the country, having been formed by Scotch convenanters in 1692. A rude meeting house was erected about five miles north of the present site. The first building on White Hill, the present location, was put up in 1731 and in 1751 this was enlarged into the present building. Since then the changes have been very few and although the structure is of wood, painted white, it is today in excellent condition.

During its early history Old Tennent was known as "The Scots Church," later taking its name from its most famous pastor, the Reverend William Tennent, Jr., who became pastor in 1733 and served for forty-three years. When at last he passed on in 1777 he was buried beneath the middle of the floor of the church, presumably because of his strong support of the colonies and the fear that a grave in the open yard might be molested by English sympathizers.

The Royal Charter of incorporation was granted to the church organization by King George II in 1749 and a handsome facsimile of this charter now hangs in the church; also may be seen the old communion table from which, it is said, David Brainerd administered the holy sacrament to his converted Indians in 1746.

The Battle of Monmouth was fought near the church on Sunday, June 28, 1778, between Generals Washington and Clinton. A desperate struggle took place over the body of Lieutenant-Colonel Monckton who was killed near the old parsonage; finally the Americans secured possession of it, carried it to the rear and buried it in the churchyard. The grave was later marked and in 1913 the New Jersey Society of the Sons of the American Revolution placed a British flag on the grave as a gallant tribute to a brave enemy.

During the battle the church edifice was pierced by bullets, the marks of which were allowed to remain until it became necessary to repair the damage in order to preserve the building. According to tradition, a dying American soldier was taken into the church after being fatally injured by a cannon ball, and to this day the stains of his blood may be seen on one of the pews. Following the battle, the church was used as a hospital and several members of the present congregation have interesting traditions in their family, their forebears having nursed the wounded there.

The Reverend John Woodhull who came as pastor in 1778 was for a time Chaplain in Washington's Army and is said to have taken part in the Battle of Monmouth. Probably the most famous traditional figure to emerge from that battle is that of "Molly Pitcher" who is said to have carried water to the thirsty soldiers, among whom was her husband, and, when the latter was overcome while working a cannon, to have taken his place and fought in the battle.

The custom of endowing pews in Old Tennent Church is of recent origin. A pew was endowed by the congregation in memory of that famous pastor, Reverend Wm. Tennent, Jr., while the Tennent Chapter, Daughters of the American Revolution, has endowed another to the memory of George Washington. There are also pews memorializing Presidents Ulysses S. Grant and Theodore Roosevelt.

The congregation of the Presbyterian Church at Lawrenceville, New Jersey, is now over two hundred and twenty-five years of age and the front of the present house of worship is pre-Revolutionary, dating back to 1764.

Lawrenceville at first bore the more picturesque name of Maidenhead and one of the early ministers serving there was the Reverend John Rowland, who, while pursuing his many duties in this and several other towns which he likewise served, was once charged with stealing a horse, thus adding yet another to the long list of tribulations and hardships suffered by the Colonial parson. At the trial he was quickly acquitted by the testimony of the Reverend William Tennent, Jr., of Old Tennent Church, and two laymen, Joshua Anderson and Benjamin Stevens, all of whom recounted that at the time the horse was stolen Mr. Rowland was absent from the colony, holding services elsewhere. It was all plainly a case of mistaken identity and the real thief, the notorious Tom Bell, had simply assumed Mr. Rowland's name in the pursuit of his illegal profession.

The first record of any settlers at Crosswicks, New Jersey, was when Friends came from England about 1677. They found already awaiting them the Indian village of Cross-weeks-ung, located upon a hillside overlooking a picturesque valley along the creek. Cross-weeks-ung means divided creek and after the Friends settled there they called the village Crosswicks, which was both easier to pronounce and easier to spell.

The first Friends' Meeting House was not built until 1693 but prior to this, from the year the Friends first settled there, it had been the custom to hold meetings for worship in the home of some Friend in the neighborhood. The first meeting house was a wooden structure and, soon proving too crowded, was succeeded in 1707 by a brick one erected not far away.

By 1773 this new meeting house was likewise too small and the subject of enlarging it was discussed. The committee appointed to consider this finally decided that it would be best not to attempt to enlarge the building but to erect a larger one near the burying ground, where the first frame meeting house had been.

About this time a new meeting house had been erected at Buckingham, Pennsylvania, and Crosswicks Friends appointed a committee of four to view the Buckingham structure, learn its expense and report back to them. At the next meeting it was decided to build one something like it, the cost to be around seven hundred and fifty pounds. There is no record of when the building was finished but most probably it was in 1776. This is the meeting house in use today.

When the British troops marched from Philadelphia on their way to Monmouth in June, 1778, a detachment attempted to cross the bridge on Crosswicks Creek. The Americans were stationed on the north side under General Dickinson and one soldier was killed while sawing off the last support in an endeavor to prevent the British from crossing. Three cannon balls were shot into the meeting house, one lodging in the wall and two going through the roof. Later the building was used by the Hessians as a barracks and on the floor are circular indentations made by jarring the muzzles of the muskets on the wood to rid them of stubborn bullets before the pieces were cleaned.

It is not generally remembered that one of the boundary lines of the early settlements of Swedes on the Delaware extended over into what is now the State of New Jersey, reaching the banks of Naraticon's Kil, so called by the Indians, paraphrased by the Swedes to Araratcung, or Ratcung, and finally Racoon. Such is actually the case, however, and the settlement was made not many years after the Pilgrims landed at Plymouth.

"In the settlement of America the romance of history has been thrown around all of the colonies," begins the Reverend Edgar Campbell in his history of Trinity Church, Swedesboro, "with the single exception of that made by the Swedes. In 1607, a band of hopeful adventurers went to Jamestown from the mother country. They were followed by the Dutch at New Amsterdam and the Pilgrims at Plymouth. The Swedes came only a few years later, but historians as a rule pass over the early efforts of these sturdy sons of the Vikings, and in a very few lines tell of their having come here."

The settlers along Racoon Creek at first attended church at Christina, Wilmington, Delaware, and in that church's records the people "on the other side of the river" are often mentioned. When the Christina structure was built the outsiders across the river generously subscribed to the building fund with the understanding that they might expect like treatment when it came time for them to erect their own church.

The long distance, severe winters and at times dangerous travel made this at length necessary but not only did the Christina church refuse to give its aid to the contemplated new building but the project was flatly opposed, as is seen from the early records. The temporary clouds soon blew over, however, and in the following year, 1703, a plot of ground was purchased and the first log church erected. In 1731 was purchased the communion service of beaten silver which is still in use.

During the time of the Revolution the rector of the church was the Reverend Nicholas Collins, D.D., who had come over from Sweden to guide the little flock and help them in determining their duty to country as well as to God. It was he who officiated at the funeral of Hester, wife of Captain Samuel Williams, who died on October 16, 1777. The story goes that during the services at the grave General Cornwallis marched by on his way to the Battle of Red Bank, but, seeing the Swedish parson officiating in the churchyard wearing vestments like those of the Church of England, gave orders that the man must not be harmed.

The following entry, taken from the old church records, tells of an interesting occurrence during the Revolution, the Battle of Swedesboro, not recorded in most histories:

The year 1778: The usual vestry meeting on the 3d day of Easter could not be observed, because of the general distraction produced by the war. Militia and continental troops on one side, and refugees with British on the other, were frequently skirmishing, and both almost equally destroying the country, plundering, marauding, imprisoning, and burning houses, with other horrid excesses, were frequent from the beginning of spring, till July, when the British Army evacuated Philadelphia. In the morning of Easter Sunday, a man who had traded with the British was tied to a tree near the burying ground and cruelly whipped. He died after a hard time. On the 4th day of April some hundred of English horsemen and refugees came to Sweedsburgh early in the morning to surprise the militia. Being disappointed they burnt the schoolhouse, alledging for a reason that some loyal subjects had been imprisoned there for some weeks before.

Following the war, the Reverend Mr. Collins remained on and a year after the conclusion of peace, persuaded his congregation to build the church that is now in use. The building was enclosed by Christmas of 1784 but the roof proved defective and a new one had to be put on before the church could be used. The Reverend Mr. Collins helped with this work—in one instance building small ovens to dry some brick spoiled by the heavy rains. A relic of this incident may be seen in the eastern gable of the church where it is easy to distinguish between the dried brick and those which were laid while wet.

Soon after the building was completed the Swedish mission ceased to take care of the church. For a time a German Lutheran minister officiated; then in 1789 arrangements were made with a candidate for holy orders in the Protestant Episcopal Church to take charge when he was ordained. Thus began for Trinity Church, Swedesboro, the long succession of Episcopal rectors which has continued to this day.

The oldest, fully organized church of Christ of any denomination within the State of New Jersey appears to be Old First Church, Newark. Before its organization ministers of the Reformed Dutch Church conducted services at irregular intervals but their flocks had no churches in which to worship and there were no organized congregations.

The early members of the First Church were New Englanders from Branford, Connecticut, where their Presbyterian leanings had made them decidedly unpopular. The original church built in

1663 was a stockaded fort prepared for defense against Indian attacks, and serving as a "town-house" as well as a place of worship. This first structure was a crude wooden building but in 1714 a substantial stone structure was put up. Concerning this second building, an early historian wrote, "It was hardly believed that the inhabitants of the town would ever be so numerous as to fill it," however, in less than fifty years it had already become too small to seat its congregation comfortably and a new edifice was necessary.

Although there is some confusion on the exact date, this, the present edifice, is thought to have been begun in 1786 and finished about five years later. It is an attractive, though plain structure, carefully planned in accordance with the American architectural church style of that period.

Within the walls of the second church structure, on Wednesday, November 9, 1748, was organized the College of New Jersey, which was to become in time Princeton University. The seventh pastor of Old First Church, the Reverend Aaron Burr, was a President of this school. Old First Church also enjoys the distinction of having given the first President to Yale University when it was organized, in the person of the Reverend Abraham Pierson, Jr., its second pastor.

Closely related in its history to the church at Newark is the First Presbyterian Church at Elizabeth, the original congregation likewise being from New England. The first church was erected soon after the settlement of Elizabeth Town and as the settlement there was commenced somewhat earlier than that at Newark, it would appear that the Elizabeth church might possibly be the older of the two. An examination of the records, however, reveals that the first minister regularly in charge was the Reverend Jeremiah Peck—1668–78—and since the Reverend Abraham Pierson is known to have officiated in Newark for a year previous to this, the seniority of the Newark organization is easily established.

At first the church was of independent or Congregational policy but became Presbyterian in 1717 or 1718. A second structure is supposed to have replaced the original building in 1724 and in 1745 the first meeting of the Synod of New York was held in this building, with the then pastor, the Reverend Jonathan Dickinson, as Moderator. During the same year David Brainerd, noted missionary to the Indians, and already mentioned in connection with Old Tennent Church, preached in Mr. Dickinson's pulpit. The germ out of which Princeton University ultimately grew was planted by the Reverend Mr. Dickinson at Elizabeth Town in the small school he conducted there in connection with the duties of his ministry.

The second house of worship at Elizabeth was burned by the British in 1780 but four years later the congregation proceeded to erect a new building upon the site of the old one, which was completed in 1789. This was like the Newark church, of similar stone, and is the edifice which remains to this day, except the addition in the rear and the tall wooden spire of extremely graceful proportions which was built to replace the one blown down by a tornado in 1899.

The Springfield Meeting House has had a very interesting history and while its most stirring moments are connected with an earlier building, the thing that makes it so exciting is the fact that this building was burned by the British; under the circumstances, as in the case of the church at Elizabeth, we must be content with a later church structure.

The first Presbyterian Church at Springfield was finished in 1746. While occupying this meeting house the congregation received a donation of one hundred acres of land, the only payment for which was to be "one pint of spring water when demanded on the premises." This wooded tract enabled the church for many years to supply the free firewood that was a part of the support promised the early pastors but whether or not the donor of the one hundred acres ever demanded payment of his rent is not recorded.

In 1761 the second meeting house was completed and when in November, 1778, this building was needed for military stores, it was gladly given and services were held in the attic of the parsonage.

In the Battle of Springfield, June 23, 1780, much of the fighting took place in the vicinity of the Springfield church. The British, under General Knyphausen, numbered five thousand, and were determined to drive Washington from New Jersey. The Patriots were poorly equipped and small in number, but equally as determined not to be driven out and to protect their supplies from destruction as well.

The farmers in the vicinity joined hands with the army and for a time the fighting was fierce. Chaplain James Caldwell was in the midst of the battle and, according to Headley's "The Chaplains and Clergy of the Revolution," when he saw the fire of one of the companies "slackening for want of wadding, he galloped to the Presbyterian meeting house near by and rushing in, ran from pew to pew, filling his arms with hymn books. Hastening back with them into the battle, he scattered them about in every direction, saying as he pitched one here and another there, 'Now put Watts into them, boys.' With a laugh and a cheer they pulled out the leaves, and ramming home the charge did give the British Watts with a will."

The enemy was shortly compelled to retreat but not until they had burned the village, including the church. After this the pastor, Reverend Jacob Vanarsdal, gathered his people in the barn of the parsonage which was fitted up in crude fashion to serve as a meeting house. The present church was built in 1791, on the old foundations. The exterior is of hand-split shingles and all hardware, even the nails, is hand-made. The interior was somewhat altered in 1880 although no great changes were made in the general lay-out of the building. A statue of a Continental soldier has been placed in front of the church in memory of the skirmish fought there.

The first Dutch Reformed Church at Hackensack, New Jersey, was built in 1696, just ten years after the congregation had been organized. This was a substantial stone structure and in 1726, when a new building was necessary, the stones from the older building were incorporated into the new.

In 1791 when it was proposed again to rebuild the church there were the usual friends and foes of the suggestion. There was much discussion both ways but finally the young people of the congregation settled the question by taking possession of the building before the time for the next appointed meeting, and tearing out the pews around the wall, removing the chairs and benches from the center of the room, and carrying them, with other fixtures to "the Green." Following this action there was no further hesitancy on the part of the meeting to rebuild and plans went speedily forward. Three times since then, in 1837, 1867 and 1911, the building has been enlarged or altered in some manner, but care was taken on each occasion not to change the original architectural lines.

The church at Hackensack is known as the "Mother" of sixteen other churches, fifteen of which were consecrated before 1814 and resemble in the main the parent church; from this the building's great influence on the design of ecclesiastical structures in the vicinity may easily be seen. Unfortunately, however, the name of the original architect is unknown.

The congregation celebrated its two hundred and twenty-fifth anniversary in 1911 and among those taking part in the memorial services was His Excellency, Woodrow Wilson, then Governor of New Jersey.

Chapter VII

DELAWARE: ONE OF THE ORIGINAL THIRTEEN

I like that ancient Saxon phrase, which calls
The burial ground God's Acre! It is just;
It consecrates each grave within its walls,
And breathes a benison o'er the sleeping dust.
—Henry Wadsworth Longfellow

Wilmington, Delaware, was not incorporated as a city until 1832 but the district was settled by a band of immigrants from Sweden almost two hundred years previous to that, in March, 1638. The site of the present city was not definitely determined, however, until the erection of Old Swedes' Church, or Trinity Church as it is now most generally called, near the close of the seventeenth century.

The church speedily became the social center of the entire Swedish population living on both sides of the Christina River and across the Delaware in New Jersey, and presently a little village sprang up, which came to be known as Wilmington.

The building of Old Swedes' Church presents an interesting picture of early pioneer life. Every member of the community helped. The stones were broken by the congregation and hauled on sleds in the winter, and after spring had set in, on carts. The boards were all sawed by hand and the nails used were forged by the community blacksmith. The dimensions of the new church were sixty by thirty feet. The stone walls were made six feet thick at the foundation and three feet at the level of the windows. On the eastern gable was inscribed a Latin sentence which, translated, read: "The light arising from on high shines in the darkness." The total cost of the building figured at ordinary prices for all material and labor was estimated at around eight hundred pounds.

The church, begun in 1698, was consecrated on Holy Trinity Sunday, July 4, 1699, and afterwards there was a celebration in honor of the occasion at the home of the church warden and all who came were feasted royally.

Old Swedes' was at first a branch of the state church of Sweden, the Evangelical Lutheran, governed directly from the home country. Among its proud possessions, and still in use today, is a communion service sent over from Sweden in 1718 as a gift to the parish.

The original roof of the church was very poorly constructed and its great weight threw the walls out of plumb so that in 1750 extensive repairs had to be made, buttresses built, and a new roof put on. The south wall was also rebuilt at this time and additional windows added. The Swedish language was gradually abandoned as English settlers in the community increased and after 1748 each alternate service was conducted in English.

When the British were in possession of Wilmington in 1776–77, two companies of soldiers were quartered in the church and public worship was therefore abandoned, although there is one record in the old vestry book of divine service having been conducted one Sunday for the soldiers by order of the British commanding officer, Captain McDonald.

By 1795 the complexion of the community had changed to such an extent that it was decided to adopt the ritual of the Protestant Episcopal Church and to seek admission into the diocese of Delaware. Today Trinity Church is in a splendid state of preservation, a restoration program having been carried on in recent years. The interior has a quaint, interesting appearance, especially the old rough brick floor and the old-fashioned white pews that are beautiful without being at all pretentious.

In the early days of the church, burial within its walls was considered the highest honor and tribute of respect that could be shown the departed and a number of the early members were interred under the brick and stone floor, some under their own pews.

Old Swedes' Church. Around this church grew the modern city of Wilmington, Del.
Photo by Sanborn Studio.

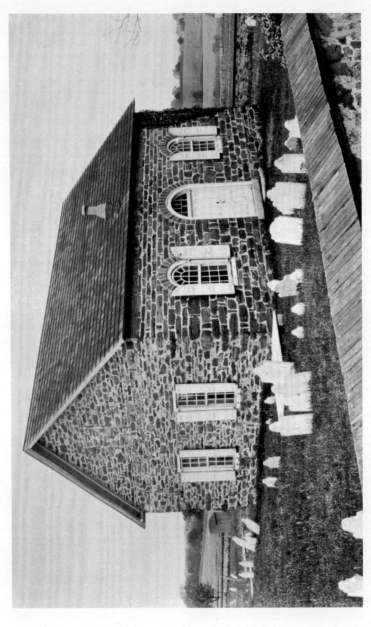

Norriton Presbyterian Church, near Norristown, Penna. The oldest monument of Presbyterian enterprise within the bounds of Pennsylvania. *From Wallace's "Colonial Churches and Meeting Houses," Courtesy Architectural Book Publishing Co.*

Delaware

The little town of New Castle is, in spite of the fire of 1824, very rich in early Colonial buildings of historic interest. As a town it has had at least eight names and has been under the flags of four different countries while its old court house is without a doubt one of the oldest state buildings in the country.

Closely entwined with the early history of the town and located just in the rear of the court house, is Immanuel Church, the oldest church of English construction on the Delaware River. The parish was organized in 1689 and the present church building begun in 1703, the same year that the young Scotch missionary, the Reverend George Ross, was sent over from England by the Society for the Propagation of the Gospel.

For fifty years he served as pastor of Immanuel, exerting a wide influence on the whole vicinity. One of his sons was George Ross, a Signer of the Declaration of Independence, and his daughter Gertrude married George Read, another of the Signers, whose tomb may be found in the rear of the church. Another son, John Ross, was a distinguished lawyer in Philadelphia, while a third, the Reverend Aeneas Ross, followed his father as pastor of old Immanuel and held the charge for thirty-eight years.

The building, which is cruciform in design, was finished in 1706. The two chalices and paten of the communion service were presented by Queen Anne, and Governor Charles Gookin contributed a flagon, all of which are in the possession of the church today.

Various changes have been made from time to time, particularly in 1724 when a gallery was added and in 1822 when the tower and spire were built under the direction of the noted Philadelphia architect, Mr. William Strickland. It was at this time that the citizens of the town united in purchasing a town clock, which was placed in the tower in charge of the city trustees, who retained ownership of it until June, 1887, when it was transferred to the control of the church.

Prominent among the contributors to the fund for making these improvements was Commodore Thomas MacDonough. It is said that when MacDonough was a young boy on a ship anchored in New Castle Harbor he with a party out on a celebration, rang the bell of the church so vigorously that it cracked and he afterwards felt a keen obligation to make some restitution, since the parish itself was never a wealthy one.

The glebe farm of the church, still owned, was given by Richard Halliwell in 1719. The congregation played an important part in the War of the Revolution and many who had a part in that historic struggle lie buried in the old churchyard.

The exact date of the erection of Prince George's Chapel, Dagsboro, is unknown, but the structure seems to have been referred to in letters as early as 1717. The history of the Society for the Propagation of the Gospel in Foreign Parts mentions the visit of the Reverend George Ross to this section in August of that year and that he visited "a place of worship about sixteen miles from Lewes. It is a small frame building erected by a few well disposed persons in order to meet together to worship God." This place of worship was very probably Prince George's Chapel; it was approximately that distance from Lewes and was a small frame structure, built originally as a chapel of ease to St. Martin's, the mother church of Worcester Parish, Maryland. In 1765 the fixing of the boundary line between Delaware and Maryland threw several churches, including Prince George's Chapel, into the bounds of the former state.

Some time about the middle of the eighteenth century the chapel was enlarged, chiefly at the expense of General Dagworthy. This was done by the addition of transepts and the building of a small sanctuary on the east end, changing the plan into the form of a Latin cross, beneath the north arm of which were later buried General Dagworthy and his wife. The length of the church was now ninety feet and the width, including the arms of the cross, fifty feet. The walls were fourteen feet high and the ceiling composed of semicircular arches, intersecting each other and giving to the whole interior a most pleasing effect. There was a large goblet-like pulpit and sounding board but the crowning glory of the church was the chancel window consisting of three sections, the center one having a circular head. This was fourteen feet high and the whole width nine feet, and the sash contained one hundred and twenty panes of glass.

In 1866 the transepts were still standing but were in such poor condition that repairs were impossible. The original chapel, however, that is, the nave, curiously enough, in view of its greater age, remained in good condition. This portion was reroofed and about ten years later the decayed portion was replaced by a small chancel intended to conform as much as possible with the design of the original structure.

Regular services were discontinued about 1847 and the old chapel exists today only as a precious relic of those early pioneers to whom the Christian cause was as important as their own fortunes.

Christ Church, Dover, was begun in 1734. It succeeded a frame structure erected about 1704 on the church glebe which had been donated that same year. In 1705 the Reverend Thomas Crawford was sent over as missionary. Conditions in Dover in those days were evidently not all they might have been and in 1708 Mr. Crawford complained to his superiors, the Society for the Propagation of the Gospel in Foreign Parts:

I can say upon the word of a minister that those three years that I have been in this place I have not had twenty pounds, Pennsylvania money, per annum, which is but a small benefice, considering it is paid me not in silver, but as the people are able in corn, etc.

Six years were required to build the present church but the structure has seen many changes since originally completed. Services were maintained with but slight interruption until the time of the Revolution. During that period the building fell into disrepair and was given to "moles and bats, cattle and boys," but was "restored to decency" about 1785.

Early in the eighteenth century William Penn granted to David Evans and William Davis thirty thousand acres of land, to be divided and deeded to settlers from South Wales, this land being ever afterwards known as "The Welsh Tract." It was partially located in Pencader Hundred, New Castle County, Delaware, and partially in Maryland. Prominent among the early settlers in "The Welsh Tract" was a little group of Welsh citizens who in 1701 decided to come to America, there to settle and make their home.

It was this little group, sixteen in number, which founded the congregation today known as the Welsh Tract Baptist Meeting House, Newark.

Soon after their arrival they erected a log meeting house and in 1746 the present house of brick was built. It is said that some of its timbers were those originally used in the first building while, according to tradition, the bricks were said to have been brought from England, landed at New Castle and then transported upon the backs of mules to the spot where the church was being built, about ten miles away. It may have been that the bricks were actually burned in New Castle; there would, at least, seem to be no practical occasion for importing bricks as late as 1746; also this would have been an extremely expensive procedure for a congregation which was never wealthy.

The little structure erected in 1746 occupies the site of the first log meeting house and is still in a good state of preservation. The two hundredth anniversary of the founding of the Welsh Tract Meeting was celebrated in October, 1903.

The first St. Anne's Church, New Castle County, was built on Appoquinimink Creek in 1705, a small and simple frame building that was destined to serve the parish for more than sixty years. The first pastor was the Reverend Thomas Jenkins sent out by the Society for the Propagation of the Gospel in Foreign Parts. After a few months of earnest effort he died "of a calenture," so reads the record, "caused by the musketoes" and for three years then, the parish was without the services of a regular minister.

It was during the early days of the church's existence that Queen Anne showed her interest in this new mission of the Church of England by presenting to it an altar cloth, a fragment of which, bearing the royal letters A. R., worked, it is said, by her own hands, is still preserved in the parish.

The present church was erected in 1768. The walls are two feet thick and the timbers of the roof, taken from the virgin forest, are far heavier than those that would be employed in a similar building today. It was a day of substantial but plain buildings and St. Anne's is no exception, being a two-story brick structure without any exterior ornament except a cove cornice which almost seems to indicate an earlier date of erection.

Delaware

The rector at the time of the Revolution was the Reverend Philip Reading. Like many other clergymen who had come from across the sea, he felt bound by his oath to use the entire English Prayer Book, including the prayer for the King; therefore following the Declaration of Independence, on August 28, 1776, having "no design to resist the authority of the new government, on one hand, and as . . . determined, on the other, not to incur the heavy guilt of perjury by a breach of the most solemn promises," he closed and locked the doors of St. Anne's Church, nor were they apparently reopened during his lifetime. He died on October 29, 1778, and was buried near the south entrance of the church.

The old building is now used only for special services. The structure is well preserved and stands surrounded by a grove of gigantic oaks, about three-quarters of a mile from Middletown, on the only ridge for miles around. This ridge, incidentally, was once described by the English commissioners sent to examine the colonies, as a "huge mountain," a description that causes a smile today.

Ivy-covered Drawyers Meeting House, located a mile north of Odessa, on the King's Highway, is one of the pioneer churches of Delaware and one of the earliest structures erected by the Presbyterians in the state. The original house was built in 1711 but in 1769 this house of worship having decayed and being "unfit to answer the purpose of a house of worship," plans were begun for a new church which was erected in 1773.

The bricks were burned on the farm of one Robert Meldrum, a member of the congregation, and for many years the ruins of the brick kiln could be seen on the northeast corner of his land.

The dimensions of the church are forty-four by fifty-six feet. The workmanship and materials are of high character and both the interior and exterior present a true picture of Colonial architecture at its very best. The graceful doorway of the meeting house is a very lovely thing, as is the old pulpit and precentor's box. The many-paned windows with their circular tops and white shutters are also much admired. Both the building and burial grounds have been well cared for by an association formed some years ago, called Friends of Old Drawyers.

The church is now commonly known as Old Drawyers Church and seems to have derived its name from the creek on whose bank it stands. Just where this creek got its title is not definitely known. The official name of the religious corporation is "The 1st Presbyterian Church in St. Georges Hundred." In the beginning it was known as Apoquinimy Meeting House.

Many famous sons and daughters of Delaware were members of the old congregation, among them being Nicholas Vandyke, Esq., Governor of Delaware in 1783. He was one of the signers of the Confederation of the States, while his son, the Hon. Nicholas Vandyke, was a well-known lawyer of his day, later a member of the Legislature of Delaware, a member of the House of Representatives of the United States and, finally, of the Senate of the United States. Commodore Thomas Brown, a son of the church, grandson of Peter Chevalier, Huguenot, was at the siege of Tripoli and, during the War of 1812, a Commander on Lake Ontario. Another well-known member was Captain Kirkwood, generally referred to as the most noted of Delaware's soldiers during the Revolution.

A great many real heroes of the Revolution rest in the graveyard of this old Colonial church. Delaware furnished almost four thousand officers and soldiers during the War of Independence and only one out of each hundred lived to return home. "The Blue Hen's Chickens," as the Delaware regiment was called, was raised and mustered at Dover before the Declaration of Independence had been made, sentiment running high in the little Diamond State. This regiment, of which Captain Kirkwood was a part, saw service at the Battle of Trenton, December 25, 1776, and at the Battle of Princeton, January 3, 1777.

The Friends first settled in Brandywine Hundred in 1682 and soon their unassuming little meeting houses began to appear here and there in the "three counties." In 1703 a meeting house was erected on the road from Port Penn. This was first called George's Creek Meeting and the location later became a Quaker burying ground when the meeting was moved to Odessa and the present small brick meeting house was erected there in 1780. During the period preceding the Civil War the meeting house became a part of the famous underground railroad, the runaway slaves being concealed in a small loft overhead. Today the building is in fair condition for its age but is no longer in active use and much of the exciting history connected with its existence has been lost.

One of the most famous Methodist historic shrines in America is Barratt's Chapel, on the du Pont Highway a mile north of Frederica, for it was in this old structure that steps were first taken to organize the Methodist Church in America.

Two smaller churches had been built by the Methodists in Delaware in the two years preceding 1780, but Barratt's Chapel was much more pretentious than the others, although the structure when viewed today impresses one as being somewhat barnlike. Still well preserved, the building stands as a monument to its founder, the pious Judge Barratt, a friend and protector of Francis Asbury during the troublous days of the Revolution.

An early writer described the chapel as being "42 feet by 48 feet, built of brick, 2 stories high" and with a "vestry room connected with it." One learns further that two generations passed away before it was completed and that the first quarterly meeting was held in the chapel in November of 1780. It is supposed that there were a thousand people in attendance.

Before the erection of the chapel, Judge Barratt had opened his home for the brethren of the church, protected the traveling preachers and exerted great influence in support of religion.

On Sunday, November 14, 1784, the Reverend Thomas Coke came to Barratt's Chapel with a message from John Wesley, in England. In the chapel on this day occurred the memorable interview between Dr. Coke and the Reverend Francis Asbury at which was appointed the first General Conference of American Methodism and plans laid which resulted in organizing the Methodist Episcopal Church in America. Several mementos of this interview may be found in the chapel, including the chair used in the pulpit on that occasion.

In his journals, Bishop Asbury refers frequently to Barratt's Chapel and the spot grew to hold a hallowed spot in his memory. The last time he spoke there was shortly before his death, when passing through the region for the last time, he ascended the old pulpit and preached once again to his flock.

Chapter VIII

IN THE LAND OF WILLIAM PENN

I love old Meeting-houses,—how my heart
Goes out to those dear silent homes of prayer
With all their quietude and rustic charm,
Their loved associations from old days,
Their tranquil and pathetic solitude,
Their hallowed memories!
— John Russell Hayes

On the site of the present "Gloria Dei" Church, Philadelphia, the early Swedish pioneers to the state first erected a block house for defense against the Indians, in case of an attack. Now within the limits of the city, the site was at first some distance from it and was known as Wicaco. It is not known when this block house was built but in 1677, for the sake of convenience, the building was converted into a place of worship. As the years passed, the remodeled structure grew more and more dilapidated and it was finally decided to build a permanent structure on the same location.

Work commenced on September 19, 1697. The new building was sixty feet long, thirty feet wide and twenty feet high. A tower was purposely left unfinished until it could be ascertained whether a chime of bells could be obtained from Sweden. The church was a simple little edifice yet when it was dedicated on July 2, 1700, the pastor, the Reverend Eric Bjork, said, "Through God's blessings we have completed a great work, and have built a church superior to any in this country, so that the English themselves, who now govern this province and are beyond measure richer than we are, wonder at what we have done."

The name "Gloria Dei" was given as a token of the thankfulness of the parishioners and the church was at first a branch of the state church of Sweden, the Evangelical Lutheran. It was from

· 172 ·

the first a very tolerant organization and in 1710 permission was granted to members of the Church of England to use the building for worship each Sunday after the Swedish services were over. As a mark of harmony, a Swedish hymn was sung at each of the Church of England services.

The Swedish language was gradually abandoned, however, and English adopted in the regular services of the church. Like Trinity Church, Wilmington, Delaware, begun a year after and finished a year sooner, Gloria Dei is now an Episcopal church, the change in ritual dating from 1789.

Although the walls of the church were very thick, nevertheless in 1704 they appeared unable to resist the weight of the roof and a sacristy erected adjoining the north end of the structure and a vestibule against the south, served as buttresses and greatly strengthened the building.

The old Norriton Presbyterian Church was erected in 1698 and the date of the deed of the grassplot adjoining—1678—marks the spot as "the oldest monument of Presbyterian enterprise within the bounds of Pennsylvania." According to tradition, the religious history of the site goes back even farther than this and there was a log church in existence here, established by the Hollander, or Reformed Dutch, as early as 1660. At any rate the plot of ground acquired in 1678 was used for a cemetery long before the present church building was erected.

Reverend Francis Makemie, organizer of the first Presbyterian church in America at Rehoboth, Maryland, wrote under date of July 28, 1685, of one Reverend Mr. Wardrope as having removed to Pennsylvania to preach. There is a tradition that Mr. Wardrope preached occasionally at Norriton and that Reverend Mr. Makemie also visited the place.

When Matthias, father of David Rittenhouse, came to Norriton he found the building already there, erected on a corner of the property that has ever since borne his name. Matthias Rittenhouse was a Mennonite but he gave clear title to the church in 1737. In 1749 he built the stone house in which his son spent the rest of his life. Benjamin Franklin was a frequent visitor in the Rittenhouse home and on Sunday he and young David undoubtedly often attended services in old Norriton Church which was within sight of the house.

The early part of December, 1777, a division of the Continental Army under Washington began its march to Valley Forge. The weather was unbearably cold and in passing by Norriton Presbyterian Church many of the weary and almost exhausted soldiers dropped out of line and for a short time sought refuge in the building. At about this time also the little structure was turned into a hospital for the army troops and several times General Washington visited the building. An interesting feature is that after the Revolution the Pennsylvania Legislature voted to permit the church to raise by lottery the necessary funds which were required to repair the damages sustained during the war.

In the old churchyard are buried many who served with distinction in the Revolutionary War or who played their part in the Colonial life which preceded that struggle. Unfortunately, however, many of the oldest stones in the cemetery are no longer there for in 1844 workmen who were repairing the church utilized the flat gravemarkers in strengthening the foundations! At the same time the old style pews were removed and replaced by others, the floors repaired, the ancient pulpit and sounding board taken down and a new roof placed upon the building.

The oldest part of the Merion Meeting House, the north end as it stands today, was built in 1695 and in 1713 this was enlarged into the present structure. The building clearly shows evidences of having been built in parts and differs in appearance from any Friends' meeting houses of the period, the smaller portion being attached to the larger in such a way as to form a cross.

The Welsh Friends who built this ancient meeting house came to America in 1682 and the first burial in the Merion graveyard was that of Catherine Reese who died "Eighth Month 23d," of that year. Merion was named for their beloved homeland across the sea, Merionethshire, a county of North Wales which in turn received its designation from a prince who had ruled there over one thousand years before.

These early Quaker pioneers first worshiped in a tent until a log cabin was built some two hundred feet east of the present building; then in 1695 the present stone meeting house was begun. This was repaired and plastered in 1829 and it has always been regretted that the old stones were covered over. It is said that another nineteenth century addition is the attic over the meeting loft.

Among the first entries in the old minute books are those which tell of paying eight shillings for cleaning Merion Meeting. These minutes were kept by women members.

During the Revolution the Welsh Friends of Merion went through some very trying days, their goods and money being taken for the support of both armies, whichever happened to be in possession of the section. Both Cornwallis' Army as well as that of General Washington are named in the old record books as taking for their needs the property of the members.

Hugh Roberts, an intimate friend of William Penn, at whose house Penn often stopped, presented the meeting with a handsome sundial which was placed in front of the house, close enough o the road so that people could see and read it while passing. It stood there until the Revolutionary War, when, on account of the large amount of lead it contained, it was confiscated by the American soldiers and melted into bullets. It was at the home of Hugh Roberts on the "second Fifth-day in Fourth month, 1634," that there was held the first meeting by Friends of Merion of which there remains any account, although services undoubtedly date from the time of the first settlement in 1682.

The interior of the meeting is very plain. The old gallery, where, it is related, a century or two ago the young people gathered when the lower part was filled to overflowing, is still in place and here may be seen the original old seats, in fairly good state of preservation, although some of them are worm-eaten.

According to tradition, William Penn worshiped in this old building and the story goes that many of the hearers were unable to understand the sermon that he preached on one occasion.

Another venerable meeting house in which William Penn is said to have worshiped is old Haverford. This was founded by the same Welsh Quakers who built the Merion structure. These Welsh friends had early purchased from the Proprietary in England, forty thousand acres of land; those who came first "took up so much of it in the west side of the Schulkil River, as made the three townships of Merion, Haverford and Radnor."

Services were first held in members' homes but in 1688 the first meeting house at Haverford, a log structure, was put up. The burying ground had been laid out four years previously. In 1697 subscriptions were taken for a new stone meeting house which was completed and ready for occupancy in 1700. This is thought to be the south portion of the building, its rougher masonry and style of building clearly marking it as the oldest part. As a matter of fact the northern section of the meeting house was erected in 1800 and is, therefore, a century younger.

One curious feature about this particular little structure is that it was heated by a kind of stove for which the fuel was supplied and piled up outside the building. "The tops of these pseudo stoves were of iron and the smoke escaped through a hole in the outer wall a few feet above the fuel supply." According to tradition, the window frames of Old Haverford were made of lead and during the Revolution they were seized, melted, and used as bullets.

As an example of the respect with which William Penn's Holy Experiment in Pennsylvania was regarded by the Friends in England is the case of John Bevan, a minister of prominence, who stated that he and his wife planned to come to Pennsylvania because they thought "it might be a good place to train up children among sober people." About 1704, with his children grown and comfortably settled, he returned to his native Wales, and, as he writes, "The aim intended by my wife was in good measure answered."

Thomas Story, one of the early leading Quaker ministers and writers, tells of attending a general meeting at Haverford in the Eleventh Month, 1699, in company with William Penn. Later Robert Sutcliff records the tradition that Penn, coming one time to Haverford Meeting, took a little bare-legged girl, Rebecca Wood, behind him on his horse and carried her on to the meeting house.

Old Radnor Friends' Meeting House, Ithan, Delaware County, was built in 1718, also by Welsh settlers of the Society of Friends.

Radnor Meeting was organized about 1686 and meetings were held in the homes of members until a meeting house could be erected. John Jermen, one of the first settlers in Radnor Township, donated the land but died before the little structure could be completed.

The building was used as a hospital during the Revolutionary War during the encampment at Valley Forge. It is recorded that "Friends were deprived of their meeting house early in 1778 in consideration of its being used by the army." The soldiers using it came from Camp Field, an outpost of Valley Forge, and officers had their headquarters in the main meeting house. Several died there and are buried in the graveyard along the adjoining wall, but no markers exist to indicate their exact resting places.

The first Kennett Meeting House, located close to the Delaware line, about four miles from the Borough of Kennett Square, was built in 1710 and this building, enlarged in 1719 and 1731 is said to be the one which stands today. It is a plain and almost austere little structure whose outward calm gives little hint of the stirring events in which it was perhaps an unwilling participant. During the Brandywine campaign Friends had gathered here to worship. British soldiers taking cover behind the stone wall of the burying ground, fired at the American troops coming down the road. It is even said that a British soldier opened the door to the meeting house but that the Friends paid no attention to this interference and continued in meeting. "Tumult without, but great calm within," wrote one who was there that day.

A tablet placed on Kennett Meeting House by the Pennsylvania Historical Commission gives the following information:

> HERE THE AMERICANS UNDER MAXWELL
> OPENED FIRE UPON THE ADVANCING
> HESSIANS, THUS BEGINNING THE
> BATTLE OF BRANDYWINE,
> SEPTEMBER 11, 1777.

The oldest portion of Old Bristol Friends' Meeting House, Bucks County, was built in 1710. Over three years were required to complete the work, this long period due in part, it is said, to the desire to secure some of the required material from England. Not many years after it was erected, a portion of the meeting house had to be taken down because its construction was faulty. Additions and repairs were made in 1735 and 1756. The original structure, as altered and repaired from time to time, still stands, however. This is a two-story brick building with two porches in front and one at the side.

During the Revolution the British occupied the meeting house as a hospital. Services were still held at the little end of the building, several members being appointed to keep that portion cleared of the troops each "First Day."

Today, Old Bristol is kept in its original state, with the walls whitewashed and the benches or seats unpainted, but with all necessary repairs made as they are needed.

The exact beginnings of Trinity Church, Oxford, are unknown but both a church and congregation were in existence as early as the year 1700, if not earlier. A tablet over the doorway in the west front of the present building states: "Church of England services were first held on this site in a log meeting house belonging to the Society of Friends." When the proprietors of this little log structure became converts to the Church of England they turned over the property for the uses of that church. It is thought that the log church, before it was donated to the uses of the Church of England, was also used by the Dutch Anabaptists and Swedish Lutherans of the neighborhood.

The oldest portion of the present church, the western end of the nave, was built in 1711 and at this time very probably the Queen Anne silver was received. The church was lengthened about 1786 or 1789 and transepts added in 1833. The structure did not receive its present cruciform shape until 1839 with the erection of the tower and vestry. Later the partition wall separating the east end of the nave from the old tower was removed and the vestry converted into a recess chancel, making the *interior* truly cruciform for the first time. In 1875 the height of the tower was reduced to conform to the rest of the building, and a new tower, with belfry and steeple, was reared at the side of the old one, giving to the building more of the appearance of the rural churches of England, after which it seems to have been modeled. While nearly every generation has added something to the old church, the original structure forming the western end of the nave has been most sacredly preserved.

In the old cemetery are buried many who played their part during Colonial times. The history of the church from 1770 until 1782 has been lost, there being no entries covering this period in the only parochial record now in the possession of the vestry. A relic and reminder of the original Quakers who first worshiped on the spot is found in the inscription on the grave of Elizabeth Roberts, which reads:

> *Here by these lines, is testify'd,*
> *No Quaker was she when she died.*
> *So far was she from Quakerism,*
> *That she desired to have baptism.*

According to tradition, the Welsh settlers at Radnor, who formed the original congregation of St. David's Church, first erected a log place of worship on the plantation of one William Davis and this log church, toward the close of the seventeenth century was garrisoned by settlers against the attacks of the Indians, subsequently burning to the ground in 1700. Historians, however, hold this story as extremely unlikely and 1700 is usually taken as the date of the congregation's birth.

The corner-stone of the present little church was laid May 9, 1715. Most of the work of construction was done during the winter months, and practically all the work fell upon the fifteen families which composed the congregation. The interior of the building remained unfinished for many years. Not until 1765 was a floor put in, the bare earth sufficing until then. Toward the middle of the eighteenth century a custom seems to have originated of selling a piece of ground within the church, on which the purchaser had the privilege of building such a pew as he desired. Some pews were also erected by the vestry and rented for the support of the church.

In 1771 a gallery was built along three sides of the interior. Heading the subscription list was Anthony Wayne, father of the famous general and a prominent member of the congregation. There is also reason to believe that at this time the church was considerably remodeled; the present Norman type door and windows being substituted for a more Gothic type.

At the beginning of the Revolutionary War the rector was the Reverend William Currie. According to tradition, the congregation refused to permit the use of the prayers for the King and royal family; when the rector insisted otherwise the doors were forcibly closed against him. The church records, however, mention no such occurrence and Mr. Currie's letter of resignation, dated May 16, 1776, expresses only affection and solicitude for his flock.

During the war, services were held only infrequently and squads of soldiers from both sides alternately made the church their rendezvous. When the Continental Army encamped in the neighborhood, all of the lead sashes then supporting the small diamond shaped window panes were cut out and molded into bullets. Following the battle of the Brandywine, sixteen unknown victims, it is said, were buried in the little hollow west of the gallery steps.

In 1811 the remains of "Mad Anthony Wayne" were removed to St. David's Graveyard where they now rest, but there is some confusion as to the exact date on which this reinterment took place. Many men prominent in national affairs attended the services held on this occasion.

Repairs have been made from time to time but in the main St. David's has been left undisturbed. In May, 1876, Henry Wadsworth Longfellow visited the old church and was greatly affected by its picturesque surroundings. One of his last productions was "Old St. David's at Radnor" in which is evidenced the deep impression the old church made on the mind of the great American poet.

> *What an image of peace and rest*
> *Is this little church among its graves!*
> *All is so quiet; the troubled breast,*
> *The wounded spirit, the heart oppressed,*
> *Here may find the repose it craves.*

In the Land of William Penn

Closely associated with the Revolutionary struggle for Independence is Christ Church, Philadelphia. The present building was begun in 1727 but the church organization goes back to 1695, under a provision in the original charter of King Charles II to William Penn, inserted through the influence of the Right Reverend Henry Compton, Bishop of London.

Christ Church is one of the handsomest of all the Colonial churches. The architect was Dr. John Kearsley and the design in a general way resembles St. Martin's-in-the-Fields, London. Dr. Kearsley, an amateur architect, although a physician by profession, was active also in arranging for the construction of the State House, later known as Independence Hall. The interior of Christ Church is much the same today as when first erected but the building itself has been extended two or three times.

The chimes, consisting of eight bells, were imported from England in 1754, purchased with money raised through a lottery run by Benjamin Franklin. On July 4, 1776, the bells pealed forth the Declaration of Independence in unison with the Liberty Bell. During the war they were taken from the city, with the Liberty Bell, for safekeeping but were later returned to the church and replaced in the tower. In the early days they were rung daily at noon and in the evenings of market days to please the citizens of Philadelphia. It was these bells that Longfellow mentions in the closing scene of "Evangeline."

*Then, as she mounted the stairs to the corridors, cooled by the east-
    wind,
Distant and soft on her ear fell the chimes from the belfry of Christ
    Church,
While, intermingled with these, across the meadows were wafted
Sounds of psalms, that were sung by the Swedes in their church
    at Wicaco.*

The "church at Wicaco" of course refers to the present Gloria Dei or Old Swedes' Church.

Shortly after the Declaration of Independence had been signed, the bust of George II was removed from Christ Church and when, a few months later, the crown on the spire was struck by lightning it was considered a good omen by the congregation!

The Protestant Episcopal Church was organized, its constitution framed and the Amended Prayer Book adopted in Christ Church, at a convention called for this purpose in 1785. Today, one of the most priceless of the church's many possessions is an original copy of the Prayer Book of Edward VI showing the alterations made at this convention.

Probably no other church in America has so much in the way of historic furniture, silver and so on. The communion silver was given by Queen Anne about 1708; the baptismal font dates from 1695; the silver bowl from 1712. The pulpit dates from 1769 and the organ from 1765. This organ has twice been renovated, but the case and as many other parts as was possible to retain, are original.

Independence Hall was built by three members of the congregation, its architect, Judge Andrew Hamilton, having been a member of the vestry. Many members of the convention which framed the Constitution of the United States in 1787 worshiped in Christ Church. In the chancel may be seen a tablet to another distinguished member, General Forbes, victor of Fort Duquesne in the French and Indian War.

The list of prominent members is practically endless. From 1790 to 1797 President and Mrs. Washington regularly occupied pew number fifty-eight; later this same pew was used by President John Adams on occasion. High officials of this and other nations, including General Lafayette when he visited America for the second time, were frequent guests in this pew, which is now preserved in the National Museum at Washington.

Other pewholders included Robert Morris, Treasurer of the Revolution; Francis Hopkinson, Signer of the Declaration of Independence, chairman of the first navy board, and designer of our flags; his son, Judge Joseph Hopkinson, author of the national hymn, "Hail Columbia"; Betsy Ross, first maker of the American flag; and General Cadwalader of the War of 1812.

In the burial ground were interred seven Signers of the Declaration of Independence: Franklin, Morris, Wilson, Hopkinson, Rush, Ross and Hewes; Michael Hillegas, first Treasurer of the United

States; General Morgan and General McCall of the Civil War, and many, many others of equal distinction. General Charles Lee, of the Continental Army, was interred beside the southwest door, and near by was laid to rest, after the Battle of Princeton, General Hugh Mercer.

Among the clergy who have officiated at Christ Church should be mentioned the Reverend Robert Blackwell, Chaplain of the American Army at Valley Forge. The Right Reverend William White, D.D., first Bishop of Pennsylvania, and long Presiding Bishop of the United States, the first in the American Episcopate derived from the Church of England, is interred before the chancel rail.

For sixty-five years all churchmen in Philadelphia worshiped at Christ Church, but the growing congregation, with the constant scarcity of seats, caused the vestry to consider the advisability of building a new church.

A petition was accordingly drawn up to the Honorable Thomas Penn and Richard Penn, Proprietaries of the province, for a "Lott on the west side of Third Street," which was part of a large section owned by them. The document was signed by many of the most prominent Philadelphians of the day and the two Penns proved themselves to be hearty friends of the Church of England by speedily donating the ground requested.

The corner-stone of Old St. Peter's was laid September 21, 1758, and the edifice was completed three years later. The church stands today practically as when first built, with the exception of a belfry tower and spire substituted in 1842 for the original quaint belfry cupola. The architecture is pure Colonial or Georgian. Its walls were built entirely of brick but these bricks were not "imported from England" as is sometimes said. There is, in fact, no building in Philadelphia built of imported brick; this tradition, held in connection with a great number of historic buildings, is in most cases simply a legend with no foundation other than that the bricks were manufactured in English style.

The interior of St. Peter's, with its old Colonial windows, its original white, square box pews, with doors in place, its wineglass pulpit and sounding board, its stone passageways, its quaint prayer desk underneath the pulpit, and its old-time galleries, is the same now as in the days when George Washington and his wife, Martha, reverently worshiped in the same surroundings. What a treat for the antiquarian to pass through the portal of St. Peter's Church!

Robert Smith was the master architect in charge of the building of this church, being assisted by Dr. John Kearsley, the designer of Christ Church. A rather unique feature of the interior is the location of the reading desk and pulpit at one end and the chancel at the other, compelling the minister to walk down the center aisle from one to the other, preceded by the verger with his mace.

St. Peter's had no trouble in filling all pews but to fill the treasury and pay off the building debt proved a task indeed and not until 1771 was the church free of this burden. St. Peter's was at first a chapel of Christ Church and not until 1832 did it become an independent congregation. In September, 1775, Jacob Duché, the senior assistant minister, was elected rector of the united churches, Christ Church and St. Peter's.

When the Continental Congress met at Carpenter's Hall, September 6, 1774, Reverend Mr. Duché gave the opening prayer, for which the "Thanks of the Congress" were voted him. The following year he opened the second session of the Continental Congress with prayer. July 20th was set aside by Congress as a day of fasting and prayer. Members assembled at Christ Church and Mr. Duché was appointed to preach before them; officiating again at the funeral of Peyton Randolph, President of the Congress. On the 7th of July he made a very patriotic address before the First Battalion of the City of Philadelphia.

After the Declaration of Independence, July 4, 1776, Mr. Duché called a special meeting of the vestry at his own house and it was voted to omit the prayers for the King in the liturgy at St. Peter's and Christ Church. St. Peter's was now definitely on the side of the colonies and its rector was appointed first chaplain to Congress, a post which he resigned about three months later, returning the hundred and fifty dollars which had been voted him by Congress. He later declared that when Independence was proclaimed he had forced himself to believe that it was a mere temporary measure adopted to terrorize the crown and thus procure favorable terms for the colonists; as it turned out, Mr. Duché was at heart a loyal British subject, something that was, in view of his past actions, hard for his congregation to understand.

On October 8, 1777, he wrote his astonishing letter to George Washington, in which, amid a mass of incoherent statements, this fact was set forth and Washington was urged to desert his cause and betray his army. Washington sent the letter to Congress and feeling over the incident ran very high.

In December, 1777, Mr. Duché sailed from Philadelphia and not until after the adoption of the Constitution of the United States, when laws excluding refugees from the State of Pennsylvania were repealed, did he return to the city. Reverend Mr. Duché never was officially connected with St. Peter's after his return, but on his death, January 3, 1798, he was buried near the east wall of the church, beside his wife, who had died a few months before.

Before returning to America Jacob Duché wrote Washington a pitiful letter asking his forgiveness and begging him not to interfere with his return to Philadelphia. The gracious Washington not only did not interfere but permitted Mr. Duché to call upon him after his return to the city. At this meeting he manifested genuine concern on observing in the limbs of the former rector of St. Peter's the effects of a slight stroke of paralysis sustained by him in England. This is an incident in the life of Washington which might well be better known than it is.

Thomas Coombe, one of the assistant ministers of the church, also remained loyal to the mother country, although he was himself a native of Philadelphia and might have been expected to be on the other side. After the departure of Jacob Duché in 1777, Thomas Coombe had both churches on his hands, remaining in the city until after the British evacuation, when he returned to England.

William White, the other assistant minister, early cast his lot with the colonies. When the British occupied Philadelphia he moved with his family to Aquila Hall, the house of his brother-in-law, in Harford County, Maryland; returning to the city in June,

1778, shortly before Thomas Coombe's resignation. In October of the previous year Congress had chosen Reverend Mr. White as one of its chaplains, in which capacity he served until the end of the war. In 1787 when William White went over to England to be consecrated Bishop he found that his former colleague, Thomas Coombe, was then one of the forty-eight chaplains to the King.

During the war the British soldiers took up the board fence around St. Peter's, for the use of their troops. At first it was promised that a "reasonable allowance for this part of their property" would be made; afterwards this allowance was refused and some years went by before a brick wall was put up.

Among the interesting personages who were pewholders in St. Peter's immediately preceding and following the Revolutionary War might be mentioned Charles Wilson Peale, the artist, and Colonel John Nixon, who first proclaimed the Declaration of Independence before the people.

On George Washington's first Sunday in Philadelphia, in September, 1774, he attended "Quaker Meeting in the Forenoon" and then to St. Peter's Church in the afternoon. The first Church of England service that he attended in Philadelphia was therefore, according to his diary, at St. Peter's. The pew in which he sat that day is not known but the date was September 25th. On the next Sunday he went to Christ Church. The pew occupied by General and Mrs. Washington during the winter following the Yorktown campaign is thought to be number forty-one, which was numbered thirty-six in 1781, on the south side of the central passageway.

St. Paul's Church, Philadelphia, was commenced in 1760 and the building was ready for use on Christmas Day, 1761. The organization of St. Paul's came as a result of the treatment accorded Reverend William McClenachan, a young minister of the Church of England, who preached at Christ Church when on a visit to the city. He was extremely popular; so popular that he was asked to become assistant pastor there.

Many of the clergymen of the province did not like the methods of Mrs. McClenachan, who was decidedly in sympathy with the Reverend George Whitefield and the "Great Revival" which was

Interior St. Peter's Church, Philadelphia, Penna. The same now as in the days when George and Martha Washington reverently worshiped in its pews. *Photo by Ph. B. Wallace.*

Augustus Lutheran Church, Trappe, Penna. The oldest unaltered Lutheran Church in the United States.

Photo by Ph. B. Wallace.

then sweeping the country, and a petition was sent to the Lord Bishop of London finding fault with the young man because of "his railings and revilings in the pulpit," and as a result of this the Bishop refused to give his consent to Mr. McClenachan's appointment.

There were many protests heard on all sides and several days after the news became generally known a meeting for the organization of a new church was held in the State House. Steps were taken at once to purchase ground and a new church edifice soon was under way in Philadelphia.

During the Revolution St. Paul's experienced some exciting moments, particularly on a certain Sunday after the British had entered the city. Many of the male members of the congregation were with Washington at Valley Forge and when the rector, the Reverend William Stringer, took for his text the line from Ezekiel 20:38, "I will purge out the rebels from among you," the use of the word rebels proved too great a strain and Mr. Stringer was forced to retire.

With the years St. Paul's suffered many unfortunate changes. In 1830 the interior was redesigned for the accommodation of the Sunday School. The high-back pews were taken out, along with the sounding board and the two wooden angels which had been placed on either side of the choir loft. These latter were happily secured by St. Peter's Church and transferred there. Some unfortunate exterior changes were also made but they were later in part corrected.

Among those who lie at rest in the old burial ground of St. Paul's are John Ross, son of the Reverend George Ross of New Castle, Delaware, and a great lawyer; and Daniel Hall, for eighteen years a partner of Benjamin Franklin in the printing business.

One of the best-loved of all Quaker shrines will be found in Delaware County. This is Concord Meeting House, established as early as 1686 and with the oldest portion of the present meeting house built in 1728. Concord Meeting was used as a hospital by the British following the Battle of Brandywine, 1777.

The Friends' Meeting House in Chester was erected in 1736 but the building underwent unfortunate modernizations in the eighties and much of its original charm was lost. The many-paned windows were replaced with commonplace sash containing two large panes, and the hoods or porches over the outside doors were replaced with porches which do not suit the building. Banished also were the old doors, the original interior woodwork and benches. The porches mar but cannot spoil the fine brick work laid in Flemish bond with black headers. The cornices of this little structure are especially fine. It was at Chester that the Friends established their first meeting in Pennsylvania. This was in 1681 although there was no meeting house erected for twelve years, services until that time being confined to private homes.

New Garden Friends' Meeting, Chester County, had its beginning in 1712, also in gatherings held in private homes but the following year a little log structure was put up. In 1743 was erected the southern end of the present meeting house, although the northern end of the building was not added until forty-seven years later.

Old Neshaminy of Warwick Presbyterian Church, on the north bank of Little Neshaminy Creek, near Hartsville, was founded in about 1726 by the Reverend William Tennent of Ireland, a cousin of the Hon. James Logan, Secretary of the Province. At the same time Mr. Tennent laid the foundations of his "log college" one of the most remarkable of pioneer schools. Mr. Tennent wanted his four sons trained for the ministry. Nine other youths wished similar training and no school being available, a little log building was erected by the minister and his prospective students. These students boarded with farmers in the neighborhood; when no other place was available Mr. Tennent himself took them in; so generous was he in caring for the school that he involved himself in financial difficulties.

All of the thirteen original students became pioneer organizers of Presbyterianism in America. Some went forth to found other institutions of learning and among these was the Reverend Samuel Finley, who established a like school in connection with his church at Nottingham, Maryland. This school is still in existence and has had some famous students, including Dr. Benjamin Rush of Philadelphia, Governor Martin of North Carolina, Colonel John

Bayard, Speaker of the House of Representatives, and Governor Herzog of Maryland.

Another pastor of Neshaminy, Reverend Charles Beatty, is permanently enshrined in the village of Hartsboro, not far from Hartsville, where in 1756 he founded a public library, one of the first institutions of its kind in America, still in existence and still occupying its own building.

In 1741 there was a split in Neshaminy Church when the followers of George Whitefield broke away from the older organization and two years later erected the present church, some five hundred yards east of the old. The two factions were reunited in 1758 in time to give loyal support to the cause of the colonies in the War of the Revolution. In 1775 when the church was enlarged some of the old walls were incorporated into the new structure. The building has been remodeled several times and has modern pews and stained glass windows but the gallery which extends around the two sides and the back reminds one of the description of the original church built across the road—probably of similar design, though smaller and simpler.

During the Revolution, after the Battle of Trenton, when Washington came down York road on his march toward Philadelphia, many of his wounded were quartered in the Neshaminy Presbyterian Church for treatment.

Over the main entrance of Augustus Lutheran Church, Trappe, is a dedicatory stone bearing the following inscription in Latin:

Under the auspices of Christ, Henry Melchior Muhlenberg with his Council, I. N. Crosman, F. Marsteler, A. Heilman, I. Mueller, H. Hass, and H. Rebner, erected from the very foundation this building dedicated by the Society of the Augsburg Confession. A. D. 1743.

It is said that this is the only known church bearing an inscription that designates the confessional document of the congregation instead of the name, Lutheran, by which it is popularly known. Augustus Church also has another point of distinction: it is the "oldest unaltered Lutheran Church in the United States," standing today just as it was when first erected nearly two hundred years ago.

The earliest traces of the Trappe Congregation are found on

March 8, 1730, when there is recorded a baptism by John Casper Stoever, an unordained minister. The Reverend Henry Melchior Muhlenberg, the first regular pastor, did not begin his service until twelve years later when it is recorded that he preached his initial sermon in a barn, on December 12th. In January of the following year the congregation decided to erect a house of worship. During this same month the first school in the vicinity was opened by the church with Mr. Muhlenberg as teacher. Here again we find one of the many instances where the church acted as a pioneer in bringing education to a civilization set up in the wilderness. It was true of the Catholics of Maryland, the Puritans of New England, and the Presbyterians of New Jersey—as we have already seen—and now it was again true of the Lutherans and Friends of Pennsylvania.

The corner-stone of the church was laid on May 2, 1743. On this occasion Mr. Muhlenberg preached in German and also made an address in English. The structure was formally dedicated for religious worship on October 6, 1745, at which time the dedicatory stone already referred to was placed in position over the main entrance.

The design of the little building is rather typical of German rural communities. All timbers were hewed and framed with tenons secured with dowels. Nails, hinges and latches were hand-forged out of charcoal iron. Native brown stone laid on the ground served as a floor until 1814 when some were removed and a board floor put down. After one hundred and twelve years this, being badly decayed, was removed and the stones relaid in concrete. About one-half of the original stones were found intact and are embodied in the present floor.

The church had no stoves but the women brought hot planks and bricks as foot warmers and the sexton covered the floor with straw. The old altar—1795—is still in place as are the original pews. Some of these have carved board doors with elaborate hinges and were evidently the property of the aristocrats. Two are equipped with locks, evidently furnished by the individuals who occupied them.

During the Revolutionary War, on the march from Brandywine to Germantown, Washington's Army passed by Old Augustus. On September 23, 1777, the regiment under General Armstrong encamped in the churchyard. At this time the church and the school house were used by the General as his headquarters. After the Battle of Germantown, October 4, 1777, the little edifice was fitted up as a hospital for the many wounded soldiers. The next day General Washington rode to the main entrance on his white horse; then dismounted, entered the church and visited with his men.

Old Augustus Lutheran Church is now maintained as a historic shrine, a newer and larger house of worship having been erected for the use of the congregation about the middle of the last century. The name Augustus, incidentally, was given in honor of Hermann Augustus Franke, whose son largely influenced Muhlenberg to accept the call to America. While pastor of Augustus Church, in 1749, Muhlenberg had Luther's catechism printed by Benjamin Franklin.

Under a marble slab close by the wall of the old church, the patriarch Henry Melchior Muhlenberg and his wife lie at rest. Their son, Major General Peter Gabriel Muhlenberg, received his early education in the Augustus school and was confirmed in the old church. In 1775, in Woodstock, Virginia, he preached his famous sermon on the text: Ecclesiastes 3:8, "There is a time for every purpose under heaven . . . a time of war and a time of peace." At the close of this sermon, he cast aside his clerical robe, revealing himself in the uniform of a Continental soldier, and declared that the time to fight had come. There were many enlistments that day as a result of this dramatic gesture.

Among the settlers in and around what is now known as Lancaster County, prior to 1730, were many German Lutherans. In 1730, the year of Lancaster's incorporation as a town, Holy Trinity Lutheran Church was also founded and four years later the first house of worship erected. This was a small stone structure with steeple and bells. On the pulpit stood a sand clock, which measured an hour and a half: the supposed limit of the sermon!

With the growth of the congregation the old structure soon became too small and when the foundations were declared unsafe, it was decided to build a new church rather than attempt to repair the old one. On Monday, May 18, 1761, the corner-stone of the present Church of the Holy Trinity was laid and five years later, on May 4th, the new church was consecrated. The building follows in a general way the architectural lines of Christ Church, Philadelphia, but the result perhaps lacks some of the grace of the former building.

In 1768 a bell that still hangs in the steeple was cast in London and in 1771 was built the pipe organ, the case of which, somewhat enlarged, is one of the chief ornaments of Trinity Church today. At the time of the Revolutionary War this was known as the largest pipe organ in America. In 1787 Franklin College was incorporated and among those present at the laying of the corner-stone was Benjamin Franklin. The first president of this college was Dr. H. E. Muhlenberg, celebrated as a naturalist as well as a theologian, who was at that time pastor of Trinity Church.

Although the church structure has been repaired from time to time, no extensive alterations have been made other than the construction of a tower in 1785. This is a very graceful spire with walls seven feet thick, and in places seventeen feet deep.

A number of Colonial officers were worshipers at Trinity, the town of Lancaster having been until 1812 the capital of the State. Thomas Wharton, Jr., President of the Supreme Executive Council of the Commonwealth of Pennsylvania, was buried with military honors beneath the brick pavement in front of the old pulpit. In 1777 when Congress was expelled from Philadelphia and took refuge in Lancaster, some of the members worshiped in this church.

The First Presbyterian Church of Carlisle, sometimes referred to as the Old Stone Meeting House, was begun in 1757 and is a substantial and dignified structure with walls of partly dressed limestone combined with a smooth faced limestone to form the arches and horizontal bands at the spring line of these arches. Owing to a division in the parish, the work of construction was delayed and the building was not completed until 1772–73. Even at this time the members were forced to bring their own benches, no pews being installed until about two years later. In 1785, when the breach in the parish was healed, galleries were added for the accommodation of the restored members. The next repairs came about 1827 when the pulpit was changed from the north side to the west side, the entrance doors from the south side to the east side, and a one-story building erected on the west side for a Sunday School and lecture room.

When the news of the Boston Massacre reached Carlisle, July 12, 1774, a meeting of freeholders and freemen was held in the Stone Meeting House with Colonel John Montgomery, an elder of the church, presiding. The meeting declared for independence and this was two years before the Declaration of Independence. Colonel Montgomery was one of Carlisle's leading citizens, a captain in Forbes' expedition in 1758 against the French and Indians at Fort Duquesne; a member of the Committee of Safety for Pennsylvania during the Revolution, having charge of all the military affairs of the Province and taking an important part in that historic struggle. Another prominent member of the church was James Wilson, a Signer of the Declaration of Independence and later a Justice of the Supreme Court of the United States by appointment of President Washington. As a member of the Continental Congress of 1777 it was James Wilson's vote that became the deciding one for the Declaration of Independence.

During the Whisky Rebellion George Washington passed through Carlisle in October, 1794, on his way to western Pennsylvania, and while there is said to have worshiped in the Old Stone Meeting House.

St. James Protestant Episcopal Church, Kingsessing, Philadelphia, is an offshoot of Gloria Dei (Old Swedes'). By 1760 the latter church had become so crowded that it was decided to make provision for some of its members elsewhere. That same year was laid the corner-stone of the church still standing, then located near Philadelphia, now a part of the city itself, in the section known as Kingsessing. In 1762 the date stone imported from England was put in place high in the gabled front and the building opened for worship. The church has seen many changes; the transepts not being added until as late as 1854, but enough of the old atmosphere is left to make St. James a picturesque reminder of the early

Swedish settlements in and around Philadelphia. In the old church-yard lie buried members of Washington's army killed in the Battle of Brandywine.

Likewise a child of Gloria Dei is Christ Church, Upper Merion, also erected in 1760, a beautiful little cruciform structure of the Gothic style of architecture, above which rises a stately square tower more than fifty-five feet high. At first Swedish Lutheran, Christ Church remained so until as late as 1831. By this time the Book of Common Prayer had come into general use and the Swedish language had gradually disappeared from customary, everyday conversation.

Like St. James, Christ Church has seen many changes. The transepts and chancel were added in 1837 along with a belfry which much later gave way to the square tower which is now so much admired. In 1886 Prince Oscar of Sweden presented a baptismal font in memory of his visit to the church on July 2, 1876.

The first meeting house built by the Friends of Birmingham was a rude structure of cedar logs erected near the Great Birmingham Road. This was in 1718 and curiously enough the house had some provisions for heating in the shape of a large flat stone on which charcoal was burned previous to the meeting. In 1763 was built the plain stone structure which figured so prominently in the Battle of Brandywine in 1777.

This is the western part of the present house, the eastern portion not having been added until 1818. Like other meeting houses of this kind, Old Birmingham faces the south, with small projecting gables over the door. It is but one story in height and is built of the rough stone found in the vicinity, the joints pointed with white mortar. The outside woodwork is painted a spotless white while the interior is devoid of all paint and ornament. Despite the additions which have been made the building today is much the same as when first built some fourteen years before the Battle of Brandywine.

When Washington's army reached Chester County during the first week of September 1777 to dispute the passage of the invaders at the fords of the Brandywine, one of the first acts of the Ameri-

Friends' Meeting House, Birmingham, Penna., which figured prominently in the Battle of the Brandywine.

Photo by Ph. B. Wallace.

St. Paul's Church, Edenton, N. C. The oldest corporation in the State of North Carolina. *Photo by Dixon's Studio, Courtesy J. H. McMullen.*

can Commissaries was to take possession of Birmingham Meeting for use as a hospital for the sick soldiers and the wounded in the impending battle. It was thought that the actual engagement would take place at Chadd's Ford with the meeting house consequently far away from the scene of battle.

On Sunday, September 7th, when the Friends assembled for worship, they found their building in possession of the soldiers. A few benches were taken out under the trees and permission was granted to hold a meeting there, but on account of the rude jests of the soldiers, the attempt was abandoned.

Four days later came the Battle of Brandywine which, contrary to expectations, was fought close to the old meeting house. Several companies of light infantry were posted in the graveyard and under cover of the low stone wall did heavy execution among the advancing British with small loss to themselves.

After the retreat of the patriots the meeting house and supplies were seized by General Howe for use as a hospital for the British. A number of amputations were performed on an improvised table and for many years the dark stains made by the blood from these operations were plainly visible. A number of British as well as American soldiers died there from their wounds and were buried in the quiet graveyard along with those who fell in the attack upon the low stone wall on the day of the battle. Few of these graves are identified but many years ago the yard was thickly planted with the evergreen trees which today grow in such profusion— with their branches almost touching—marking a sacred spot as nothing else could.

In 1825 General Lafayette during his stay in America made a special visit, July 25th, to Birmingham Meeting. To his son and companions he pointed out the familiar scenes of the countryside and then "proceeded to the meeting house where a large concourse had assembled to receive him."

The first Buckingham Friends' Meeting House was a log structure erected about 1706. Although undoubtedly a crude little structure there was no thought of anything finer for many years, until some time between 1721 and 1725 when the building was enlarged by the addition of a stone end.

A new meeting, built entirely of stone, was put up in about 1729, at least there is a record in the minutes at this time telling of the necessity for a new meeting house and the plans being made to carry these plans into execution but with this entry all further mention of a new meeting house ceases.

The present Buckingham Friends' Meeting House, the third structure erected by the Friends there, was built in 1767. The building was called by a visiting Friend "one of the most substantial and imposing country meeting houses in seven of our states." The structure is exceedingly well proportioned and with its walls of warm colored stone, quarried from the neighborhood, its deep cornice, its hooded doorways, its many-paned windows with their heavy sashes, and the white cedar woodwork of its interior to which age has given a satin finish, is almost the same now as when it came from the hands of its builders in 1768. It will be recalled that the Friends' Meeting House at Crosswicks, New Jersey, is modeled after Buckingham Meeting.

During the Revolution Old Buckingham was used by the British as a hospital. However, on meeting days the soldiers very kindly put one half of the building in order for services and many of these soldiers attended meeting. Some of those who died in this improvised hospital today lie buried in the churchyard. George Washington and his army marched directly past Old Buckingham, after leaving Valley Forge, on their way into New Jersey.

But it was not its historic associations that inspired John Russell Hayes of Swarthmore College, to write his poem "Old Buckingham," but rather the tranquil, peaceful life that once flourished around this old meeting house located in the Land of William Penn's Holy Experiment.

Here in the heart of this old, old Quaker shire,
Founded in far-off years by William Penn
And named for his homeland county well-beloved,
This ancient stronghold of Friends has seemed to me
Endeared anew as we think of the vanished years,
The long rich years that have blest the peaceful vale
That environs this antique shrine as with loving arms.

In the Land of William Penn

Early in the year 1739 John Wesley and George Whitefield began open-air preaching, visiting various parts of Great Britain and addressing vast audiences. In the same year Whitefield came to America for the second time, making a tour through several of the colonies and speaking to great throngs. Among the cities he visited was Philadelphia.

Though Whitefield organized no society it is known that there were converts to Methodism who banded together, awaiting the opportunity for organization and the leader who could accomplish it. The leader and organizer appeared first in the person of Captain Thomas Webb, an officer in the British Army, converted under and licensed by Wesley as a local preacher. Probably as early as 1767 he first visited Philadelphia and gathered about him a faithful band of worshipers.

On October 21, 1769, two regularly ordained missionaries of the denomination came to Philadelphia, the first missionaries sent by John Wesley to America. One of these, Mr. Joseph Pilmoor, learning of the existence of a Methodist society there, decided to remain on and further the cause of Methodism in the Quaker City. Mr. Pilmoor preached in Franklin Square and, when the weather would not permit this, in a house in Loxley's Court which had been used by the struggling little group for some time past.

In 1763 members of the Dutch Reformed Church started erecting a building on the spot where St. George's now stands, intending it to be their place of worship. Not being able to complete the structure, after the erection of the walls, the sponsors were imprisoned for a time for the debts they had contracted and in 1769 the church building was advertised for sale.

Among the bidders was a young man of feeble mind and his offer being the highest, he was declared to be the buyer. His father began at once to seek a purchaser who would take off his hands a church for which he certainly had no use and he finally succeeded in selling the property to the Methodist congregation in the city.

The building when first purchased appears to have been a mere shell. For a long time it was unfinished and unfurnished and was only half floored, with rough boards. A wide square box served for a pulpit. The unfinished condition of the room made it difficult for the congregation to keep comfortable in the winter season, and the women were accustomed to bring little "wooden stoves" for the feet, such as were used in the market. The church, however, was regarded as of immense proportions and its size was a matter of comment everywhere. It had been the intention of the original builders to call their house of worship the George Church, probably in honor of the reigning King of England and no doubt this fact was responsible for the later decision of the Methodists to name their new church St. George's after the patron saint of England.

During the Revolutionary War, while the British were in possession of Philadelphia, St. George's Church was used first as a hospital and later as a "riding school" for cavalry. Long after peace had been declared, implements of war and relics of the Revolutionary struggle were to be found in and about the church. When the British Army left Philadelphia the Methodists immediately began to repair their shattered edifice which was now in a worse condition than when it first fell to their lot nine years before.

The first conference of American Methodism was held at St. George's and the Reverend Francis Asbury, the first American Bishop of the denomination, presided. Francis Asbury was the third pastor of St. George's and his first sermon in America was preached within its walls. In process of time the church was floored from end to end and more "comely" seats were put in. The house was not plastered until 1784 and the galleries not added until 1790 or 1791.

St. George's stands as our only memorial of pre-Revolutionary Methodism, "the only structure of the kind which has survived until the present time." The old church structure has been in continuous use longer than any Methodist edifice in the world and it is the oldest Methodist Episcopal house of worship in the world.

The Pine Street Presbyterian Church was built in 1767 and was the third church of that denomination erected in Philadelphia. When sufficient funds were not forthcoming to complete the work of construction, a lottery was held and this yielded some twenty-five hundred pounds. A lottery in those days was a common device for raising money for all purposes.

The original building was of one story and the specifications called for a church not to exceed the dimensions of eighty feet long by sixty feet wide. The edifice stands upon its original foundations, a distinction not held by any other colonial Presbyterian church in Philadelphia; however, in 1837, extensive repairs were made and the single story with gable ends gave place to a two-story church, keeping the original walls intact but raising the top bodily and then building a new roof over the entire structure, enclosing the gable ends and roof of the original building. The visitor who climbs to the loft may see these old gable ends with their circular windows.

In 1771 George Duffield began his pastorate at Old Pine Street. Of the one hundred and ten men who signed the call to him, sixty-seven served in the army during the war. This historic document is still in the possession of the congregation. Dr. Duffield from the first was a stanch supporter of the cause of the colonies and the patriots of the first congress flocked to his church. Four months before the Declaration of Independence, in a talk delivered before several companies of the Pennsylvania militia and members of Congress, he urged such a declaration. So outspoken was he all through the war and so great was his influence, that the British offered a reward of fifty pounds for his capture.

Two days after the Declaration of Independence Dr. Duffield was made "Chaplain of all the Philadelphia Militia"; later he served as Chaplain of the Continental Congress in conjunction with Reverend William White.

When the British entered Philadelphia the Pine Street Church was commandeered for a hospital. The pews and interior furnishings were torn out and upwards of one hundred Hessian soldiers were buried in the churchyard. Later the building was even used as a stable for the dragoons.

When Dr. Duffield returned to Philadelphia after its evacuation by the British, he found a great part of his congregation homeless and the new Pine Street Church dismantled, the graves around the church dug up and the entire burial ground desecrated. The picture presented to the returning pastor must have been a dismal one but undaunted, he again took up his duties and in a comparatively short time the congregation was once more a thriving one. Dr. Duffield died in 1790, a martyr to his call in the yellow fever epidemic, and lies buried under the center aisle of the church.

Among the original trustees of Pine Street might be mentioned Dr. William Shippen, Jr., first professor of medicine in America and Director-General of all hospitals during the Revolution; and John Tittermary, ropemaker to the Continental Army. President John Adams was a member of the church and Dr. Benjamin Rush, Signer of the Declaration, attended services there and his mother was a member. Other distinguished communicants included General John Steele, aide-de-camp to Washington in New Jersey and field officer on the day Cornwallis surrendered; Colonel William Linnard, a member of the company which attempted to prevent the British from crossing the Brandywine, and Colonel William Latimer, a soldier so feared by the British that, as in the case of Dr. Duffield, a reward was offered for his capture.

On the Sunday following President Lincoln's assassination, April 16, 1865, old Pine Street was draped in mourning and special memorial services were held. The pastor during the Civil War period, the Reverend Thomas Brainerd, was a strong supporter of Lincoln and the Union cause, although he always urged moderation and there was in his deliverances and attitude none of the fanaticism of the extreme abolitionist.

Falckner's Swamp Lutheran Church, Pottstown, a gray and brown stone structure, was built in 1767. Daniel Falckner was an early settler in the region now known as Hanover Township, Montgomery County, and was a land agent as well as a Lutheran preacher. The twenty-two thousand and some odd acres of land he disposed of became known as Falckner's Swamp and the name has clung ever since to the Lutheran Church he founded as early as 1700, which is said to make the congregation the oldest Lutheran body now in existence in America. Two log structures were followed by a sturdier building which finally gave way to the present edifice, which has lasted well over a century and a half. During the Revolution an effort was made to use this church as a hospital but whether or not the pastor's refusal to allow this was finally overruled is a much discussed question today; the records themselves remain respectfully silent.

In the Land of William Penn

Along Meeting House Road, between Boothwyn and Twin Oaks, Delaware County, will be found Chichester Friends' Meeting House built after the original meeting house of 1689 burned in 1768. After the Battle of Brandywine British troops in marching on to Chester and Philadelphia defaced the building considerably by firing their muskets into the shuttered windows and into the door. Some of these bullet marks are still visible. Membership has dwindled but meetings are held at least twice a year in the little gray-walled building which has seen so much exciting history in the making.

According to tradition, the first Presbyterian Church was built in Newtown in 1734. The deed for the original church property, however, is dated December 1, 1744, so either the land was purchased and used for some years before the deed was given or else there was no building erected until 1744.

This early place of worship was used until 1769, then the present historic stone building on Sycamore Street was erected. The heavy walls of this church—the east and south walls constructed of nicely dressed stone, with the north and west walls built of stone as it came from the quarry—are still standing and in good repair. The structure was remodeled in 1842. At this time the present alcove for the pulpit was built, the entrance changed to the east end and a gallery built around the north, east and south sides. In 1901 were added the two stained glass memorial windows, one on each side of the pulpit alcove.

In the early days, funds to cover the cost of repairs were occasionally raised by holding lotteries under authority from the state. The following is a copy of one of these lottery tickets:

Newtown Presbyterian Church Lottery—1761—No. 104. This ticket entitles the bearer to such prize as may be drawn against its number if demanded within six months after the drawing is finished. Subject to such deduction as is mentioned in the scheme.

Jno. De Normandie.

History informs us that after the Battle of Trenton, George Washington commandeered Newtown Presbyterian Church for use as a prison house for the Hessian prisoners.

The first Mennonite Meeting House in America was a log structure erected at Germantown some time around 1683. William Rittenhouse, who in 1690 built the first paper mill in America, was the first minister. His son, David Rittenhouse, was born in the old Rittenhouse homestead—which is still standing not far from old Norriton Presbyterian Church—and became the friend of Benjamin Franklin and Thomas Jefferson.

The present Germantown church was built in 1770. It is a stone structure, since this was the cheapest and most enduring material to be procured, and is built along severely simple lines which suggest a Quaker meeting house more than anything else. Its windows are of the many-paned colonial variety and in its churchyard lie buried many of those who were leaders in old Germantown.

The congregation was never a wealthy one but in spite of this fact the early minute books record many instances of charitable acts on the part of the early worshipers. In 1771 a grant of five pounds was made to Abraham Swartz. The same year five pounds was paid for the freight of Jacob Smith, a newcomer, and two pounds for the freight of Jacob Swentzer. These last two men were probably redemptionists, that is, in lieu of fare money their services had been sold for a period of years by the captains of the ships that transported them to America. This practically amounted to peonage—in some sections these poor unfortunates were looked down upon and treated as such—and frequently friends came to their rescue by paying the obligation and saving them from a long period of service.

The present Germantown church is said to have suffered during the presence of the British in Germantown, the officers being angered by the action of the citizens who, from behind the church wall, fired on the troops and fatally wounded Brigadier-General Agnew.

Just a short distance from Germantown Mennonite Church will be found the Church of the Brethren, or Dunkard Church, as it is popularly known. The Germantown Dunkard Church was organized in 1723 and is the mother church of that denomination in the United States. The Dunkards came from Germany to Germantown in 1719. The oldest part of the present church building was erected in 1770. In 1797 the rear wing was added and this portion was further enlarged in 1915. The front part, however, is not greatly changed except that where the round window is now, there was at first a door leading into the loft, this door being reached by an outside stairway which has long since disappeared.

Probably the most important members of the congregation in the early days were the Senior and Junior Christopher Sower (or Saur). The elder Sower in 1742 published the first American quarto edition of the Bible. His son who became Bishop of the Church of the Brethren, was likewise a publisher of the Holy Book.

Sower had so little type that he could print only four pages at a time. When these were finished he would lay the sheets aside to dry; then distribute the type and set up four more. Because of the lack of room in his printery for the storing of the sheets until they were thoroughly dried, Christopher used the loft of the little Dunkard Church for this purpose.

At the time of the Battle of Germantown a quantity of sheets of the third edition of his Bible were stored in the loft and the British soldiers took these pages and scattered them under their horses as bedding on the frosty October night following the battle. The edition, of course, was ruined and only those that had been sold are still in existence, with the exception of a few copies which Christopher Sower gathered from the mud, after the retirement of the British soldiers, and bound into copies which he gave to his own children. One of these copies is in the possession of the Germantown church.

As is well known, many a colonial Quaker braved the wrath that was sure to descend upon him and took an active part in the Revolutionary struggle. Thus Elizabeth Griscom, or Betsy Ross as she is more popularly known, persisted in making flags for congress and was "read out of meeting," and Lydia Darragh's revelation of a British plot, overheard in her own home, which saved the army of Washington at Whitemarsh from a surprise attack, also caused her to be "read out of meeting."

Many of those who were thus publicly disowned remained silent until the close of the war; then some of these outcasts sought to have their Quaker birthright restored. This was a somewhat difficult procedure and could only be done by "condemning the violations for which disownment had been meted out to them." Some did this but others were unwilling to compromise their views; at the same time they had no desire to ally themselves with any other religious body.

As a result of this situation "The Religious Society of Friends" was formed. In their first minute book, in February, 1781, they spoke of themselves as Free Quakers and this is the name by which the group was afterwards most generally known. The new society attempted to include all that was best in Quakerism, adapted to the changing times. No one was to be read out of meeting for any cause. If a member erred the others should endeavor to restore him to grace, and most important of all the changes, members were encouraged to perform civil and military duties for the defense of the country.

The new organization having no meeting house, a request was framed to the Friends of the three monthly meetings in Philadelphia for the "use of the meeting house . . . in common with them, and also to the burial ground." Naturally this request was ignored and when the case was appealed to the Pennsylvania General Assembly the petition was denied.

The Free Quakers now decided to erect a meeting house of their own. A site was purchased at the corner of Fifth and Arch Streets and donations to a building fund solicited. Public sympathy was with the little group and contributions were plentiful and generous. Among those who contributed to the simple building which still stands were Benjamin Franklin and George Washington. Upon this building is the inscription:

> By General Subscription,
> For the Free Quakers, Erected
> In the year of our Lord, 1783
> of the Empire 8

When asked the meaning of the last line, one of the early members replied, "I tell thee, Friend, it is because our country is destined to be the greatest empire over all the world."

Among the one hundred or more original members might be mentioned: Christopher Marshall, whose Revolutionary day-by-day diary of Philadelphia is so valuable; Timothy Matlack, a colonel in the Revolutionary Army and Secretary of the Executive Commission of Pennsylvania; and Betsy Ross and Lydia Darragh whose brave exploits have already been mentioned. Meetings continued in the old building for over half a century. Then the membership became small and in 1836 meetings ceased entirely.

Conewago is simply the church and attached farm of the old Jesuit mission; it is situated near a stream called "Little Conewago Creek," a branch of the "Big Conewago" that flows through Adams and York counties, emptying into the Susquehanna River. The nearest railroad station is the town of Hanover located some one hundred and ten miles due west from Philadelphia. Conewago is an Indian name meaning "the rapids" but since the current in both Big and Little Conewago is slow and unbroken, the exact significance of the term as applied to this section is unknown.

For nearly a century and a half the old stone church at Conewago has been a landmark for the entire neighborhood. For more than half a century before its erection Jesuit missionaries had conducted religious services in a large stone dwelling which is still standing and in fine condition. It is safe to say that Conewago was the earliest Catholic settlement in Pennsylvania. Of eighteenth-century Catholic church structures—aside from the missions of the Southwest—there are very few yet standing in the United States. The Church of the Sacred Heart at Conewago is one of these and although enlarged and remodeled several times, most of these changes have been in the nature of additions and a great deal of the original structure remains.

The settlement at Conewago began as early as 1727 and perhaps before this but since the wear of time has removed all traces of the records cut into the stone tombstones of the old graveyard, all hope of discovering with certainty the names of those who first administered to the spiritual needs of this congregation is lost. The early settlers were Germans and it is safe to say that the adjoining community gradually grew up about the church.

According to tradition, the Reverend Joseph Greaton was the

first Jesuit to visit Conewago and a certain room in the old Conewago stone dwelling is even yet pointed out as the room in which he conducted religious services. The story further goes that Father Greaton, dressed as a Quaker, passed through the Conewago settlement on his way to Philadelphia to found the Church of St. Joseph and this might well be true. Jesuits as well as other Catholic clergymen wore no clerical costume in those days, but customarily dressed as gentlemen of means. In adopting the Quaker costume Father Greaton would simply be dressed like the most common secular gentlemen.

First services were, as we have seen, conducted in the old stone house that is still standing but in 1741 a log church was erected. This consisted of a chapel to which dwelling rooms were attached. Outwardly the structure presented the appearance of a common farm house and in this manner avoided conflict with the penal laws of England. In 1753 this building was enlarged by the addition of another room and the size of the chapel was increased. In this same year Conewago was given its first resident pastor.

In 1763 the Reverend James Pellentz became pastor and it was he who built the present church on the spot formerly occupied by the humble chapel. The new structure took two years to build and was opened in 1787. Father Pellentz dedicated his church to the Sacred Heart, the first church in North America to receive this designation. When he died on March 13, 1800, he was buried just outside the sanctuary, the spot being marked by a marble tablet in the wall.

The Church of the Sacred Heart was allowed to stand as erected until 1850, at which time the original structure was enlarged by the addition of transepts at each side and the construction of an apsidal east end which added depth to the sanctuary. The enlarged building was then decorated by Mr. Franz Stecher and many of his murals are still in a fair state of preservation and much admired. The artist took as his theme the intense personal love of Christ and did much of his work while lying at full length on his back or holding a mirror in his left hand while painting. The spire surmounted with its gilded ball and cross which adorns and completes the church was not added until 1871.

In the Land of William Penn

Old St. Joseph's Church, Philadelphia, is interesting not because of any particularly ancient building, for unfortunately that has not been preserved, but simply because it is a Metropolitan Catholic church located in one of the thirteen original colonies which can trace its history from pre-Revolutionary days. It is the proud boast of St. Joseph's that for its humble beginnings one must go back as far as 1733, some two centuries ago. This is truly remarkable when one considers that the Catholic Church did not commence to get a firm foothold in America until as late as the nineteenth century.

It is from a spot known as Bohemia, Maryland, about thirty miles south of Philadelphia, that we first catch a glimpse of the early Jesuit missionaries going out through the provinces of Pennsylvania, New York and New Jersey, disguised in the garb of Quakers, to administer at stated times to the faithful few, and it is known that Catholic religious services were held in Philadelphia as early as 1707 because a certain colonial minister in another state, who had previously expressed his dislike of the Quakers, further complained about them in this year: "I saw Mr. Bradford in New York. He tells me that Mass is set up and read publicly in Philadelphia, and several people are turned to it, amongst which Lionel Brittan, the church warden, is one and his son is another. I thought Popery would come in amongst Friends, the Quakers, as soon as any way."

Father Joseph Greaton, the founder of St. Joseph's, is known to have been in the city as early as 1729. The deed to the ground bought by him for his house and church is dated May 14, 1733. This lot was near Fourth Street facing the south side of Walnut Street. It adjoined a larger lot on the south side, alongside the Quaker Almshouse, built in 1713, and later made famous by Longfellow's "Evangeline."

Close to the Quaker Almshouse, and far back from the street, so as to be as inconspicuous as possible, Father Greaton built his two-story residence of English bond brick. The little chapel attached was apparently a kitchen "with a chimney instead of a cross" and was eighteen by twenty-two feet in size.

When the chapel was first being built there were some objections raised and an appeal was made to Governor Patrick Gordon that it was contrary to the laws of England, particularly the twelfth and thirteenth of King William III, for a "Popish Chapell" to be thus erected in an English colony. Father Greaton, sometimes *alias* Mr. Josiah Crayton, pointed out that the Charter of Privileges had been granted by the late Honorable Proprietor and confirmed by Queen Anne four years subsequent to the law of William III. *"We are,"* he insisted, *"and of right ought to be, free and independent* of any civil law restricting or debarring our right to religious liberty. We claim the right from William Penn."

Governor Gordon, now somewhat alarmed, submitted the question as to which enactment should prevail to the Provincial Council, but that body was loath to assume the responsibility of a decision and tabled the matter. As a result of this, unqualified religious liberty, promulgated by William Penn, and unlike that offered in any other of the colonies at the time, prevailed, and continued in practice until time and use completely confirmed it. In this manner true religious independence was established in the little chapel with a chimney instead of a cross, forty years before civil liberty was declared at Independence Hall only a stone's throw away. "It is odd and significant," writes M. Maury Walton in the little booklet prepared for the occasion of the congregation's two hundredth anniversary, "that part of the very phraseology proclaiming civil liberty should have been the very same a Jesuit priest used four decades earlier, in insisting on religious freedom."

Father Greaton's little chapel was enlarged in 1757 to forty by sixty feet and enlarged again in 1821. The present church of St. Joseph was commenced on June 5, 1838, and finished on February 11th of the following year. In 1890 the structure was somewhat altered, with new pews and new floors installed, the old pulpit discarded, the columns supporting the galleries removed and the altars reconstructed.

Although occupying an obscure position in the backyard of Willing's Alley, St. Joseph's has come to have a permanent place in the city and today is tenderly spoken of by many as *St. Joe's, The Alley, Old Point Comfort,* and the like. With the change in neighborhoods that comes in any great city, the little church is now, after two hundred years, "back whence she started, obscure, lowly, poor and hidden away from the rushing world like her gentle Patron." It is interesting to note in passing that Count Thaddeus Kosciuszko, the Polish patriot and later the American one, was a parishioner of St. Joseph's.

St. Mary's Church, Philadelphia, was built in 1763 as "Mission No. 1" of St. Joseph's. The enlarged chapel had by that time become too small and it was proposed to erect a larger house of worship to be used for Sunday services. Not until 1821 were the two churches set off as separate parishes.

St. Mary's is a real Catholic Colonial shrine. George Washington and John Adams attended a vesper service there in 1774, the former noting in his diary, under date of October 9th: "Went to Presbyterian meeting in the forenoon and the Romish Church in the afternoon." Washington was there again on Sunday, May 27, 1787. In the new church he first Independence Day celebration was observed July 4, 1779, by the first Te Deum sung in the new nation. The Abbé Bandole, Chaplain of the French Embassy, delivered an address to a distinguished group that included George Washington, the Marquis de Lafayette, members of Congress and the Supreme Executive Council and the Assembly of Pennsylvania. Their presence had been requested by M. Gérard, the French Minister, his avowed purpose being, as expressed in a dispatch to his own government, to win over all the Catholics to the side of the Revolution, by showing them that the French alliance would give them a guarantee of liberty.

At least four times from 1776 to 1781 the Continental Congress came to St. Mary's in official attendance. One of these occasions was the funeral of M. du Coudray, a French engineer officer who had been drowned in the Schuylkill, and was, by order of Congress, buried with the honors of war. The most notable religious service held at St. Mary's was that of November 4, 1781, in solemn thanksgiving for the practical ending of the war by the surrender of Cornwallis and his army at Yorktown. This service was attended by the Continental Congress and members of the French troops under Rochambeau and Dillon, and the armies of the Republic under Washington, and Wayne, and Moylan, assembled in Philadelphia, the nation's capital. Again, by invitation, many of the principal men then in the city attended.

The following year considerable improvements were made in the church. New pews were added and the galleries were erected.

In 1800 St. Mary's was draped in mourning for the death of Washington, there being a special commemorative service held on February 22nd, with an address on the "Father of His Country" by Reverend Matthew Carr, O.S.A., then residing at St. Joseph's.

With the appointment of Bishop Egan to the new see of Philadelphia a brief period of added greatness was opened in the history of St. Mary's with the Bishop's decision to make the old church his cathedral. The building was enlarged in 1810, the west end extended twenty feet and the north side twenty-two feet and it is in this form that the church exists today, although the interior has been completely rearranged. The positions of the entrance and sanctuary have been reversed, the former being originally at the west end and the latter next to the street. This was done in 1886 at which time new stained glass windows were added and a new floor put in.

St. Mary's was from early days ruled by a Board of Trustees which later led to difficulties. An amusing entry in the old Trustees' book under date of February 25, 1811, is probably a hint of the stormy days which were to follow:

This meeting having been convened for the purpose of taking into consideration the best mode of preventing a Mrs. Mary Nowland from further trespassing the Rules of the church, respecting Pew No. 17, South Aisle, the owner of which she has for several Sundays annoyed and prevented from peaceable possession of the same wherefore Resolved and Unanimously agreed to that a Committee be appointed to wait on Mr. Jos. Hopkinson in order to get his opinion of the conduct of the said Mrs. Nowland relative to Pew No. 17 South Aisle, to which she has no claim whatever.

At the next meeting Mrs. Nowland appeared before the Board and offered to subscribe to the pew but the Trustees informed her that the seat had already been assigned to another. The quarrel then disappears from the minute book but the parish was presently involved in another a great deal more serious.

This was the famous "Hogan Schism" which plunged the diocese into four long years of turmoil and strife. The climax came on April 9, 1822, when the two disputing factions met in open conflict at a Trustees election at St. Mary's, during which the railing and a portion of the wall were torn away. St. Mary's was finally placed under an interdict, that is, closed temporarily against the holding of religious worship, and St. Joseph's made the parish church. Happily the quarrel was ended by 1826 when the interdict was removed, although smoldering embers of discontent continued for many years and the church was closed again for a brief period in 1831.

Since then the history of St. Mary's has been a calm and peaceful one. With the encroachment of business and the loss of regular parishioners, the picturesque little brick church stands today a wayside shrine, "gently linking with its memories—the Quaker City of today with its romantic and colorful yesterdays."

A few years older than the church is the burial ground which adjoins it. Here are laid to rest many companions in arms of Washington and the friends and associates of Lafayette. Here will be found the tomb of Commodore John Barry, the Father of the American Navy, to whom the Continental Congress gave command of the first warship it owned, and who brought into the capital the first vessel captured under our flag. Close by in an unmarked grave lies Stephen Moylan, aide-de-camp and private secretary to Washington at the siege of Boston. He was likewise Chief of the dashing corps known as Moylan's Dragoons, and after the death of Pulaski, the Commander of all the Cavalry Forces of the new Republic. Here also lie Meade, the father of the victor of Gettysburg, and Mathew Carey, the "pamphleteer of the Republic." A little farther along the pathway is the son of the Marshal of France whom Napoleon sent as his representative to transfer Louisiana to America.

The third Catholic Church erected in Pennsylvania was the Chapel of St. Paul, built in 1741 at Goshenhoppen, later known as Churchville, and still later as Bally. The Reverend Theodore Schneider, S.J., was the first Catholic missionary to this section and in a settlement that was, like Conewago, largely German, he found many willing hands to aid him in his work. It is recorded that not only Catholics but also the Mennonites and Hernhutters helped him gather his material and construct his church. From France came an old bell cast in 1706 to hang in this "Jesuit Shrine of Colonial Days." The dimensions of the little building are given as fifty-five by thirty-two feet and it is referred to in the old records as "a very magnificent chapel."

An interesting historical fact is the establishment of the first Catholic parish school in the United States by Father Schneider in 1743, many of whose graduates fought for the colonies in the War of the Revolution. The lives of the early Catholic missionaries were not without their moments of excitement. The founder of the Chapel of St. Paul once made his way to New York disguised as a doctor and ministered to the spiritual needs of the few Catholics then living there. This disguise was necessary because the Governor of the colony had placed a price upon his head; not infrequently did the duties of this colonial pastor threaten to cost him his life.

The present Church of the Blessed Sacrament at Bally was erected in 1827 and with what the historian John Gilmary Shea calls "a respect for antiquity worthy of praise," the walls of the old chapel of the last century were retained as a part of the present church. It will be seen, then, that the entire church is over a hundred years old while St. Paul's Chapel, carefully preserved in the rear of the present building, has reached nearly twice this age. The old altar in this chapel is thought to be the one used by Father Schneider, who lies buried before it. In the church will be found several remarkable paintings, among which might be mentioned "The Holy Family," judged to be an original Rubens of the sixteenth-century Flemish school of art; and "The Last Supper" dated 1767, a gift from the ex-Prince-elect of Saxony to Father Schneider, S.J., the founder of the mission.

When the town of Churchville was given a post office in 1883 the name was changed to Bally in honor of the Reverend Augustin Bally, a native of Antwerp, Belgium, who came to the parish in 1837 and won a place in the hearts of the entire community.

The oldest Baptist church in Pennsylvania is Pennypack,

founded in 1688 although the congregation was so small that no place of worship was erected for nineteen years. This, according to the records, was a humble little building which was soon replaced by a more commodious structure and in 1805 another edifice was built which stands to this day, near the banks of the Pennypack Creek on Krewstown road in the extreme northeastern section of Philadelphia, and is a fine example of the severely plain colonial architecture. There is a high mounted pulpit in the front, galleries around the three sides, a very lovely Palladian window in the second story, and the pews have doors attached. Pennypack was one of the first churches to install a stove for the comfort of its worshipers. It is said that one of the factors influencing its installation was the fact that the stamping of the feet of the members endeavoring to keep warm frequently drowned out the voice of the preacher!

The Baptists of Pennsylvania were from earliest days noted for their scrupulous regard for the rights of conscience and played a very important part in the establishment of American religious liberty as it exists today. When Governor Gordon submitted the question of the propriety of a "Popish Chapell" in Philadelphia, the Baptists were among those who came to the assistance of the Catholics, pointing out the fact that all sects were protected by the laws which had been established by William Penn and all were equally entitled to religious liberty. This defense by another group probably played its own important part in the refusal of the Council to interfere and in this manner the high ideals of William Penn's colonization efforts found their practical fulfilment.

Chapter IX

DOWN SOUTH ALONG THE ATLANTIC SEABOARD

Yes, give me the land that hath legends and lays,
That tell of the memories of long vanished days;
Yes, give me a land that hath story and song!
Enshrine the strife of the right with the wrong!
Yes, give me a land with a grave in each spot,
And names in the graves that shall not be forgot;
Yes, give me the land of the wreck and the tomb;
There is grandeur in graves—there is glory in gloom.
—Abram J. Ryan

THE oldest town in the State of North Carolina is that of Bath and it seems somewhat appropriate then that in North Carolina's oldest town should be found the state's oldest church building.

St. Thomas', Bath, was not the first church built within the province as that honor belongs to the first St. Paul's Church, a wooden structure erected near Edenton, but of all the buildings now standing, St. Thomas', Bath, has always been acknowledged the oldest.

The church was erected in 1734 and practically the entire building stands today as first built. The roof is, of course, new, as are the windows, but the old pine dor and the window and door frames are the original ones placed there two hundred years ago. Considering the wear and tear of the years, they are in a remarkable state of preservation. All of the wood trimming for the interior was manufactured locally of Carolina pine, a saw mill having been in operation in the town as early as 1731. Tradition says the bricks were imported from England but it seems more probable that they were burned locally in English style.

The three men who founded the town of Bath in 1705, John

Lawson, Joel Martin, and Simon Alderson, are memorialized in a tablet to the right of the doorway; at the opposite side is another tablet to the memory of one Thomas Boyd, identified simply by the epitaph, "An Honest Man." Just above the door is a brick with the inscription: "Bath 1705—Church 1734." Some years ago this brick disappeared but it was later discovered in the Metropolitan Museum in New York and soon afterwards was returned to its place over the door.

The pews now in the church are quite old but are not the original seats placed there. It is estimated that perhaps sixty early members are buried beneath the crude brick pavement of the floor. It is said that many times this was done to keep the Indians from finding out the colonists were subject to death; also this was the English custom in vogue at the time.

The early vestry minutes of St. Thomas' have disappeared but a number of priceless heirlooms are still to be found there. Perhaps the most interesting is the old Bible, published in England in 1703. It has large, thick covers and the pages in spite of their antiquity are well preserved. This Bible is kept in a glass covered case but the attendant who is on duty every day is always glad to open it up for the benefit of visitors. According to tradition this old Bible was used in the first services held in the building. The candelabra upon the altar were the gift of King George II of England. The original bell was given by Queen Anne in 1710 and at first hung in a wooden belfry standing apart from the church. This belfry has long since been removed.

The old church at Bath has made at least one excursion into literature; having been used by Edna Ferber in her novel "Show Boat." The structure as she presents it is located in Tennessee but aside from some legitimate romantic additions in the way of sagging pillars and vine covered walls, the house of worship she describes is very plainly St. Thomas' and the old Bible unmistakably the one kept in the glass case and observed by all visitors.

The oldest corporation in the State of North Carolina is St. Paul's Church at Edenton, the first permanent settlement in the colony, although not the first incorporated town. The parish was organized in 1701 and the present church building was commenced in 1736; however, construction dragged along to such an extent that the building was not completed until as late as 1760.

The church is a solidly constructed brick structure with the old familiar square entrance tower, on top of which rests a tall wooden steeple. The walls of this tower, incidentally, are some thirty-six inches thick. Very few changes have been made in the building except that during the Revolutionary War it fell into disrepair and afterwards had to be restored; then about 1850 the chancel was rearranged and the stained glass window and altar put in as a memorial to Josiah Collins, the benefactor who made possible the repairs after the Revolutionary War; in the main though, St. Paul's is today very much as it was when first erected and stands as perhaps the most interesting of the several eighteenth century churches yet remaining in the state.

One of the most unique features about the early days of St. Paul's was its system of collecting money for support, through a tax levy on all parishioners, so that all might have equal rights in their house of worship, instead of the procedure usually followed of selling pews to members; although the right to build a pew in the church was now and then granted by the vestry.

Colonel Edward Mosely in 1725 contributed the communion silver that is still in use. In a letter to London written in 1713 the vestry complain that they have "no ornaments belonging to a church." This is in reference to the library of books sent to the church at Bath, which they claimed should have come to them. These books made up the first public library in the province but only one volume from the original shipment has come down to us today: a copy of Gabriel Towerson's "Application of the Church Catechism," London, 1685, bound in leather, handsomely stamped on the back, in gold, "Belonging to ye Library of St. Thomas' Parish in Pamlico."

On June 19, 1776, the vestry of St. Paul's signed "The Test" which was a set of patriotic resolutions protesting against certain features of British rule. This was fifteen days before the national Declaration of Independence was issued by the Continental Congress. Joseph Hewes, a Signer of the Declaration, was a member of the vestry of St. Paul's.

During the Civil War the church's bell was contributed to the Southern Confederacy and became one of the bells cast into four cannon of the "Edenton Bell Battery." In the beginning burials were made in vaults beneath the tile floor but these are no longer permitted and the present floor is of wood.

The first Moravians coming to America settled in Georgia during the years 1735–40. When the Georgia colony broke up, the members went to Pennsylvania where they were joined by another group coming direct from Germany. The two groups combined forces and purchased a large section of land in Pennsylvania, calling the city they founded there, Bethlehem.

In 1753 a small party of Moravians settled in North Carolina, calling the region "Wachovia" to perpetuate the name of the beautiful ancestral estate of Count Zinzendorf who had extended them his protection and patronage in Saxony, Germany.

In 1766 was begun the town of Salem and the first place of meeting was consecrated on March 26, 1768. This was a hall on the second floor of a structure generally called "the two-story house," which gives an excellent idea of the size of houses in Salem in that day!

The second place of worship was consecrated on November 13, 1771. This was also a second floor meeting hall of the "Gemein Haus" or Congregation House, which contained rooms for the ministers and so on. This place of worship was used until the present church was erected in 1798. Thereafter it was used for many years as a chapel for the congregation and for the girls' school at Salem. All of the Revolutionary stories center around this second meeting place. Here services were attended by the Continental forces in the vicinity and here the "Hymn of Praise" for the coming of peace was sung on July 4, 1783; here President Washington attended a song service in 1791 while on his southern tour, and here services in his memory were held on February 22, 1800. Unfortunately, however, this "Gemein Haus" was torn down in 1854 to make way for the main hall of Salem Academy.

The present church is constructed of brick which were burned close by. The original tile roof has been replaced by slate but the clock in the tower is as originally placed there, while the bell in the steeple is considerably older than the church building itself. There is a very interesting and artistic hood over the front door. The original hand-wrought iron railings are still in place on either side of the front steps, which are of stone. The structure stands at the northeast corner of Salem Square, just north of the site of the "Gemein Haus," or second place of worship.

The congregation in time outgrew the old church but instead of adding to it, or erecting a larger structure, new churches were built in different parts of the community. Each of these churches is independent, yet all are united. Each has its own individual board but there are two boards on which all are represented. The old church came to be known as the Home Church because it furnished members for the daughter congregations growing up about it, whose members "came home" for certain anniversary services.

Easter is the main festival of the Moravian year, even more important than Christmas. For the special Easter sunrise service the congregation gathers in the square in front of the church, then marches north to the graveyard where the service is concluded. "The Lord is risen!" is the yearly message given by the Bishop from the hooded doorway of the Home Church and impressively, in the manner of the early Christians, the modern congregation answers, "The Lord is risen indeed."

Ever since the Easter of 1773, soon after the first interment in the Salem graveyard, the annual sunrise service has been held ther. On the "Great Sabbath" afternoon, that is, on the Saturday afternoon preceding Easter Sunday, a special Lovefeast service is held. Large buns and mugs of steaming coffee, with cream and sugar, are passed quietly among the congregation by designated men and women. After all have partaken, the Bishop of the church bids them pray silently for the persons beside them, whether they be friends or strangers. The Easter morning service is scheduled so as to end just as the sun begins to flicker through the eastern trees, but many visitors linger on after it has ended, to view the graveyard, decorated and resplendent.

In going over our list of historic churches we find that many of them are interesting because during some war they were either damaged, turned into hospitals or used for purposes far less glorious, but now we come to a church that is famous for none of these reasons, but distinguished because of the fact that although it was in the very thick of battle during the days of the Revolution, it was not harmed in any way.

This is St. James Church located some eighteen miles from Charleston in that section of South Carolina known as Goose Creek, and the reason it was spared was because of the fact that the royal arms of England were emblazoned on the wall above the chancel and allowed to remain there notwithstanding the Revolution, or at least this is the tradition that has come down to us! These arms still shine in red and gold while the "hatchment" of one Ralph Izard may yet be seen upon another wall.

There is an interesting story concerning a Ralph Izard of Goose Creek Church that has been preserved and while it is not definitely known that this is the same Ralph Izard whose "hatchment" may be seen on one of the walls, this fact seems most probable.

It seems that the Reverend Mr. Ellington who officiated at the church during the troublous days of the Revolution was an intense loyalist. For a time his parishioners sat quietly in their seats but undoubtedly the lion and the unicorn above the chancel must have caused some of them to squirm impatiently.

On one particular Sunday Mr. Ellington uttered the usual petition, "That it may please Thee to bless and preserve our Sovereign Lord King George," but instead of the usual response, "We beseech Thee to hear us," all that greeted Parson Ellington was a silence that soon became protracted. Finally, the surcharged air was punctuated by resonant tones from the Izard pew, "Good Lord deliver us!"

Needless to say, Mr. Izard was promptly warned that deviations from the usual litany would not be tolerated. A gentleman then told the rector that if he repeated the prayer for the King the following Sunday he would throw his Prayer Book at him. The rector did read the prayer, the Prayer Book was hurled as promised and after that the clergyman refused to hold services.

The Parish of Goose Creek was laid off by Act of Assembly, November 30, 1706, but even before the establishment of the

Church of England in the province by law, the Goose Creek district had become thickly settled. The present church was erected under the rectorship of the Reverend Francis Le Jau, D.D., a native of Angers, France, and a former canon in the Cathedral Church of St. Paul, London. Before this, two clergymen had done missionary work in the district, the Reverend William Corbin and the Reverend Samuel Thomas, the first missionary sent to South Carolina by the Society for the Propagation of the Gospel in Foreign Parts.

There is some slight confusion as to when the present church was built. Some say 1714; others 1712; the year 1713 is frequently given, while another group insists that the building dates from 1706. The arms above the pulpit are those of George I whose reign commenced in 1714, while the vestry records indicate that final work, at least, was not completed until 1719. The building was probably started about 1712; this seems the most likely date.

"It was," says a description published in 1820, "a handsome rough-cast brick edifice," with "four arched sash windows on each side." At the east end was a large window against which the pulpit was erected. Upon the sill of the window was the following scriptural quotation: "Come unto me all ye that labour and are heavy laden: For I am meek and lowly in heart and ye shall find rest unto your souls." Above the window was inscribed, "Glory to God on high, on Earth peace, Good Will towards men." "The sides of the altar are adorned with four Corinthian Pilasters, supporting a cornice, and between them are marble tables of the Decalogue, Apostles' Creed, and Lord's Prayer . . . at the west end of the church is a large and convenient gallery. There are twenty-five large double pews on the ground floor and the aisles are paved with flagstones."

This old description of St. James is still very good with the exception that a year or so ago the church was repainted, inside and out, and a high wall placed around the yard as a protection against fire. In 1844 the building was greatly in need of repair and St. Michael's Church, Charleston, contributed the money necessary to do this work. The royal arms had suffered defacement and the artist selected to do the necessary retouching "adhered as closely as possible to the original designs." These arms had to be repaired again after the earthquake of 1886. The communion silver all disappeared during the War Between the States and no trace of it has ever been discovered.

Services are still held in the old building once a year and occasionally a wedding is also held there. Not so long ago the autographed "Book of Common Prayer" of the Reverend Mr. Ellington, the Revolutionary minister already referred to, was found in a second-hand bookshop in Charleston and is now owned by Goose Creek Church. This book is always on display at the annual services conducted there.

Sole survivor of the village of Childbury is old Strawberry Chapel, a little brick church, located beneath the arms of the mighty oaks that surround it, on the banks of the Cooper River. The chapel originally was intended to form a nucleus for the once ambitious South Carolina Colonial town. This was laid out by one James Child on a hill above the river. Mr. Child designated and donated a square of land to be used for a university, another for a free school, a location for the schoolmaster's house and one acre and a half to be used for the building of a church and burying ground.

The plat for the town seemed practically ideal. Streets were laid out, wide and straight, each side lined with great oaks. Today these deserted streets, the great oaks and the little chapel are all that remain of one man's dream of a city beautiful.

Strawberry Chapel was erected as early as 1725, as a chapel of ease to Biggin Church, the parish church of St. John's, Berkley, for the convenience of the inhabitants of the lower part of the parish. As Biggin Church has been in ruins for many years, Strawberry Chapel has been for a long time the sole place of worship for the parish and services are still held there once a month. The little building stands as a link between the present day, with all its progress and accompanying hustle and bustle, and the Colonial period, when time was abundant and leisure no luxury. It derived its name from the close-by Strawberry ferry, which for many years was used by the rice planters on the many fine old plantations along the Cooper River.

In spite of the fact that it was threatened and slightly damaged by the earthquake of 1886, Strawberry Chapel is still in good condition. The balcony was removed many years ago and also the old doubledecker pulpit. On the walls are to be seen mural tablets placed there in memory of illustrious sons of the parish. Two of these were removed from the ruins of Biggin Church.

The silver communion service, which was a present from King George, was stolen during the Federal raid following the evacuation of Charleston by the Confederate Army in 1865. With this was hidden a silver chalice presented to the parish in 1778 and said to have been used by the Huguenots in France before their persecution set in, and this invaluable piece, too, disappeared.

On the old vestry records will be found the signatures of such men as Sir John Colleton, who donated the glebe plantation from which the chapel drew its sustenance for many years; Henry Laurens, who refused liberty when imprisoned fourteen months in the Tower of London, with the immortal words, "I will never subscribe to my own infamy and to the dishonor of my children"; William Moultrie, whose defense of Charleston is eulogized wherever American children study history, and for whom the fort is named; Governor Thomas Broughton, speaker of the Commons House of Assembly; and the intrepid Francis Marion.

The family vaults around the church are said to have been requisitioned by the British troops during the Revolution and no one knows to this day what they did with the bodies found therein. The vaults were used to imprison patriots, some of whom were left behind when Francis Marion put the foe to flight, and were rescued by the "Swamp Fox." And, the story goes, the British also stored their ammunition within these deserted burial places.

The Church of England was established in South Carolina in 1706 and the province set off into parishes. Many of these old Colonial parishes are no longer in active existence and the parish churches have long since fallen into ruins, as, for instance, the old Church of St. George's, Dorchester, at one time a lovely and graceful creation, but others still continue to flourish as in the long ago.

The parish of Prince George, Winyah, in Georgetown County, belongs in this latter group. At first a part of the mother parish of St. James, Santee, Prince George's was set off as a separate unit by Act of Assembly in 1721 and consisted of "upwards of 500 Christian souls, besides Indians and negroes."

The first church, a wooden structure, was erected shortly afterwards at a spot about twenty miles from Georgetown known as Brown's Ferry. Soon it became apparent that the center of population was to be the little seaport town of Georgetown and plans were laid to build a large permanent structure there. It was some time, however, before these plans matured. Finally, the Colonial assembly passed an act devoting to the building fund all proceeds received from the importation of spirituous liquors into the port of Georgetown for a period of three years.

The church was completed about 1750 and has been in continuous use ever since. It is a very beautiful old Georgian structure surrounded by a graveyard thick with mossy oaks, palmettos and cedars and the graves of early settlers prominent in the history of South Carolina. The land on which the church stands was donated by the Reverend William Screven, the first Baptist minister to come to Carolina, and his son, Elisha Screven, who it was that laid out the straight and wide streets of the city of Georgetown, on land granted by the crown.

During the Revolution the interior of the church was burnt, but it was repaired shortly afterwards on a scale more pretentious than before. In 1820 the present chancel at the east end and the tower at the west were added, and a gallery was also built.

During the Civil War the vestry found itself confronted with great financial difficulties due to the fact that most of its funds had been invested in Confederate bonds and these had shrunk greatly in value. An entry in the vestry book shows that the rector left Georgetown on February 23, 1865, and two days later the town was occupied by the naval forces of the United States. Happily, however, the precautions and care taken to preserve the church were successful and its doors were kept open all during this period.

At present the church is in a splendid state of repair and is often referred to as one of the "finest specimens of English church architecture in America." The communion plate, consisting of a flagon, a chalice, a paten and basin, donated in 1750 by the Reverend Thomas Morritt, is still in the possession of the parish and is used on special occasions even now.

St. Michael's at Charleston, South Carolina, is one of the most interesting of the southern churches and it has figured prominently in three wars.

At the beginning of the Revolutionary War, the rector being a Tory and most of the vestry being Patriots, the rector resigned, leaving affairs in a somewhat jumbled condition. Later the beautiful tower of the church was painted black lest it prove a guiding beacon to the British fleet, hardly a fortunate act since black against a light blue sky was a much better landmark than the white tower had been. During the British occupancy of the city the church was used as a stable for the city horses, and the leaden roof was melted to form bullets. After the evacuation of the British and the re-entry of the South Carolina troops, the chaplain of one of these held services regularly in St. Michael's for many months.

The bells hanging in the tower have an unusually sweet tone and a most interesting history, having made five trips across the Atlantic. Cast in London in 1757 they were carried away by the British troops and sold in London as spoils of war. A former Charleston merchant, a Mr. Ryhmer, or Ryhiner, then residing in London, learned of this, purchased the bells and sent them back to Charleston. The moment they arrived in the city the overjoyed parishioners took possession of them and rushed them up into the steeple. Mr. Ryhmer was later paid for the chimes through popular subscription.

Then for over seventy years the bells regulated the social life of the city, calling the faithful to worship and announcing all occasions of public joy and suffering as well as ringing a curfew at night.

In 1811 and 1812 the church played a prominent part in the second war with Great Britain and many patriotic meetings were held within its walls.

During the Civil War the history of the famous bells of St. Michael's almost came to a close as they were sent to Columbia to be melted into ammunition. They were not used for this purpose but during Sherman's march to the sea were discovered in hiding and smashed into a hundred pieces.

There was at that time no record in Charleston of where the bells came from but despite the great poverty in which the parish then found itself on account of the ravages of the war, the rector wrote to a friend in London, a Mr. C. R. Prioleau, to inquire as to the cost of a new set.

Mr. Prioleau, after a thorough search of the city at last found the company which had cast the original set for St. Michael's Church and in their books were recorded the exact proportions of the metal, the size of the bells and so on, and the firm was engaged to turn out a new set.

In the services of this firm was found an old man who had been an apprentice under the very foreman who more than a hundred years before had cast the original set and he, spurred on by the example of Mr. Prioleau, did not rest until he had found the original molds for the castings! All fragments were gathered together and sent to London to be recast, along with some new metal, in these original molds.

And then, the historic bells of St. Michael's made their final voyage across the Atlantic to be returned to the church steeple, where until the installation of a modern fire alarm system in 1882 they gave warning of all fires in Charleston, and where they still hang today! No set of church bells in this land has a firmer hold on a community than the bells of St. Michael's Church have upon the people of Charleston. They are universally loved and no visit to the city is complete without hearing them peal out their sweet tones.

St. Michael's Church was begun on February 17, 1752, the Governor of the state laying the corner-stone. The architect was very probably James Gibbs, who was then at the height of his career, a surmise borne out by the building itself which is said to resemble greatly certain English churches designed by this architect, but not St. Martin's-in-the-Fields as is sometimes suggested.

The structure is of brick covered with stucco. The length of the building with its portico is one hundred and thirty feet and the width sixty feet while the tower is one hundred and sixty-eight feet high. The roof is of slate and the belfry of wood. At the time of its construction St. Michael's was considered one of the finest church buildings in the United States.

At the top of the steeple is a gilt ball, made of black cypress and covered with copper. Once, during a storm, this ball was hurled to the ground below, making a dent in the pavement but curiously enough not injuring the ball itself, which was patched up and later restored to its original position. On St. Valentine's Day, 1865, a shell from the Federal batteries on Morris Island entered the east end of the chancel, causing great destruction, knocking down some of the furnishings and destroying all pews within range and bursting out the panels of the pulpit. Following this disaster the building was "plundered by thieves by night and by day." The United States Government took possession of Charleston during the same month and St. Michael's suffered greatly during their stay. Followers of the army broke into the church and defaced it, breaking off from the pilasters the gilded and carved ornaments, and taking from the front of the pulpit the initials I.H.S. which were inlaid in ivory. Some years later these lost initials were restored by a northern clergyman with the strange explanation that he was returning them since there was no place for them in his church!

George Washington once worshiped in St. Michael's Church while on a trip to Charleston. The pew in which he sat is still pointed out to visitors. Also pointed out is the grave of Mary Ann Luyten in the churchyard. When she died, in 1770, her place of burial was marked in a unique manner, the head of her bedstead serving as a monument. After one hundred and sixty-six years in the open this bedstead monument still continues to give service.

In addition to receiving the scars of war, St. Michael's has suffered from fire, windstorm and earthquake but each time has been speedily repaired along the original lines so that the architecture has very fortunately been unchanged through the years. St.

St. Michael's Church, Charleston, S. C. The bells in the tower made five trips across the Atlantic. *Photo by Geo. W. Johnson.*

Wambaw Church, near Wambaw Creek, S. C., whose ponderous folio Bible was presented by Mrs. Rebecca Motte, the South's most celebrated Colonial heroine. *Photo by Howard R. Jacobs.*

Michael's has played an important part in the history of its city, of its state, and of its nation, and it is fortunate that it has been so well preserved.

On the outskirts of the little town of St. Stephens, on the Santee River Road, will be found old St. Stephen's Chapel, one of the finest Colonial churches of the state. Like that of Prince George, Winyah, the old parish of St. Stephen was originally a part of the parish of St. James Santee, being set off as a separate unit by act of assembly, May 11, 1754. The original church was a small wooden structure, built as a chapel of ease to St. James. The communicants soon realized that this was not a fitting place of worship; neither was it large enough to accommodate the growing congregation. They therefore petitioned for a new parish church, and the necessary act permitting this was passed May 19, 1762. Five years later the new structure was completed.

Dr. Frederick Dalcho, historian for the Episcopal Church in South Carolina, wrote in 1820: "This church is one of the handsomest country churches in South Carolina, and would be no mean ornament to Charleston. It is built of brick and neatly finished. It stands upon the main river road about twelve and one-half miles from the Santee Canal. The north and south sides are ornamented with six Doric pilasters, and each end with four of the same order. Upon a brick at the south side is inscribed A. Howard, Ser. 1767; and on another, F. Villepontoux, Ser. 1767, the names of the architects. At the east end is a large sashed window and the usual tables of the commandments. At the west end is a large gallery, pewed. There are forty-five pews on the ground floor, which is tiled. It has a handsome mahogany pulpit; on the front panel are the initials I.H.S. The ceiling is finished in the same style as that of St. Michael's in Charleston."

The Santee country was to a great extent populated by French Huguenots who had fled their native country to escape religious persecution; however, St. James, lower down the river, was looked upon as the true French settlement while St. Stephens was known as English Santee. Gradually the French settlers moved up the river into the new parish and St. Stephens therefore became but an extension of the earlier St. James. At one time the population of the new parish exceeded that of any portion of the state outside of Charleston.

There is, then, something strangely pathetic in viewing the little chapel of St. Stephen today, with its great congregation swept away by economic changes, by war and by pestilence . . . yet something that is somehow rather noble and inspiring to observe is yet standing there, a silent marker of other days.

Professor Frederick A. Porcher, writing in the *Southern Quarterly Review* of April, 1852, said: "The church tells a story of former grandeur and of present desolation. Though not large, it indicates a respectable congregation. It is finished with neatness, with some pretentions even to elegance, and the beholder involuntarily mourns over the ruin to which it is doomed."

However, in spite of its many and varied vicissitudes, the little chapel stands today in a good state of repair, and happily the ruin feared by Professor Porcher has never come to pass. Regular services were discontinued in 1808 but twice since has the building been repaired and saved from destruction. During the earthquake iron pipes were run through at each end, from front to back, and from side to side, to save the building from threatened collapse. Occasional services were held there from time to time and in 1932 the church was again reopened for regular worship and services have been held bi-monthly ever since.

Among the early Huguenot parishioners might be mentioned Gabriel Marion, a liberal subscriber to the building fund and a church warden in 1765. His famous brother, General Francis Marion, is believed to have been without doubt a worshiper within the church's walls as were many others who counted not the cost personally when the call was made to free the colonies from the yoke of oppression.

Located on a fine bluff on the eastern branch of the Cooper River will be found old Pompion Hill Chapel, in point of location perhaps the most picturesque of all South Carolina churches. Whether approached by water or by land, the spot is a charmed one, and whoever was responsible for the selection of the site had a very keen appreciation of the beauties of nature and, artistically at least, the choice was a happy one.

The chapel derives its name from Pompion Hill Plantation, later corrupted into Punkin Hill. The first building on the site was a cypress structure erected as early as 1703. The funds for its construction were furnished very largely by Sir Nathaniel Johnson, who was then governor. Governor Johnson, an ardent and devoted churchman, was largely instrumental in making the Church of England the established church of the province.

Pompion Hill Chapel is located in St. Thomas Parish. The parish was not formed until 1706 and the parish church not finished until 1708, the original chapel antedating it by five years. By an act of 1747 Pompion Hill was made a chapel of ease to St. Thomas Church and the rector required to perform services in the chapel every third Sunday of the month.

By 1763 the building had fallen into a bad state of repair and the present structure of brick, forty-eight by thirty-five feet, with a slate roof, was erected. Among those contributing to the building fund was Gabriel Manigault who gave fifty pounds and nine hundred and sixty brick tiles for the floor. This is mentioned because after one hundred and seventy-three years of service these tiles are still in good condition. Services, however, have not been held at Pompion Hill for many years and it is doubtful if they will ever be resumed as there are but two or three families to attend. So the old chapel presents the sad spectacle of a church without pastor or congregation, but stands as a precious relic of early days in Carolina.

The parish of St. Andrew was laid off in 1706 and a plain brick church erected on the Ashley River near Charleston. The parish must have been a populous one for in 1723 it was necessary to enlarge the original church to take care of the growing congregation. The structure now took the form of a cross, forty feet long and fifty-two feet wide, with a handsome chancel twelve feet deep and twenty-four feet wide. At the west end was a gallery originally intended for those who had no pews, but afterwards appropriated for the use of the slaves who accompanied their owners to worship.

The church was destroyed by fire and rebuilt in 1764, such portions of the older building as remained standing no doubt being utilized in the new structure, and it now remains as one of the comparatively few structures which have escaped the warring hand of two revolutions. Many persons prominent in history have worshiped in this little church, much of whose history has been unfortunately lost.

The first church of the parish of St. James, Santee, was, of course, the Huguenot Church; later this was merged into the Church of England and, after the Revolutionary War, into the Protestant Episcopal Church, which has come down to our day. The original building was erected of wood about 1706 at Jamestown, a settlement on the Santee River; the second, also of wood, on Echaw Creek in 1714; the third, of brick, on the same spot in 1748; and in 1768 the present brick church, near Wambaw Creek, was finished. This is a fine old Colonial church, now in excellent state of repair and still used occasionally for religious services throughout the year. The structure is without any great architectural pretensions but the front pillars are very unusual, being constructed of curved brick. In late years the Colonial Dames of Charleston have taken a great interest in the old building and only recently a new asbestos shingle roof was put on and the church completely restored and renovated.

The parish has had many distinguished members, among these being Thomas Lynch, Jr., a Signer of the Declaration of Independence, who worshiped in the old church as a boy. In 1773 Mrs. Rebecca Motte, probably the South's most celebrated Colonial heroine, presented the congregation with a ponderous folio Bible and two Prayer Books. These were stolen during the Revolutionary War by British soldiers who conceived the idea of carrying them back to England as souvenirs. Afterwards they were offered for sale in a book stall, where they were purchased by an officer who recognized the name on the cover of the books as that of the lady he had known in South Carolina and returned them to her. Mrs. Motte replaced the books in Wambaw Church and they are still in possession of the vestry and are used in the special annual services held there each April. These services serve as a special homecoming day for many families who are descendants of the early parishioners.

The silver communion service has also had an exciting history;

one piece, thought to have been a plate, was taken from the home of the warden during the Civil War by raiding gunboat men, but was later recovered. It had been given by the captain to a carpenter on the boat as pay for his services. Later on, feeling that it was wrong to have it in his possession, he returned it to the church. The oldest piece of the communion service, the chalice, was acquired in 1756. Another set, acquired in 1773, did not fare so well, having been lost or stolen during the Revolutionary War and never recovered.

The old church still lingers on, a lonely sentinel upon the stage road between Charleston and Georgetown, still pointing out the righteous way to the passing wayfarer, her own children and all others who will heed her advice; the same now as in the days when beautiful ladies, in hoop skirts and poke bonnets, attended services year in and year out with their husbands and families, sitting upright in the high-backed pews that separated one family from another. . . .

Old St. David's Church in the little town of Cheraw, South Carolina, has had a curious connection with two of our wars. During the Revolutionary War the 71st Scottish Regiment, a part of Cornwallis' army and known as the "Prince of Wales' Regiment," used the building as a hospital. About fifty of the British soldiers and officers succumbed to the epidemic of smallpox, which then raged, and lie buried under a low marble dome at the back of the church. A grave close by is said to be that of an English general.

During the Civil War a skirmish took place at the near-by river bridge between the Confederates under General Hardee and the Federal forces under Generals Benjamin Harrison and James Garfield, both of whom became Presidents of the nation. At this time the church was again used as a hospital, and for many years bloodstains, resulting from this service, could be seen on the floor when the carpets were lifted. A great many Confederate dead are buried in the churchyard, along with veterans of the War of 1812, the Seminole War, the Mexican War and the last great conflict. In the midst of the Confederate graves stands the first monument ever erected in memory of the soldiers of the South, an impressive granite shaft.

St. David's Church was commenced about 1770 and finished some four years later. The original building, described as "a frame building, on a brick foundation, 53 feet long, 30 wide and 16 high in the clear, with a cove ceiling and arched windows: the chancel 10 feet by 6," still stands, but its plan has been altered and added to with the years. The vestibule and steeple were added in 1826. In the latter was hung a bell purchased the year before. This being the only church bell in the whole country around, caused St. David's to be commonly called "The Old Bell Church" for many years. The interior arrangements have been remodeled several times and the old square style pews have been missing for many, many years. The building is no longer used for purposes of worship except once each year, at Easter.

For half a century the little structure was kept in repair with funds collected from all who would contribute and the building was used in common by all the denominations. In 1823, when the Episcopalians laid exclusive claim to it, strong opposition was aroused but the finding of the old parish records, proving it to be one of the established churches, showed that the claim was justified.

The exact beginning of Old Brick Church, Fairfield County, South Carolina, is not known. Before the Revolutionary War there was a log church on the spot and the present structure was completed in 1788. Today it stands almost the same as when first built: four unadorned walls of hand-made brick and small windows, while inside may be found plain wooden benches and a small gallery at the back which was originally for the use of the slaves. A wall of granite surrounds the grounds and there are several "horse blocks" or steps of granite which were used by the ladies to mount and get off their horses in the early days.

It was within the walls of Old Brick Church, originally known as "Ebenezer" and later as "Little River Church," that the Synod of the Carolinas, which is now the "Associate Reformed Presbyterian Synod of the South" was organized on May 9, 1803, the centennial of which was celebrated in 1903.

The church stands in a grove of oaks and hickory trees, a short distance from Kincaid's bridge over Little River. During the Civil

War Confederate soldiers, when retiring before Sherman in his march through the state, destroyed the bridge over Little River. Sherman's men then tore up the flooring and sleepers of the church and rebuilt the bridge. Someone in the company was so affected by this that he wrote in pencil on the door facing of the church these words which are legible today:

Citizens of this community: Please excuse us for defacing your house of worship so much. It was absolutely necessary to effect a crossing over the creek, as the rebs destroyed the bridge.

> A Yankee

The war played havoc with the fortunes of Old Brick Church. Out of the great number of men who went out to serve the Southern Confederacy only a few returned. The homes of many of the parishioners had been burned by Sherman's army. So great was the blow from the war that the church declined and finally disappeared from the rolls of the presbytery until about 1891 when it was reorganized by the Reverend A. G. Kirkpatrick.

Each year the descendants of those who lie buried in the cemetery of the church gather to clean the graves of weeds and to consider means of preserving the premises from decay. A copper roof was recently put on the building to preserve it from fire and the window blinds repaired. The old communion service with its waiter, tankard, cups and Irish linen more than a century old, is still in the possession of the congregation.

Hopewell Meeting House, or Old Stone Church as it is now called, near Pendleton, South Carolina, was built in 1789. Colonel Robert Anderson and General Andrew Pickens, both famed as Indian fighters and Revolutionary soldiers, solicited the funds for its erection. General Pickens donated the pulpit and seats and the church was called Hopewell as a compliment to him, the house of worship at Abbeville, his former home, having borne that title.

The building was constructed by John Rusk, also a Revolutionary War soldier and a skillful rock mason. He and his wife are buried in the cemetery of the church. Later, his son, Thomas Jefferson Rusk, emigrated to Texas where he served as United States Senator from 1846 to 1856 and was second only to Sam Houston in the public affairs of the Lone Star State. General Pickens and Colonel Anderson became the first elders of the church, which was truly a product of frontier life, and later John Calhoun was among those who worshiped in the old building.

Old Stone Church is an exceedingly plain structure and through the years has suffered greatly from vandals. The furnishings are even yet almost austere in their rugged simplicity. There is no organ and only the plainest of benches and pulpit. The prosperous days of the congregation really ended in 1824 with the erection of a Presbyterian Church in the thriving village of Pendleton, although regular services continued to be held at Hopewell for some time after that. In the last twenty-five years, however, only occasional services have been held there. The cemetery is still in use and many come to seek the simple marker erected to the memory of General Pickens and some, unfortunately, linger long enough to chip away pieces of it for souvenirs!

A few years ago the United Daughters of the Confederacy erected a rock amphitheatre near the church where annual tribute is paid to the Confederate dead buried in the cemetery.

"The Westminster of South Carolina" is the name fondly given to St. Philip's Church by the people of Charleston, because of the many distinguished men buried in its churchyard and in the vaults under the church; indeed, St. Philip's is a church of perhaps more tradition than any other church in the South. It is not known when the first place of worship was erected but it was on the site of the present St. Michael's Church which was itself erected by the congregation of St. Philip's and continued as a chapel of the mother church until 1797, when the congregations were formally divided.

When first erected St. Philip's was known as "The English Church" to distinguish it from the French Huguenot organization in South Carolina. The present building dates from 1835 and is the third church of St. Philip's erected in Charleston, a second building having been destroyed by fire in that year. This second building was several times threatened with destruction by fire before the end finally came, and was once saved only through the bravery of a spirited negro slave who climbed up the steeple and tore off a burning brand lodged there, together with several shingles which had caught fire.

For this courageous act the vestry is said to have purchased his freedom and the incident became the subject of a long poem which at one time appeared in a great many school readers and was used as a recitation at school entertainments. Although this poem is entitled "How He Saved St. Michael's" the althor was apparently in error here as the best facts obtainable show that it was St. Philip's Church which was saved in this manner, not St. Michael's. The fire in question occurred on June 13, 1796. Like most recitation pieces, the literary value of this effort is decidedly questionable, but no doubt many a young orator was able to put considerable feeling into the lines:

Slowly and steadily mounting, unheeding aught save the goal of fire,
Still higher and higher, an atom, he moves on the face of the spire.
He stops! Will he fall? Lo, for answer, a gleam like a meteor's track,
And, hurled on the stones of the pavement, the red brand lies shattered and black.

Once more the shouts of the people have rent the quivering air;
At the church-door mayor and council wait with their feet on the stair;
And the eager throng behind them press for a touch of his hand,
The unknown savior whose daring could compass a deed so grand.

But why does a sudden tremor seize on them while they gaze,
And what meaneth that stifled murmur of wonder and amaze.
He stood in the gate of the temple he had periled his life to save.
And the face of the hero, my children, was the sable face of a slave!

The second structure known as St. Philip's was erected some time around 1723 and was modeled after the Jesuit Church in Antwerp. The present building follows this second structure to a great extent and is in fact constructed on the old foundations. The chancel end was extended some twenty feet and a spire added to the tower which formerly was topped by a cupola—adding several more incongruities to the poem just quoted! The present building was built from designs of Mr. J. Hyde and the spire by Edward B. White.

The vestry of St. Philip's had great power in Colonial days, regulating civil affairs with such severity, for instance levying fines on those who walked about the streets while divine services were being conducted, that many citizens of the town petitioned against it. As a result of this, some of the vestry's power was removed. A hospital was built, known as St. Philip's Hospital, and did great service in the several yellow fever epidemics which swept the state prior to the Revolutionary War. In addition to its hospital, St. Philip's also conducted a school for whites as well as a separate school for negroes which lasted for some twenty years.

The church in the colonies suffered greatly from the fact that no provision had been made by the government or Church of England for the Episcopal supervision of the clergy who came out to America, some of these latter being outcasts of the church at home and, some times, even men of the lowest character. The Bishop of London finally decided to send out commissaries charged with the general administration of the church and supervision of the clergy. In 1707 the first of these was sent to South Carolina in the person of the Reverend Gideon Johnson to act as "commissary in Carolina and minister of Charles Town."

Mr. Johnson had a very tedious passage across and was finally forced to transfer to a small sloop, with other passengers, to proceed to the town. A sudden squall drove the sloop on a sand bank and some days elapsed before he reached the city. There he found further trouble awaiting him in the person of Richard Marsden, who was apparently not an ordained minister at all but simply an impostor who had in some manner obtained possession of the rectory of St. Philip's and the charge of the church.

In a letter to his Bishop, Mr. Johnson poured forth his distressed feeling, declaring that he had never repented anything so much, his sins only excepted, as coming to this place and describing the people there as "the vilest race of men on earth, with neither honor, honesty, nor religion." Mr. Marsden was finally ousted, however, and the Reverend Mr. Johnson then became himself the rector, remaining in this charge long enough to become greatly beloved by his flock.

St. Philip's was the first Church of England established in South Carolina and, in fact, the first established south of Virginia. During the War Between the States the chimes of the present church were contributed to the Southern cause and were cast into cannon. During this period the tower of the church served as a target for the great guns with which the city was bombarded. Ten or more shells entered the walls, destroying the chancel, piercing the roof in several places and demolishing the organ.

Among the distinguished men buried in the churchyard and in the vaults under the church are John C. Calhoun, Generals William Moultrie and Thomas Pinckney and Bishop Gadsden, as well as many Colonial governors, chief justices and officers of the colony. It has been said that there is probably no churchyard in this country which contains the remains of so many men who have been prominent in its history—in church and state—as does that of St. Philip's.

Huguenots were among the first settlers in South Carolina and there was undoubtedly some form of Huguenot society in existence from the moment that they arrived. In 1680 Charles II sent out a group of these French Protestants to "cultivate oil, wine and silk" and in 1681 appears what is apparently the first public notice of any Huguenot organization in South Carolina: the recording of a warrant in which the present church lot was granted to one "Michael Lowell" with the notation on the margin "ffrench church". The right of incorporation did not exist for many years afterwards and title to property was always taken by an individual, which explains why the grant was made to Michael Lowell instead of to the Huguenot society.

From the date of its founding, 1680, until now, the Huguenot Church has undergone many disasters, having suffered from fire and flood, war and earthquake, but somehow has always managed to survive them all, although the danger of closing its doors has many times been imminent.

The first Huguenot Church in Charleston was built on the same site where the modern church now stands. According to tradition, this first church was burned in the fire of 1740 and all the early records destroyed, but this is now thought to have been a mistake and very probably it was the records alone which were then destroyed. In 1796, however, the building was blown up in an attempt to arrest the progress of the great fire which swept over Charleston at that time. The church was immediately rebuilt but in 1844 this second building was torn down and the present Gothic structure erected. This was opened for public worship the following year. The architect was Edward B. White who also designed the spire of St. Philip's Church.

During the bombardment of Charleston the Huguenot Church was in the direct line of fire and for a time services were held in the Second Presbyterian Church; but when in time the shells also reached this structure all services were discontinued and the congregation to a great extent disbursed to other parts of the state. The church was in poor repair at the close of the war due to injuries suffered in the bombardment, but extensive repairs were made as soon as possible. In 1886 the building was very badly damaged by the earthquake but was restored through the generosity of Mrs. Charles Lanier of New York.

The Charleston church is rich in tradition. It is the only Huguenot Church in America and as such retains even today the liturgy, form of government and confession of faith of the Huguenot Fathers. Its service has always been liturgical, but in the early years, at least, an extemporaneous prayer was frequently interpolated. The liturgy now in use is a translation and an adaptation from that of the churches of Neufchatel and Vallangin, with additions from the liturgy of the Protestant Episcopal Church.

Until 1828 the services were conducted in the French language, but this language having gradually ceased to be used and understood by the members, services since 1836 have been conducted in the English tongue. Frequently in its early days the church was forced to close because of the great difficulty of securing a French pastor.

The present church is famous for its mural tablets adorning the walls, in memory of illustrious Huguenots, the first pastor, the Reverend Elias Prioleau, and the early immigrants who figured so prominently in the early history of Charleston and of the province which is now the State of South Carolina. These tablets have earned for the church the title a "Second Notre Dame des Victoiries," the church in Paris whose walls are covered from floor to ceiling with white marble tablets on which are votive inscriptions.

Founded by sturdy Puritan immigrants from New England and originally a rich and flourishing community, the old Georgia town of Midway is today but a rich memory. The settlement had its beginning on May 16, 1752, and the first house of worship was put up two years later. This was a temporary log building and was soon replaced with a more permanent structure. This second church was burned by the British in 1778. The third church was also a temporary structure but the fourth house of worship, finished in 1792, still stands.

In appearance Old Midway Congregational Church greatly resembles the meeting houses found all over New England but, located not in New England but hundreds of miles away in the southeastern portion of the State of Georgia, the old church has an added interest not found in the meeting houses of the Pilgrim Country.

The Province of Georgia was at first divided up into parishes and the towns of Midway and Sunbury, a port nine miles distant, were in St. John's Parish. In 1776 one-third of the wealth of the colony was in this parish and Sunbury was a rival shipping port of Savannah. The principal export crop was rice, the low swamp lands being particularly adapted to its culture.

The fourth meeting house followed the general outlines of the church destroyed by the British. It was built of cypress, weatherboarded with wide beaded siding and originally contained a door in the north end, one in the west end and one in the south end. The pulpit was at the east end, with a gallery for the use of the slaves across the south end. A window sash from Old Midway was exhibited at the Chicago Century of Progress Exposition. After one hundred and forty-one years of service the red cypress of which it was constructed was still in splendid condition.

In 1849 various repairs were made, the pulpit removed to the north end and the gallery built across the west and east sides. Two of the doors were closed and the steeple placed on the south end. A door to the left of the main entrance leads to the gallery. The key to the main door was lost years ago and a faithful old colored caretaker now enters through the gallery and then opens the main door which is fastened from the inside. No provisions were ever made for heating the building, no doubt as a precaution against fire.

Midway suffered greatly during the Civil War. Most of the near-by houses were burned during General Kirkpatrick's occupancy of the churchyard and later Sherman's army used the yard as a pen for horses and cattle. The melodeon, which had been removed to the gallery for safety, was thrown down to the lower floor and used as a block for cutting up meat brought from the slaughter pen in the cemetery. Later a beautiful table was made from the rich wood of this melodeon and this table now stands in front of the pulpit and is used on special occasions.

Happily the building was spared by the soldiers although the Baptist Church at Sunbury was burned. It was said to have been a structure similar to the Midway Church.

With the close of the war the great days of Midway were over. The old families, with their fortunes swept away, moved to larger towns and cities and many plantations were left uncultivated. Forests grew more dense and the wild growth of the swamp lands created an almost impenetrable barrier in places.

For a time, from 1867 to 1887, Old Midway was used as a colored church, but both church and cemetery are now owned and kept in repair by descendants of the founders and their friends, a committee of five direct descendants having control.

Many famous sons and daughters have gone forth from Old Midway. Two of Georgia's Signers of the Declaration of Independence—Dr. Lyman Hall and Button Gwinnett—were from

St. John's Parish. The latter's signature recently sold for twenty-two thousand, five hundred dollars. Dr. Hall represented Midway Parish in the Continental Congress of 1775, and after Georgia became aligned with the federation he represented the colony. Although his home was at Sunbury, Dr. Hall, like so many others in that town, was an active member of the Midway Church.

The list of congressmen, United States Senators, governors, ministers, writers, artists and professional men and women coming from Midway Parish reads like a page from Georgia's hall of fame, or indeed from the hall of fame of the nation, for the living descendants of the original founders have spread out and reached the four corners of the United States.

Dr. Nathan Brownson, a member of the Federal Constitutional Convention of 1787, was a member of Midway, and ten men of the parish sat in the First Provincial Congress of Georgia, held at Tondee's Tavern in Savannah on July 4, 1775. It will be seen that the Midway people played quite as important a part in the War of the Revolution as those of their patriotic brethren who settled in New England and rallied to the midnight cry of Paul Revere.

The last minister to serve the Midway congregation was Dr. I. S. K. Axson, the grandfather of the first Mrs. Woodrow Wilson and later pastor of The Independent Church at Savannah. Another famous pastor was the Reverend Abiel Holmes, father of the celebrated writer, Oliver Wendell Holmes.

President Theodore Roosevelt was a lineal son of Old Midway, being a great-grandson of General Daniel Stewart, who lies buried in the old churchyard. General Stewart, a hero of the early Indian wars, and General James Screven, a hero of the Revolutionary War, were both honored by a joint memorial shaft erected by the Congress of the United States in 1914. This stands in the center of the old churchyard.

Many quaint epitaphs are to be found in the cemetery. The following, marking the grave of one William Fraser, is a good example of these: "He was diligent about his own concerns, unmeddling in those of others. Reader, go thou and do likewise." One cannot help remarking that this advice seems as good today as when first placed on the old stone marker so many years ago.

Another of the distinguished "dead" towns of Georgia is Ebenezer, the site of the Salzburger colony in Effingham County. This county is one of the original constitutional counties of the state and is today peopled largely by descendants of those early pioneers who came out to make a new home in a new land.

The first location selected was four miles south of the present town of Springfield, at a spot now known as Old Ebenezer. This was abandoned after two years and with the consent of General Oglethorpe a new location laid out on a high ridge within a short distance of the Savannah River. Thus it will be seen that there are really two "dead" towns of Ebenezer: "Old" Ebenezer, settled in 1734, and "New" Ebenezer, settled two years later.

The first building erected in the new town was an orphans' home, said to have been the "first established in America," which was also used as a place of worship until the first church, a frame structure, was built in 1744. This was supplanted by a brick church erected in 1767 and still standing today in excellent condition. The first church having been known as Jerusalem Church, the same name was retained for the new structure.

The walls of the church are twenty-two inches thick and tradition has it that no iron nails were used in the construction of the entire building. For the most part the materials of which this church was constructed were prepared by the Salzburgers themselves, the bricks, for instance, being burned close by, but the money necessary for the construction came from friends in Germany. The two bells now hanging in the tower were brought over by the Salzburgers from the old country.

The church as erected was a two-story structure, surmounted by a belfry on the top of which was a metal swan. A swan was Martin Luther's coat of arms and such a decoration is frequently seen on the spires of Luthern churches in Germany. The completed building is described by an early writer as "plain but substantial and in every respect creditable to those who planned and erected it."

Jerusalem Church is the oldest ecclesiastical building in Georgia and is the only public building in the state built in Colonial times which has been used continuously since its erection.

The Salzburgers were leaders in education as well as religion. Their pastors were usually skilled teachers and their library contained a large stock of books in all languages. Silk and rice culture led in the colony and there are early references to the splendid quality of Ebenezer sauerkraut and Ebenezer lager beer. The people were thrifty and industrious and the town prospered, reaching its supremacy in 1774 with a population of about five hundred.

The great majority of the parish of Jerusalem Church was decidedly loyal to the American cause in the Revolution. Prominent among the leaders in this connection was Governor John Adam Treutlen, the first governor of the state under the constitution of 1777.

Ebenezer was taken by the British in the first days of January, 1779, and turned into a prison camp for the detention of American captives. The church was first used as a hospital for the sick and wounded and later as a stable and commissary. The soldiers fired at objects on the wall, reducing the interior to ruins. Many of the old records were destroyed and the metal swan adorning the spire of the steeple was pierced by a bullet from an English musket. In 1783 General Anthony Wayne took possession of Ebenezer and the Salzburgers were free to return to their homes. They found their church in a deplorable state of filth, but as quickly as possible it was put into good condition once more.

Religious services were held in German until 1803 when through the efforts of Reverend Christopher F. Bergman, the English tongue was adopted.

But Ebenezer as an enduring town was not to be and under changed conditions the leading citizens moved away to more prosperous communities, leaving behind Jerusalem Church as a fitting monument to the one-time glory that had flourished there but which was no more. The main reason for the breaking up of the town was the prevalence of malaria fever in the adjacent swamp region. Also, of course, a great many homes had been destroyed by the British and depleted fortunes made rebuilding impossible.

The church, however, has a large membership at the present time, drawn for the most part from farmers in the surrounding community.

Descendants of the original congregation of Ebenezer have banded themselves into a society known as The Georgia-Salzburger Society and every year, on March 12th, celebrate their natal day with fitting exercises at Old Jerusalem Church, Ebenezer, on the Savannah River.

The First Presbyterian Church at Augusta, Georgia, was organized in 1804. The present building was begun in 1809 and completed in 1812, the first service being held in the new church on May 17th of that year. The main entrance remains unchanged today but the steeple and the pews in the galleries were added in 1818, the steeple not being called for in the original plans. The first pulpit was placed high above the people in conformity with the tradition of the church in Scotland.

It was on December 18, 1857, that the Reverend Joseph R. Wilson, D.D., then pastor of a church in Staunton, Virginia, was called and accepted charge of the Augusta church. The pew occupied by his family is now marked by a bronze tablet, for his son, Woodrow Wilson, who sat in that pew as a boy, grew up to become a President of Princeton University, a Governor of the State of New Jersey, and the twenty-eighth President of the United States.

During the pastorate of Dr. Wilson occurred the Civil War and the separation of the Southern Presbyterians from the General Assembly took place in May, 1861. On December 4, 1861, the "General Assembly of the Presbyterian Church in the United States"—the Southern Assembly—was organized in the Augusta church with Dr. Wilson as permanent clerk. The chair used by the moderator, the Reverend Benjamin Morgan Palmer, D.D., of New Orleans, at this historic convention is preserved in the building today as a relic of that memorable occasion.

After the Battle of Chickamauga in September, 1863, the church was used for a time as a Confederate hospital and its yard turned into a detention camp for Northern prisoners. During these eventful days the building itself naturally sustained considerable damage but was completely renovated in 1892. At that time the side galleries were removed and a choir loft and new organ placed back of the pulpit.

In May, 1904, the church celebrated its centennial anniversary and a marble tablet was placed over the main entrance to commemorate this event. A bronze tablet commemorating the use of the church as a Confederate hospital will be found on the chancel wall.

Shortly after his nomination for the Presidency in 1912, Woodrow Wilson visited Augusta. He worshiped in the church of his boyhood on Sunday morning and took dinner in the manse. Woodrow Wilson frequently said that one of the most memorable events of his life occurred while he made his home in the Presbyterian Manse at Augusta and in one of his public addresses referred to the "delightful memory of standing, when a lad, for a moment by General Lee's side and looking up into his face."

Christ Church in Savannah is the oldest church organization in Georgia, really having its beginning when the good ship *Ann* sailed from Gravesend on the Thames in November, 1732, with colonists under command of James Edward Oglethorpe, to establish the colony of Georgia, for among the passengers was the Reverend Henry Herbert, going "without any allowance" to perform all religious offices in the colony. The beginning of Christ Church, then, is really the beginning of the Province of Georgia.

The third rector of the church was the Reverend John Wesley who assumed charge in 1736. During his stay his residence was on the lot in the rear of the present church and religious services were held in the court house. Savannah at that time had about a hundred and fifty to two hundred houses and a population of some five hundred people.

It was while at Christ Church that the Reverend Mr. Wesley started a Sunday School which is still in existence; under him, Mr. Charles De La Motte, a young man who came to America with him, instructed the children of the church in Biblical truths every Sunday morning. This was nearly fifty years before Robert Raikes began this form of Sunday instructions in Gloucester, England and it is therefore believed that the Christ Church Sunday School is the oldest in the world.

At the beginning of the Revolution the pastor was the Reverend Hadden Smith. He was a pronounced Tory and gave such offense to the parishioners that in 1775 the doors of Christ Church were closed against him and he was forced to flee the colony with his family. Services were discontinued during the war but resumed after the British captured the city.

In May, 1791, George Washington visited Savannah and while there he attended divine services in Christ Church. Five years later the church building was destroyed by fire, rebuilt in 1803, partially blown down the following year and again rebuilt in 1810. The present building was erected in 1838. It follows the Grecian Ionic order of architecture and is a very pleasing structure. The architect was Mr. James Hamilton Couper, a rice planter, who was connected with the church and apparently this was the only thing he ever did in an architectural way. According to tradition, he did not intend the building to have any basement and was very much disturbed when on his return from a trip to Europe he found a basement had been put in.

Big Buckhead Church in Jenkins County, Georgia, derives its name from the stream on whose east bank it is located. It is a plain wooden structure in good state of repair but no longer possessed of a regular pastor although services are still held there occasionally.

The exact date of the church's organization is not recorded but it is known that there was some sort of a Baptist congregation in existence at this spot prior to the Revolutionary War. The minister at that time was the Reverend Matthew Moore, an ardent loyalist who, from motives of personal safety, left Georgia in company with the British forces after peace was declared.

Reorganization of the congregation took place in 1787 and this date is frequently given as the beginning of Big Buckhead Church but it would seem as though a much earlier date would be justified since it is known that the Reverend Mr. Moore baptized a negro slave at this spot two years before the Revolutionary War.

There have been in all four houses of worship on the present site, or very close by. The first was a simple log structure which lasted until 1807, at which time a frame building took its place. Twenty-three years later the congregation erected a brick church but the construction proving faulty, the present frame building was substituted in 1858.

The church has several points of historic interest. It was the birthplace of the Baptist Convention of the State of Georgia, the Hephzibah Baptist Association having been organized in the first log structure on September 27, 1794.

Then in the spring of 1831 at the annual meeting of the Georgia Baptist Convention, a resolution was adopted "to establish a classical and theological school, the main object of which was the improvement of the rising ministry." From this resolution, introduced in a humble little country church, grew the thriving Mercer University, Macon, Georgia, as it exists today, although the original institution was located at Penfield, Green County.

It was, however, during the Civil War that Big Buckhead Church experienced the most historic and unique phase of its long career, and these incidents are connected with the existing church edifice.

A detachment of General Wheeler's cavalry approaching Buckhead Creek, in retreat from General Sherman's forces, found the water too high for crossing and at flood stage. A bridge was hastily constructed from the pews taken from the church and after crossing safely the Federal forces were defeated in a skirmish. The pews were returned to the church where they are still in use today, many of them covered with hoof prints from Confederate cavalry, marks which are held in reverence along with the sacred traditions of the church. Considerable fighting took place in the neighborhood. The church bears bullet marks and a near-by tree shows itself to have been pierced by a cannon ball.

All church architects consider it a necessary part of their education to visit the Independent Presbyterian Church of Savannah, Georgia, sometimes simply called The Independent Church, and a religious body that is really independent in practice as well as name. There was at first no presbytery in Georgia with which it could unite and when a presbytery was organized, the congregation at Savannah continued in its independent relation.

The land upon which the church rests was granted by George II on January 16, 1756, and the grant stipulated that the annual rent, if ever demanded, would be "one pepper corn."

The first pastor was the Reverend John Joachim Zubly, a prominent figure among the patriots of the early years of the Revolution. Dr. Zubly preached a sermon for the First Provincial Congress of Georgia when it met in Savannah on July 4, 1775, an address which won for him the public thanks of that body. He was also a member of the First Continental Congress held in 1774 and a member of the Second Continental Congress held in 1776.

During the Revolutionary War the church building was badly injured and for a time used as barracks by the British troops. In 1784 the building was repaired and services resumed. Dr. Zubly, however, was missing from the pulpit, he having resigned in 1778 after deserting the colonies and declaring his allegiance to Great Britain.

In 1796 fire destroyed the original building and a new church was built. Then in 1817 a much larger structure was erected, modeled after St. Martin's-in-the-Fields, London, and requiring over two years for its construction. It is thought that the design was by an English architect named Jay, although this is not certain. President James Monroe and members of his cabinet were among those who attended the dedication services in 1819.

It was indeed a sad day for all Savannah when this beautiful building was destroyed by fire on April 6, 1889, but the whole city declared that it must be rebuilt. A new church was erected, which was an exact replica of that which had been there before, and it is this building that is standing today. The original structure was of wood and the present structure is of white marble; however, photographs of the old and new buildings are hardly distinguishable since the proportions of the original wood structure were followed exactly, measured drawings of the old work having been made. For this reason, and because of its unusual excellence along architectural lines, the church, although of comparatively late origin, is included in this work.

The spire above the tower is of wood and is frequently pointed out as a model of all that a church spire should be, the proportions of each story being almost perfect. Although the photograph

Pompion Hill Chapel and its picturesque surroundings on the Eastern Branch of the Cooper River, S. C.

Photo courtesy Rev. Wallace Martin.

The Independent Church, Savannah, Ga. Visited by all church architects as a necessary part of their education. *Photo by Foltz Studio.*

might tend to indicate that The Independent Church is an oblong structure, it is in fact square, as are so many of the older American churches.

The interior is roofed with a flat dome, supported by four columns which also support the galleries. There are three aisles, the center aisle eleven feet wide and the two side aisles each four and a half feet wide. The broad and graceful center aisle leading up to the historical pulpit backed by an arched window, strikes the dominant note of the building which is one of simple beauty.

Dr. I. S. K. Axson was pastor of The Independent Church from 1857 to 1889 and the marriage of his granddaughter, Miss Ellen Louise Axson, to Woodrow Wilson, took place in the manse of the church.

St. Augustine, Florida, passed from Spain to England in 1763 but with the return of the Spaniards in 1784 work was at once resumed on the parish cathedral, some portion of the walls of which seem to have already been erected when the British governors had taken possession of the town in 1763. Just how long they had been built at the time work was abandoned is unknown, but historically the present church stands as a definite relic of that change in the flag that flew over the wild and uncharted territory that is now the State of Florida. This statement is equally true if the walls of the cathedral were not begun until after the return of the Spaniards, as some insist.

The parish of St. Augustine is by far the oldest in the land, having been fully organized more than half a century before the Pilgrims landed at Plymouth and for more than a quarter of a century before the first permanent English settlement at Jamestown, and it is its unique privilege to have a full set of records, baptisms, marriages and so on from the year 1594! For many years these records were missing, having been carried to Havana at the beginning of the English occupation in 1763, and they were not recovered until about 1906. They are very carefully kept but are in a poor state of preservation and greatly in need of the help of some rich patron to bring about their restoration.

The history of the parish, prior to the erection of the cathedral, has been set down in only the most meager form; it was known,

however, to be very extensive and early records found in Quere-
taro, Mexico, refer to some twenty-eight Florida missions, not one
of which is standing today.

Unfortunately, in the building of the Cathedral of St. Augustine, two earlier churches, "Nostra Señora de la Leche" and "Our
Lady of the Angels" were torn down and the materials sold for
the benefit of the new church which was finished in 1797, with the
aid of a substantial appropriation by the Spanish Government. The
year 1797 is frequently given as the year of the erection of the
cathedral; but this is really the year in which it was completed;
it was apparently many years in the building.

The original St. Augustine Cathedral was an attractive structure
not unlike the early Texas and California missions. In the top of
the front wall, which extended above the roof, were four niches
in which were hung four bells. One of these bells carried the inscription "Sancte Joseph Ora Pro Nobis D 1682" proving it to be
many, many years older than the most ancient part of the building
in which it found a resting place; other than that its early history
is unknown. The interior of the old church was free from columns
except two at the entrance which supported the gallery.

In 1887 the old structure was destroyed by fire but the historic
walls, as well as the façade containing the four bells, were left
standing and form the nave and façade of the present cathedral,
which was erected the same year upon the ruins of the older
structure.

Two wings were added, giving the church the form of a cross,
the sanctuary lengthened and the tower built. The high altar was
not completed until as late as 1902 and quite recently a marble
altar rail and marble sanctuary steps were added. The main altar
is worthy of more than a passing note, being of the Renaissance
model and constructed of the finest Carrara marble.

A solid silver, embossed sanctuary lamp hangs from the center
of the sanctuary ceiling. This is at least a century and a half old
and may be much older than that. According to legend, it was the
offering of a Spanish sea captain who was in danger of losing his
life in a storm at sea and made a vow that if he reached port safely
he would present a precious sanctuary lamp to the church.

Chapter X

OLD CHURCHES OF THE DEEP SOUTH

I wish I was in de land ob cotton,
Old times dar am not forgotten,
Look away! Look away! Look away!
  Dixie Land.
In Dixie Land whar I was born in,
Early on one frosty mornin'
Look away! Look away! Look away!
  Dixie Land.

Den I wish I was in Dixie, Hooray! Hooray!
In Dixie Land, I'll take my stand
To lib and die in Dixie;
Away, away, away down south in Dixie,
Away, away, away down south in Dixie.
                              —Dan D. Emmett

THE region in Kentucky known as Cane Ridge was the favorite hunting place of the state's First Citizen, Daniel Boone. Robert W. Finley, the founder of the Cane Ridge Meeting House, was, like Boone, a native of Pennsylvania and it was from Boone's own lips that he learned of the great fertility of the lands comprising Cane Ridge and of its many advantages.

It was in 1784 that Finley organized a small party of his neighbors and first penetrated into the wilds of Kentucky. Although no permanent settlement was attempted, the explorers were greatly impressed with the country and in 1788 Finley organized another party and set out once more. Several spots were tried and it was not until 1790 that the canebrake section was finally reached.

One of the first acts of all the early pioneers seems to have been to erect a house of worship so it is, therefore, not surprising that these Kentucky settlers also decided to build a meeting house, which was completed the following year, 1791.

The building was a log structure and after suitable timber had been selected, cut, hewed and notched where it fell, it was necessary for men to climb trees to find the location of the building, owing to the dense growth of cane which was from eight to ten feet in height. At first there was a gallery which was entered from the outside by means of a ladder, but in 1829 the gallery was removed, the meeting house weatherboarded, a ceiling placed above and new benches added. In 1882 more repairs were made, more comfortable seats introduced and the interior repaired and redecorated.

The original structure, however, still stands and services are yet conducted within its ancient walls. The old logs remain where they were placed in 1791 and are once more exposed to view after having worn a weatherboard dress for nearly a hundred years. Various other changes are planned in order to restore the meeting house to as near its original appearance as possible.

Many pioneer citizens are buried in the graveyard which lies to the east of the building. Barton W. Stone, one of its most famous ministers, is buried there. Barton W. Stone was a Marylander by birth but most of his early life was spent in Virginia. He assumed the pulpit of Cane Ridge Church in 1796 after Robert W. Finley had removed to Ohio.

It was in 1801 that the great union revival was held at Cane Ridge with a crowd estimated at from twenty to thirty thousand in attendance. People came in droves from all parts of the state and from Ohio as well and the roads for miles around were crowded with wagons, carriages and men on foot and horseback. Pulpits were arranged at various spots and frequently seven ministers would be speaking at the same time. At night hundreds of camp fires lit up the entire countryside. Conversions were estimated at three thousand.

Under Finley the Cane Ridge Meeting House had been a Presbyterian church; later Barton W. Stone introduced the Christian denomination there. A document dated February 12, 1829, shows that the meeting house was used by the Christian and Presbyterian churches, "but free for other societies to worship in when not occupied by these churches."

The Cane Ridge Log Cabin Seminary was founded by Finley at the same time as the old meeting house and stood about a quarter of a mile away, near a fine spring which is still known as Finley's Spring. Although in existence but for a brief period, five years, the seminary had the distinction of educating a number of men who afterwards achieved genuine distinction in their various professions. Prominent among the graduates was Robert Trimble who became a member of the Supreme Court of the United States under Chief Justice John Marshall. The seminary building was destroyed by lightning soon after being erected and only fragments of its foundation may be seen today.

St. Joseph's Proto-Cathedral, Bardstown, Kentucky, was the first cathedral to be built west of the Alleghenies. It was in 1808 that the episcopal see of Bardstown was created and the Right Reverend Benedict Joseph Flaget appointed Bishop, but it was not until July 16, 1816, that the corner-stone of St. Joseph's was laid.

The architect and builder was John Rogers who brought the perfected plans of the building with him on his removal from Baltimore to Bardstown in 1815. The style of the architecture is largely Corinthian and at the time of its erection the church was one of the loveliest to be seen in the new world. It still is, although over a hundred years of active service have passed since its erection and the episcopal see of Bardstown is no more, having been transferred to Louisville in 1841. The building is one hundred and forty feet long, seventy-four feet wide and sixty feet high. Across the front is a portico with six Ionic columns. The materials used in its construction came from the immediate vicinity; the tall pillars being trees cut in the surrounding forest, hewed, sawed and shaped without the aid of modern machinery: the result is certainly a rare tribute to the patience and painstaking care exercised by the pioneer builders.

Many travelers have been struck dumb with astonishment to find the beautiful Cathedral of St. Joseph projecting itself up before them in the little Kentucky town where Stephen Foster, a visitor, is sometimes said to have composed his "My Old Kentucky Home" but it is not alone its beautiful architecture, its setting, or its age that makes St. Joseph's so interesting to us today, but rather is it because this church stands as a mark of the affection held by a King of France for a priest and his flock who were carving out a home for themselves in the wilderness of the new world.

Bishop Flaget was a Frenchman, having been born of respectable parents at Contournat, a village in the commune of St. Julien near the town of Billon, France. In 1787 while a young priest in Havana, Cuba, he met Louis Philippe, then an exile from France, and had occasion to render several acts of kindness and these courteous acts were well remembered many years later when Louis Philippe was King of the French and the young priest was the Bishop of Bardstown.

In the cathedral will be found nine superb paintings which were the gift of the French monarch and his brother-in-law Francis I, King of the two Sicilies. These are: "The Crucifixion" by Van Brée; "The Flaying of St. Bartholomew" by Reubens; "The Winged St. Mark," "St. Peter in Chains," and "St. John the Baptist" by Van Dyck; "The Crowning of the Blessed Virgin" by Murillo; "Descent of the Holy Ghost" and "The Annunciation" thought to have been painted by Van Dyck; and "St. Aloysius Teaching the Youths," artist unknown: truly a priceless group to be in the possession of a single church in a little country town! "The Flaying of St. Bartholomew" by Reubens is considered the most valuable painting in the collection.

But this is not all, for the tabernacle, upon which is engraved the royal French coat of arms, was also the gift of Louis Philippe while many of the vestments used in the services are said to be the handiwork of the Queen and her maids. On the back of one of these vestments is yet traceable the outline of the French royal coat of arms which is said to have been removed by Bishop Flaget because he felt this savored too much of autocracy for use in the land of liberty.

The bell now hanging in the tower is also probably the gift of Louis Philippe but has been recast, due to cracking, since first given.

There has been a story more or less indulged in that Louis Philippe was for a time actually in exile in Kentucky and sheltered in the rectory of St. Joseph's Cathedral but the tale was

St. Joseph's Proto-Cathedral, Bardstown, Ky. The first cathedral built west of the Alleghenies, which contains many precious paintings given by Louis Philippe.
Photo by Caufield & Shook, Inc.

Hermitage Church, Nashville, Tenn. Built by Andrew Jackson for his wife.

Photo by Wiles.

never regarded as anything more than a pleasant though fanciful tradition by the older residents of the town who actually knew the real facts in the case. The kind acts on the part of the Reverend Benedict Joseph Flaget, which Louis Philippe repaid so generously in the way of gifts to the church, occurred not in Kentucky but in Havana, Cuba, as has already been pointed out. These consisted, among other things, in making up a purse for the exiled monarch, the presentation being made by Reverend Father Flaget.

Old Strother's Meeting House was erected some time during the last decade of the eighteenth century, near Cottontown, Sumner County, Tennessee. It is not definitely known when the first congregation was organized but it is thought probable that the location was one of the first preaching places established by Benjamin Ogden, the first Methodist preacher in what is now the Tennessee Conference.

The name came from "Brother Strother" on whose land the meeting house was built. Several were put up about the same time but Strother's seems to have been one of the best known and most conveniently located—it may have even been the first but this is not known—and no doubt for these reasons was selected as the place for holding the first Methodist Conference west of the Cumberland Mountain Range on October 2, 1802. This, incidentally, is the first mention of the meeting house in the records of the Methodist Church. At this conference Bishop Asbury, whose name is so important in Methodist history, presided, and William McKendree—six months later to become a Bishop—was present as presiding elder.

Strother's was a tiny little church: a rude shelter of beech logs erected in the woods. Its actual size is about twenty-two by twenty-one feet and the fact that it has been preserved all these years is truly miraculous. According to one account it was originally named Ebenezer but all other historians of Methodism call the structure Strother's Meeting House, subsequently named Bethel.

About the middle of the nineteenth century a new Bethel Church was built and the old Strother's presently began service as the corn crib of a barn. This bit of ignominy was not without its good effect for being enclosed on all sides the structure was protected from the wear and tear of the weather.

In 1931, at the request of Bishop Horace M. Du Bose, the old log church was removed to the campus of Scarritt College, Nashville, and there, with a new roof, stands in perfect restoration to its original appearance. The meeting house now serves as a Methodist museum, housing many relics of early church days. Among these is the table over which Bishop Asbury and William McKendree held the first cabinet meeting known to American Methodism.

Hermitage Church, Nashville, Tennessee, was erected by General Andrew Jackson in 1823, on his own plantation, to please his wife. It is a substantial little structure built of brick burned in the same kiln from which the brick used in the construction of the first Hermitage came and, as originally constructed, had a brick floor, detached benches with backs and was heated by two large log fireplaces.

In 1838, due to changes in the boundaries of Hermitage Estate, it was necessary to make some changes in the church and at this time the doors were changed to the south end, the north fireplace closed and converted into a place for the pulpit as it is today. Stationary pews with doors were installed and a plank floor introduced but two aisles of bricks were left exposed.

The church was incorporated into the presbytery in 1823 as Ephesus Church and supplied with a minister. Mrs. Jackson joined immediately and General Jackson "sympathized with her in her resolves, and strengthened them by all the means within his power" but he, himself, did not join. When his wife earnestly requested that he unite with her in partaking of communion at the church, he replied, "My dear, if I were to do that now, it would be said by my enemies I did it for political effect. I cannot do it now, but I promise you when once more I am clear of politics I will join the church."

General Jackson kept his word. His presidential campaigns kept him in politics for a number of years after his wife's death but shortly after his return from the Presidency in 1837, he joined the little church.

· 256 ·

On Sundays the General always said to his guests, "Gentlemen, do what you please in my house; I am going to church," and many times these guests went along with him. When it was proposed to make him a ruling elder, Jackson said, "No, the Bible says be not hasty in laying on hands. I am too young in the church for such an office. My countrymen have given me high honors but I shall esteem the office of ruling elder in the church of Christ a far higher honor than any I have ever received."

In 1841 an effort was made to partition off a part of the church for a school, which would have necessitated the removal of the negroes' benches in the rear. General Jackson did not approve of this and the change was never made and the benches were never removed.

However, without the partition, the little church was used as a neighborhood school for a time and by 1889 was in a most dilapidated condition. It was then that Mrs. Bettie M. Donelson, whose father, Andrew Jackson Donelson, was reared and educated by General Jackson, interested herself in its repair and preservation and gave an "Old Folks' Concert" at the Vendome Theatre in Nashville. Later at the request of Mrs. Andrew Jackson III, who was then living in the Hermitage mansion, the concert was repeated in the church.

With the proceeds from these concerts the church was repaired, the missing bricks put in, the foundation pointed, the chimneys capped, a new roof put on and two windows filled in. Today the little structure is in a good state of preservation and stands as a worthy monument to the hero of the Battle of New Orleans.

The name of Leonidas Polk occurs frequently in any discussion of historic churches of the South. After having been graduated from the United States Military Academy in 1827, he entered the Seminary at Alexandria, Virginia, the following year. Finishing his studies and being ordained a priest in 1831, he first traveled abroad for a time and then returned to his father's home in North Carolina.

Colonel William Polk, father of Leonidas and an officer in the Revolution, had acquired a tract of land in Maury County, Tennessee, which he had divided up among his four sons and where three of them, Lucius J., Rufus K., and George W., were already living when Leonidas decided to join them in 1835.

The four brothers decided to build a comfortable chapel in the neighborhood, to be known as St. John's Church and which would make the "wilderness bud and blossom as the rose." Leonidas donated six acres for the church and burial grounds, conveying this to James H. Otey, Bishop of the Diocese of Tennessee, for and in consideration of one dollar and the love and affection which he felt for the church.

The actual building began in 1839. Leonidas wrote back home for the donation of things that could not be built by hand and as a result of this the silver communion service, still in use today, was presented by the widow of Colonel Polk and the marble baptismal font by his daughter. The donors of the organ, bell and other furnishings are unknown as the parish register, no doubt giving this information, was destroyed by fire in the early seventies. It is known, however, that the chancel and altar railings were made from a wild cherry tree which grew upon the site occupied by the church.

St. John's is described by an observer at the dedication services on September 4, 1842, as a "neat brick church of chaste and simple Gothic architecture; its interior plain but beautiful, capable of seating, with a small end gallery, about 500 persons." The building is set in a grove of beautiful oaks while a cluster of ivy clings to the old tower in beautiful array. In the early days the congregation was urged to select pews as close to the chancel as possible; the rear of the church and the gallery being reserved for the use of the slaves.

The Reverend Leonidas Polk became the first rector of St. John's and the first interment made in the churchyard was that of Rufus K. Polk who died in 1843. The remains of two other of the brothers who helped to build the church also rest in the old churchyard while Leonidas Polk is buried in the crypt of the new St. Paul's Church, Augusta, Georgia.

During the Civil War regular services were discontinued at St. John's. When the Federal commander General Buell marched south from Nashville to join General Grant near Shiloh, his army passed down the Columbia and Mt. Pleasant turnpike running in front of St. John's. A squad of his soldiers gained entrance into the church, wrecked the organ and removed a number of the pipes which they held aloft as they marched along.

During the Confederate General Hood's march into Tennessee in the fall of 1864, a few days prior to the Battle of Franklin, General Pat Cleburn, while passing in front of the church, was so struck with the charm of the spot that he turned to one of his staff officers and remarked, "It is almost worth dying for to be buried in such a beautiful spot," thereby, seemingly, giving lie to the old proverb:

> *No churchyard is so handsome anywhere*
> *As will straight move one to be buried there.*

A day or two later he fell while leading his troops in the Battle of Franklin. His body was first placed in a cemetery near Franklin but mindful of his remarks as he had passed St. John's only a few days before, was later transferred to the old churchyard where it remained for many years. Five Confederate generals who fell in the Battle of Franklin were also buried here but all have now been claimed by their own states and today rest under appropriate monuments in their native soils.

While General Hood occupied middle Tennessee, St. John's Church was used as a hospital. The pews were temporarily pushed to one side and replaced by cots and the ladies of the parish took care of the sick and wounded.

The corner-stone of St. Mary's Cathedral, Nashville, was laid in 1845. Immediately following this, objections were raised by certain people who seemed to sense something sinister in the fact that a Roman Catholic church was to be erected in such close proximity to the state capitol, with the result that work on the structure was delayed.

Presently though, the opposition quieted down and construction went speedily forward. This is much the same sort of welcome that greeted the proposal to build King's Chapel, the first Episcopal house of worship—or Church of England as it was then—in New England, and both churches—King's Chapel and St. Mary's Cathedral—have existed long enough to prove the fears expressed in their behalf to have been entirely misplaced.

On November 1, 1847, the church edifice was completed. Its dimensions are one hundred by sixty feet. A flight of stone steps leads directly to the vestibule, which is separated from the auditorium by a spacious portico. The inside is well arranged and has three aisles separating six rows of pews. The church was dedicated under the title of the "Blessed Virgin of the Seven Dolors" but has always been known by the more familiar title of "St. Mary's."

During the Battle of Nashville the cathedral was converted into a hospital and afterwards had to be refitted and renovated. During the last decade of the nineteenth century the interior was transformed into the beautiful and artistic picture which it now presents. The idea is drawn from the basilicas of Rome, and the brush of the painter, intensified by the symmetrical arrangement of the myriads of electric lights, added later, gives to the interior of the church edifice a splendor that is truly very lovely.

With the passing of the years it became apparent that the Catholic population of Nashville was following the general trend of the city's growth and extending westward. In 1909, with the completion of the Pro-Cathedral of the Incarnation, St. Mary's lost its standing as a cathedral and in the years following became greatly in need of repairs. On October 24, 1924, Bishop Smith once more appointed a resident pastor and two years later this pastor, with the help of the Bishop, began the work of improvement and decoration which was so necessary.

This historic church, which saw service as a hospital during the War Between the States and has therefore become a historic relic of those stirring times, and which was dedicated over eighty-eight years ago to the worship and service of God, still continues to function as a downtown church for the benefit of hotel residents, with its interior once more returned to its pristine beauty, so that today, even to the casual visitor unacquainted with its history, there is a certain feeling of reverential awe as one crosses the threshold of old St. Mary's Cathedral. . . .

The present First Presbyterian Church, Nashville, was not commenced until April 28, 1849, and the building dedicated on Easter Sunday two years later, but the congregation dates from as early as November 14, 1814. The church was organized at the courthouse by the Reverend Gideon Blackburn assisted by the Reverend Robert Henderson of Murfreesboro, and consisted of seven members: six women and one man! This early solitary male member, Robert Smiley, became the church's first ruling elder and continued as such until his death. Apparently the male citizens of Nashville had more important matters to occupy their attention in those days than that of going to church for at the end of Mr. Blackburn's ministry, although the congregation had grown from seven to forty-five, only two or three of these were men.

The first church edifice was commenced in 1812—two years before the congregation was actually organized—and although unfinished, was first used for services in the fall of 1816. This place of worship was erected by general subscription of the citizens and when not in use by the Presbyterians was open for use by other denominations. It was in this early structure, on July 4, 1822, that General Andrew Jackson was presented with a sword on behalf of the people of Tennessee. The building was destroyed by fire in 1832 and a new structure erected the following year.

In this second church James Knox Polk took the oath of office as Governor of Tennessee, with General Jackson and William Carroll, another hero of the Battle of New Orleans, among the spectators.

The second church structure was destroyed by fire in 1848 and the present building completed three years later. The architect was William Strickland, the builder of the state capitol, and the architecture is chiefly Egyptian, with two towers one hundred and four feet high.

The church has suffered from two storms, having been unroofed in 1855 and partially so in 1859. Then from December 31, 1862, until June, 1865, the church was under the control of the Federal Government and turned into a hospital, with the congregation left without a place for worship. The building was greatly damaged during its service as a hospital and afterwards Congress appropriated seventy-five hundred dollars for making repairs. In 1914 a further claim for twelve hundred dollars was allowed.

Mrs. James Knox Polk was for a great many years a member of the First Presbyterian Church. Her portrait hangs in the White House, a gift of the women of the North and South in recognition of her example as mistress of the executive mansion. Her pew in the church is still occupied by her descendants.

The Chelsea Avenue Presbyterian Church in Memphis, quite frequently referred to simply as "The Old Brick Church," has passed through many trying times since its erection shortly before the War Between the States.

Its first pastor, the Reverend Mr. Porter, served as chaplain in the Confederate Army. During that time the upper floor of the church was used as a hospital for Union soldiers and its lower floor as a storage place for feed for army mules and horses.

It was during this period that an incident occurred which reflects honor upon General Ulysses S. Grant. An elder of the church complained to him that certain of his soldiers, when they went to secure feed for their horses, tarried long enough to indulge in gambling games back of where the feed was stored and that he complained not of the church's being used as a hospital for the sick and wounded but that it did hurt him to think of its being employed for gambling purposes. General Grant promised that it should occur no more and promptly censured and moderately punished the offenders.

The outside of the church with its tower stands just as it did when first erected, except for the fact that the brick has been covered with concrete in an effort to keep out moisture; the interior has been remodeled and today presents a very attractive appearance.

Montgomery, the capital of Alabama, is a city of many historic associations. The State capitol building is the birthplace of the Confederacy and a metal star set in the capitol steps marks the spot where Jefferson Davis stood when he took the oath of office. Inside may be found the composer's original draft of "Dixie," the song that quickens the pulse of every Southerner, no matter where he may roam.

It is no great surprise then to learn that Montgomery also has a church that is intimately tied up with the history of the town, the church in which Jefferson Davis and his family worshiped during the early days of the Confederacy when Montgomery was its capital.

St. John's Episcopal Church was organized in 1834 but the first church was not erected until 1836. The present structure was built during the term of the fourth rector, the Reverend Nicholas Hammer Cobbs, and was consecrated on December 9, 1855.

Most churches to be found in Alabama in the fifties were of log or frame construction but St. John's was one of the notable exceptions, being a substantial brick structure, designed by Wills, Dudley and Humbage, a New York firm. The style was early pointed Gothic. The original pews were hand-carved, simple and beautiful. There was an attractive pulpit and a tower entrance, square at the bottom but changing to octagon shape about forty feet up.

In 1861, with the formation of the Confederate States of America with Montgomery as the first capital, President Jefferson Davis became a communicant of St. John's Church. The tall and slender Jefferson Davis made a striking figure with his black broadcloth coat and pants, cut in "Prince Albert" fashion, white shirt and black tie. He always wore gloves and carried a high silk hat in his hand as he and his family walked up the aisle to their pew.

On Whitsunday, 1925, a tablet dedicated as a memorial to Jefferson Davis was unveiled in St. John's Church. This tablet embodying the Great Seal of the Confederate States of America is set in the east wall and marks the location of the pew which President Davis and his family occupied. The tablet reads: "IN MEMORIAM JEFFERSON DAVIS PRESIDENT OF CONFEDERATE STATES OF AMERICA A COMMUNICANT OF SAINT JOHN'S CHURCH WHILE RESIDING IN MONTGOMERY 1861."

A very interesting historical program was printed for this occasion, containing personal recollections of President Davis by Mrs. Mary Phelan Watt, reading in part:

Among the treasured recollections of the days that are gone is that of seeing President Jefferson Davis and his family walk up the aisle of

St. John's to Mr. Davis's pew, about the middle of the church on the right center aisle. . . . I saw him in his pew at St. John's regularly during the months when the capital of the Confederacy was at Montgomery. Generally he was accompanied by his wife (formerly Varina Howell of Natchez) and by two small children.

As soon as Mr. Davis and his little family entered their pew all devoutly kneeled and recited the brief prayer customary among church people. He and his wife followed closely the services as found in the Book of Common Prayer and their voices mingled audibly with the congregation's responses. He was very devout in his devotions, and never left the church until the benediction had been pronounced. Then with quiet dignity he moved with his family down the aisle, receiving and returning in kindly spirit the greetings of his fellow worshipers, many of them high dignitaries of the Confederate Government, and others just friends and neighbors.

As long as the Confederate capital was at Montgomery, Mr. Davis was a regular communicant of St. John's.

A most historic Prayer Book was used in the dedication services, one of four ordered as samples by a publisher during the war. One he gave to General Robert E. Lee and another to President Davis. It is not known to whom he presented the other two. A thousand dollar order for these Prayer Books was sent in but the shipment was confiscated and the four samples were the only ones that got through the lines; for this reason they were always known as the thousand dollar Prayer Books. President Davis gave the copy presented to him to Thomas Hill Watts, Attorney General in his cabinet, and it is today owned by his granddaughter, Mrs. Albert James Pickett of Montgomery.

In the program prepared for the dedication is a very fine photograph of Jefferson Davis with the inscription "The Man Whose Only Sin Was We Made Him Leader."

During the period of the Confederacy a prayer for the President of the Confederate States of America was always included in services at St. John's. Following the fall of the Confederate Government, Bishop Wilmer of Alabama directed all Episcopal clergy to omit this prayer and further stated that when civil authority had been restored the prayer for the President of the United States should be used. When the Federal troops attempted to enforce this provision in 1865, the Bishop refused to direct the

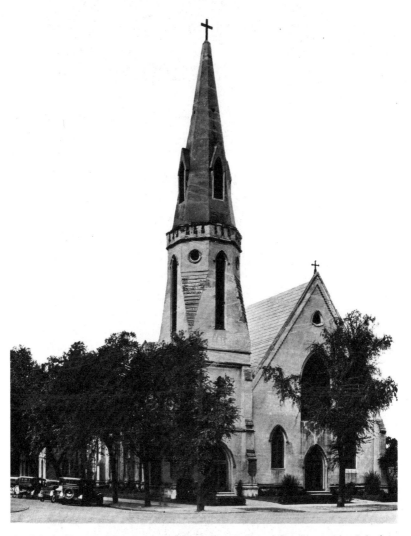

St. John's Church, Montgomery, Ala., where Jefferson Davis worshiped during the early days of the Confederacy. *Photo by Sexton's Studio.*

College Hill Presbyterian Church, College Hill, Miss. Built by early pioneers alongside the old Indian Trail.

Photo by Cofield's Studio, courtesy Mrs. J. B. Anderson.

use of the prayer at the dictation of the military authority, or while the state was under military control. As a consequence St. John's was closed by the troops. Stirring days now set in for the church. The congregation attempted to meet in Hammer Hall, a school building, but were dispersed by soldiers at the point of the bayonet. In spite of this, services were regularly held in private houses until, finally, Bishop Wilmer won out in his contention, the order closing the church was rescinded and regular services resumed.

Trinity Church, Natchez, Mississippi, is now twelve years beyond the century mark, having been organized in 1822 and the church structure completed the following year. The building was an oblong one, topped with a large tin covered dome which glistened in the sunlight and could be seen for a great distance, earning for the building the title of "Round Top Church."

Prominent among the early vestrymen was Joseph Emory Davis, brother of Jefferson Davis, who came to Natchez in 1820 to practice law. During the period 1824–26 he was President of the Board of Trustees of Trinity Church.

In 1827 it was decided to erect an additional gallery for the accommodation of the choir and to appropriate "the present spacious and convenient one solely for the use of such well disposed people of color and servants as are desirous of being instructed in the knowledge of God, the principles of the church and the genuine duties of piety and religion." It was not, however, until 1838 that any extensive repairs took place. At this time revolutionary changes were made, both inside and out, and two years later, on Easter Sunday, the building was reconsecrated by the Right Reverend Leonidas Polk, then missionary Bishop of Arkansas and Bishop in charge of Mississippi.

These repairs occurred during the pastorate of the Reverend David C. Page. It was the Reverend Mr. Page who officiated at the marriage of Miss Varina Howell and Hon. Jefferson Davis, who were not long afterwards to become the First Lady and Chief Executive of the Confederacy. In 1826 Varina Howell had been baptized in the church and in 1823 her parents, William Burr Howell and Margaret Louisa Kempe, had been married there.

The Reverend Albert A. Muller officiated at this wedding and Joseph Emory Davis acted as best man.

During the Civil War the members of the church, of course, rallied to the Southern cause and the bell of Old Trinity was offered as metal to be molded into cannon. This bell, however, was never used for this purpose. After the war came the Reverend Charles B. Dana to act as rector during the most trying period of all, the early days of post-war reconstruction. Fortunes had been swept away and much work had to be done before the depressed condition of the parish showed any improvement. Dr. Dana was for many years the rector of Christ Church, Alexandria, Virginia, and at that time it was his distinguished honor to present General Robert E. Lee to his Bishop for confirmation.

From then on the history of Trinity Church has been a particularly happy one. Various changes have been made in the building from time to time, the beautiful recess chancel added and a parish house erected. The exterior alterations and repairs were not so successful but happily at the close of the World War, to which the congregation contributed a generous quota of young men, it was decided to restore the columns and steps of the front of the church to their original Greek form, which has now been done.

Another Mississippi church built about the same time as Trinity is St. Paul's Episcopal Church at Woodville, the frame of which was raised on the 9th of September, 1824. The records of this church are not in very good condition so that much of the history of the parish has been lost. It is recorded, however, that the church contributed its bell to the cause of the Confederacy, to be "melted into cannon for the defense of our wives and children, homes and property," as the old resolution reads. Jefferson Davis lived for a time near Woodville and worshiped in St. Paul's. Several of his relatives were communicants. Woodville no doubt had many an exciting moment during the War Between the States. Alongside the record of the visitation of the Right Reverend Wm. M. Green, D.D., in October, 1864, is written "Yankee alarm during the visitation.—W.F.A." That is all—but it hints at much more that has unfortunately not been preserved.

Old Churches of the Deep South

It was nearly a hundred years ago that a certain group of brave pioneers left their but recently made homes in Tennessee and set out in their ox wagons for the newly opened up strip of Indian country embracing the northern portion of the State of Mississippi. These sturdy immigrants settled in the neighborhood of what is now the village of College Hill and one of their first acts was to build a temporary log meeting house alongside the ancient Indian trail which ran by the spot they had chosen as their home. A few years later work was commenced on a permanent structure which would bear comparison with the churches they had known back in the Carolinas before emigrating to Tennessee.

The bricks were burned close by and the lumber sawed and polished by hand. The building which they erected is still standing today and its splendid state of preservation after about eighty-five years of constant use is a rare tribute to its early builders who did their work so well.

The land for the church and burial grounds was contributed by Captain Goodloe W. Buford, the first white settler in the neighborhood. There were, in fact, six Buford brothers who settled in the vicinity of what is now College Hill. The land was thickly timbered and Indian tents, mud huts and cabins were to be seen at frequent intervals.

The church erected was rectangular in shape with a spacious vestibule supported by large Doric columns, the architecture of the "Old South" so richly developed in Virginia and in the Carolinas from where the builders of this church came. Down the center of the interior ran a row of heavy columns supporting the ceiling. At one end was a platform and pulpit; at the rear a spacious balcony which was for the use of the slaves accompanying their masters to church. The old family high-backed pews are still in use, each pew having an entrance door from the aisle, equipped with a strong latch. This was so any children who grew restless could not run out into the aisles and disturb the services.

After the erection of the church the members of the College Hill community also erected a school consisting of two brick buildings, one for the boys and one for the girls, for coeducation was not practiced in those days. This Presbyterian academy was the first school of higher learning in northern Mississippi and long before the establishment of the university at Oxford, this old school was the educational center of the state. Many men who went forth to battle in the Mexican War and in the War Between the States were educated there. The home of Reverend Dr. Wallace, for a number of years the President of the school as well as pastor of the church, is still standing, but all trace of the two buildings of the academy is gone.

In the rear of the church is the old cemetery. It is very well kept and beautiful monuments mark the last resting places of the founders and early members, who brought civilization to northern Mississippi. Here are buried Captain Goodloe W. Buford and Reverend Mr. Mecklin, an early pastor, whose family settled historic Mecklinburg County, North Carolina, sometimes referred to as the "Birthplace of American Liberty." The bodies of twenty Confederate soldiers who fell on the battlefields of the South were brought back to the church after the war and buried in the cemetery side by side with their ancestors.

On December 1, 1862, General Sherman with a force of more than thirty thousand men invaded the community and took over the church as living quarters. The yards and burial grounds were dotted with tents, camp fires, and soldiers with sabers and bayonets. Later General Grant's forces, on their way to Vicksburg, camped near the church.

Only recently a very interesting bit of history connected with this period has come to light. A former resident of College Hill advertised in a Chicago paper in an effort to locate some relics and family heirlooms of his family carried away when his home was ransacked during the war period.

An old Union soldier, in his nineties, read the advertisement and answered that he had none of the relics in question but that he did have a diploma issued by the University of Mississippi, which he had picked up near College Hill while marching with Grant's Army to Vicksburg!

The diploma, bearing the signature of the famed Lucius Q. C. Lamar, was one issued to the son-in-law of Captain Goodloe W.

Buford, Jacobus Jones Quarles, honor man of the class of 1851 at Ole Miss. It turned out that this diploma was the first ever given by the University of Mississippi and it is now in the hands of the son of the man to whom it was issued. This son incidentally was one of the framers of the Oklahoma Constitution and is now a resident of that state. Thus does the shadow of the old church at College Hill reach out and cast its influence on neighboring states and on the nation.

The old town of Washington is often called the "Cradle of Arkansas History" and many of the good people of that state are descendants of the early Washington pioneers.

In the old town may be seen the very tavern—now degenerated into a private dwelling—in which Sam Houston drank raw whisky and dreamed of a liberated Texas; here also may be seen the home of W. H. Etter, founder of the Washington "Telegraph," the oldest weekly newspaper west of the Mississippi and which has had continuous publication since its start. In Washington lingered Davy Crockett and William B. Travis to partake of the hospitality of the town and here lived James Black, named by some as the inventor of the Bowie knife.

In 1863 Washington became the Civil War capital of Arkansas and many precious relics of this period are yet to be seen, particularly the old Civil War Capitol building which has recently been restored, largely through the efforts of Mrs. Charlean Moss Williams, who has done much in the way of helping to preserve the town's historic landmarks. It was in the old capitol, incidentally, that Sam Houston and his council are said to have planned the revolt of Texas!

Probably none of Washington's landmarks is regarded with so much reverence as the old Baptist Church, erected some time around the year 1830 and still in use today. Prominent among the founders was John H. Toland, one of the early pioneers of the state.

During the Civil War this old church became a Confederate hospital and the good women of the congregation took care of the sick and wounded soldiers. Many were saved but many passed on and were buried in a corner of the Presbyterian cemetery not far away. Their valor is today commemorated by a beautiful monument erected some years ago.

In the old Washington Baptist Church the first negro school of the state was organized, right after the War Between the States, by a teacher from the North. It was not very successful at first, however, because the young negroes of the community were so adverse to the idea that they fled to the woods and had to be hunted down and led back into the building!

On April 6, 1932, the state convention of the Daughters of the American Revolution met in the church and afterwards adjourned to the "old" cemetery to conduct memorial services over the graves of five Revolutionary soldiers who are buried there. The "old" cemetery contains graves dating from 1799 and the "new" cemetery, from 1860. Most of the graves were removed from the "old" cemetery about thirty years ago when a Mr. Wiederman claimed the land and threatened to plant the spot in corn. This man was later adjudged insane but not before many persons had moved the bodies of their relatives.

The old Washington Church formerly had a square belfry adorning the front of the building but this was removed several years ago. The porch columns are of hand-hewn pine, and measure about twenty inches thick, with the exception of the one at the extreme left of the porch which is constructed of machine-hewn planks. The story goes that during the war it was necessary to remove this column and use it as firewood to help keep warm the sick and wounded soldiers inside the church and that it was afterwards replaced in the present manner.

Grace Church, St. Francisville, Louisiana, was organized in 1827 and the first church was an exceedingly plain brick structure, unplastered and unceiled, with a balcony for the slaves who worshiped with their masters. Later the simple building was ceiled, plastered and painted and for thirty years served as a worshiping place for the faithful. In 1858 plans were laid for a much handsomer building in early English style, rather severely plain, "without tracery or clustered columns, but beautiful in its chaste simplicity and admirable proportions. Set amidst carefully laid out grounds, planted with live oak and other trees, it only required time to make it an object of rare beauty and interest."

This building was opened for service April 28, 1860, and it is hardly possible that any of the thankful worshipers in the church that day realized that in a few short years much of their work would be lost for, during the War Between the States, the sacred structure was a target for the Federal gunboats on the Mississippi. Several shells passed through its walls and its furniture was entirely destroyed. In this way the church became a relic of war on the river during the Civil War period of our history and as such it may be regarded today.

At the close of the war the rector, despairing of repairing the structure, accepted another call and it was not until 1883, under the rectorship of the Reverend A. Gordon Blakewell, that the half-wrecked Grace Church was restored to its former appearance. This was done with great fidelity to detail and with discriminating taste, and the church today is indeed very beautiful. There is a grove of live oaks in front, festooned with gray garlands of southern moss, and the cemetery lying on the side and at the rear is adorned with beautiful trees as well as tasteful monuments and richly growing flowers. The setting is a perfect one for a house of worship and the impression gained from a first view of the church lasts a long time.

If we could turn time backward and drop in on the City of New Orleans on January 23, 1815, we would find the place wild with joy because of the glorious victory achieved by General Andrew Jackson over the British forces led by General Pakenham! Let us imagine ourselves doing that and attempt to re-create a picture of what took place. . . .

Citizens of all creeds have gathered to celebrate and in the square in front of the St. Louis Cathedral a triumphal arch has been erected. Extending out from this arch, arranged at proper intervals, are two rows of young ladies of the city, attired in flowing white veils, a silver star gleaming on their foreheads! In one hand they carry a flag on which is written the name of the state they represent; in the other a basket of flowers trimmed with blue ribbons. Behind each is a shield, also inscribed with the name of a state and held upright with the aid of an attached lance stuck in the ground. Both rows are linked together with verdant festoons which form a lane leading from the arch to the doors of the historic cathedral itself.

And then there is heard the boom of artillery together with military music, and faces grow expectant and eager.

Suddenly the crowd screams forth its approval and handkerchiefs and flags are waved excitedly. General Jackson has passed under the triumphal arch and has now started down the lane leading to the cathedral.

At a given signal hundreds of children start singing and presently the whole crowd joins in with them in repeating the words of the famous song:

> *Hail to the chief! who hied at war's alarms,*
> *To save our threaten'd land from hostile arms,*
> *.... Jackson, all hail! our country's pride and boast....*
> *Remembrance long shall keep alive thy fame,*
> *And future infants learn to lisp thy name.*

At the door of the cathedral the returning hero is welcomed by Abbé Dubourg and presented with a wreath of laurel. Modestly he accepts it, "Reverend Sir, I receive with gratitude and pleasure the symbolical crown which piety has prepared. I receive it in the name of the brave men who have so effectually seconded my exertions for the preservation of their country. They will deserve the laurels their country will bestow. . . . I thank you, Reverend Sir, most sincerely, for the prayers which you offer up for my happiness. May those your patriotism dictates for our beloved country be first heard, and may mine for your individual prosperity, as well as that of the congregation committed to your care, be favorably received! The prosperity, the wealth, the happiness of this city will then be commensurate with the courage and other qualities of its inhabitants."

Through the church doors is heard the mighty peal of the organ and then, on the arm of Abbé Guillaume V. Dubourg, the rugged warrior from Tennessee is escorted to his seat near the altar for the solemn thanksgiving services which are to follow.

Cathedral of St. Louis, New Orleans, La., where Andrew Jackson's great victory over the British was publicly celebrated. *Photo courtesy New Orleans Association of Commerce.*

Rehoboth Methodist Church, near Union, West Virginia. The oldest Protestant church west of the Alleghenies.
Photo courtesy Rev. Chas. A. York.

The story of the Cathedral of St. Louis is the story of New Orleans itself, so deeply entrenched is it in the early history of the city. The archives of the parish date from the erection of the earliest wooden and adobe chapel which was obliterated by a tornado in 1723. A brick church followed and lasted for sixty years, until Good Friday, 1788, when a great fire swept over New Orleans and destroyed it.

Then came Don Andrés Almonaster y Roxas, a native of Mayrena, in the Kingdom of Andalusia, public benefactor in the days of Spanish supremacy, through whose munificence the present Cathedral of St. Louis was erected in 1794. He was a man of noble birth and a distinguished citizen of his day; no history of New Orleans would be complete without him.

The present cathedral bears the marks of several architects. At first there were only the two side towers but about 1814 these were topped with low spires and the upper portion of the face decorated with four gigantic blocks of granite. About ten years later a belfry was erected in the center, to match the side towers. At the request of the mayor, this belfry became the city watch tower and each night a guard was stationed there to give warning in case of a fire.

One still hears the assertion that in 1850, or thereabouts, the St. Louis Cathedral was completely torn down and rebuilt but this is not true. At that time the principal tower fell, injuring the roof and the walls to a great extent. Naturally a great deal of repair work had to be done; the upper portion *was* torn down and a new design was suggested by Louis Pilié and adopted by the wardens. At the same time the cathedral was enlarged by the addition of the present sanctuary and vestries. As a matter of fact, however, a greater part of the structure stands as originally erected than most people realize.

Many men, famous in the early regime of Louisiana, lie buried under the stones of the cathedral sanctuary. Like St. Philip's in South Carolina, the Cathedral of St. Louis is truly the Westminster of its own state, Louisiana.

CHAPTER XI

HISTORIC CHURCHES ALONG THE WAY WEST

One place there is—beneath the burial sod,
Where all mankind are equalised by death
Another place there is—the Fane of God,
Where all are equal who draw living breath.
                                    —Thomas Hood

OLD REHOBOTH METHODIST CHURCH, Monroe County, West Virginia, is the oldest Protestant church west of the Alleghenies.

By 1784 a representative group of Methodists had settled in what is now Monroe County, West Virginia, and were making plans for the erection of a house of worship. Early in 1784 Bishop Francis Asbury, a leader in the organization of the Methodist Church in America and the first Bishop of American Methodism, as we have already observed, appointed Reverend William Phoebus as preacher in charge. Services were held in a near-by schoolhouse and in the homes of the settlers but in June, 1786, a church building was completed and dedicated by Bishop Asbury. The church is still standing in a good state of preservation and is used for special services each year.

The building is of large hewn logs with a gallery at the rear and on both sides. This gallery is quite large and strongly supported, for like so many of the early structures of its day, Rehoboth Church was built to last.

There are several windows high up from the floor but all of the rude furniture with which the church was furnished has long since disappeared with the exception of the communion table which is in use in the newer church erected a few yards away. This battered poplar stand is greatly treasured by all members of the congregation. By it knelt the early pioneer builders to receive communion from the hands of Bishop Asbury . . . around it cling hallowed memories. . . .

It was Edward Keenan, an early settler in the district, who first petitioned Bishop Asbury for a minister and it was through the efforts of this same Edward Keenan that the erection of the church was made possible. He donated the lot and five acres for the church and burying ground and today he lies at rest at the northeast corner of the church, just as he requested when he gave the land.

Edward Keenan more than once acted as a good samaritan to the congregation, at one time turning the preacher's horse into his field of oats to graze, for feed was scarce and he was the only farmer in the community who had a crop that year.

While the church was being built every man brought along his rifle for defense if attacked by the Indians, which probably gives a better picture of conditions in those times than anything else that could be told.

A small pile of rocks now marks the spot where a bonfire used to be built by the churchgoers in winter time. It was said that the people gathered around this fire to keep warm until the preaching started, at which time they entered the church and the preaching was then supposed to keep them warm!

Bishop Asbury held three conferences in Rehoboth Church and many of the famous preachers of the day spoke there. During the eighty-four years that this church was in regular use, it was served by one hundred and six pastors, but thirty of these were junior preachers or assistants.

In 1886 the centenary of the dedication of Rehoboth Church was celebrated and over two thousand people attended. Again in 1909 when Monroe County observed its homecoming, the celebration was held in a grove near the old church because of its historic associations and the ties that bound it to the community. Over ten thousand people were in attendance on this occasion.

Old Rehoboth Church is located on the Union-Sweet Springs Turnpike, two miles east of Union, West Virginia.

The Presbyterian Church in Lewisburg, West Virginia, was organized in 1783 when a temporary building was erected by the early settlers. It was made of unhewn logs covered with clapboards. The present structure, known as the Old Stone Presbyterian Church, was erected in 1796 and has been used as a place of worship ever since.

The building, a very plain structure, rectangular in shape, is in an excellent state of preservation today. It is built of native stone and appears essentially as it did at the beginning although certain changes have been made. One or two openings have been closed, the main entrance changed, the doors removed from the pews and the pulpit altered in connection with the installation of a pipe organ.

The pews are very plain and there is a gallery extending across the rear and down both sides. These galleries were at first and for many years afterwards reserved for the slaves who had their membership in the church along with their white masters and who appeared regularly at the services.

The name most prominently identified with the development of the old church is that of the Reverend John McElhenny, D.D., who became pastor in 1809 and continued his connection with the congregation for nearly sixty-three years. Dr. McElhenny frequently rode as far west as the Ohio River and through his great missionary work became the father of Presbyterianism in a large section of what is now West Virginia. Many churches throughout this section acknowledge him as their founder.

In addition to his work as a missionary, Dr. McElhenny was also a great educator. In 1812 he opened in Lewisburg a small school and as it grew many went out from it to places of usefulness and prominence. One remarkable thing about this school was that it was coeducational from the beginning. The two fine schools located in Lewisburg today, Greenbriar College for Women and Greenbriar Military School, trace their beginning to the little school opened in 1812.

In the Civil War, sympathy and active participation was on the Southern side. A not very important but hotly contested engagement was fought between artillery stationed on opposite hills overlooking the town. Marks of shots that fell short are still to be

Old Stone Presbyterian Church, Lewisburg, West Virginia. Sturdily built by early pioneers along the western frontier.
Photo courtesy West Virginia Department of Agriculture.

Kirtland Temple, Kirtland, Ohio. The oldest place of worship of the Church of Jesus Christ of Latter Day Saints. *Photo by J. A. Wolf.*

seen on some of the old buildings of the town but the church, although directly in the line of fire, was passed over and not struck.

The Colonial Dames of America have placed a memorial tablet in the church commemorating the services of Colonel John Stuart and Colonel John Donnally in the defense of the frontier. The name of Colonel Stuart is prominently mentioned in connection with the erection of the church and his home, "Stuart Manor," built a little earlier, and also of stone, is one of the interesting buildings of this section.

Colonel Stuart prepared the inscription to be found over the doorway of Old Stone Church. Cut on rather rudely quarried stone, it is clearly the work of an amateur in such matters. It reads as follows:

THIS
BUILDING WAS
ERRECTED IN THE YEAR
1796 AT THE EXPENCE
OF A FEW OF THE FIRST
INHABITANTS OF THIS
LAND TO COMMEMORATE
THEIR AFFECTION &
ESTEEM FOR THE
HOLY GOSPEL OF
JESUS CHRIST

READER
IF YOU ARE INCLINED
TO APPLAUD THEIR
VIRTUES GIVE GOD
THE GLORY

The little Temple of the Church of Jesus Christ of Latter Day Saints at Kirtland, Ohio, was started a century and three years ago, in 1833, and was finished some three years later. Kirtland played an important part in the early history of that faith, the opening scene for which was laid in Manchester, New York, where an angel is said to have appeared to Joseph Smith and called him to labor in the work of the Lord. He was told that a record of the Indian progenitors, containing an account of their origin and a history of God's dealings with them, had been written centuries before and had been hidden away in the earth, but soon would be revealed to him and the power given him to translate it and publish it to the world.

In 1827 the plates containing that record are said to have been given to Joseph Smith and in 1830 the Book of Mormon, so named after the man who abridged the plates, was translated and published and on April 6th of the same year the Church of Jesus Christ of Latter Day Saints was organized.

Early in 1831 Joseph Smith and fifty families came out from New York and from then on, for seven years, Kirtland was the hub of missionary effort for these people. In the building of the Kirtland Temple Joseph Smith himself labored in the stone quarry while Sidney Rigdon, an early minister, worked on the walls during the day and helped watch the structure at night to protect it from the hands of those who would tear it down.

The temple was dedicated on March 27, 1836, and in its essential details has changed but little since that day. It is a massive structure of hewn native stone and is plastered both without and within. The dimensions are fifty-nine by seventy-nine feet and the walls are sixty-nine feet high with a tower one hundred and twenty feet in height. The main auditorium is located on the first floor and the two pulpits in this hall constitute the most interesting feature of the interior. The pulpits, one located at each end of the room, represent the two priesthoods of the church, the Melchisedec and the Aaronic. Each is divided into four sections, to represent the four grades of presiding officer, and each section contains three seats, for the officer and his two counselors. In this manner there are twelve pulpits in one, the number being symbolical of the Twelve Apostles.

Even while the Temple was being built the storms of opposition were gathering fast above the heads of the Saints. They were driven from Missouri and in 1838 were forced to leave Kirtland for the city of Nauvoo, Illinois, on the banks of the Mississippi.

On June 27, 1844, Joseph and Hyrum Smith were killed by a mob at Carthage, Illinois, and the church then split into several factions. Brigham Young led one group across the plains and set up a colony on the shores of Great Salt Lake. Others refused to follow his leadership and settled down in small groups throughout Iowa and Illinois. In 1852 these Saints reorganized the church and soon, under the leadership of the slain prophet's son, went ahead with their original mission. The title to Kirtland Temple was obscured for a while but by the findings of the Court of Common Pleas, Lake County, Ohio, February 23, 1880, it was decided that the Reorganized Church was in true succession to the original church and was identical in faith and practice with the first teachings of Joseph Smith, the Prophet. The temple is now in possession of the Reorganized Church and visitors and tourists are always welcome.

The first Protestant mission station on Mackinac Island was established in 1823 at a time when the island was a strategic point in military affairs and trading interests. The present Old Mission Church was the outgrowth of the mission and was built in 1829. It was Presbyterian in form and was connected with the presbytery of Detroit.

The island at that time had a very colorful population and with the teachers, mission pupils, Indians and half-bloods, the various workers of the fur company, traders and soldiers, all sitting side by side, the congregation that worshiped in Old Mission Church must have presented an extremely interesting picture, to say the least. Forty soldiers from the white fort on the hillside, built in 1783, marched down from the hill each Sunday, and placing their arms by the church door would detail one of their number to stand guard while the rest of the company attended church.

In those days Mackinac rivaled Detroit as one of the chief towns of Michigan but its prosperity was short lived. The Indians left for less disturbed spots and John Jacob Astor's retirement from the fur company drove many other residents away. In 1837 the pastor likewise departed and for sixty years Old Mission Church was without minister or congregation.

A laundry firm once used the basement as a place of business and for a time this same basement served as the village school. The main auditorium answered as a hall for political speeches, and once a theatrical troupe, summering on the island, secured the old sanctuary for their performances, with stage and scenic effects installed. During the Civil War, when some Southern prisoners were confined to the fort, a detachment of troops was on guard and their chaplain, Reverend Mr. Knox, held preaching services in the church. Through all its darkest days, however, the old building managed to keep its head up and to endure the wear and tear of time in surprisingly good fashion so that today it stands very much the same as when first built.

In 1895 a number of the summer visitors, joined by some of the island residents, purchased the church and it is now preserved "as an historic relic of the island and a memorial of the early mission work and, secondly, as a chapel for union religious services when summer tourists crowd the island." The exterior is left unpainted and wears a gray weather-worn appearance. The old-fashioned high pulpit, square pews and gallery stand exactly as at first, as does the tin-tipped belfry.

The old mission house has for many years served as a hotel, and it was on the veranda of this quaint hostelry that Dr. Edward Everett Hale began his well-known story, "The Man Without a Country."

Cahos, or Cahokia, Illinois, was an Indian settlement, its beginnings lost in antiquity, when the first white man discovered it. The first church there was built soon after the fur traders began to arrive in 1700. This church was destroyed by fire in 1735. Not long after this disaster the Seminary of Quebec sent Father Nicholas Laurens with twenty-five hundred livres for the purpose of restoring the mission. At this time, it is thought, the second church was erected at Cahokia, which served the parish until November, 1762, when Father Forget Du Verger, the last of the French seminary priests, sold all of the mission property and returned to France. This sale was afterwards invalidated and the property returned to the congregation; however, for a number of years the Catholics of Cahokia were without a regular house of worship; and were, in fact, deprived of everything pertaining to divine worship, except a bell, a monstrance, a chalice, a paten, and a missal printed in 1668.

A house was rented in the village where services could be conducted by the visiting priests but nothing more seems to have been done until 1786 when a parsonage was erected for the new pastor,

Old Mission Church, Mackinac Island, Michigan. Built at a time when Mackinac rivaled Detroit as one of the chief towns of Michigan. *Photo by Detroit Publishing Co.*

Holy Family Church, Cahokia, Illinois. The oldest church structure in Illinois.

Photo by F. Crawford.

the Reverend Paul de Saint Pierre, and it was proposed that the stone walls of the former parsonage be utilized in the building of a new church. Work seems to have been begun on this but apparently was afterwards abandoned as impractical and the present church was not begun until 1789.

According to local tradition, the new place of worship was built by the Voudrie brothers. They and their men are said to have cut the timbers in the wood lot of the Cahokia Commons, which contained about twenty-two hundred acres, heavily wooded. The church records are silent on this point but it would seem that a great many people must have had a hand in the erection of this little church which was ten years in the making. Just what caused all the delay is not known but the church was not actually completed until the coming of Father Donatien Olivier in 1799. The finishing touches were put on under his regime and the building dedicated to divine service in September of that year by Father John Rivet of Vincennes.

This is the quaint little church that is still standing and which is acknowledged to be the oldest church structure in the State of Illinois. The church, now known as Old Holy Family Church, is built upon a stone foundation thirty-one by seventy-four feet. The walls are hewn walnut logs, the floor split cottonwood and the roof timbers are oak squared to the dimensions four by six inches. Originally these were covered with cypress clapboards. In the construction of the walls the logs were placed upright six inches apart, the sides facing each other being beveled to a depth of two inches to receive and hold the mixture of stone and mortar with which the interstices are filled. Not a nail was used in the building but large wooden pegs were used where needed. The floor slopes gently from the front wall to the communion rail with a fall of six inches.

"Originally the church had no sacristy," wrote the Reverend Robert Hynes, pastor of St. Mary's Church, East St. Louis, Illinois, for the "Illinois Catholic Historical Review" in April, 1919, "but this need was supplied in 1833 in the form of a small chapel projecting from the north wall. In the same year a corresponding chapel was built out from the south wall to accommodate the organ and choir. Later in 1840, a larger sacristy was added to the rear of the building, and a confessional was placed in the north chapel. The church as it came from the hands of the builders one hundred and nineteen years ago is substantially intact today. Additions have been made, indeed, but practically nothing of the original building has been removed."

The oldest church building in Chicago is to be found at the corner of Des Plaines and Adams streets, St. Patrick's Church, a familiar landmark known to all, located in one of the grimiest, busiest parts of the city, and serving a parish that has had a long and colorful history.

The first St. Patrick's was erected in Haymarket Square in 1846. It was a frame building and cost seven hundred and fifty dollars. Four years later the present site at Adams and Des Plaines was purchased and on Christmas Day, 1856, first services were held in the new church, the present St. Patrick's. The building survived the Chicago Fire, which started in its very neighborhood, and in the passing years has seen much of its great parish swept away by the inroads of business and the shifting of population that goes on in any great city's development.

During the Civil War it was from St. Patrick's that the famous Irish Legion, the 90th Infantry, went forth to fight for the Union. The pastor of the church, Reverend Dennis Dunne, was affectionately known as the "Father of the Regiment," and at the end of the war a touching scene was enacted when the remnant of the Legion marched to Father Dunne's house, there to be welcomed by their sponsor.

In 1912 the church was completely renovated and restored by the well-known artist, Thomas O'Shaughnessy. The Book of Kells, the Irish classic of twelve hundred years ago, was used as a source of inspiration, with such success that the church is now known the country over as a notable example of the Irish mode of decoration.

The walls are tinted a soft green, matching the coloring in the superb stained glass windows. These windows each contain a motif from the Book of Kells and are built of the "unpainted mosaic pot-metal glass of the ancients," an art lost for many centuries but now recovered. The "Faith" window at the rear of the church is valued at one hundred thousand dollars. More than two hundred and fifty thousand single pieces of glass went into its making and it contains more than two thousand color tints.

Various dates have been given for the settlement at Vincennes, Indiana, but the most generally credited version is that a short time prior to 1702 a band of Frenchmen, accompanied by a Catholic priest, first located there and it is known that the first Church of St. Francis Xavier was erected in 1702.

This structure was built of timbers set on end and the interstices were filled with adobe. In the Quebec annals it is stated that many Indian converts assisted in the erection of this crude little house of worship which had only dirt for a floor, a few rough benches and a rude sort of altar. There were no windows or openings, except the door in the northwest end.

The last pastor of the old log church, which deserves a large place in American history, was Father Pierre Gibault, the patriot priest, a man of fine education, commanding presence and possessing magnetic qualities. On July 4, 1778, George Rogers Clarke, with his one hundred and forty Virginia frontiersmen, captured Kaskaskia, Illinois, without the firing of a single shot and it was here that Colonel Clarke met the humble little priest, Gibault, who divided his time between Kaskaskia and Vincennes, a compatriot Clarke sorely needed for the Vincennes expedition. Colonel Clarke had the utmost faith and trust in his newly found friend and when the latter volunteered his services, offering to go to Vincennes and apprise his parishioners of the happenings at Kaskaskia and to win them over to the cause of the American Revolution, this offer was speedily accepted.

On July 20, 1778, the inhabitants hearing the little church bell ringing came to the old church where they were surprised to find that their friend and priest had returned. He at once prevailed on them to aid the Americans in making this land free from British rule and accordingly administered an oath of allegiance—which is on record—to the American cause.

The fort at Vincennes, known as Fort Sackville, was at that time unoccupied but the British flag flying overhead was brought down, wrapped around a stone and thrown into the near-by Wabash River. A flag of red and green stripes, the material for which was supplied by Father Gibault, was hauled to the top of the fort and again the little church bell pealed forth, this time in glorification of the birth of new American territory. For his services to the American cause, Father Gibault received the formal thanks of the Virginia Legislature.

The British authorities afterwards retook the town and the fort but on February 25, 1779, Colonel Clarke and his newly organized volunteers, many of whom were supplied by Father Gibault, surprised the British garrison and recaptured the fort, forever putting an end to British domination in the entire territory.

The following year Father Gibault erected a second log church. It was ninety by forty-two feet and upon its completion the old church was fitted up for use as his pastoral residence. The present church, the third on the same site, was started in 1825 but was not finally finished until about 1850. The second church, the log one, was torn down, however, after the present brick church had been roofed over.

High in the belfry of the present Old Cathedral of St. Francis Xavier hangs the original little bell which in the first log church proclaimed the birth of a new Vincennes. This bell, known as "The Little Liberty Bell of the Northwest Territory," was cast in Paris and into its casting pot are said to have gone precious gold and silver jewels contributed by European monarchs. In about 1745 it came to its home in the new land and now for over one hundred and ninety-one years it has called the faithful to prayer or tolled sorrowfully at the passing of some faithful parishioner. On February 25, 1779, this little bell pealed forth its most joyful tones at the surrender of Colonel Henry Hamilton, British commander of the fort, to Colonel George Rogers Clarke. This meeting between the two men is said to have taken place before the door of the old log church and secured for the United States the vast Northwest Territory.

At three o'clock in the morning of November 11, 1918, the little bell again made history by announcing to the citizens of Vincennes the welcome tidings of the Armistice, which marked the close of the World War.

Next door to the Old Cathedral stands a small brick building that houses one of the most remarkable collections of books and manuscripts in America. It stands, in reality, as a memorial to the scholarly attainments of Bishop Brute, the first Bishop of Vincennes. This great and good man was born in France and educated at the University of Paris. He inherited a love of books from his parents who were printers to the royal court. When he came to Vincennes in 1834 to become the head of the diocese he brought with him a large library of rare books, printed in many languages and covering the broad fields of history, theology and philosophy.

Bishop Brute was a most remarkable man. President John Quincy Adams, himself a great scholar, said of him that he was the "most learned man of his day in America." In the Cathedral Library, maintained much as Bishop Brute left it, one may see exquisite old hand-illuminated manuscripts laboriously penned by the monks of the middle ages, some of the very earliest examples of the printer's art, and hundreds of volumes of some of the rarest books extant.

In addition to these, there are many other objects and relics pertaining to the history of Catholicism in Vincennes. When one recalls that the parish with which this institution is connected has been in continuous existence now for more than two centuries one can appreciate the age of the community and the changes that time has wrought. One can only agree with the statement made in the little circular issued by the Chamber of Commerce: "This library is well worth a visit because it proves in a most striking manner that there were men of culture and learning in this far western country while it was merely an outpost in the wilderness."

Old Bethel Meeting House was built in 1807 on a slight elevation some three hundred yards distant from the residence of Nathan Robertson. This Nathan Robertson was the first member of the Methodist faith to settle in the State of Indiana and his home was located three miles from the village of Charlestown, in Clark County.

There was at first no provision made for the heating of Bethel Meeting House but pioneer ingenuity resorted to the happy expedient of burning a log-heap the day previous to the preaching service in order to obtain a bed of live coals; these were placed in large iron kettles and carried into the church. The building was well "chinked and daubed" and thus the bottled-up heat over night insured some degree of comfort for the worshipers.

The church has had a restless sort of existence, having been rebuilt no less than four times. In 1837, following the death of Nathan Robertson and the consequent change in ownership of the land, the meeting house was moved to the farm of James Robertson and then after twenty years was abandoned as a place of worship since the church in Charlestown was more central and more comfortable.

For a number of years, then, the building did service as a sheep barn but was finally rescued from this plight and once more removed, this time to a spot near the Lexington Highway. In 1903 the Indiana Conference authorized J. Edward Murr to purchase the building for fifty dollars and to rebuild it on its original foundation where it had been placed in 1807. This was accordingly done. Not until July, 1925, was it decided to move the church to its present location in Charlestown where it now rests on a concrete slab much larger than itself, with another roof over the entire building, and is visited each year by many people from over a wide range.

The logs comprising the present structure are the original ones throughout without any alterations in the building plans, except that two logs had decayed beyond the possibility of further use and had to be replaced. This was in 1903 when preparations were being made to place the old meeting house on its original site and at the same time the Nathan Robertson barn was being dismantled. Not without some degree of appropriateness, oak logs from this barn were used to take the place of the decayed yellow poplar logs of the meeting house. A relic of the period in which the building ceased to be used as a church and was experiencing its many changes is to be found in the opening in the north side for a stove pipe.

The first church structure in St. Louis was a log Catholic church built in 1770 on land assigned by Pierre Laclede-Liguest, the founder of the city. The church was blessed on June 24th of that year by Father Sebastian Meurin, S.J., the "pioneer priest of St.

Louis." Incidentally, the first official record of a Christian missionary in St. Louis is a baptism administered by Father Meurin
on May 9, 1766, "in a tent for want of a church."

The little religious structure became the hub around which the
town wheel revolved. Crime was almost unknown and justice was
administered in a fatherly way by the officiating priest or some
one chosen from "the ancients," as the elder citizens were styled.
Even the announcements of sales and other publications were made
on Sundays from the church steps.

This early place of worship soon gave way to a more permanent
structure erected in 1776 while St. Louis was under Spanish rule
and sometimes referred to as "The Church of the Palisades." At
the close of the War of 1812 when General Jackson obtained his
victory over the British at New Orleans, the town of St. Louis was
illuminated and a solemn Te Deum and thanksgiving service was
held in this church and a patriotic sermon delivered by Father
Savine, the priest then in charge.

Bishop Du Bourg came to St. Louis in 1818 and at once determined upon the erection of the first cathedral in the city. The
corner-stone was laid on March 29, 1818, and solemnly blessed two
years later. Although this first cathedral was destroyed by fire before the days of photography we know that it was a brick structure
one hundred and thirty-five feet in length. At the front of the
building was a steeple in which hung bells brought over from
France. Inside were to be found many beautiful and precious things
in the way of paintings, gold embroideries and sacred vessels, many
of them donated by the royalty of Europe.

In 1830 Bishop Rosati decided upon the erection of the Old
Cathedral which still stands on Walnut Street between Second
and Fourth streets, the corner-stone being laid on August 1, 1831,
and the building completed in the fall of 1834.

When finished, the church was considered of rare architectural beauty. In length it was one hundred and thirty-six feet;
eighty-four feet wide and forty feet high. The entire façade was
of beautiful polished stone, much like marble, and the portico was
sustained by four columns of the Doric order, after the fashion of
the ruins of Poestum, near Naples. This is the same classic model

which served as a guide in the building of the Custis, or Robert E. Lee Home, at Arlington Cemetery. On the interior there were alongside the wall in front, several spacious galleries, these being so arranged that the men would be separated from the women and the boys from the girls. There were also two spacious galleries reserved for the negro slaves and freedmen who attended services.

October 6, 1834, was set apart for the solemn consecration of the cathedral. The militia from the Government barracks participated in the demonstration in full uniform and during the services three American flags were lowered over the balustrade of the sanctuary, with drums beating the reveille, a deafening discharge by the artillery, and the bells of the cathedral being rung again and again.

The Old Cathedral of St. Louis of France is now entirely surrounded by business houses and its regular parishioners are few, yet every Sunday and special Feast Day its pews and aisles are well crowded and hundreds drop in each day to offer a prayer or a word of thanksgiving before one of its beautiful shrines. It is the most richly indulgenced church in America, offering the same benefits to those who visit its three altars as are attached to the seven basilicas of Rome.

The building is affectionately enshrined in the minds of the people of St. Louis as evidenced by a newspaper write-up published in 1875, which said:

It is fitting that all who cherish memories of the past, who have regard for the preservation of this the most important historical monument left to us, should join in the work of maintaining and keeping in order the Cathedral of St. Louis. It is not alone a work for the Catholics to do, but in a large sense it is a special work for the Protestants as well. It belongs to all; it is historical.

The oldest Protestant Church to be found west of the Mississippi River is old McKendree Chapel, seven miles northwest of Cape Girardeau, Missouri, organized in 1806 and with the present church structure, standing on a site which has been used for camp meetings from the time the church was first organized, completed in 1819. The original chapel was of logs. Later the house was weatherboarded. The interior, however, has remained practically

Old Cathedral of St. Louis of France, St. Louis, Mo. St. Louis'
most historic shrine. *Photo by Charles Trefts*.

An old church of the Indian Territory, Wheelock Mission, Millerton, Okla.
Photo courtesy Wheelock Academy.

unchanged and today is as near its original condition as it has been humanly possible to make it.

Regular services were held in the church for about eighty-three years. After 1844 the congregation was small as many of the members joined the southern branch of Methodism after the division in 1844–45. Gradually the old chapel was deserted and the road leading to it, closed. The building was all but forgotten in its desolation and in danger of complete obliteration when interest in its restoration and preservation was aroused and a McKendree Chapel Memorial Association formed to bring this about. First a new foundation was built; the underpinning of the house was made secure; a fireplace and chimney was erected as nearly like the original as possible; a new hand-made cypress slab roof was put on; well-preserved material was obtained from other old buildings and this was used to replace the missing weatherboarding.

Old McKendree Chapel, located in a magnificent grove of two acres, with one of the finest springs in the state, is now in a condition to last another half-century. It is proposed to have an annual meeting at the chapel, on the second Sunday of October, and thereby perpetuate the active membership in the memorial association.

The most interesting religious structure in the State of Kansas is the old Shawnee Mission, originally established by the Methodist Episcopal Church at Turner, about 1830. Eight years later it was decided to move the mission to its present site three miles from Westport.

The Reverend Thomas Johnson remained in charge of the mission, which, after its removal, was known as Shawnee Indian Manual Labor School. For the first buildings much of the lumber was shipped in from Cincinnati and the bricks from St. Louis; but presently a brick kiln was put up and all the material used in the later buildings was home-made. The two main brick buildings on the south of the road, the largest of these serving as a schoolhouse and chapel, were completed in 1839 and in 1845 was added an additional large brick structure on the north of the road. In addition to these main buildings, smaller log structures were erected to serve as tool shops, a grist mill, a brickyard, trade shops and so on, and here the Indian boys were taught practical arts which would enable them to earn their daily bread. They were taught to be expert farmers, brickmasons, carpenters; while the girls learned to spin and weave, to cook and sew and keep house. The young people living at the mission led busy, contented lives.

The period during which the old Shawnee Mission flourished was the most troublous in all American history. The whole United States was at that time torn up over the question of slavery and presently this penetrated even into the peace and quiet of the mission chapel.

Thomas Johnson was of southern birth and when the Methodist Church separated into a northern and southern division, he naturally chose the southern branch, especially since in the division of territory by the church his institution fell into that branch. At the same time he could not find it in his heart to abandon and betray his northern friends and associates. The situation was an extremely difficult one.

Andrew H. Reeder was appointed the first territorial governor of Kansas in June of 1854. At first he located his headquarters temporarily at Fort Leavenworth but soon transferred them to the old mission. By virtue of this the Shawnee Mission became in reality the first territorial capital of Kansas. Governor Reeder located the future seat of government at Pawnee but the Missourians objected strenuously to the location, saying it was selected simply because of his land holdings in that vicinity. The legislature assembled there but in a few days adjourned to meet at the Shawnee Mission which once again became the capital of the territory.

With the fight over slavery growing more heated, the old quiet life at the mission was commencing to be a thing of the past. Funds for its support dwindled and in 1854 the manual training shops had to be closed. Finally, ten years later, the school was abandoned. During the Civil War the old brick buildings making up the mission were used as barracks for the troops and marching soldiers took the place of the Indian school lad, with the bugle substituted for the former school bell.

Thomas Johnson was killed on the night of January 2, 1865. Despite the fact that he had altogether renounced whatever southern sympathy he might naturally have been expected to have, in his loyalty for the Union, and despite the fact that his oldest son was at that time fighting for the North, he was looked upon as legitimate prey by one of the many lawless and vicious bands who murdered and stole under the black flag of guerrilla warfare. Mrs. Edith Connelley Ross tells the story of his tragic end in her interesting little pamphlet "The Old Shawnee Mission":

It was late on a bitterly cold night, and Thomas Johnson and his family had been asleep for hours, when they were awakened by shouts and halloes in the yard below. Thomas Johnson went down to the front door and flung it open fearlessly. He asked them what they wanted, and, when they asked, directed them on their way to Westport. To keep him standing there and talking, they asked for water to drink. He called their attention to the cistern in the side yard and told them to help themselves. Too late he perceived their drawn guns and started to close the door. They fired. Though fatally wounded by a ball that passed close to his heart, he managed to turn the lock of the door as he sank to the floor. His wife caught him as he fell, lifted his head into her lap. But he never spoke again, and within a few minutes he was dead.

With the passing of the years the old mission buildings gradually fell into disrepair. One of them was considerably damaged by a cyclone, but the main building in which the legislature held its sessions remained in fairly good condition. Finally, at the instance of various civic and patriotic bodies, the grounds and mission buildings were purchased by the state and are now being preserved as a historic spot.

The first church and school established in the Choctaw Nation was organized December 9, 1832, by a company of some six hundred persons who in that year removed from Mississippi and settled in what is now McCurtain County, Oklahoma. The trip from their old home to their new settling place west of the Mississippi River was so difficult that many died on the way and as a result of this the road over which they traveled was called the "Trail of Tears." This is one of the saddest incidents in American history but not many people are aware that there is an old stone church still standing in Oklahoma which was built as a result of this tragic removal.

Soon after the arrival of these new settlers a mission was established and a church organized and named Wheelock Mission, in memory of the first President of Dartmouth, a personal friend of the Reverend Alfred Wright who founded the mission. First services were held under a large tree, with rude split log seats and a common wooden box serving for a pulpit, and it must have been with a twinge of sadness that the Choctaws gathered to sing the old songs they had learned back in Mississippi. At the first meeting some thirty people were received into the church, from those who had been members before their removal to their new home, and some seven others on profession of faith. At first the mission was almost wholly a religious organization but very soon after it was founded a school was opened up as an important part of it. This was at first a day school for Indian children; later a boarding school for Indian girls.

Still standing is the old stone church built in 1842 under the direction and supervision of the founder of the mission, Reverend Alfred Wright, a native of Connecticut who labored many years among the Indians. The church that he built of native stone taken from the ground a few rods south of the site, is today the only one of the original buildings of the mission that is left. Some time during the sixties the main dormitory caught fire and a strong northwest wind carried the sparks to the school and church; when the day was done nothing remained of the old mission except the home of the Wrights and the walls of the church.

Later it was the mute appeal of the walls of the old stone church which brought Wheelock back to life about 1883. The church was then repaired and new school buildings erected. Today the school is still in existence but the church membership was removed to the little town of Garvin in 1912. Since then the old stone building has been used by various denominations; it is privately owned and in a very bad state of repair. It should belong to the entire Choctaw people and kept as a memorial to their tribe.

The first church built in Oklahoma, in other words in the original territory of Oklahoma, was the Presbyterian Church at Beaver City in what was then known as "No Man's Land," a strip of land some one hundred and sixty-four miles long by thirty-four miles wide—public domain tolerant of the squatter's rights. The church, put up in 1887, is still being used by the Presbyterian Congregation at Beaver City. The lumber was hauled from Dodge City, and Kansas friends of the first minister, the Reverend R. M. Overstreet, donated the money for the church's erection.

In their haste to complete the structure the builders simply ran the stove pipe out through the roof, without any protection for the wood, with the result that the building caught fire while the first Sunday School was being held, but with the aid of a ladder and a few buckets of water this fire was easily extinguished and the faulty construction was later remedied.

Reverend Mr. Overstreet contributed a vivid description of early conditions in "No Man's Land," as he found them, which was published in Sturms "Oklahoma Magazine" in December, 1908:

It was Sunday morning when I first looked out on this place. . . . There appeared in the glen a group of cowboys, lined up at Jim Lane's saloon, and a gang of loose horses grazing around a chuck wagon on the bottom, all in appearance as if a round-up was on hand. There were stakes set here and there over a section of land, to represent the plat of a townsite that had just been laid out by a company from Wichita, Kansas. . . . The whole "strip" was little else than a stock range, and seemingly fit for nothing else, and had been so regarded up to that time . . . desolate, forbidding, and by no means promising as the abode of a civilized community. It was pre-eminently droughty and barren. No federal or municipal law was as yet established or prevailed as a terror to evildoers and a praise to them that did well. . . . The settler could enter and take a claim on a quarter section of government land and hold it by maintaining continuous residence—by might, or such protection as the community of interests afforded the individual. This was an anomalous, uncertain and hazardous condition, and yet the people—men, women and children—came in, taking chances, resolved to make the best of things as they might find them. They were here to build homes and the state. To say the least, they were a gritty and hazardous people. This was in 1886. That year and the following, as many as three thousand people came in to make settlement, and engage in such business pursuits as the country afforded; most of them with good intent, battling for the right, for home and for country. A large element, unfortunately, were freebooters, and at first well might hold control. It was a field for the rough and the lawless. Such was the condition of things at the beginning of settlement of No Man's Land.

It was these "gritty and hazardous" pioneers who organized and built the Beaver City Presbyterian Church. "All lent a willing and helping hand," wrote Reverend Mr. Overstreet, "and so the walls went up. It drew us together in a fellow feeling, and had its influence for good ever afterwards."

St. Gabriel's Catholic Church, Prairie du Chien, is the oldest permanent church building erected in the State of Wisconsin. It is a stone structure put up in 1836 by Father Samuel Mazzuchelli, O.P., who in 1832 made the trip from Green Bay to Prairie du Chien over the old Indian Trail, on horseback. Much earlier he had erected a frame mission church at Green Bay and there opened the first school in the entire state, but very little is known concerning the buildings themselves and so far as I have been able to find out, there are no pictures of them in existence today. Father Mazzuchelli was indeed a great builder for according to early records he was responsible for no less than twelve churches in Iowa and was the designer of that state's first capitol building which, with its lovely hanging staircase, is still preserved at Iowa City as a historic relic.

Although the settlement at Prairie du Chien is of very early origin, there is no record of a church or missionary established there until 1817, when the Trappist monk, Joseph Marie Dunand, opened the church records with a large number of entries and, in addition, opened and blessed a cemetery and urged the building of a church. Father Dunand came to Prairie du Chien at the urgent invitation of the French Catholics who lived at that remote point. The journey from Florissant, Missouri, was by canoe and consumed thirty-four days, with the little party suffering great hardships because of the extreme cold and privations of all kinds. The second entry made in the parish register tells of the scalping of a woman by the Indians which gives a hint of conditions in the old French town as the first known visiting missionary found them.

In front of the church is buried Reverend Father Galtier, a

former pastor of St. Gabriel's who later put up the first mission church in what is now St. Paul, Minnesota. It was he, in fact, who gave that city its name, changing it from Pig's Eye to St. Paul.

In 1908 the Reverend Peter Becker enlarged the original church erected in 1836, by adding a new front with two towers, keeping the old building intact, however. It will be observed that this oldest portion of St. Gabriel's will just this year reach the century mark.

Another old Wisconsin place of worship is the mission church on Madeline Island in Lake Superior. In 1818 Lyman M. Warren came to La Pointe, Madeline Island, to engage in the fur trade. He was a member of a distinguished New England family and with such a background it was only natural that he should feel the need of religious influence on the island. Mr. Warren asked the American Board of Commissioners for Foreign Missions, in Boston, to send out a missionary to the Indians but for some time the proper person to undertake this charge was not to be obtained.

Finally, in 1831, the Reverend Sherman Hall came as a missionary to the island. With him came his wife and Mrs. John Campbell, as an interpreter. It took the little party twenty-five days to make the trip from Mackinaw to La Pointe.

One of the most distinguished services rendered by Mr. Hall was his translation of the New Testament into the Ojibwa language. Soon after his arrival, work was begun on a mission house at a spot half-way between the Old Fort Settlement and the New Fort Settlement, where the present village of La Pointe was just beginning to take form. Seventeen months were required to construct this mission house. Lumber was whip-sawed out of logs according to the custom of the day and the bricks for the chimney were made from clay found near by. The house was dedicated on August 20, 1833, and on the same evening was organized a Congregational Church, the first of that denomination in Wisconsin.

Six years later the Old Mission Church was built on Crescent Bay. It became the meeting place for preaching, Sunday School, and other religious gatherings and filled a long-needed want as the brick basement of the mission house had become too small to accommodate the growing congregation. The pleasant tradition exists that when the church was put up the members of the Catholic community on Madeline Island generously gave them aid; then in 1841 when the Catholic mission was removed and rebuilt, the Protestant settlement in turn helped with this work. The church was constructed in much the same manner as the mission house—with whip-sawed lumber, sectional wooden walls, hand-split cedar strip criss-cross lathing, clay mud plaster and old-fashioned small paned windows.

In 1901 the church was moved to its present site overlooking the old mission house. The original stove which furnished warmth to the early members may yet be found in the vestibule while the old bell is still used to call the summer visitors to Sunday morning worship. Mr. Warren's Bible, bearing his autograph and the date 1834 on its fly-leaf, is still used by the visiting preachers who officiate every summer.

The first Christian ceremony in the State of Iowa seems to have been that celebrated in 1833 by a roving Catholic missionary at the home of one Patrick Quigley in Dubuque, which at that early date had a population of about two hundred and fifty people. Two years later, Father Samuel Mazzuchelli, already mentioned in connection with St. Gabriel's Church, Prairie du Chien, Wisconsin, came to Dubuque and within a month after his arrival, this energetic pioneer had drawn the plans for a church, engaged workmen and made the site ready for the laying of the corner-stone. The ground, incidentally, was donated by the same Patrick Quigley in whose home the first services had been celebrated.

The whole town attended the laying of the corner-stone, at which the structure was dedicated to the Archangel Raphael, and both Catholics and Protestants alike contributed to the building fund.

The present St. Raphael's Cathedral, the successor to Reverend Father Mazzuchelli's first stone church, was started on July 15, 1857, on a lot adjacent to the earlier structure. It seems a safe conjecture, in the light of all the evidence available, that Father Mazzuchelli was likewise the architect for the present cathedral which is of Gothic design and more than three times as large as the one which preceded it. "The proportions are classic, perfect;

the central arches are supported by slender Corinthian columns, which also form the base for the smaller side arches. There are more arches from pillar to pillar, making a lacework of inter-twining curves beautiful to behold." The main body of the cathedral was finished in 1858 but the tower was not completed until 1876. It is twenty-six feet square at the base and is one hundred and sixty feet high.

Reverend John de Padilla, a Franciscan friar, was the first Christian clergyman to officiate in the State of Nebraska while St. Mary's Episcopal Church at Nebraska City was the first church edifice erected in the state; but of the structures now standing, the Presbyterian Church at Bellevue is the oldest.

Bellevue is a very historic spot, being one of the stopping places of Lewis and Clarke on their expedition up the Missouri, in 1804, to explore the Louisiana Purchase. It was also the seat of the first white settlement in 1810, the American Fur Company establishing a trading post there in that year, and is the oldest existing town in the state. In the early years of its existence, Indians constituted the chief population of the town, as well as of the state, the very name of the latter coming from the Otoe Indian word for the Platte River—Ne-brath-ka, meaning Flat Water.

In 1834 a Presbyterian mission was located at Bellevue among the Omaha Indians and in 1847 the Pawnee Mission was established there. This was a substantial log structure containing ten rooms.

With the coming of more white settlers, a Presbyterian Church was organized as early as 1855 and meetings were held in the Pawnee Mission building. The present church structure was begun in 1856 and the walls of stone and cement erected that year. Substantial additions have been made to the old edifice, the vestibule and tower being built a number of years afterwards and other additions and changes have been made from time to time, but the main part of the old building erected in 1856–58 still stands and still continues to give service as a house of worship.

St. Mary's Mission, Stevensville, Montana, was first established as a mission for the Selish Indians, commonly known as the Flat Heads, by the Reverend Peter John De Smet, S.J., who with his companions reached the spot on September 24, 1841. Hewing down a couple of trees they very shortly constructed a large cross which presently was planted in the ground to the chant of the Vexilla Regis. The premises and the mission were both called St. Mary's and work was soon begun on a shelter for the coming winter and a chapel for divine service. This, the first Catholic mission in Montana, was a primitive little structure, measuring twenty-five by thirty-three feet, was constructed of cottonwood trees and had two galleries, one on each side. A year or so later this chapel was replaced by another whose dimensions were somewhat larger; that is, thirty by sixty feet.

"The Black Robes," as the early missionaries were known, came to teach the Indians not only to pray but to toil as well, hence the building of the chapel and winter shelter were their first lessons in manual labor. Preparations were made to cultivate the ground but since the Indians had no seed at hand to sow in the newly prepared fields, a trip had to be made to Fort Colville, three hundred miles away, to secure potatoes, wheat and oats. Curiously the Indians watched the plowing and the sowing. When told that what had been planted would itself grow and multiply they were incredulous and many could be seen day after day, perched on the fence for hours, waiting for the seed to start growing. When the new shoots began to appear they were both delighted and astonished. This was actually the first farming done in Montana.

The Reverend Peter John De Smet made many trips into neighboring territory and is today known as the "Apostle of the Northwest." Early missionary life was fraught with many dangers and life at St. Mary's was often beset with difficulties. Scarcely once a year did these pioneer fathers hear from the outside world and always there was danger of an attack by hostile bands.

Not quite ten years after its establishment, St. Mary's was temporarily abandoned and for sixteen years only occasional services were held there. The mission was reopened in September, 1866, and continued in existence as an Indian mission until 1891, with the final removal of the Flat Heads to the reservation which the Government set aside for them on the Jocko.

Thus fifty years after it was founded St. Mary's was discontinued as an Indian mission but many precious memories of great and noble deeds still cling to the spot.

The Minnesota Historical Society advises that it is extremely doubtful if there are in Minnesota today any churches which are of sufficient interest to be included in a work of this nature. There are a number of interesting church and mission sites scattered throughout the state and reaching back to the earliest days of white settlement in the northwest area but congregations that were organized in the period of early settlement in practically no instances are located today in their original edifices and few of them remain on their original sites.

The same condition apparently holds true in Wyoming, South Dakota, Nevada and Colorado. The history of the early Catholic and Protestant missionaries who first invaded these states, carrying the torch of Christianity to the Indians and ministering to the early settlers, constitutes a thrilling story but it does not have its place in this work which is a discussion of church buildings—for the humble structures erected by the pioneers have long since been replaced by more elaborate buildings of brick and stone. The urge to build and rebuild has thus far operated all too effectively to prevent the development of some interesting associations and traditions among the churches.

In Washington much the same condition exists. The first Protestant church there was erected in Steilacoon by a Methodist Minister who arrived via the Isthmus of Panama in the month of August, 1853. This building was torn down several years ago and an appropriate granite marker placed on the site.

There is an old Methodist church built at Claquato in 1858. The entire community helped to put up this little wooden structure, with contributions of money, labor and material. Architecturally the building is of the New England type, with a square tower surmounted by an octagonal tower.

Following the removal of the county seat from Claquato to Chehalis, three miles east, in 1873, the center of Methodist activities was transferred there. Prior to this, however, from 1866 to 1870, the little church was occupied for school purposes, the school being known as Claquato Academy. Later, the Methodist organization deeded it to a community organization formed at Claquato to take over the church and hold it for religious services of any communion that might desire to occupy it and also for public gatherings, such as singing schools and so on. Its occupancy was finally abandoned about 1890.

In 1926 the St. Helens Club, a literary organization of Chehalis, undertook its restoration and in its renewed condition the little church has been turned over to the Washington State Historical Society.

The oldest Icelandic church in the two Dakotas is now in use by the parish at Mountain, North Dakota. This is the Vikur Lutheran Church built in 1884. The building is apparently the first one erected by Icelanders on the continent. Icelandic settlements are, of course, quite infrequent and are to be found probably only in the Dakotas and in the State of Minnesota.

In St. Paul, Oregon, is located the first brick church erected in the Pacific Northwest, St. Paul's Catholic Church, built in 1846, at a time when the little town was a thriving community and gave promise of perhaps developing into something even larger.

Closely connected with the early settlement of Utah is the famous temple of the Latter Day Saints at Salt Lake City, or the Mormon Temple as it is popularly known, begun in 1853 but not fully completed until some forty years later. The whole early history of the Mormon faith is the story of various colonization efforts in the long trek of its members across the United States. We have already read of the building of a temple in Ohio. After the death of Joseph Smith one group under Brigham Young moved westward to what is now the State of Utah and there founded the present City of Salt Lake.

The first place of worship was a primitive structure known as "The Bowery" and built of timber and tree boughs. Less than six years after the pioneers arrived the foundation walls of the present temple were laid. This massive granite structure is reserved for sacred ceremonies and is open to none but members of the faith and only to those in good standing. The granite used in its construction was hauled by oxen from the Wesatch Mountains twenty miles distant, and the timbers from Cottonwood Canyon the same distance away. Before the structure was completed a railroad was built to the quarry, greatly expediting the work. The foundation walls are sixteen feet thick and the walls above the ground vary in thickness from nine to six feet.

Adjacent to the temple stands the tabernacle, the one story elliptical building famed for its acoustical properties. It is capable of seating eight thousand people and its organ is one of the largest in the world. A free recital is given each week-day at noon and all are welcome to attend.

The most interesting and historic church in Idaho is the old Coeur d'Alene Mission of the Sacred Heart at Cataldo, on the Yellowstone Trail between Coeur d'Alene and Kellogg. Father De Smet, the founder of St. Mary's Mission at Stevensville, Montana, chose the site of the Mission of the Sacred Heart about 1846 but its history was in the making nearly fifty years before, for with the Lewis and Clarke Expedition of 1805 and that of John Jacob Astor in 1811, many French-Canadian adventurers had penetrated into the unknown depths of the Northwest. Most of these explorers were members of the Catholic faith and in a sense they prepared the way for the Jesuits, or "Black Robes" as they were affectionately termed by the Indians, who were to come later.

At first a temporary chapel made of bark was erected, and the work of the mission carried on. At the same time plans for a larger church were being drawn by the Reverend Anthony Ravalli, S.J., then stationed at St. Mary's in Montana. The church was begun in 1848 and required about two years to build. The plans called for an edifice some ninety feet long, forty feet wide and thirty feet high. The uprights and rafters were cut from the mighty pines which grew in such abundance. The sawing was done with an improvised whipsaw and a broadax was the only tool available for planing and shaping the boards. As no nails were to be had, holes were bored in the uprights and rafters and these were then joined by wooden pegs. The six large columns which support the porch are beautifully and laboriously planed by hand and present a remarkably smooth surface, resembling greatly a machine-made product.

When St. Mary's Mission in Montana was closed temporarily,

Father Ravalli, the architect-builder, was placed in charge of the Coeur d'Alene Mission and quickly set about completing the interior of the church. Three altars were built and the walls were decorated with pictures painted by some of the best old world artists and transported to the wilds of Idaho by the Black Robes. Above the two side altars pictures representing "Heaven" and "Hell" were placed. For some reason the latter painting was once removed and lay for a time at the bottom of a pile of rubbish. Finally a visitor to the mission secured permission from the wife of the Indian caretaker in charge to carry it away. The picture was removed and the new owner spent many hours removing the accumulations of the years with the result that it was completely restored and retains all its original brightness of color. When the work of reclaiming the mission was begun the owner of this picture very graciously agreed to replace it in the church and it now occupies its old position above the altar of St. Joseph.

The mission contains much in the way of very fine wood carving, including the nine large and eight small ceiling panels and the statues of the Blessed Virgin and of St. John, the Evangelist, which adorn the tops of two small pillars at the entrance to the sanctuary.

The Mission of the Sacred Heart was opened for services in 1852 or 1853 and the finished structure stood as a monument to the ability and perseverance of the Reverend Anthony Ravalli who had made so much out of so little and who had been undismayed by the task set before him.

In October, 1853, Isaac Stevens, the new Governor of the whole Oregon Territory, stopped at the mission for three days on his way to Olympia to assume his new duties and observed the Indians being tutored in the many tasks required of an average farmer. Two years later Governor Stevens again stopped at the mission, this time to receive the oath of allegiance to the United States from the Jesuit fathers, all of whom were Europeans.

By 1877 the last days of the mission had set in. The United States Government set the bounds of the Indian reservation in that year and the mission did not lie within the new limits. After the departure of the Indians to their new home at Desmet, Idaho, the church was used but little.

Early in 1925 the late Bishop Gorman, realizing the historic importance of the venerable landmark, appointed a committee to plan its rehabilitation. This proposal immediately struck a responsive chord in the hearts of the people of the Coeur d'Alene. Several near-by cities organized an automobile pilgrimage to the church in September, 1926. About two thousand people visited the mission on this occasion.

Plans were laid and two years later the work of restoration was begun. The foundation of the old church has now been strengthened, the floor made firm, the walls covered with new sheathing, the pillars of the portico properly aligned, the façade repaired and the whole exterior painted white.

Details of the interior have been renewed but no changes were made; the desire being to return the church to its original appearance but not to allow it to suffer any so-called "modernizations." Every effort has been made to preserve the quaint architecture throughout and, as is pointed out by the Reverend Edmund R. Cody, M.A., in his little booklet on the mission, "despite the many repairs, the visitor may yet see the old adobe walls showing the fingerprints of the original masons, and the interlaced saplings bound with coarse grass which formed the original walls."

Chapter XII

MISSIONS AND SHRINES OF TEXAS

Thermopylae had her messenger of defeat, the Alamo had none.

I⊤ is surprising to find in San Antonio a cathedral of such venerable old age as San Fernando, when the fact is considered that this ancient structure never, in its whole existence, saw service as an Indian mission but was from the first a parish church.

For over two hundred years there has been a sanctuary lamp burning in a San Fernando Church: first in the ancient chapel; then in the old San Fernando; and now in the improved and enlarged cathedral. At one time, in 1839, its rector, the Reverend Refugio de la Garza, is said to have been the only living Catholic priest in Texas. Since he remained on, the continuity of the oldest parish in the state remains unbroken.

The Texas Franciscan missions, as such, were abandoned many years ago. Their once huge and impregnable buildings have slowly crumbled into dust. Some are gone entirely, others are a mass of ruins, impressive in their desolation, while a few are in a fairly good state of preservation. Services are still held in portions of these ancient buildings but of their once flourishing settlements where the savage Indians were civilized, cared for, and taught, there remain but fragments of their glorious history.

For San Fernando, however, a happier fate was decreed. Founded as a parish church over two centuries ago, it still exists as such and for the last half-century, and more, has assumed the dignity of a cathedral.

In 1716 the Presidio of San Antonio de Bexar became by royal decree the military outpost of the King of Spain. With the coming of thirteen families from the Canary Islands in 1731, at the ex-

The old San Fernando Church as it looked when Santa Anna stormed the Alamo. The rear portion is a part of the modern San Fernando Cathedral, San Antonio, Texas. *Photo by E. Raba.*

The Alamo Chapel, San Antonio, Texas. "Thermopylae had her messenger of defeat, the Alamo had none." *Photo by Harvey Patteson.*

pense and under the protection of Philip the Fifth, ruler of Spain, a military barrack was hastily turned into a chapel to serve the purpose of a parish church. This was the ancient Chapel of San Fernando. . . .

After seven years the population had increased to such an extent that a more spacious building was necessary and efforts were put forth to raise funds for a new church. King Philip again displayed his friendship for the parish by giving five thousand dollars to the building fund; Don Prudencio Basterra, Governor of Texas, two hundred dollars; the pastor, Reverend Juan Recio de León, twenty-five dollars, the remainder necessary being contributed by the congregation.

The corner-stone of the new church was laid on the 11th day of May, 1738, with the ecclesiastical and civil authorities both in attendance. On the lid of this corner-stone were carved the names of the patrons of the future church; Our Lady of Candelaria, Our Lady of Guadalupe, San Fernando, and San Antonio. Our Lady of Guadalupe was chosen, according to the old records, because the people showed special devotion to her; San Fernando, in memory of the Prince of Spain, Ferdinand the Sixth, the second son of Philip; and San Antonio, to honor the Viceroy of Mexico, Marquis Antonio de Valero, who delivered the five thousand dollars presented by the King of Spain.

Eleven years passed by before the old San Fernando Church was completed. The plan formed a perfect Latin cross with the transepts and dome all of solid rock.

This old church had great historic interest as is carefully pointed out by the Reverend Father Camilo Torrente, C. M. F., in his little essay "Old and New San Fernando." In the early days it was the very center of life in the community. Its bells gave warning to the peaceful citizens of the impending Indian incursions or tolled in solemn tones the passing of the monarchs of Castile, while its zealous pastors went out to minister impartially to the conqueror as well as to the vanquished foe who battled at El Rosillo, at Alazan Creek and Medina during the struggles for Texas Independence, blessing alike the banners of the victors and the grounds of the dead.

From the tower of San Fernando Johnson raised the flag of victory after the Battle of La Concepción, December 12, 1835, and here the Texas sentinels first sighted the enemy in February, 1836. Only shortly afterwards Santa Anna floated from this tower the blood-red flag of "No Quarter" at the siege of the Alamo, which carried its merciless message to the men within the fort.

Another interesting historic incident is the marriage of Colonel James Bowie, hero of Texas Independence, which was solemnized in San Fernando by the Reverend Refugio de la Garza on the 25th day of April, 1831.

Then lately, in 1922, the Generalisimo of the World War, Ferdinand Foch, was given a magnificent reception in the new cathedral, being honored by a sermon preached in French by Archbishop Arthur Jerome Drossaerts of San Antonio.

The basis of San Fernando Cathedral today is the old church erected in 1738 for, when the structure was enlarged into a cathedral in 1868, portions of the old church were included in the new. When complete, on October 6, 1873, the old front and heavy tower with the choir and baptistry were torn down and taken away. The new church had its formal opening at this time—although services had never actually been discontinued—and in attendance was F. Giraud, Mayor of San Antonio, who had furnished the architect's plans and specifications, thus completing the chain, the ecclesiastical and civil authorities again being in attendance.

The old Romanesque style of architecture was abandoned in the changes of 1868 in favor of the light and gracious, and cheaper, ogival style, since there was neither time nor money available to build the additional domes, arches and walls of the size which were needed to make of the old and of the new construction one solid, uniform and larger San Fernando.

Sidney Lanier, writing from San Antonio in 1873, gives a very interesting description of the cathedral:

By far the finest and largest architectural example in the town is the San Fernando Cathedral, which presents a broad, varied, and imposing facade upon the western side of the Main Plaza. Entering this building, one's pleasure in its exterior gives way to curious surprise; for one finds inside the old stone church built here more than a century ago, standing, a church within a church, almost untouched save that parts of some projecting pediments have been knocked away by the builders. In this inner church services are still regularly held, the outer one not being yet quite completed. The curious dome, surrounded by a high wall over which its topmost slit windows just peer—an evident relic of ancient Moorish architecture, which one finds in the rear of most of the old Spanish religious edifices in Texas—has been preserved and still adjoins the queer priests' dormitories, which constitute the rear end of the cathedral building.

The oldest portion of the cathedral takes the form of an apsidal chapel, of octagonal design, with massive walls, stunted buttresses and a low flat dome. Were the present main altar located fourteen feet beyond the place where it is now, the broken lines of the old architecture could be perceived more distinctly.

The archives of San Fernando form a priceless collection of ancient documental history, dating back to the beginning of San Antonio. One interesting civil document to be found in the archives is that dated August 10, 1759, in which special funeral services were ordered in memory of the King of Spain, Ferdinand the Sixth. Just across the Military Plaza on which San Fernando fronts will be found the Old Spanish Governor's Palace, only recently restored, a fascinating reminder of the days when viceroys ruled San Antonio in the name of the King of Spain. The iron cross atop the dome of the cathedral is still, after two centuries, the geographical center of San Antonio.

To understand properly the Texas missions, it is necessary to know something of the factors which led to their founding. The government's main purpose was to establish itself firmly and thereby prevent France from coming in and obtaining a foothold; with the church it was, of course, a desire to convert the Indians.

The early missionaries to Texas experienced untold hardships, the full of which could never be told for unfortunately, not all of this has been preserved as carefully as it might have been. "One of the most illustrious Franciscans," writes Adina De Zavala, "around whose name cluster legends and romance, is claimed by Texas with much pride, although Mexico City possesses his tomb." This was the venerable Anthony Margil, one of the earliest pioneers of the state, "author, philanthropist, teacher and founder of the first public schools of San Antonio and Texas, industrial, agricultural and literary. . . . The people of California stress the wonderful labors and long journeys on foot of Padre Junipero Serra, but the people of Texas could, perhaps, prove far more wonderful deeds and labors accomplished by Padre Margil if they were familiar with his life." He was greatly loved by the Indians and there was universal weeping when he died. The pretty tradition exists to this day that at the moment of his death all the Texas mission bells rang of their own accord, without aid.

The first Texas mission was established in 1690 but not until 1715 did the government make any really aggressive endeavors to establish their claims. In that year the Duke of Linares, Viceroy of Mexico, dispatched Don Domingo Ramon to Texas with a party of troops and some Franciscan friars to take steps for the permanent occupation of the country. Ramon established several forts and missions; among these being a fort, or presidio, on the western bank of the San Pedro River, about three-fourths of a mile from the present Main Plaza of the modern city of San Antonio, and we have already read how this presidio later became by royal decree the military outpost of the King of Spain.

Captain Ramon is said to have become a great favorite among the Indians, who adopted him as a son and voluntarily assisted in the work of erecting the humble cabins which served as the first living quarters of the new settlers; in time these structures were replaced by the more elaborate and substantial presidios and the work of transforming the wild Indian tribes into civilized laborers began. In due course came the erection of the various other presidios and missions, the ruins of which stand in such magnificent splendor today.

These buildings were usually arranged around a square or military plaza and comprised a church, dwellings for the priests, officers and soldiers, a storehouse, a prison, and a hospital, while a short distance away were the huts of the neophytes. The garrison at each presidio was supposedly two hundred and fifty men although this number was not maintained at all times and was, for various reasons, generally less. So much trouble was experienced with the mission soldiers that in 1731 the Spanish Government became impressed with the recommendations of the Marquis de Aguayo, that settlers be substituted for mission soldiers as a factor in gaining the affections of the Indians, and a group of colonists was brought from the Canary Islands with the consequent formation of the town and parish of San Fernando.

In 1716 the Reverend Antonio San Buenaventura y Olivares established a mission which he called San Antonio de Padua; in 1718 the name was changed to San Antonio de Valero in honor of the Viceroy of Mexico, and an earlier mission—that of San Francisco Solano, founded in 1700—was merged with it. It was the Mission of San Antonio de Valero, with its little church of the Alamo, which afterwards won so much glory in the Texas Revolution.

In 1732 the mission was moved to what is now the Military Plaza of San Antonio and in 1744 the present historic site on the opposite bank of the river was chosen and work on the present church was begun. It was also about this time that the little chapel began to be called the Alamo, signifying Poplar Church. Although started in 1744 the building was not finished until 1757, which date appears on the front door of the building today.

The name San Antonio de Bexar, more particularly the designation Bexar, early attached itself to the military post, or presidio, its exact origin being unknown. The town of San Fernando clustered around the old San Fernando Church was still so called at this time and there was also the mission settlement of San Antonio de Valero. In the course of years these three settlements grew into the modern city of San Antonio.

From the year of its completion until 1793 the Alamo served as a mission church combined with a fort, well armed and available as a rallying point to resist invasion. In 1793 the Valero mission records were transferred to the archives of the Villa of San Fernando and the mission lands divided up among the Indians. After that the building was used only occasionally for religious services.

When San Antonio fell into the hands of the Texans in December of 1835 the Mexicans lost their last foothold in Texas and the town therefore became a point to be held at all hazards, a fact appreciated by William B. Travis, David Crockett, James Bowie and their men when they retired into the Alamo on the afternoon of February 23, 1836, with the coming of Santa Anna and his Mexican troops. The siege of the Alamo which followed was certainly one of the bloodiest battles in all history and the little group of one hundred and eighty-two patriots quartered in the ancient mission of San Antonio de Valero died to the last man rather than surrender, thereby earning for themselves and for the building in which they perished, a permanent place in the pages of history. Of course there was much more to the Alamo mission than the familiar little chapel; it however is the part which has been most carefully preserved and it has popularly come to signify the whole; also the final acts of the siege all took place within its walls.

When admittance to the mission was finally gained the wounded survivors were cruelly butchered. Santa Anna's dead were ordered buried in the cemetery but no such respect was accorded the remains of the slaughtered garrison; they were instead laid in three heaps, mixed with fuel—huge piles of dry brush, kindling wood and bodies—and burned. The final siege occurred on the morning of March 6, 1836. Four days before, the Independence of Texas had been proclaimed by the delegates of the people of Texas in general convention at Washington on the Brazos River. The interesting fact has been pointed out that the heroes of the Alamo, therefore, died for a republic of whose existence they never knew. The battle cry of "Remember the Alamo!" carried the Texans to victory at San Jacinto on April 21st of the same year, and the Republic of Texas came into actual existence.

On the 25th of February, 1837, the bones and ashes of the defenders were, by order of General Houston, collected as well as could be done by Colonel Juan N. Seguin and interred with military honors. Colonel Seguin was political chief of the Department of Bexar; he espoused the Revolutionary cause and entered the Alamo with Travis but escaped the massacre by reason of the message he was commissioned to bear to Fannin at Goliad.

Colonel Seguin's disposition of the remains of the Alamo heroes has been a much discussed question and since it is one that is intimately connected with several historic churches it seems desirable to take it up here. The funeral services were conducted from the old San Fernando Church; most versions seem to agree on this; but the exact location of the place of burial remains as much of a mystery today as in 1878 when Captain Reuben M. Potter wrote in the January issue of the "Magazine of American History":

The stranger will naturally inquire where lie the heroes of the Alamo, and Texas can reply only by a silent blush. A few hours after the action the bodies of the slaughtered garrison were gathered by the victors, laid in three heaps, mingled with fuel and burned, though their own dead were interred. On the 25th of February, 1837, the bones and ashes of the defenders were, by order of General Houston, collected, as well as could then be done, for burial by Colonel Seguin, then in command at San Antonio. The bones were placed in a large coffin, which, together with the gathered ashes, was interred with military honors. The place of burial was a peach orchard, then outside of the Alamo village and a few hundred yards from the fort. When I was last there, in 1861, it was still a large enclosed open lot, though surrounded by the suburb which had there grown up; but the rude landmarks which had once pointed out the place of sepulture had long since disappeared. Diligent search might then have found it, but it is now densely built over, and its identity is irrecoverably lost. This is too sad for comment.

Captain Potter's article in the "Magazine of American History" was the outgrowth of an earlier and shorter account published in the San Antonio "Herald" in 1860. Even at this early date, just twenty-four years after the siege, the exact burial place of the Alamo heroes was unknown for in the "Herald" article Captain Potter wrote:

The place of burial was in what was then a peach orchard outside the town and a few hundred yards from the Alamo. It is now a large enclosed lot in the midst of the Alamo suburb, but has fortunately not been built upon. The rude landmarks which once designated the place of burial have long since disappeared, and it would now require diligent search to find the exact locality. It is to be hoped that search will not be delayed until it is too late.

But the exact locality has not been found, not to this day, and, all the more cause for regret, the second article, written eighteen

years after the first account, seems to infer that no real determined effort was made at the time to find it!

The "peach orchard," however, is not the only claimant for the
honor. In the "Telegraph and Texas Register," Columbia, for
March 28, 1837, is given a vivid account of the burial although
this, like all other contemporary accounts, omits many details
which would be greatly treasured today and there is no exact
identification of the place of burial.

According to this report: "In conformity with an order from the
general commanding the army at headquarters, Col. Seguin, with
his command stationed at Bexar, paid the honors of war to the remains of the heroes of the Alamo; the ashes were found in three
places, the two smallest heaps were carefully collected, placed in a
coffin neatly covered with black, and having the names of Travis,
Bowie and Crockett engraved on the inside of the lid, and carried
to Bexar, and placed in the parish church, where the Texas flag, a
rifle and sword were laid upon it, for the purpose of being accompanied by the procession, which was formed at 3 o'clock on the
25th of February; the honors to be paid were announced in orders
of the evening previous, and by the tolling knell from day-break
to the hour of interment; at 4 o'clock the procession moved from
the church in Bexar. . . . The procession then passed through
the principal street of the city; crossed the river; passed through
the principal avenue on the other side; and halted at the place
where the first ashes had been gathered. The coffin was then placed
upon the spot, and three volleys of musquetry were discharged
by one of the companies; the procession then moved to the second
spot, whence part of the ashes in the coffin had been taken, where
the same honors were paid; the procession then proceeded to the
principal spot and place of interment, where the graves had been
prepared; the coffin had been placed on the principal heap of
ashes," when Colonel Seguin delivered a short address in Spanish,
followed by an address by Major Western in English. "The coffin
and all the ashes were then interred, and three volleys of musquetry were fired by the whole battalion."

The newspaper account then closes with the following para-
graph:

Thus have the last sad rites of a christian burial been performed over the remains of these brave men. In after times when peace shall have returned to smile upon our prosperous country, a towering fabric of architecture shall be reared by their grateful countrymen above their ashes—designating Bexar as the monumental city of Texas, where long after the massive walls of the Alamo have crumbled into dust, the votaries of freedom shall yearly assemble to celebrate at *this tomb of heroes,* the mighty achievements of the unreturning brave.

This might be taken as rather bitterly sarcastic in view of the way things have worked out. Or is it? Has a "towering fabric of architecture" actually been reared above the resting place of the ashes? In the July, 1900, issue of "The Quarterly of the Texas State Historical Association," in the article "A Retrospect of San Antonio" by Mrs. Emily B. Cooley, is to be found the following statement:

East Commerce Street was called the *Alameda* as late as 1875, and on this street, in the vicinity of St. Joseph's Church, tradition tells of a huge grave filled with the mortal remains of the heroes of the Alamo.

and Miss Adina De Zavala, Historian of the Texas Historical and Landmarks Association, gives the following information:

It is true that the old settlers, many of whom I knew and talked with, pointed out the places on the *Alameda* where the bodies of the Alamo heroes were burned, and they always stated that St. Joseph's Church designated one of these places. The others are east of the church on the *Alameda,* and are designated by tablets.

One of these tablets is placed on the M. Halff Bro. building on the corner of East Commerce and Rusk streets, and the other almost opposite, on the Salvation Army Chapel, on the north side of Commerce Street.

Is it a possibility, then, that St. Joseph's, the German church of San Antonio, whose corner-stone was laid in 1868, and which is located only a few hundred yards from the Alamo, stands as a monument above the graves of the Alamo heroes? The answer to this must be a negative one.

First of all, the funeral procession, according to the account in the "Telegraph and Texas Register," halted first at the place where the first ashes had been gathered; then passed on to the other two. This would mean that the first spot was the one nearest San Fernando Church, as the procession came from there. Now since the other two sites are, by tradition, placed east of St. Joseph's, with San Fernando to the west, it would suggest that the German church of San Antonio stands somewhere near the place where the procession first stopped.

This same process of reasoning cannot be followed in the case of the other two funeral pyre locations for the account in the paper is confusing on this point. After leaving the first spot the funeral procession moved to the "second spot," not necessarily the second pile of ashes as found, but simply the second spot from "whence part of the ashes in the coffin has been taken." This was, in fact, according to tradition, the third pile of ashes found—that is the third in point of distance from the Alamo. The procession then proceeded to the principal spot and place of interment, its location completely unidentified in any way by the article.

The most dependable tradition is that the place of interment lies in the "vicinity of St. Joseph's Church"—a wide and elastic statement. The exact location of any one of the three places on the *Alameda* where the bodies were burned has been hopelessly lost. The traditional place of burial, pointed out for years by the old residents of San Antonio, is, however, in the immediate vicinity of the Salvation Army Chapel which stands at 313 East Commerce Street, and this fact is so stated on the tablet which has been placed there. Almost directly across the street another tablet marks the general location of what was apparently the second pile of ashes mentioned in the newspaper account.

For the one objection to East Commerce Street as the place of burial we must go back to the year 1889. At this date the exact location of the tomb of the Alamo heroes had become a confused question. Many traditions were extant; nothing definite was known.

Colonel Seguin had removed to Mexico many years before and was believed to be dead until General Hamilton Prioleau Bee got in touch with him in 1889. Here at last seemed a chance to settle the puzzling question once and for all but Colonel Seguin's contribution instead of helping matters tended to confuse them all the more. His letter, which is given in full, sheds an entirely new light on the burial place of the Alamo heroes and records a version which, in spite of the fact that it was attacked on all sides, by the clergy of San Fernando and the old residents of San Antonio, yet persists and is still heard very frequently today.

Laredo, Tamaulipas
March 28, 1889.

Hamilton P. Bee, Esq.
San Antonio
Dear Sir:

This is in answer to your favor of the 9th instant which I have not answered before because I have not been well.

The remains of those who died in the Alamo were ordered burned under instructions of General Santa Anna, and the small fragments I ordered put in an urn; I had a grave dug in the Cathedral of San Antonio, near the sanctuary, that is, in front of the railings but very near the steps.

That is all I can tell you in regard to the matter.

Very truly yours,
Juan N. Seguin

If you are the son of him who was Secretary of War during the Republic of Texas, I shall never forget him and I offer you my friendship.

Seguin

Just what is the answer to this most puzzling question? Did Colonel Seguin's memory play him false after a lapse of fifty-two years? * How can one reconcile his statement " the small frag-

---

* The majority opinion has always been that Colonel Seguin was mistaken. This year when it was decided to move the main altar of San Fernando Cathedral back to a spot where the main altar stood, approximately, one hundred years ago—in order to provide more room—all agreed that the moment was opportune to attempt to learn more definitely whether the remains of some of the Alamo heroes rested there. Excavations were made July 28th and at a depth of about four feet was found a strata of a brown substance, indicating the top of a box. Several nails were next uncovered and a piece of metal identified by H. H. Flores, superintendent of the cathedral, as a casket ornament. Then came a number of bone fragments, some of which were said to bear evidence of having been burned, a lower jaw with most of its teeth intact, small bits of moldering cloth and a few buttons.

Whether these findings actually constitute the remains of some of the Alamo heroes

ments" with the large amount of bones and ashes mentioned in other accounts? Is it possible that there were in fact two interments; with "the small fragments" placed in an urn and buried in San Fernando in a symbolic ceremony, and the remainder, consisting of much wood ash and so on, impossible of identification, buried outside the city? If so, why was no mention of this made in the account of the burial published in the "Telegraph and Texas Register" or in the various articles published in the Texas "Almanac"? Or, was the account as published in the "Telegraph" all a hoax, as one writer insists? Again, if so, why was such a hoax perpetrated? Why should the Alamo heroes have been buried in such an obscure indefinite place as the center of a peach orchard so that just twenty-three years after the burial the rude landmarks which had once pointed out the place of interment had long since disappeared? Why were they allowed to disappear? Is it possible that Colonel Seguin's later account was true after all?

But all of these puzzling questions must remain unanswered; to not one of them can we give a definite reply not limited to some extent by our own opinion. St. Joseph's, San Fernando and the Alamo hold their secrets well, remaining completely mute to our every plea. If only inanimate walls could talk. . . .

The quaint old Alamo chapel with its simple façade is now owned by the state and stands as a memorial to the men who fought there. In it will be found many interesting relics connected with the historic struggle in which it played the most decisive part.

The Alamo is located in the heart of San Antonio and then at a distance of about two miles away begins a series of truly re-

---

will probably be a much discussed question for some time to come. The "box" or "casket," mentioned in newspaper accounts, hardly agrees with Colonel Seguin's statement, "the small fragments I ordered put in an urn." It seems strange also that the San Fernando burial site apparently never came to the attention of Captain Reuben M. Potter who was in San Antonio as early as 1841, and later, and who knew and talked with Colonel Juan N. Seguin, obtaining from him "many additional and interesting details" which went into the "Magazine of American History" article, apparently nothng new, though, regarding the burial place of the Alamo heroes.

On the other hand, the bits of human bones located under the sanctuary floor of San Fernando Cathedral were found at a spot which corresponds to the location given in Colonel Seguin's letter, "near the sanctuary, that is, in front of the railings but very near the steps," of the old San Fernando church, and many well-known authorities on early Texas history, including Miss Adina De Zavala, whose opinions the author respects, insist that the San Fernando tradition has been completely vindicated.

markable missions, built in eighteenth-century Spanish style and each remembered for some particular reason of its own.

At Mission Purísima Concepción it is the twin towers and the near-by tablet marking the site of a battle between Mexicans and Texans several months preceding the fall of the Alamo; at San José it is the exquisite carving that catches one's eye; at San Juan Capistrano it is the general air of desolation that is remembered, although a chapel has been restored; and finally San Francisco de la Espada because here was used the first text book in the Province of Texas, a book of religious instructions written by Father Bartholome Garcia of the mission and published in Mexico in 1760, truly a historical fact of importance.

It would have been a very difficult thing to have translated the catechism into all of the different Indian languages spoken in the vicinity of the mission so Father Garcia simply prepared his "Manual" in the Coahuiltecan language which was the most common, thereby preserving that particular dialect in permanent form as a number of the Garcia manuals are still in existence. The title page is marked "Printed with the necessary permission," which simply means with both civil and ecclesiastical authority, as this was necessary for all printing in those times.

According to tradition, some of the mortar used in the construction of Espada, and of Concepción as well, was mixed with asses' milk and the name of the former came from the old tower built as it was in the form of the hilt of a sword. The cruciform door is unmistakably Moorish, while in the elevated front, fitted with arches, hang the three original bells of the mission. The structure is still in use and there is even yet a little mission school conducted by nuns who live in the restored barracks which form a part of the old walled-in enclosure. Espada is one of the most interesting of the old missions but since it is off the regular route is frequently missed by the tourist. It was somewhat rebuilt in 1845 but the outside appearance of the church remains unchanged, the present façade being a part of the old structure. The square of this mission was the first camping ground of the Texas Army of Independence in the campaign about Bexar, in 1835.

Mission Concepción still has its great dome and the interior is a miniature Alamo, giving the visitor a good idea of the original appearance of that historic structure. The Church of the Alamo was a ruin by 1762 for its two towers, dome and arched roof are said to have fallen in previous to or about that year and it was never restored or fully rebuilt. Following Santa Anna's siege there was more desolation than ever and it was not until many years later that the building was repaired and reroofed, which accounts for the comparatively modern lines, as well as the lack of harmony, of the present covering. "For many years," writes Adina De Zavala in her "History and Legends of The Alamo and Other Missions," "the Alamo was abandoned as a great tomb, a place of horror to many who recalled the story of the frightful sacrifice of the heroes of 1836."

The front of Concepción was originally frescoed in the brightest colors of which the Franciscans were capable and must have presented a gorgeous appearance to the early Indian worshipers. The well dug by the padres is still there.

Much has been written of San José de Aguayo, so named in honor of the Marquis de Aguayo, and its famous façade, pillars, doorways and windows, but not half enough, for to many travelers this great treasure of art is still unknown. The famous "Rose Window" is a lovely thing but no finer than other bits of carving found within and upon the same walls: figures of saints, cherub heads, ornate pillars, a truly exquisite door facing. . . .

From Spain came Juan Huicar, one of the best artists of his day, to the frontier to decorate the exteriors of the more important missions, his best work finding expression in San José de Aguayo. There is, for instance, the famous window already referred to. According to tradition, Huicar, a descendant of the architect who designed the Alhambra, poured into the creation of the Rose Window all the agony of a broken heart over a lost love.

The story most generally told is that Huicar was preparing to return to Spain to claim an inheritance and wed the girl who had sworn to wait for him, but the very ship on which he intended to return to his betrothed brought him news that she had wed another. Cut to the quick, the sensitive young artist cursed all women

Mission San José de Aguayo, near San Antonio, Texas, whose carved facade is something to marvel at, even today. *Photo by Harvey Patteson.*

Mission San Francisco de la Espada, near San Antonio, Texas, with its unusual facade and Moorish door. *Photo by Harvey Patteson.*

and determined to devote his entire life and talents to the church. During the twenty years that remained of his life, most of which time was spent in carving the façade and baptistry of San José, Huicar is said to have aged rapidly and changed from a young, eager boy into a morose, embittered old man. Of course part of this tale may be the purest of fancy but it makes a very pretty story and adds a touch of romance to the old mission.

Just how these traditions arise, if not with some foundation of fact, would be difficult to conjecture. Another story exists with reference to the old bells that hang in the tower. In this case it concerns one Don Luis Angel de Leon, a young Spanish nobleman who came to Texas with a group of adventurers, there to be slain in an Indian raid which, so the tale continues, was not far from the Mission of San José.

When the news reached Spain the bells for the mission were just being cast and Luis' fiancée, the Señorita Theresa, stricken with grief, removed the golden ring and cross her lover had given her and cast them into the molten metal so that these bells would carry a message to him when they reached their resting place far over the sea. Other people who were present were much affected and followed her example, throwing their gold and silver ornaments into the caldron, and although some authorities scoff at the use of gold and silver in church bells, it is a fact well known that many of these mission bells have a peculiar sweetness of tone not found in any other bells; it is also definitely known that the custom of donating precious jewelry to be used in the casting of such bells was actually followed in Spain for many years. This same legend is told of the well-known bells of San Gabriel Mission, California.

San José was abandoned as a mission in 1803 and in 1868 the dome and parts of the arched roof fell. The statues have been wilfully disfigured and the delicately carved work on the front ruthlessly defaced. A massive pile of gray stone, San José has been referred to as the most magnificent ruin in America. A restored model of the mission was a part of the Texas exhibit at the Chicago Century of Progress Exposition.

Sidney Lanier wrote of this mission:

Down the river a couple of miles one comes to the Mission San José de Aguayo. This is more elaborate and on a larger scale than the buildings of the first mission, and is still very beautiful. Religious services are regularly conducted here; and one can do worse things than to steal out here from town on some wonderfully calm Sunday morning, and hear a Mass, and dream back the century and a half of strange, lonesome, devout, hymn-haunted and Indian years that have trailed past these walls.

Some of the Texas missions go back to the seventeenth century, San Francisco de la Espada being an outgrowth of a mission originally founded on May 23, 1690. The existing missions of Concepción, San Juan and Espada were all commenced in 1731. San José was founded in 1720, but the corner-stone of the present stone church was not laid until 1768. A rehabilitation program is now under way at this mission and it is to be hoped that a complete restoration will some day be effected, in which all that is original will be retained and saved for posterity. It will be noticed that all of these missions date back prior to the Revolution and that most of them were flourishing churches at the time George Washington was born! All of them, with the exception of the Alamo, still possess one or more of their original chimes, sent over by the King of Spain two centuries ago.

We must not leave Texas without visiting the presidio chapel to be found near Goliad, for much history lingers around this old building.

It was in 1749 that the Presidio La Bahia and Mission Espiritu Santo were established under Spanish protection. Mission San Rosario, the third unit in the early Spanish settlement at Goliad, was built in 1754, on the San Antonio River, about four miles from the presidio and is now in complete ruins.

Of the presidio, all that remains is the chapel, fairly well preserved; the rest is now a mass of crumbling ruins although the barrack quarters and other portions of the fort are partially traceable in visible foundations and broken walls. Religious services are still held in the chapel which is built along very pleasing lines.

The Presidio La Bahia was captured by the Texans under the

command of Collingsworth and Milan in 1835. In December of that year, meeting within the walls of the presidio, the first formal declaration of Texas independence was promulgated by Collingsworth's garrison of troops.

On March 19, 1836, was fought the Battle of Perdido, just across the river from La Bahia, near Mission Espiritu Santo. Greatly outnumbered, the Texans under the command of Colonel J. W. Fannin, Jr., decided to surrender. Although they were promised treatment accorded ordinary prisoners of war, the little group of three hundred and thirty men were taken back to the presidio where they were imprisoned for a week. Then on Palm Sunday, March 27th, they were marched out in several divisions, in as many directions, and shot down by order of General Santa Anna.

The victims of the massacre were, like the heroes of the Alamo, thrown in piles, mixed with dry fuel and burned, but happily the bones and ashes did not have to wait so long for decent interment. General Rusk, in command of the Texas army, reached Goliad on June 4th and under his direction the remains were gathered from the places where they had been scattered and assembled in one spot for burial, not far from the presidio. The exact place of burial is known and is at last being appropriately marked by a memorial structure of stone and bronze.

Mission Espiritu Santo stood about half a mile from the presidio. At the time of the Battle of Perdido this mission had fallen into a ruinous state but it was repaired about 1848, for use as a school, later becoming a part of Aranama College, one of the earlier chartered colleges of Texas, and named after an Indian tribe. Later the structure was reduced to ashes by a fire. This mission is located within Goliad State Park, a large tract of over two hundred acres, presented to the state by the city and county of Goliad. A CCC camp is located in the park and under the direction of the National Park Service is engaged in the work of restoring the mission. Excavations and much research work have revealed the comparative magnitude of the original structure and it is hoped that a complete restoration can be made. The CCC camp, incidentally, blends in a touch of modern conditions with the old, offering a vivid contrast as probably nothing else could.

CHAPTER XIII

HISTORIC CHURCHES OF THE SOUTHWEST

The Mission is no more; upon its walls
  The golden lizards slip, or breathless pause,
Still as the sunshine brokenly that falls
  Through crannied roof and spider-webs of gauze;
No more the bell its solemn warning calls—
  A holier silence thrills and overawes;
And the sharp lights and shadows of to-day
Outline the Mission of San Luis Rey.
                    —Francis Bret Harte

SAN MIGUEL CHURCH of Sante Fé, "City of the Holy Faith," is most generally referred to as the oldest church structure in America and, although this claim cannot be historically authenticated, according to the tradition glibly passed on to the tourist, it was built by Coronado in 1541! Various writers have assigned different dates for its construction, the years 1607 and 1636 being among those given.

The most Reverend J. B. Salpointe, D.D., has the following to say in his book "Soldiers of the Cross":

The city of Santa Fé was founded by Oñate in 1605 or 1606, and San Gabriel was deserted at the time. . . . The new town having been assigned its site, there cannot be any doubt but that Oñate and his people, faithful to the Spanish traditions, thought at once of building a church for holding divine services. This, we are inclined to believe, was that of San Miguel. . . .

The Right Reverend Salpointe was the second Bishop of New Mexico and his book on the old missions of the Southwest is considered authoritative. His statements concerning San Miguel, while merely expressing an opinion, are probably as nearly correct as any reasonable conjecture can be and it is extremely doubtful if anything more definite will ever be known. So while there seems little reason to believe that the walls of San Miguel were built by Coronado in 1541, there actually is some reason for believing they were built in 1605 or 1606.

The church is located in what is now the oldest part of the town of Santa Fé. Fray Alonso de Benavides in his famous report of 1630 presented to the King of Spain in person, in Madrid, points out that the population of Santa Fé consisted of "perhaps two hundred and fifty Spaniards, only fifty of whom can be armed," and perhaps two hundred Indians. He goes on to say, "They lacked only the principal (thing), which was the church. The one they had was a poor hut, for the religious attended first to building the church of the Indians they were converting and with whom they were ministering and living. And so, as soon as I came in as Custodian (1622) I commenced to build the church and monastery—and to the honor and glory of God our Lord; it would shine in whatsoever place."

This report quite obviously accounts for the fact that San Miguel has always been known as the oldest church in the town since the section of the city in which it is located is always referred to in the old maps as being settled by the Mexican Indians and, according to Benavides' reports, the Indians of New Mexico (and of Santa Fé presumably) were well cared for in the matter of churches—it was only the Spaniards who had no suitable house of worship.

Little more is known of the history of this ancient house of worship until 1680, the year of the Pueblo Revolution, for all of the early records were destroyed in the general conflagration of documents in the center of the plaza after the Spanish retreat. On the morning of August 15, 1680, "about five hundred Indians appeared in the fields near the chapel of San Miguel, across the Santa Fé River, in that part of town occupied by the Tlascalan Indians who had settled there from Mexico." Within two days all of the buildings of the capital were burned with the exception of the palace.

We know, however, that only the woodwork of San Miguel Church was destroyed in the fire of 1680 because in 1693, soon after the reconquest by De Vargas, the church was repaired and there is no mention of any stone or adobe or other like material being used in the walls which are referred to as still standing. Temporary repairs were soon made and with the coming of a new Governor these repairs were made more permanent, all work being completed in 1710, as appears from an inscription, still plainly legible on the great square beam near the west end of the building, which reads:

El Señor Marquez de la Peñuela hizo esta fabrica, el Alfres Real Don Agustin Flores Vergara, su criado. Año de 1710.—The Marquis de la Peñuela erected this building. The Royal Ensign Don Agustin Flores Vergara, his servant. The year 1710.

Recently this beam was made the subject of a scientific study by Mr. W. S. Stallings, Jr., of the Rockefeller School of Anthropology and its antiquity upheld, thereby corroborating one phase of the church's history.

It can be said for San Miguel, in support of its claim, that it certainly looks old. Its ancient walls are fully five feet thick, one reason why the building has withstood the attacks of fires, battles and earthquakes of the years and has now come down to us as a connecting link between the undoubtedly wild and at times savage days of its early existence and the calm serenity of Santa Fe today; naturally, however, and in some cases unfortunately, repairs have had to be made from time to time.

In 1830 a new roof took the place of the old and a few minor changes were put into effect. At that time the church had a triple tower, each story diminishing in size, but in 1872 a severe storm wrecked the upper part of this tower and when the building was repaired and stone buttresses constructed on each side of the front to prevent further damage, unhappily this tower was not restored. This is indeed a pity and it is to be hoped that some day this will be done, for many pictures of the church as it existed prior to 1872 are in existence and an exact reproduction of the tower could easily be made and, judging from old photographs, the church with its ancient tower had a certain charm that is lacking in the building as it exists today.

Considerable Spanish and Mexican carving may be found in the church, particularly upon the puncheon floor of the gallery, which is most interesting. The architecture of the interior is also worth studying by those interested, being along the general lines of all of the old mission churches which, unlike the colonial ecclesiastical structures of the Atlantic Coast, were most usually rectangular instead of square.

The paintings on the altar always attract much attention. Many of them have a richness and beautiful blending of color that is almost unbelievable considering their age and the further fact that they have not always had the best of care, particularly the large rectangular paintings of the Annunciation by Giovanni Cimabue whose thirteenth-century paintings so adorn the great Church of St. Mary in Florence, Italy. In the early days these paintings were brought out only on certain feast days and carried in procession and one of them has two narrow holes which it is said were made by hostile Indians while it was being carried along the street.

One of the most interesting objects in San Miguel Chapel is its ancient bell. It weighs seven hundred and eighty pounds but is not so large as its weight might seem to indicate, being fully four inches thick. There has been much discussion as to its age and early history but like the beginnings of the church itself, nothing is definitely known; neither is it known just when it found a resting place in the chapel. Some say it was first used in another church and later given to San Miguel; others think that it has been in its present home from the early days; while still others declare that it is of more modern construction. The Reverend W. J. Howlett in his life of Bishop Machebeuf carefully recounts the legend of this old bell:

In a little room at the base of the tower of San Miguel is the sweetest-toned bell in America, and perhaps the richest. It, too, has its history, filled with poetry and romance of the ages of the faith.

In 1356, so the legend runs, the Spaniards were fighting the Moors. Battle after battle was fought and lost by the Christians, until the people vowed a bell to St. Joseph as a gage of their confidence in his assistance. They brought their gold and silver plate, their rings and their bracelets, their brooches and ear-rings, and cast them into the melting-pot with the other metal. The bell was cast, and in its tone were the richness of gold and the sweetness of sacrifice. It sounded the defeat of Moslemism in Spain, and then came to ring in the birth of Christianity in Mexico, and with the Padres it found its way up the Rio Grande to rest and ring out its sweet notes over the City of the Holy Faith.

In the old adobe church stands the bell—
From the ancient tower its notes have ceased to swell
O'er the houses, quaint and low,
Whence it summoned long ago,
Spanish conqueror, Indian slave,
All to gather 'neath this nave.
Pealed it many a bygone day
O'er the roofs of Santa Fé
And before that, century long,
Had it sent its sacred song
O'er the hills and dales of distant, sunny Spain,
Six long centuries have passed
Since the ancient bell was cast,
And sounded forth its first long sweet refrain.
Strike it now, and you shall hear,
Sweet and soft, and silver clear,
Such a note as thrills your heart
With its tender magic art,
Echoing softly through the gloom
Of that ancient, storied room,
Dying softly, far away,
In the church at Santa Fé.

Since the publication of Willa Cather's "Death Comes for the Archbishop" the Cathedral of St. Francis has come to have an added interest. It seems appropriate therefore that something of its history should be told here. While the main portion of the building is not of ancient construction, it does have chapels which go back to the early part of the eighteenth century.

We have read in the history of San Miguel Church how Fray

Alonzo de Benavides soon after his arrival in Santa Fé began the erection of a church and monastery to the honor and glory of God. As Benavides came to New Mexico in 1622 it is assumed that the first parish church was begun that same year, on the same spot where the cathedral now stands. This building was almost completely destroyed in the Pueblo Revolution of 1680 and was not rebuilt until 1713–14.

The story of Bishop Lamy, later Archbishop Lamy—the Bishop Latour of "Death Comes for the Archbishop"—and how his great plans and wishes for a suitable cathedral were at last answered, has been much too beautifully told by Willa Cather for me to attempt even a résumé here. After reading the account of his indefatigable energy in the face of many trials and hardships, even those of us who are historically minded can easily forgive the good Bishop for taking down the church of 1713 and substituting the present cathedral, for through Willa Cather's book, Bishop Lamy and his church have in themselves become historic in much the same manner that the California missions were popularized by Helen Hunt Jackson's "Ramona."

The new Cathedral of St. Francis was built around the adobe church of 1713, the corner-stone being laid on July 14, 1869. When the roof was at last completed the old structure, with the exception of the east end, was taken down and carried away. The building from the front to the arms of the transept is one hundred and twenty feet long and sixty feet high, with a height in the middle nave of sixty-five feet. The walls are of native stone while the ceiling is of very light volcanic tufa of a dark red color, brought from a mountain twelve miles distant. The two towers are eighty-five feet high and both remain unfinished to this day, a fact which carries with it a twinge of sadness in view of its builder's great plans.

In the key-arch at the main entrance, Archbishop Lamy had a triangle placed and in it the word "Adonoi" in Hebraic letters. This was in honor of various Jewish friends who were helpful to the Archbishop in his work and who made generous contributions to the building fund.

There was at one time in Santa Fé a church popularly known

as "The Castrense"—"belonging to the military profession"—
although its real name was "Church of Our Lady of Light." This
church contained a magnificent stone reredos, carved under order
of Governor Francisco Antonio Marin del Valle who served from
1754 to 1760. When "The Castrense" was taken down in 1859
the great reredos was carefully removed to the old Church of
St. Francis and placed in its proper position in the rear of the altar.

There it remains, for that portion of the old church, the east
end, has never been destroyed, and serves to connect the ancient
with the modern, keeping its history in an unbroken continuous
line. The two transept chapels are a part of the old church of
1713 now made a part of the cathedral proper. The chancel of the
old church, however, is now walled off from the newer building
and forms a little chapel behind the present high altar. This room
has an especial interest for the historian because in it are buried
some of the martyred Franciscan fathers who lost their lives in the
revolt of 1680. Here also is found the great stone reredos, that
amazing piece of stone sculpture already referred to.

Its dimensions are eighteen feet wide by fourteen feet high and
it was executed out of native stone by artists brought from Mexico.
Many figures are worked into the design: "St. Anthony of Padua,
with the Holy Child and a tree; St. Ignatius, with a book and
standard; St. John Nepomuceno, with cross and palm; St. Francis
Xavier baptizing Indians, the water being poured from a shell;
while crowning all is a representation of St. Joseph and of the
Virgin and Child." Carved arabesque columns separate the various
sections and the whole is painted in appropriate colors.

The cathedral since its erection has been gradually beautified by
fine stained-glass windows and other furnishings but to the visitor
its greatest interest lies in the rare old pictures and statues which
have been in the possession of the parish for generations. The great
stone reredos, being in a separate room, is frequently missed by the
tourist; however, there is nothing more interesting to be seen in
Santa Fé.

The mission church at Acoma, New Mexico, is said to be the
oldest European structure now extant in the United States in anything like its original form. This was built in 1629 and is said to

Old church at Acoma, New Mexico. Said to be the oldest European structure now extant in the United States in anything like its original form.
Photo by Mullarky.

be almost the only edifice that survived the Pueblo Revolution of 1680. When De Vargas visited the Rock of Acoma in November, 1692, he found the walls "stood firm in spite of heavy rains which break the windows and sky lights of the said church." This is ample evidence that the building was in a good state of preservation even before the reconquest had been effected. When that was accomplished the Acoma church was repaired and although some insist that an entirely new church was built at this time, this seems somewhat unlikely.

The famous pueblo of Acoma is truly a city of the sky, being located on a giant rock which rises perpendicularly nearly four hundred feet from the great plain below, which is itself over seven thousand feet above the sea. Its church is of enormous proportions: one hundred and fifty feet long, thirty-five feet wide and forty feet high and exceedingly massive. The adobe walls are ten feet thick at the base while the roof beams are logs forty feet long and fourteen inches in diameter.

These measurements are given in some detail so as to make more impressive the fact that every particle of material that went into the building of this old structure had to be brought up from the plain below. There was no road or trail in those days; only an almost perpendicular crevice in the great cliff. The timbers for the roof were first carried by the men twenty miles from the San Mateo Mountains; then the perilous journey upward began. One misstep meant certain destruction. It is hard, almost impossible, for modern man to contemplate the work involved or in just what manner it was accomplished but in some way the dizzy height was scaled and the church at last completed.

Two unique institutions adjoin the church: a large monastery which the Indians built for the early Franciscan missionaries and a cemetery. The great rock on which Acoma stood was entirely devoid of earth so the Indians built a stone wall nearly two hundred feet square and forty-five feet high. This they gradually filled with earth brought up in sacks from the depths below and in this manner was the cemetery finally made.

The story told of the conversion of the Indians of Acoma by Fray Juan Ramirez is an interesting one. Journeying all the way from Santa Fe alone and afoot, a shower of arrows was his first greeting from the natives high above; however, none of these touched him. At this moment it happened that a little girl of eight suddenly fell over the cliff and landed unhurt near Fray Ramirez. He picked her up and carried her to the summit of the great rock where he restored her to her mother and father. The Indians, being unable to see where she had fallen, believed she had been killed; her restoration by Fray Juan was received as a miracle, and the natives speedily accepted Christianity. Fray Juan remained at Acoma for many years. It was he who built the great church there and later a trail to the summit by which horses could ascend.

Not far away from the giant rock of Acoma is the even higher Enchanted Mesa, which, according to tradition, was the original site of the city. According to the story which has been handed down from one generation to another, the summit of this rock was accessible only by means of a narrow perpendicular pathway, in which little niches cut in the rock made a ladder of stone up the great height. And then one day when every man and almost every woman was busy in the fields of the valley far below—with only three old women left above in the deserted town—there came a terrible storm. The lightning struck the great stone cliff right where the dizzy stone stairway was cut, knocking away a portion of the huge rock and cutting off the sole means of communication with the world above. A return to the old home being impossible the Indians built a new city on the top of the adjacent cliff; this is the Acoma of today. The three old women left alone on the Enchanted Mesa were naturally forced to live out the remainder of their lives there, separated from their kindred.

No account of Acoma would be complete without some mention of the famous picture of St. Joseph which it possesses. This was brought to Acoma in 1629 by Fray Ramirez, to whom it had been presented by Charles II of Spain. The picture was supposed to possess miraculous power and whenever an attack from the Apaches was expected or whenever the pueblo was in need of rain; in short, whenever things were not going exactly as they should, St. Joseph was always appealed to and, it is said, always with fruitful results. This picture was once the subject of as strange a lawsuit as has ever passed through the courts, that of the "Pueblo of Acoma vs. the Pueblo of Laguna" in 1857.

It seems that the Pueblo of Laguna had been suffering from a period of unfortunate occurrences. The crops had been small, there had been much sickness and too much rain; they therefore sent a commission to Acoma asking the loan of the picture of St. Joseph in the hope that he would restore order out of chaos! The Acoma Indians, however, refused to allow their beloved picture to leave them, with the result that a band of Laguna warriors broke into the chapel and carried it away. Naturally there was much excitement when the theft was discovered but the Reverend Mariano de Jesus Lopez, the superior of the Franciscans, persuaded the Acomans to be generous and let the Lagunans have the benefit of the influence of the miraculous picture for a few months, with the understanding that they would agree to return it at the end of that time.

This seemed like a fair solution but alas! so successful was the picture in changing the condition of the Lagunans that when the time agreed upon had passed they refused to return it. The matter was finally carried into court and this was the reason for the contest already referred to. It is said that the lawyers' fees made both pueblos poor but finally a decision was rendered in favor of the original owners and the Acomans then appointed a delegation to bring the saint home. But when they had journeyed half-way to Laguna they found the picture resting against a mesquite tree and many firmly believed that when St. Joseph heard of the decision of the court he was so anxious to get back to his home that he started out by himself!

The old Acoma church is generally considered to be a splendid example of the most perfect type of New Mexican architecture and at the Panama Exposition at San Diego served as the model for the New Mexico Building.

The finest, best preserved and in many ways the most interesting of all the Spanish missions in North America is undoubtedly San Xavier del Bac, nine miles south of Tucson, Arizona, on the Papago Indian Reservation. A halo of romance crowns the spot while an air of unbelievable medieval richness pervades the interior of the building. San Xavier was first established as a Jesuit mission by Padre Francisco Eusebio Kino in 1692 and it was from the first one of the most prosperous of all the south-western missions.

Padre Kino died in 1711 but although some have said that there were no priests in southern Arizona for twenty years after his passing, this is now known to be incorrect for the Mission of San Xavier del Bac continued to operate until the Franciscans came to take the place of the Jesuits. Some of the old journals tell us that the surrounding Indian settlement was the garden spot of the desert, where grew in abundance such trees as fig, orange and pomegranate and the farm products and vegetables introduced by the Spanish Fathers. The mission is situated in a very fertile and well-watered valley and even yet the Papago Indians have excellent fields immediately adjoining the mission lands.

The Franciscans took charge in 1768 and the present church was begun about 1783 and completed in 1797, this latter date being carved upon the inside of the sacristy door. Fray Belthasar Carrillo, Fray Narciso Gutierrez, and Fray Francisco Thomas Garces were the missionaries there during the time of its construction but the actual designer of the great church is unknown.

There is also some confusion concerning the foundations of the present church. Some writers insist that these were laid by Padre Kino in 1700 but this is not borne out by the tradition of the Indians who point out a spot nearer the Santa Cruz River as the site of the earlier mission. Neither do the physical surroundings of the present mission agree with the site described by Padre Kino.

The Church of San Xavier del Bac is of the Moorish style. It is built of stone and brick and is one hundred and five by twenty-seven feet within the walls. Its form is that of a cross, the transept forming chapels twenty-one feet square on each side of the nave. "The building has only one nave," wrote the Most Reverend John B. Salpointe, first Bishop of Tucson, "which is divided into six portions, marked by as many arches, each one resting on two pillars set against the walls. Above the transept is a cupola of about fifty feet in elevation, the remainder of the vaults in the building being only about thirty feet high.

"The altars and especially the principal one, are decorated with columns and a great profusion of arabesques in low relief, all gilded or painted in different colors according to the requirements of the Moorish style."

The building was never finished, as is evidenced by the incomplete tower and the sketched-in paintings in the nave. Regarding this unfinished tower there are a dozen or more legends in circulation, one being that a priest fell from it and was killed and the work never taken up again after that. Just why this should likewise have stopped the work on the paintings in the nave is not explained. As a matter of fact, the reason the church was never completed was because the Franciscans were expelled before they had a chance to finish it; afterwards there was never available the money necessary to do the work. All the various legends told in connection with the unfinished tower are actually without any foundation in fact.

Following the expulsion of the Franciscans, after Mexico gained her independence from Spain, the Mission of San Xavier del Bac remained without a priest for a long time. In 1859 the territory of Arizona was attached to the Diocese of Santa Fé, and the Right Reverend J. B. Lamy sent his Vicar General, the active and energetic J. P. Machebeuf, to investigate conditions there. Father Machebeuf found the church of San Xavier to be the only one in Arizona which was not in complete ruins. Even here though, the vaults of the once beautiful temple had been greatly injured by leakage and Father Machebeuf remained long enough to burn lime and put a coat of mortar on the outside surface to prevent any further damage. These repairs undoubtedly saved the mission for posterity.

Nor had the Indians of the old mission forgotten the things they had been taught by the missionaries many years before. As soon as they heard that a priest was coming back to them they rushed to the church and rang the bells joyously to welcome him, and when the Reverend J. P. Machebeuf at last arrived they brought out from hiding a chalice and other sacred vessels and furnishings of the altar which they had kept hidden all those years lest they should be carried off by strangers. There is something very beautiful and altogether romantic in the picture we get of these Indian neophytes clinging to the teachings of the Spanish missionaries when through several generations they were without the services of a guiding hand to show them the way.

The story of Father Machebeuf's stay among the Papago Indians and his labors in preserving San Xavier del Bac have been beautifully recounted by Willa Cather in her "Death Comes for the Archbishop" in which Father Machebeuf becomes the brave, inspiring little Father Vaillant so popular in that story.

In 1906 the work of restoring San Xavier del Bac was begun under the direction of Bishop Granjon of Tucson. The brick wall which formerly surrounded the church was replaced and the building thoroughly repaired. No picture or fresco was retouched, the interior being allowed to remain exactly as the old padres left it, except for one modern statue of St. Francis Xavier, and the pews, which are new.

In 1927 the Legislature of California named Padre Junípero Serra, the father of the California missions, as one of the state's two representatives to stand in Statuary Hall in the Capitol at Washington. The little Spanish priest so signally honored by the Pacific Coast state began his labors in California with the founding of San Diego Mission in 1769. Because of this San Diego is sometimes referred to as the "Plymouth of the Pacific Coast," for it was here that California really began, the designation being somewhat of a misnomer, of course, since the Atlantic Coast did not actually begin at Plymouth.

Junípero Serra was born in the little town of Petra, Island of Jamorca, in the year 1713. He was fifty-six years of age when he founded his first mission in California and from then on until his death in 1784 his life was one of constant toil but his unconquerable spirit and the intense devotion he felt for his work made the many difficulties in some manner surmountable.

To present even an outline of the work accomplished by the Spanish missionaries in California would require an entire volume

San Xavier del Bac, near Tucson, Ariz. A church pervaded by an air of unbelievable medieval richness.
Photo by Campbell Studio.

Royal Presidio Chapel, Monterey, California, the sole survivor of the Presidio at Monterey.
Photo courtesy Hotel Del Monte.

in itself; in a book of this nature, therefore, one can only visit a few of the more important and more interesting structures and let that suffice. As a matter of fact the history of one mission is practically the same as that of another. By stopping at a few of them we shall attempt to obtain a picture of the whole chain and at the same time avoid the monotony of repetition.

From 1769 to 1823 some twenty-one missions were erected by the Franciscan Fathers, starting at San Diego and ending at Sonoma and during this time San Diego Mission flourished, exerting great influence on the Indians who were induced to lead a settled life and to take up civilized pursuits. All that is left at the San Diego mission site now is the façade and a few remnants of the lateral walls of the third structure which flourished there. This was begun in 1808 and finished in 1813. A few old trees of the once thriving olive orchards live on as do a few ancient palms, silent reminders of a past glory that has now departed.

San Carlos Borromeo was the second mission founded by Padre Serra and while not so often sung about in legend and story, in real historic and religious interest it surpasses all of the California missions.

When Padre Serra reached the Bay of Monterey in 1770 the first duty accomplished was to erect a shelter of boughs for worship. Once this was safely accomplished, the ground was sprinkled with holy water and after Mass had been said, the possession of the land in the name of Charles III of Spain was proclaimed. A site for the presidio and mission was next selected. Within a short time a number of huts, one of which served as the chapel, and a stockade of logs around the whole group, were finished. The presidio was known as "El Presidio Real"—Royal Fort—and its chapel "La Capilla Real"—Royal Chapel—since it became the place of worship of the royal governors, representatives of the King of Spain in California.

For his mission Padre Serra selected a spot on the shores of beautiful Carmel Bay, south of Monterey. The interesting fact has been pointed out by Rexford Newcomb in his "The Old Mission Churches and Historic Houses of California" that in many ways San Carlos Mission may really be considered the first cathedral of

California for although not a bishop in the true ecclesiastical sense, Padre Serra had permission to confirm and otherwise perform duties corresponding to those of a bishop and it was from San Carlos that he directed his labors. It was here that he made his home and when at length the time came for him to cease his earthly labors, his body was laid to rest in the sanctuary of the church on the Gospel side.

This was in the second structure erected upon the spot by Padre Serra himself. The first church was of a temporary nature and was not long used. The present mission was begun in 1793. Father Serra had said, "I wish you to bury me in the church next to Father Fr. Juan Crespi, for the present, and when the stone church is built, you may place me where you will." As there is nothing to indicate that the bodies were ever removed, it seems probable that the present San Carlos is erected on the foundations of the older mission.

In 1852 the mission having fallen into disrepair, the roof collapsed and for thirty-two years the church remained a mere shell without a cover. Tiles and stones were carried away to be used in buildings in the near-by town of Monterey and the old San Carlos Mission fell into a shameful state. Finally various prominent Catholics of California awoke to the fact that the early mission landmarks of their faith were gradually being lost to history, and a drive was launched to restore many of them to as near their original appearance as possible, among these being San Carlos Borromeo. The building was reroofed and the interior put in perfect repair.

At the time of this restoration, 1882, Father Casanova instituted a search for the graves of Padres Crespi and Serra by digging "in the sanctuary on the Gospel side," as set forth in the old burial record. Both bodies were discovered and the tombs opened on July 3rd in the presence of several hundred people who had congregated for the event.

The bell tower of San Carlos gives to the church a certain oriental flavor and was no doubt inspired by some structure of old Spain. The star window over the entrance is very unusual and the doorway of the chapel is one of the most elaborate to be found in any of the California missions. The chapel was added to the church some time between 1811 and 1820; whether the doorway was added at this time or has been there from the first, is not known.

The sole survivor of the presidio at Monterey is La Capilla Real, the oldest portion of which was built in 1795. It is the only presidio chapel to survive from colonial times and although there have been changes made in the structure through the years, the façade remains almost exactly as erected. The church was not cruciform at first, the transept not being added until 1858. The curious pavement in front of the building is composed of the vertebrae of whale utilized as paving blocks.

The chapel and plaza were the scene of many brilliant festivities. Perhaps none of these surpassed the inauguration ceremonies of Governor Pablo Vicente de Solá, last of the Spanish governors, in 1815. The revolution against Spain had already begun in Mexico and since the people of Monterey and the new Governor were of the royalist party, his arrival was naturally a time for great demonstration. In the evening a great ball was held at the Governor's residence with music furnished by the best local talent assisted by the mission Indians who had played at the services held at the chapel in the morning.

In the yard at the rear of the church may be seen the remains of a once flourishing oak tree. A tablet at the base of this tree tells its own story:

THE JUNÍPERO OAK: At Monterey June 3, 1770, the ceremony of taking possession of California by Spain was enacted by Father Junípero Serra under the shade of this tree. Placed here for preservation by R. H. Mestres and H. A. Green, 1909.

San Gabriel the Archangel was founded September 8, 1771, and today is one of the best known of all the missions because of its favorable location between Pasadena and Los Angeles. The mission was famous for its fine products, not the least in importance being the fine wines and brandy made at the mission distillery. Padre Zalvidea, who was minister in charge from 1808 to 1826, gave a great deal of attention to viticulture and it was during his time that San Gabriel grapes and wines became famous.

The present mission was begun in 1794 and not completed until 1806. Before this there had been two temporary chapels and an adobe church. The present church is of stone and has about it a Moorish atmosphere that impresses the visitor with its strangeness. The design is thought to have been influenced by the Cathedral of Córdova, formerly the Mosque. The two buildings show some points of similarity and since Córdova was the home of Padre Cruzado, the architect of San Gabriel, this supposition seems quite likely to be true.

The altar of this mission is said to be the only one of ancient days still in place. It is much older than the church itself and came originally from Mexico. The companario in which hang the bells of San Gabriel, the chimes made famous in story and verse, dates from 1812, having been erected after the earthquake.

The mission has been a parish church since 1850 and since 1908 in charge of the Missionary Sons of the Immaculate Heart of Mary who have taken a very splendid interest in preserving the ancient relics of the church. A museum has been opened up in the mission house for the display of the old books from the mission library, a number of ancient Spanish paintings, architectural fragments, and so on. The oldest book in the library is the "Summa Alex. Ales," published in Spain in 1489. There is a much treasured confirmation record dated November 7, 1778, with the title page in the handwriting of Padre Serra himself.

Picturesque Santa Barbara was founded in 1786. Padre Serra planned the first church but died two years before the work was actually started. The original structure was only a temporary chapel but in 1789 a more permanent building was begun. Three years later this new church was already too small and another structure was put up. This stood until the earthquake of 1812. The corner-stone of the present great stone church was laid in 1815 and completed five years later.

The façade of the mission is most unusual in California mission architecture. Padre Ripoll, who was the designer, had access to a book still to be seen in the mission library: a Spanish translation of the Latin Vitruvius containing plates of the orders of architecture

Mission Santa Barbara, Santa Barbara, California. One of the most picturesque of all the missions. *Photo courtesy Santa Barbara Chamber of Commerce.*

Old Russian Chapel, Fort Ross, California. The site of an early Russian colonization effort. *Photo courtesy W. H. Turk.*

and one of these plates is thought to have been the basis for the design of the mission.

The stations of the cross adorning the walls of the nave were brought from Mexico in 1797 and are very beautiful. Santa Barbara has one of the best and most complete of any of the mission libraries. In addition to its books this library contains much in the way of documentary and archival material that is invaluable in the writing of California history.

On June 13, 1798 was founded San Luis Rey De Francia, named for the saintly Louis IX of France. None but Serra himself was endeared to the Indians like Padre Peyri of San Luis Rey and when at last, an old man, he desired to return to Spain, he so dreaded the pangs of parting that he stole away in the night. The next morning, so the story goes, several hundred of the Indians drove furiously to San Diego, forty-five miles distant, and arrived in time to see Padre Peyri on board ship on his way to Spain. From the boat he blessed them, these his beloved children, and bade them farewell.

After the overthrow of the Spanish regime the prosperity of the missions waned and two years after Padre Peyri's departure, San Luis Rey was secularized and turned over to Captain Pablo de la Portilla. In 1843 Governor Micheltorena restored the mission to the padres. It is now in the hands of the church and has been since 1865 when President Lincoln signed the title deed authorizing this.

The present structure was not begun until 1811 and in many ways it is the grandest of all the old missions; it is at any rate the most harmonious in all of its details of those existing at the present time. The work of restoring the mission started in 1892. Two years later it was rededicated and turned over to the Franciscans who yet serve there. All of the restoration work is being done after the primitive fashion by the lay brothers and novices. The church has been repaired and redecorated, the cemetery walls rebuilt and the gardens and orchards rehabilitated. An idea of the size of this mission may be had from the fact that on one side of the structure was a corridor of some two hundred and fifty arches. At the pres-

Old Historic Churches of America

ent time San Luis Rey presents a perfect appearance of a prosperous Spanish monastery.

The feathery, red-berried "pepper tree" was first introduced into California by the Spanish padres. According to tradition, the seeds were actually brought to this country by a sailor from Lima, Peru, and given to the padre in charge at Mission San Luis Rey. These seeds were planted and eventually a row of pepper trees set out in front with one tree left in the patio. Those in front have long since disappeared but the tree in the patio still remains.

In its day San Juan Capistrano, built in 1797, probably surpassed San Luis Rey in grandeur. The earthquake of 1812 did a great deal of damage and, later, well meaning but misguided restoration efforts did more harm than good, but even in ruins this mission is a thrilling one. Engineers and architects come to marvel at the long line of corridors with triple archwork and to view the massive stone walls. The church originally was one of the two cruciform churches of California—the other being San Luis Rey De Francia—and contained much that was exceedingly fine in the way of carving and cut stone work. A chapel has been restored and the spot is one favored by tourists.

While the Roman Catholic Church progressed westward across Europe and the Atlantic to Mexico, with a string of missions northward in California, its most westward outpost being the mission in Sonoma County—the Greek Catholic Church, on the other hand, was working eastward, from Russia through Siberia to Alaska, and down the western coast, the tiny chapel at Fort Ross, Sonoma County, being its most eastern outpost. Thus the two churches, in their respective journeys around the world, met and lingered for a time in this historic county of California.

The Russian settlement at Fort Ross began in 1812 with the arrival of Captain Alexander Kudkof and ninety-five Russians, armed with orders to found a settlement immediately, in an effort to obtain furs and Spanish trade along the California shores.

A site was selected nine miles north of the Russian, or Slavianska River and in a short time a fortified village sprang up there. It was ready for occupancy on September 10th and the name of Ross was given to the new settlement, this designation having its origin in the name of the mother country of the new settlers, after several variations in spelling. With its impregnable position on a steep cliff by the sea, its armament, and its ever-present sentinels, Fort Ross early had the appearance of a formidable fortress.

Inside the enclosure were fifty-nine little buildings, including a chapel that is still standing today. This quaint little building, surmounted by two pointed towers or turrets, and decorated on the interior with paintings brought from Russia, was an outstanding structure in the village.

The Russians were the first white settlers in that portion of California but unfortunately not a great deal is known concerning the colony and for many years all that was left to remind the visitor of the once flourishing colonization project was the two-turreted chapel and a few houses in half-ruinous condition.

In 1906 the State of California acquired the property and in 1928, through the efforts of the Native Sons of the Golden West, the chapel was restored and marked with a bronze tablet, and plans for further restoration of the fort are now being carried forward. One of the chapel bells afterwards hung for more than half a century in the fire station at Petaluma; after the rehabilitation of the chapel the city graciously allowed it to be rehung in its original home. Once a year religious services are conducted in the old Russian Chapel in conjunction with a patriotic celebration by the Native Sons of Sonoma County.

THE END

CHURCHES COVERED IN THIS WORK

Listed According to Date of Erection

IN MOST cases the date given is the year in which work on the present structure, or oldest portion of it, was commenced. Where this is not known, the traditional date is given. Sometimes these traditional dates are open to serious question and text should always be consulted.

San Miguel, Santa Fe, New Mexico	1606
Acoma Mission Church, New Mexico	1629
St. Luke's, Smithfield, Va.	1632
Tower of Church at Jamestown, Va.	1639
St. George's, Accomac County, Va.	1652
Merchant's Hope, Prince George County, Va.	1657
St. Mary's White Chapel, Lancaster County, Va.	1669
Old Ship, Hingham, Mass.	1681
Friends' Meeting House, Easton, Md.	1684
Trinity, Dorchester County, Md.	1690
Ware, Gloucester County, Va.	1690
Hungar's, Northampton County, Va.	1691
Merion Friends' Meeting, Penna.	1695
Grace, Yorktown, Va.	1696
Gloria Dei, Philadelphia, Penna.	1697
Haverford Friends' Meeting, Penna.	1697
Norriton Presbyterian, Montgomery County, Penna.	1698
Trinity, Wilmington, Del.	1698
Sleepy Hollow Dutch Reformed, Tarrytown, N. Y.	1699
St. Peter's, New Kent County, Va.	1701
Immanuel, New Castle, Del.	1703
Old St. Mary's, Burlington, N. J.	1703
Yeocomico, Westmoreland County, Va.	1706
Rehoboth, Somerset County, Md.	1706
St. Paul's, Wickford, R. I.	1707
Bruton Parish, Williamsburg, Va.	1710

Churches Covered in This Work

Farnham, Richmond County, Va.	1737
Glebe, Nansemond County, Va.	1738
San Fernando, San Antonio, Texas	1738
St. Paul's, Norfolk, Va.	1739
Westover, Charles City County, Va.	1740
Hebron Lutheran, Madison County, Va.	1740
Hickory Neck, James City County, Va.	1740
Ballou Meeting, Cumberland, R. I.	1740
Poplar Hill, St. Mary's County, Md.	1740
Dutch Reformed, Fort Herkimer, N. Y.	1740
St. Paul's Chapel, Bally, Penna.	1741
St. John's, Richmond, Va.	1741
St. Mary's, North East, Md.	1742
St. Thomas, Baltimore County, Md.	1743
New Garden Friends' Meeting, Chester County, Penna.	1743
Augustus Lutheran, Trappe, Penna.	1743
Neshaminy Presbyterian, near Hartsville, Penna.	1743
The Alamo, San Antonio, Texas	1744
Welsh Tract Baptist, Newark, Del.	1746
Unitarian, Cohasset, Mass.	1747
Middleham Chapel, Calvert County, Md.	1748
Augusta, Staunton, Va.	1749
La Bahia, Goliad, Texas	1749
King's Chapel, Boston, Mass.	1749
Church of Prince George, Winyah, Georgetown, S. C.	1750
Tennent, Tennent, N. J.	1751
St. Michael's, Charleston, S. C.	1752
Eastern Shore Chapel, Princess Anne County, Va.	1754
Abingdon, Gloucester County, Va.	1755
St. John's, Nansemond County, Va.	1755
St. Martin's, Worcester County, Md.	1756
All Hallows, Snow Hill, Md.	1756
Timber Ridge Presbyterian, Timber Ridge, Va.	1756
St. Paul's Chapel, New York City	1756
The Old South, Newburyport, Mass.	1756
Old Meeting House, Harpswell, Maine	1757
First Presbyterian, Carlisle, Penna.	1757
Aquia, Stafford County, Va.	1757
St. Peter's, Philadelphia, Penna.	1758
Meeting House, Danville, N. H.	1759
St. George's, Schenectady, N. Y.	1759
Jewish Synagogue, Newport, R. I.	1759
St. Paul's, Philadelphia, Penna.	1760
Christ, Upper Merion, Penna.	1760

St. James, Kingsessing, Philadelphia, Penna.	1760
Christ, Cambridge, Mass.	1761
Holy Trinity, Lancaster, Penna.	1761
Congregational, Wethersfield, Conn.	1761
Herring Creek, Anne Arundel County, Md.	1762
First, Dedham, Mass.	1762
Park Hill Congregational, Westmoreland, N. H.	1762
St. Stephen's, St. Stephens, S. C.	1762
Pompion Hill Chapel, Eastern Branch Cooper River, S. C.	1763
Old Birmingham Meeting, Penna.	1763
Cathedral of St. Augustine, St. Augustine, Fla.	1763
St. Paul's, Eastchester, Mt. Vernon, N. Y.	1763
St. Mary's, Philadelphia, Penna.	1763
St. George's, Philadelphia, Penna.	1763
Presbyterian, Lawrenceville, N. J.	1764
St. Andrew's, near Charleston, S. C.	1764
All Faith, St. Mary's County, Md.	1765
St. Andrew's, below Leonardtown, Md.	1766
St. Paul's, King George County, Va.	1766
Old Buckingham Meeting, Penna.	1767
Christ, Alexandria, Va.	1767
Old Falls, Falls Church, Va.	1767
Pine Street Presbyterian, Philadelphia, Penna.	1767
St. Francis Xavier's, Newtown, Md.	1767
First Church of Christ, Longmeadow, Mass.	1767
Old Jerusalem, Ebenezer, Ga.	1767
First Church, Kennebunk, Maine	1767
Swamp Lutheran, Pottstown, Penna.	1767
Chestnut Hill Meeting House, Millville, Mass.	1768
Wambaw, near Wambaw Creek, S. C.	1768
St. Anne's, Middletown, Del.	1768
San José de Aguayo, San Antonio, Texas	1768
Newtown Presbyterian, Newtown, Penna.	1769
Pohick, near Alexandria, Va.	1769
Christ, Shrewsbury, N. J.	1769
Lambs Creek, King George County, Penna.	1769
Trinity, Fishkill, N. Y.	1769
Chichester Friends' Meeting, Delaware County, Penna.	1769
St. David's, Cheraw, S. C.	1770
German, Waldoboro, Maine	1770
Trinity, Brooklyn, Conn.	1770
Dunkard, Germantown, Penna.	1770
Palatine, Mohawk Valley, N. Y.	1770
St. Andrew's, Richmond, Staten Island, N. Y.	1770

Germantown Mennonite, Germantown, Penna.	1770
First Church of Christ, Farmington, Conn.	1771
St. Andrew's, Princess Anne, Md.	1771
St. Barnabas, Leeland, Md.	1772
Christ, Port Republic, Md.	1772
Walpole, Bristol, Maine	1772
Crosswicks Friends' Meeting, Crosswicks, N. J.	1773
Union, West Claremont, N. H.	1773
Drawyers Meeting House, Odessa, Del.	1773
Old Meeting House, Sandown, N. H.	1773
Old Presbyterian Meeting House, Alexandria, Va.	1774
First Baptist, Providence, R. I.	1775
Barratt's Chapel, Frederica, Del.	1780
Friends' Meeting, Odessa, Del.	1780
Free Quaker Meeting, Philadelphia, Penna.	1783
San Xavier del Bac, Tucson, Ariz.	1783
First Presbyterian, Elizabeth, N. J.	1784
Trinity, Swedesboro, N. J.	1784
Burlington Friends' Meeting, Burlington, N. J.	1784
Congregational, Southampton, Mass.	1785
St. Ignatius, St. Inigoes, Md.	1785
Church of the Sacred Heart, Conewago, Penna.	1785
Old Rehoboth, Monroe County, W. Va.	1786
First Presbyterian, Newark, N. J.	1786
Old Thetford Hill, Thetford, Vt.	1787
Congregational, Enfield, Mass.	1787
Old Rockingham, Rockingham, Vt.	1787
Old Brick, Fairfield County, S. C.	1788
Old Stone, Pendleton, S. C.	1789
Meeting House, Alna, Maine	1789
Holy Family, Cahokia, Ill.	1789
Cane Ridge Meeting House, Paris, Ky.	1790
Dutch Reformed, Hackensack, N. J.	1791
First Presbyterian, Springfield, N. J.	1791
Midway, Georgia	1792
Flatbush Dutch Reformed, Brooklyn, N. Y.	1793
San Carlos Borromeo, California	1793
First Church of Christ, East Haddam, Conn.	1794
San Gabriel the Archangel, San Gabriel, California	1794
Cathedral of St. Louis, New Orleans, La.	1794
La Capilla Real, Monterey, California	1795
Old Strother Meeting House, Nashville, Tenn.	1795
St. Marks, New York City	1795
Old Stone Presbyterian, Lewisburg, W. Va.	1796

Churches Covered in This Work

San Juan Capistrano, California	1797
St. Ignatius, Charles County, Md.	1798
Home Moravian, Winston-Salem, N. C.	1798
Congregational, West Springfield, Mass.	1799
Pennypack Baptist, Philadelphia, Penna.	1805
Old First Church, Bennington, Vt.	1806
Cathedral of Assumption, Baltimore, Md.	1806
Bethel Meeting House, Charlestown, Ind.	1807
St. John's, Portsmouth, N. H.	1807
San Diego De Alcalá, San Diego, California	1808
First Presbyterian, Augusta, Ga.	1809
San Luis Rey De Francia, near Oceanside, California	1811
Cathedral of St. John, Providence, R. I.	1811
Monumental, Richmond, Va.	1812
Old Russian Chapel, Fort Ross, California	1812
St. John's, Washington, D. C.	1815
Santa Barbara, California	1815
St. Joseph's, Bardstown, Ky.	1816
McKendree Chapel, Cape Girardeau, Mo.	1819
New York Avenue Presbyterian, Washington, D. C.	1820
Trinity, Natchez, Miss.	1822
Hermitage, Nashville, Tenn.	1823
St. Paul's, Woodville, Miss.	1824
Old Cathedral of St. Francis Xavier, Vincennes, Ind.	1825
Old Mission, Mackinac Island, Mich.	1829
First Baptist, Washington, Ark.	1830
Cathedral of St. Louis of France, St. Louis, Mo.	1831
Kirtland Temple, Kirtland, Ohio	1833
St. Philip's Charleston, S. C.	1835
St. Gabriel's, Prairie du Chien, Wis.	1836
Old St. Joseph's, Philadelphia, Penna.	1838
Old Shawnee Mission, Kansas	1838
Christ, Savannah, Ga.	1838
St. John's, Maury County, Tenn.	1839
Old Mission, Madeline Island, Wis.	1839
Trinity, New York City	1841
Wheelock, Millerton, Okla.	1842
St. Mary's Mission, Stevensville, Montana	1843
The Huguenot, Charleston, S. C.	1844
St. Paul's, Richmond, Va.	1844
St. Mary's Cathedral, Nashville, Tenn.	1845
St. Paul's, St. Paul, Oregon	1846
Coeur D'Alene Mission of the Sacred Heart, Cataldo, Idaho	1848
College Hill Presbyterian, College Hill, Miss.	1849

First Presbyterian, Nashville, Tenn.	1851
Salt Lake Temple, Salt Lake City, Utah	1853
St. John's, Montgomery, Ala.	1855
Bellevue Presbyterian, Bellevue, Neb.	1856
St. Patrick's, Chicago, Ill.	1856
Cathedral of St. Raphael, Dubuque, Iowa	1857
Methodist, Claquato, Wash.	1858
Big Buckhead, Jenkins County, Ga.	1858
Grace, St. Francisville, La.	1860
Chelsea Avenue Presbyterian, Memphis, Tenn.	1860
Lee Memorial Chapel, Lexington, Va.	1866
St. Joseph's, San Antonio, Texas	1868
Vikur Lutheran, Mountain, N. D.	1884
Presbyterian, Beaver City, Okla.	1887
Independent Presbyterian, Savannah, Ga.	1889

ACKNOWLEDGMENT

THE author wishes especially to thank the clergy attached to the various churches for without their aid this work could not have been started. That it has been finished is due in large measure to their splendid, whole-hearted cooperation in every respect. Then there are the countless newspapers who published the author's appeals for information; the hundreds of people who responded to these appeals; the different libraries, clubs and chambers of commerce who assisted so splendidly when they were called upon; and the historical societies of the various states, all of which helped in some way and only one of which refused to do so by failing to answer his letters. The quotations from Longfellow, Whittier and Harte are used by permission of, and arrangement with Houghton Mifflin Company.

Many people aided in the production of this book; aided by hunting for old photographs, taking new ones, searching through old records, collecting the best founded traditions of the neighborhood and so on. It would be impossible to name them all but the author takes this occasion to thank the Chicago Public Library, The Newberry Library, Chicago, Free Library of Philadelphia, Texas Library & Historical Commission, Miss Adina De Zavala, Mrs. Samuel Lapham, Jr., Mrs. Eugenia A. McMasters, Mrs. William Slade, Mrs. Lane Taylor, Reverend Victor R. Stoner, and Messrs. H. R. Dwight, Horace B. Folsom, Charles L. Kuhn, R. W. Kelsey, George Morgan Knight, Jr., Percy G. Skirven, and W. H. Turk. To these and to all of the others who likewise played a very important part in the making of this book, the author can offer only his thanks, realizing at the same time that the work was done as a real labor of love and that words of thanks on his part are, therefore, not needed.

Acknowledgment

Lastly, the author wishes to thank Miss Eleanor Enright and
Mr. Edmund Enright, the latter, especially, for his kindness in
doing research for him in the various libraries of New York City,
and both because their generous hospitality in the spring of 1931
made possible his trips to Old Christ Church, Alexandria, Virginia,
and St. Paul's Chapel, New York City, making them both, therefore, in a measure responsible for this book.

BIBLIOGRAPHY

AUGUSTA CHURCH, by J. N. Van Devanter, The Rose Printing Co., Staunton, Va., 1900.

ANNALS OF TRINITY CHURCH, Newport, R. I., by George Champlin Mason, Newport, R. I., 1890.

ANNALS OF HENRICO PARISH, DIOCESE OF VIRGINIA, by Lewis W. Burton, Williams Printing Company, Richmond, Va., 1904.

AUGUSTINE LUTHERAN CHURCH, Trappe, Penna., Published by the Church, 1931.

AMERICAN METHODISM, by Abel Stevens, LL.D. Printers Phillips & Hunt, New York, Walden & Stowe, Cincinnati.

THE ARCHITECTURAL RECORD: an illustrated monthly magazine of architecture and the allied arts and crafts.

ANNALS OF THE SWEDES ON THE DELAWARE, by the Rev. John Curtis Clay, D.D., Philadelphia, H. Hooker & Co., 1858.

ANNALS OF KING'S CHAPEL, by Henry Wilder Foote, Boston, Little Brown and Company, 1882 and 1896.

BUCKINGHAM MONTHLY MEETING, Bucks County, Pennsylvania, Walter H. Jenkins, Philadelphia, Penna., 1923.

A BROCHURE ON OLD TENNENT CHURCH, Published 1931 by the Trustees.

BULLETIN OF FRIENDS' HISTORICAL ASSOCIATION, Vol. 13, No. 2.

COLONIAL CHURCHES AND MEETING HOUSES, by Philip B. Wallace, Architectural Book Publishing Company, Inc., New York City, 1931.

COLONIAL CHURCHES IN VIRGINIA, by Henry Irving Brock, The Dale Press, Richmond, 1930.

THE CHURCHES OF ALABAMA DURING THE CIVIL WAR AND RECONSTRUCTION, by Walter L. Fleming, W. M. Rogers & Co., Montgomery, Alabama, 1902.

THE CALIFORNIA HISTORY NUGGET, Published by the California State Historical Association.

CHRIST CHURCH, Salem Street, Boston, A Guide, Boston, Published by the Church, 1930.

THE CANE RIDGE MEETING HOUSE IN BOURBON COUNTY, by James R. Rogers, Standard Publishing Company, Cincinnati, 1910.

COLONIAL CHURCHES IN THE ORIGINAL COLONY OF VIRGINIA, Southern Churchman Company, Richmond, Virginia, 1908.

CATHEDRAL RECORDS: FROM THE BEGINNING OF CATHOLICITY IN BALTI-

Bibliography

MORE TO THE PRESENT TIME, Published by The Catholic Mirror Pub. Co., Baltimore, 1906.

THE CATHOLIC ENCYCLOPEDIA: AN INTERNATIONAL WORK OF REFERENCE ON THE CONSTITUTION, DISCIPLINE AND HISTORY OF THE CATHOLIC CHURCH, Encyclopedia Press, 1907.

CHRIST CHURCH DIRECTORY, Dover, Delaware.

THE CHRONICLES OF BALTIMORE, by John Thomas Scharf, Baltimore, 1874.

THE CHAPLAINS AND CLERGY OF THE REVOLUTION, by J. T. Headley, Charles Scribner, New York, 1864.

THE DAYS OF MAKEMIE: OR THE VINE PLANTED, by the Rev. L. P. Bowen, Philadelphia, Presbyterian Board of Publications, 1885.

THE DEAD TOWNS OF GEORGIA, by Charles C. Jones, Jr., Savannah Morning News Steam Printing House, 1878.

DOWN WHERE THE SOUTH BEGINS, Published by Richmond, Va., Chamber of Commerce.

DELAWARE, Published by the Bureau of Markets of the State Board of Agriculture, State of Delaware, 1932.

EARLY AMERICAN CHURCHES, by Aymar Embury II, Doubleday, Page & Co., New York, 1914.

EARLY ARCHITECTURE OF DELAWARE, by George Fletcher Bennett, Historical Press, Inc., Wilmington, 1932.

THE EARLY BAPTISTS OF PHILADELPHIA, by Rev. David Spencer, Philadelphia, William Syckelmoore, 1877.

THE FALL OF THE ALAMO, by Captain R. M. Potter, Old South Leaflets No. 139, Boston.

FIRST REFORMED DUTCH CHURCH, Fishkill, by Francis M. Kip, D.D., Wynkoop & Hallenbeck, New York, 1866.

FIRST REFORMED (DUTCH) CHURCH, Hackensack, N. J., by Rev. Theodore B. Romeyn, Board of Publication R.C.A., New York, 1870.

THE FIRST PARISHES OF THE PROVINCE OF MARYLAND, by Percy G. Skirven, The Norman Remington Company, Baltimore, 1923.

FRIENDS ON LONG ISLAND AND IN NEW YORK, by Henry Onderdonk, Jr., Lott Van De Water, Hempstead, N. Y., 1878.

THE GEORGIAN PERIOD, American Architect and Building News Company, Boston, 1899.

GEORGE WASHINGTON, ST. PETER'S AND THE EPISCOPAL CHURCH, by C. P. B. Jefferys, Published by The Washington Bicentennial Committee of St. Peter's Church, Philadelphia, Penna.

HISTORICAL SKETCHES, Daniel H. Mahony, Philadelphia, 1895.

HISTORY OF THE HEBRON LUTHERAN CHURCH, by Rev. W. P. Huddle, Pastor, Henkel & Company, New Market, Virginia, 1908.

HISTORY OF KENT COUNTY, MARYLAND, by Fred G. Usilton.

HISTORY OF THE CHURCH IN BURLINGTON, by Rev. George Morgan Hills, D.D., William S. Sharp, Printer, Trenton, N. J., 1876.

Bibliography

HISTORY OF OLD ST. DAVID'S CHURCH, by Henry Pleasants, The John C. Winston Co., Philadelphia, 1915.

HISTORIC SHRINES OF AMERICA, by John T. Faris, Geo. H. Doran Co., New York, 1918.

HISTORIC CHURCHES OF AMERICA, by Nellie Urner Wallington, Duffield & Company, New York, 1907.

HISTORIC VIRGINIA HOMES AND CHURCHES, by Robert A. Lancaster, Jr., J. B. Lippincott Company, Philadelphia.

HISTORY OF THE FIRST PRESBYTERIAN CHURCH, Nashville, Tenn., Published by the Church, 1914.

HISTORY OF ST. PAUL'S CHAPEL, New York City.

HISTORIC CHURCHES OF THE WORLD, by Robert B. Ludy, M.D., The Stratford Company, Boston, 1926.

HISTORY OF OLD PINE STREET CHURCH, by Hughes Oliphant Gibbons, The John C. Winston Company, Philadelphia, 1905.

HISTORY OF THE ARCHDIOCESE OF ST. LOUIS, by Rev. John Rothensteiner, St. Louis, Mo., 1928.

HISTORIC CHURCHES OF AMERICA, THEIR ROMANCE AND THEIR HISTORY, H. L. Everett, Philadelphia, 1890.

HISTORICAL SKETCH AND GUIDE TO THE ALAMO, by Leonora Bennett, San Antonio, 1902.

HISTORICAL SKETCHES: A COLLECTION OF PAPERS PREPARED FOR THE HISTORICAL SOCIETY OF MONTGOMERY COUNTY, PENNA., Norristown, Pa. Herald Printing and Binding Rooms, 1905.

HISTORY OF TALBOT COUNTY, MARYLAND, by Oswald Tilghman, Williams & Wilkins Co., Baltimore, 1915.

THE HISTORY OF OLD ALEXANDRIA, VIRGINIA, by Mary G. Powell, The William Byrd Press, Inc., Printers, Richmond, Virginia, 1928.

A HISTORY OF THE FIRST CHURCH AND PARISH IN DEDHAM, by Alvan Lamson, D.D., Dedham, 1839.

THE HISTORY OF TRURO PARISH IN VIRGINIA, by Rev. Philip Slaughter, D.D., George W. Jacobs & Company, Philadelphia, 1907.

HISTORICAL SKETCH OF BRUTON CHURCH, Williamsburg, Va., by Rev. W. A. R. Goodwin, A.M., The Franklin Press Company, Petersburg, Virginia, 1903.

HISTORY OF THE CATHOLIC CHURCH IN THE UNITED STATES, by John Gilmary Shea, New York, 1886–92.

HISTORIC SKETCH OF THE FIRST CHURCH OF CHRIST IN WETHERSFIELD, by A. C. Adams, The Allen & Sherwood Co., Hartford, Conn., 1877.

AN HISTORICAL ACCOUNT OF THE PROTESTANT EPISCOPAL CHURCH IN SOUTH CAROLINA, by Frederick Dalcho, M.D., E. Thayer, Charleston, 1820.

HISTORIC GRAVES OF MARYLAND AND THE DISTRICT OF COLUMBIA, by Helen W. Ridgely, The Grafton Press, New York, 1908.

Bibliography

HISTORY OF DELAWARE, by J. Thomas Scharf, L. J. Richards & Co., Philadelphia, 1888.

HISTORY OF THE OLD SOUTH CHURCH, by Hamilton A. Hill, Boston, 1890.

HISTORY OF THE TOWN OF HINGHAM, MASSACHUSETTS, Published by the Town, 1893.

HISTORIC HOMES AND LANDMARKS OF ALEXANDRIA, VIRGINIA, by Mary Lindsey, Alexandria, Va., 1931.

HISTORY OF MOUNT ZION METHODIST EPISCOPAL CHURCH, SOUTH, by Louis Biles Hill, Standard Printing Company, McMinnville, Tennessee, 1928.

A HISTORY OF ST. GEORGE'S CHURCH IN THE CITY OF SCHENECTADY, by Willis T. Hanson, Jr., A.M., Schenectady, Privately Printed, 1919.

HISTORY AND REMINISCENCES OF ST. JOHN'S CHURCH, Washington, D. C.

HISTORICAL CATALOGUE OF THE MEMBERS OF THE FIRST BAPTIST CHURCH IN PROVIDENCE, RHODE ISLAND, Compiled and Edited by Henry Melville King, F. H. Townsend, Printer, Providence, R. I., 1908.

A HISTORY OF THE FABRIC: THE MEETING HOUSE OF THE FIRST BAPTIST CHURCH IN PROVIDENCE, by Norman M. Isham, F.A.I.A., Providence, 1925.

A HISTORY OF THE HEPHZIBAH ASSOCIATION, by W. L. Kilpatrick, 1894.

HISTORY OF OLD ST. GEORGE'S METHODIST EPISCOPAL CHURCH, Compiled by Francis H. Tees, Pastor, Philadelphia, Pennsylvania, 1933.

HISTORY OF THE OLD FORT HERKIMER CHURCH, by W. N. P. Dailey, D.D., St. Johnsville Enterprise and News, St. Johnsville, N. Y.

HISTORIC HOUSES OF SOUTH CAROLINA, by Harriette Kershaw Leiding, J. B. Lippincott Company, Philadelphia, 1921.

A HISTORY OF CAROLINE CHURCH, Setauket, L. I., N. Y., prepared by Edward P. Buffett, Historian, Published by Caroline Church, 1923.

HISTORY OF CHRIST CHURCH, Shrewsbury, N. J., by Anna V. Jennings.

HISTORY OF MARYLAND, by J. Thomas Scharf, John B. Piet, Baltimore, 1879.

HISTORY AND LEGENDS OF THE ALAMO AND OTHER MISSIONS IN AND AROUND SAN ANTONIO, by Adina De Zavala, San Antonio, December, 1917.

HISTORY OF ALNA-DRESDEN-EDGECOMB-PITTSTON-WISCASSET, verified by Bertram E. Packard, State Commissioner of Education in Maine, August 1933.

HISTORY OF THE COEUR D'ALENE MISSION OF THE SACRED HEART, by Rev. Edmund R. Cody, M.A., 1930.

HISTORY OF THE TOWN OF FLUSHING, LONG ISLAND, NEW YORK, by Henry D. Waller, Flushing, J. H. Ridenour, 1899.

IN AND AROUND THE OLD ST. LOUIS CATHEDRAL OF NEW ORLEANS, by Rev. C. M. Chambon, Philippe's Printery, New Orleans, 1908.

Bibliography

ILLINOIS CATHOLIC HISTORICAL REVIEW, Published by Illinois Catholic Historical Society.

INDIAN AND WHITE IN THE NORTHWEST, by L. B. Palladino, S.J., Wickersham Publishing Co., Lancaster, Pa., 1922.

JAMESTOWN, WILLIAMSBURG, YORKTOWN, Published by Virginia State Chamber of Commerce, Richmond, 1931.

JOURNAL OF THE PRESBYTERIAN HISTORICAL SOCIETY, Published by the Society, Philadelphia.

KING'S HANDBOOK OF NOTABLE EPISCOPAL CHURCHES IN THE UNITED STATES, by the Rev. George Wolfe Shinn, D.D., Moses King Corporation, Boston, 1889.

KIRTLAND TEMPLE, REFORMED CHURCH OF JESUS CHRIST OF LATTER DAY SAINTS, 1928, Independence, Mo.

LIFE OF PATRICK HENRY, by William Wirt, New York, 1834.

LIFE OF THE RIGHT REVEREND JOSEPH P. MACHEBEUF, D.D., by W. J. Howlett, Pueblo, Colorado, 1908.

MARYLAND'S COLONIAL EASTERN SHORE, Swepson Earle, Editor, Baltimore, Maryland, 1916.

MISSOURI'S CONTRIBUTION TO AMERICAN ARCHITECTURE, by John Albury Bryan, St. Louis, Mo.

MISSIONS AND PUEBLOS OF THE OLD SOUTHWEST, by Earle R. Forrest, The Arthur H. Clark Company, Cleveland, 1929.

THE MEMORIAL OF FRAY ALONSO DE BENAVIDES: 1630, translated by Mrs. Edward E. Ayer, Chicago, Privately Printed, 1916.

MEMORIAL OF THE CENTENNIAL ANNIVERSARY OF THE FIRST PRESBYTERIAN CHURCH, Augusta, Georgia, May, 1904.

MEMORIAL SERMON DELIVERED IN OLD TRINITY CHURCH, Brooklyn, Conn., Hartford, 1871.

THE MORAVIANS IN GEORGIA, 1735–1740, by Adelaide L. Fries, Edwards & Broughton, Raleigh, N. C., 1905.

MIDWAY CONGREGATIONAL CHURCH: A PATRIOTIC PARAGRAM, by H. B. Folsom, Mt. Vernon, Ga., 1929.

OLD CHURCHES AND FAMILIES OF VIRGINIA, by Bishop Meade, J. B. Lippincott Co., Philadelphia, 1861.

THE OLD MISSION CHURCHES AND HISTORIC HOMES OF CALIFORNIA, by Rexford Newcomb, M.A.M., Arch. A.I.A., J. B. Lippincott Co., Philadelphia, 1925.

THE OLD BRICK CHURCHES OF MARYLAND, by Helen West Ridgely, Anson D. F. Randolph and Company, New York, 1894.

OLD CHURCHES AND MEETING HOUSES IN AND AROUND PHILADELPHIA, by John T. Faris, J. B. Lippincott Company, Philadelphia, 1926.

THE OLD PARISH CHURCHES OF VIRGINIA, by Francis Marion Wigmore, United States Government Printing Office, Washington, 1929.

Bibliography

OLD NEW ENGLAND CHURCHES AND THEIR CHILDREN, by Dolores Bacon, Doubleday Page & Company, New York, 1906.

ONE HUNDRED YEARS WITH "OLD TRINITY" CHURCH, Natchez, Miss., by Chas. Stietenrogh, Natchez Printing & Stationery Co., Natchez, Mississippi, 1922.

THE OLD MEETING HOUSE AND FIRST CHURCH IN ROCKINGHAM, VERMONT, by Lyman S. Hayes, and William D. Hayes, Bellows Falls, Vt., 1915.

THE 175TH ANNIVERSARY OF TRINITY LUTHERAN CHURCH, by J. E. Whitteker, D.D., 1905.

OLD SAINT JOSEPH'S, PHILADELPHIA, Notes compiled by M. Maury Walton with the assistance of the Bicentenary Committee of the Jesuit Fathers of Old St. Joseph's Church, The Dolphin Press, Philadelphia, Pennsylvania, 1933.

THE OLD PALATINE CHURCH, Press of the Enterprise and News, Saint Johnsville, New York, 1930.

OLD MISSION CHURCH OF MACKINAC ISLAND, by Rev. Meade C. Williams, D.D., Published by the Trustees, 1912.

THE OLD SHAWNEE MISSION, by Mrs. Edith Connelley Ross, for The Shawnee Mission Memorial Foundation, 1928, Topeka, Kansas State Printing Plant.

THE ONE HUNDRED AND FIFTIETH ANNIVERSARY OF THE BUILDING OF THE MEETING HOUSE OF THE FIRST CHURCH OF CHRIST CONGREGATIONAL AT FARMINGTON, CONNECTICUT, 1922.

OLD AND NEW SAN FERNANDO, by Rev. Father Camilo Torrente, C.M.F., The Claretian Missionaries, 1927.

OLD TIME NEW ENGLAND, The Bulletin of the Society for Preservation of New England Antiquities, 1922.

THE ORIGIN AND GROWTH OF KING'S CHAPEL, by Rev. John Carroll Perkins, D.D., Boston, Mass., 1929.

PICTURESQUE CHARLESTON, Published by Walker, Evans & Cogswell Co., 1930.

THE PROVINCIAL AND REVOLUTIONARY HISTORY OF ST. PETER'S CHURCH, PHILADELPHIA, by C. P. B. Jefferys.

PROCEEDINGS OF THE MASSACHUSETTS HISTORICAL SOCIETY, October to November 1876 inclusive.

PROCEEDINGS AT THE CENTENNIAL CELEBRATION OF THE INCORPORATION OF THE TOWN OF LONGMEADOW, Published by the Town, 1884.

QUARTER MILLENNIAL ANNIVERSARY OF THE REFORMED DUTCH CHURCH OF FLATBUSH, NEW YORK, 1904.

RECORDS OF THE AMERICAN CATHOLIC HISTORICAL SOCIETY OF PHILADELPHIA.

RETROSPECTS AND PROSPECTS, by Sidney Lanier, Charles Scribner's Sons, 1899.

Bibliography

THE ROMANCE OF OLD NEW ENGLAND CHURCHES, by Mary C. Crawford, L. C. Page & Company, Boston, 1903.

REVISED HISTORY OF DORCHESTER COUNTY, MARYLAND, by Elias Jones, The Read Taylor Press, Boston, 1925.

REPORT UPON THE HISTORIC BUILDINGS, MONUMENTS, AND LOCAL ARCHIVES OF ST. AUGUSTINE, FLORIDA, by Prof. David Y. Thomas, American Historical Association Annual Report, 1905.

RECORDS OF THE MORAVIANS IN NORTH CAROLINA, Edited by Adelaide L. Fries, North Carolina Historical Commission, Raleigh, N. C., 1922–1930.

THE RESTORATION OF SAINT PAUL'S CHURCH, CEMETERY AND RECTORY AT EASTCHESTER IN NEW YORK, 1930.

RECORDS OF THE WELSH TRACT BAPTIST CHURCH, PENCADER HUNDRED, New Castle County, Delaware, Delaware Historical Society, 1904.

SPANISH MISSION CHURCHES OF NEW MEXICO, by L. Bradford Prince, LL.D., The Torch Press, Cedar Rapids, Iowa, 1915.

SOME OLD TIME MEETING HOUSES OF THE CONNECTICUT VALLEY, by Charles Albert Wight, B.A., 1911.

SOLDIERS OF THE CROSS, by the Most Rev. J. B. Salpointe, D.D., Banning, California, 1898.

SPANISH MISSIONS OF THE OLD SOUTHWEST, by Cleve Hallenbeck, Doubleday, Page and Company, Garden City, New York, 1926.

ST. LOUIS CATHOLIC HISTORICAL REVIEW, Published by the Catholic Historical Society of St. Louis, St. Louis, Mo.

STORIES OF OLD NEW CASTLE, Compiled by Anne R. Janvier.

ST. MICHAEL'S CHURCH, MARBLEHEAD, MASS., N. A. Lindsey & Co., Inc., Marblehead, 1924.

A SHORT HISTORICAL SKETCH OF THE OLD MERION MEETING HOUSE, Merion, Penna., 1917.

ST. PAUL'S CHURCH, RICHMOND, VIRGINIA, ITS HISTORIC YEARS AND MEMORIALS, by Elizabeth Wright Weddell, The William Byrd Press, Inc., Richmond, Va., 1931.

THE STORY OF ARCHITECTURE IN AMERICA, by Thomas Eddy Talmadge, 1927.

ST. PAUL'S, Eastchester, Mount Vernon, N. Y., St. Paul's Parish, 1930.

THE STORY OF KING'S CHAPEL, by Rev. Howard N. Brown, 1928.

THE SALZBURGERS AND THEIR DESCENDANTS, by Rev. P. A. Strobel, T. Newton Kurtz, Baltimore, 1855.

THE SOUTH CAROLINA HISTORICAL AND GENEALOGICAL MAGAZINE, Published quarterly by the South Carolina Historical Society.

SAN ANTONIO HISTORICAL AND MODERN, Passing Show Publishing Co., San Antonio, 1909.

THE SETTLEMENT AT RACOON AND THE BUILDING OF TRINITY CHURCH, SWEDESBORO, N. J., by Edgar Campbell, 1922.

Bibliography

THE STORY OF THE OLD MISSION ON MADELINE ISLAND, by Wilfred A. Rowell.

TIDEWATER MARYLAND, by Paul Wilstach, The Bobbs-Merrill Company, Indianapolis, 1931.

200TH ANNIVERSARY OF THE FIRST BAPTISM AND LOVE FEAST HELD IN THE OLD MOTHER CHURCH, Germantown, Philadelphia, Pa., 1923.

TENNESSEE HISTORICAL MAGAZINE, Published by The Tennessee Historical Society.

TRINITY CHURCH, OXFORD, Directory, 1930.

THE TWO HUNDRED AND NINTH ANNIVERSARY SERVICE OF ST. ANNE'S CHURCH, Middletown, Delaware, 1914.

THE VESTRY BOOK OF SAINT PETER'S, New Kent County, Va., Published by The National Society of the Colonial Dames of America in the State of Virginia, Wm. Ellis Jones, Richmond, 1905.

VIRGINIA, "THE BECKONING LAND," Issued by State Commission on Conservation and Development, Richmond, Va.

VIRGINIA HISTORIC SHRINES AND SCENIC ATTRACTIONS, Issued by Virginia State Chamber of Commerce, Richmond, 1931.

WASHINGTON'S CHURCH: AN HISTORICAL SKETCH OF OLD CHRIST CHURCH, Alexandria, 1888.

WHERE ABRAHAM LINCOLN WENT TO CHURCH, by Rev. Joseph Richard Sizoo, D.D.

YEAR BOOK, CITY OF CHARLESTON, SOUTH CAROLINA, FOR YEARS 1885, 1886 AND 1896.

YEAR BOOK OF THE GENERAL CONFERENCE OF THE MENNONITE CHURCH OF N. A., Mennonite Book Concern, Berne, Indiana, 1933.

INDEX

Index

Bell Church, The Old, 232
Bell, Tom, 155
Bellevue, Neb., 297
Bellevue Presbyterial Church, Neb., 297
Bells, old, 4, 10, 52, 60, 61, 65, 71, 83, 133, 147, 181, 192, 212, 214, 215, 224, 232, 250, 254, 284, 319, 320, 325, 326, 338
Bells of St. Michael's, 225
Benavides, Fray Alonso de, 323, 327
Benjamin, Asher, 91
Bennington, Vt., 91
Bennington, Battle of, 91, 93
Bergman, Rev. Christopher F., 243
Berkeley, Rev. George, 77
Bernon, Gabriel, 77
Berry, Sarah, 121
Bethel Church, Tenn., 255
Bethel Meeting House, Charlestown, Ind., 285
Bethlehem, Penna., 217
Bevan, John, 176
Bibles, old, 37, 39, 60, 61, 63, 97, 111, 114, 152, 215, 230, 296
Big Buckhead Church, Jenkins County, Ga., 246-247
Biggin Church, S. C., 221, 222
Billings, Capt. Timothy, 71
Birch, Harvey, 137
Birmingham Friends' Meeting, Penna., 194
Bjork, Rev. Eric, 172
Black, James, 269
Blackburn, Rev. Gideon, 261
Blackwell, Rev. Robert, 183
Blakewell, Rev. A. Gordon, 271
Blandford Church, Petersburg, Va., 17-19
Blue Hen's Chickens, The, 170
Bohemia, Md., 207
Boone, Daniel, 251
Bootleggers, church used by, 117
Boston churches, 52, 54, 57
Boston Tea Party, 56
Boucher, Rev. Jonathan, 118
Boush, Samuel, 23
Bowen, Rev. L. P., 123; Samuel, 41
Bowery, The, 300
Bowie, Col. James, 306, 310, 312; Rev. John, 115
Bowie knife, 269
Boyd, Thomas, 215
Braddock's army, 38, 54
Brainerd, David, 154, 160; Rev. Thomas, 200
Brandywine, Battle of, 177, 187, 190, 194, 195, 200, 201
Branford, Conn., 158
Brattle, Thomas, 99
Brattle organ, 99-100
Brattle Street Church, Boston, Mass., 99
Braxton, Carter, 17
Brick Church on Wells' Hill, 17

Brickhead, Anne, 116
Bridge, Rev. Christopher, 75
Bridger, Joseph, 5, 7
Bristol Friends' Meeting House, Bucks County, Penna., 177-178
Brittan, Lionel, 207
Britton, William, 105; Temperance, 105
Broad Creek, Md., 111
Broadwater, Col. Charles, 38
Brookhaven Township, N. Y., 135
Brooklyn, Battle of, 136
Brooklyn, Conn., 85
Brooklyn, N. Y., 146
Broughton, Gov. Thos., 222
Brown, Rev. Arthur, 97, 98; John, 83; Joseph, 83; Lieutenant, 63; Commodore Thomas, 170
Browne, John, 135
Brownson, Dr. Nathan, 241
Brute, Bishop, 285
Bruton Parish Church, Williamsburg, Va., 3-5
Bryan, William Jennings, 129
Buchanan, James, 127, 128
Buckhout, John, 133
Buckingham Friends' Meeting House, Penna., 195-196
Bucks County, Penna., 177
Buell, General, 258
Buford, Capt. Goodloe W., 267, 268
Bulfinch, Charles, 60
Bunker Hill, Battle of, 63, 83, 85
Burgoyne, General, 56, 91, 141
Burling, William, 135
Burlington Friends' Meeting House, N. J., 151
Burlington, N. J., 149
Burr, Aaron, 142, 152; Rev. Aaron, 159; Rev. David, 7
Burroughs, Dr. Charles, 100
Burton, Rev. Asa, 90
Burwell, Major Lewis, 29; Rebecca, 29
Byrd family, 24

Cadwalader, General, 182
Cahokia, Ill., 280
Caldwell, James, 161
Calhoun, John, 234, 237
California missions, 334-341
Calvert County, Md., 119
Calvert, Gov. Leonard, 101, 102
Cambridge, Mass., 62
Campbell, Rev. Edgar, 156
Cane Ridge Meeting House, Ky., 251-253
Canier, Dr., 53
Cape Girardeau, Mo., 288
Capilla Real, La., 335, 337
Carey, Mathew, 211
Carlisle, Penna., 192
Carlyle, Col. John, 36, 41
Caroline Church, Setauket, N. Y., 135-136

Index

Index

Index

Index

Index

Index

Index

Index

Index

Index

Swartz, Abraham, 202
Swedesboro, Battle of, 157
Swedish settlements, 156, 163, 172, 174
Swentzer, Jacob, 202

Taft, William Howard, 127
Talbot, Rev. George, 149, 150, 151
Talbot County, Md., 119
Tallmadge, Thomas Eddy, 125
Taney, Roger B., 125
Tarrytown, N. Y., 131
Taylor, Zachary, 127
Tennessee churches, 255-262
Tennent Church, Tennent, N. J., 153-155
Tennent, Rev. William, 188; Rev. William, Jr., 154, 155
Test, The, 216
Texas missions, 304-321
Theodore, Colonel, 100
Thetford Hill Church, Vt., 90
Thomas, Rev. Samuel, 220
Thousand Dollar Prayer Books, 264
Three decker pulpit, 32
Timber Ridge Presbyterian Church, Va., 29-31
Tittermary, John, 200
Tlascalan Indians, 323
Toland, John H., 269
Tompkins, Daniel, 148
Torrente, Rev. Camilo, 305
Touro, Rev. Isaac, 80, 81
Trail of Tears, 291
Trappe, Penna., 189
Travis, William B., 269, 310, 312
Trenton, Battle of, 170, 189, 201
Treutlen, Gov. John Adams, 243
Trimble, Robert, 253
Trinity Church, Brooklyn, Conn., 85; Dorchester County, Md., 108-109; Fishkill, N. Y., 143-144, 148; Natchez, Miss., 265-266; Newport, R. I., 72, 76-77; New York City, 135, 138; Oxford, Philadelphia, 178-179; Swedesboro, N. J., 156-158; Wilmington, Del., 163, 173
Truro Parish, 33, 37
Tucson, Arizona, 331
Twelves, Robert, 55
Tyler, Henry, 3; John, 3, 4, 127

Undertaker, 32
Union Episcopal Church, West Claremont, N. H., 95-96
Union, W. Va., 275
Unitarian churches, 48, 52, 62, 64
Unitarian Church, Cohasset, Mass., 62
United Daughters of the Confederacy, 234
University of Mississippi, 269
Unknown Soldier of the Revolution, 41
Upjohn, 138
Upper Merion, Penna., 194
Utah churches, 300

Valero, Marquis, Antonio de, 305, 309
Valentine, Edward V., 46
Valle, Gov. Francisco Antonio Marin del, 328
Vanarsdal, Rev. Jacob, 161
Van Buren, Martin, 127
Vanderbilt, John, 147
Van Dyke, Nicholas, 170
Vauter's Church, Essex County, Va., 16
Vergara, Don Augustin Flores, 324
Vermont churches, 89-93
Victoria, Queen, 6
Vikur Lutheran Church, Mountain, N. D., 300
Vincennes, Indiana, 283
Vinegar Bibles, 39, 60, 63, 97, 114, 152
Virginia churches, 1-47
Voudrie Brothers, 281

Walpole Church, Bristol, Maine, 73
Wallace, Rev. Dr., 268
Walton, M. Maury, 208
Wambaw Church, S. C., 230-231
Wambaw Creek, S. C., 230
Ward, Rev. Jonathan, 73
Wardrope, Rev. Mr., 173
Ware Church, Gloucester County, Va., 9
Warner, Col. Augustine, 29
War Between the States, 6, 8, 9, 10, 11, 13, 18, 24, 25, 29, 32, 34, 36, 38, 39, 40, 56, 67, 128, 170, 182, 200, 217, 221, 222, 223, 224, 226, 230, 231, 232, 237, 238, 240, 244, 245, 247, 258, 259, 260, 262, 263, 264, 265, 266, 268, 269, 270, 271, 276, 277, 280, 290
War of 1812, 6, 12, 14, 22, 41, 104, 105, 108, 110, 224, 231
Warren, Father Henry, 105
Warren, Lyman M., 295, 296
Washington, Augustine, 34
Washington, George, 3, 6, 7, 10, 26, 29, 33, 34, 35, 36, 37, 38, 39, 40, 41, 42, 52, 54, 59, 60, 62, 63, 69, 80, 81, 85, 97, 111, 112, 118, 138, 140, 151, 154, 155, 174, 182, 184, 185, 186, 189, 191, 193, 194, 196, 201, 203, 204, 209, 210, 211, 217, 226, 246, 320
Washington, Martha, 3, 4, 10, 41, 63, 118, 140, 182, 184, 186
Washington, Ark., 269
Washington, D. C. churches, 126-130
Washington College, 46
Washington and Lee University, 30, 47
Washington State Historical Society, 300
Washington churches, 299
Watt, Mrs. Mary Phelan, 263
Watts, Thos. Hill, 264
Wayne, Anthony, 180, 209, 243
Webb, Capt. Thomas, 197
Weeks, Rev. Joshua Wingate, 51
Weems, John, 117; Rev. Mason L., 34

Index

Welsh Tract Baptist Meeting House, Newark, Del., 167-168
Welsh settlements, 167, 174, 175, 176, 179
Wentworth, Gov. B. W., 97, 98; Michael, 98
Wesley, John, 171, 197, 245
West Claremont, N. H., 95
Western, Major, 312
Westminster of Louisiana, 273
Westminster of the South, 45
Westminster of South Carolina, 234
Westmoreland Congregational Church, N. H., 93
Westmoreland County, Va., 12
West Springfield, Mass., 71
Westover Church, Charles City County, Va., 24-25
Westport, Kansas, 289
West Virginia churches, 274-277
Wethersfield, Conn., 84
Wharton, Thomas, Jr., 192
Wheaton, Comfort, 83
Wheelock Mission, Millerton, Okla., 291-292
Whisky Rebellion, 193
White Church, 71
White, Father Andrew, 101, 102
White, Edward B., 236, 238; Rt. Rev. William, 183, 185, 199
Whitefield, George, 18, 61, 186, 189, 197
White Haven, Md., 112
White Plains, Battle of, 142
Whiting, Rev. Samuel, 90
Whittington, Bishop, 108, 111
Wicaco, Philadelphia, 172, 181
Wiederman, Mr., 270
Wilhelmina, Queen, 148
Willard, Rev. Samuel, 55
William and Mary College, 4
William and Mary, Reign of, 63, 115
Williams, Mrs. Charlean Moss, 269; Rev. Eleazer, 66-67; Eunice, 66; Hester, 157; Roger, 82; Capt. Samuel, 157; Rev. Stephen, 66; Thomas, 66

Williamsburg, Va., 3, 29
Williston, Father, 70
Willing's Alley, Philadelphia, 208
Wills, Dudley and Humbage, 263
Wilmer, Bishop, 264
Wilmington, Del., 163
Wilson, James, 182, 193
Wilson, Woodrow, 4, 5, 128, 162, 244, 245, 249; Mrs. Woodrow, 241, 249
Winslow, Ebenezer, 68
Winston-Salem, N. C., 217
Winthrop, Governor, 49
Wisconsin churches, 294-296
Witchcraft, 20, 55
Witch Duck, 20
Wood, Rebecca, 176
Woodhull, Rev. John, 154
Woodruff, Capt. Judah, 87
Woodstock, Va., 191
Woodville, Miss., 266
Woonsocket, R. I., 81
Worcester County, Md., 115
World War, 72, 231, 266, 284
Wren, Sir Christopher, 36, 60, 130; James, 35
Wright, Rev. Alfred, 292
Wye Mills, Md., 111
Wyoming churches, 299
Wythe, George, 3, 26, 28

Yale University, 159
Yeardley, Governor, 15
Ye Merchant's Hope, 8
Yeocomico Church, Westmoreland County, Virginia, 12-13
Ye Olde Yellow Meeting House, 152-153
Yorktown, Va., 10, 85
Young, Brigham, 278, 300

Zavala, Adina De, 307, 313, 316, 318
Zalvidea, Padre, 337
Zinzendorf, Count, 217
Zubly, Rev. John J., 248

WITHDRAWN